A Celebration of Poets

East
Grades K-6
Fall 2013

creativeCOMMUNICATION
A CELEBRATION OF TODAY'S WRITERS

A Celebration of Poets
East
Grades K-6
Fall 2013

An anthology compiled by Creative Communication, Inc.

Published by:

creativeCOMMUNICATION
A CELEBRATION OF TODAY'S WRITERS

PO BOX 303 • SMITHFIELD, UTAH 84335
TEL. 435-713-4411 • WWW.POETICPOWER.COM

Authors are responsible for the originality of the writing submitted.

All rights reserved. No part of this book may be reproduced or transmitted in any form or by any means, electronic or mechanical without written permission of the author and publisher.

Copyright © 2014 by Creative Communication, Inc.
Printed in the United States of America

Thank you to our student artists whose work is featured on the cover: Ariea Xu - Grade 11, Bruce Cai - Grade 12, DJ Wang - Grade 12, Dorosi Valle - Grade 12, Drew Ledbetter - Grade 7, Dylan Hazel - Grade 2, Kyle Coward - Grade 5, Mia Niikkonen - Grade 9, Nolan Morris - Grade 3, Polly Clarchick - Grade 12, Savannah Fernandes - Grade 11, Stephanie Lutfallah - Grade 11, and Valerie Tsai - Grade 12. To have your art considered for our next book cover, go to www.celebratingart.com.

ISBN: 978-1-60050-602-4

FOREWORD

Dear Reader:

The poems in this book are the best entries that were entered into our Fall 2013 poetry contest. There are a lot of contests these students could have entered. Some contests require an entry fee. Some contests accept everything that is entered and just want to sell books. Creative Communication is glad to be different. For over 20 years our contests have been free to enter and there has been no required purchase to be published. Our staff is comprised of teachers and many of our judges are students in the Education and Writing Composition programs at Utah State University. Each entry is individually read and evaluated with the top 45% of the students who enter being invited to be published.

I had a professor tell me that once you have been published, it is something that can never be taken away. You will forever be a published writer. These students could have put their time and talents into many activities. They chose to take a chance and they have now been rewarded with being published. Having worked with thousands of student writers over the past 20 years, I have many cases where a student contacted me thanking Creative Communication for giving them their first publication. A first publication that later resulted in many first novels, or as in the case of Taylor Swift, who was a contest winner when she was in fifth grade, a first publication that resulted in a life of writing and performing music lyrics. In reality though, most of these student writers will end their writing career once school ends. However, we are pleased that for each of these published writers, Creative Communication has played a role giving them a bit of confidence and recognition in their academic career. We hope you enjoy these poems as much as we have enjoyed putting this anthology together.

Sincerely,

Thomas Worthen, Ph.D.
Editor
Creative Communication

WRITING CONTESTS!

Enter our next POETRY contest!

Enter our next ESSAY contest!

Why should I enter?
Win prizes and get published! Each year thousands of dollars in prizes are awarded throughout North America. The top writers in each division receive a monetary award and a free book that includes their published poem or essay. Entries of merit are also selected to be published in our anthology.

Who may enter?
There are four divisions in the poetry contest. The poetry divisions are grades K-3, 4-6, 7-9, and 10-12. There are three divisions in the essay contest. The essay divisions are grades 4-6, 7-9, and 10-12.

What is needed to enter the contest?
To enter the poetry contest send in one original poem, 21 lines or less. To enter the essay contest send in one original non-fiction essay, 100-250 words, on any topic. Please submit each poem and essay with a title, and the following information clearly printed: the writer's name, current grade, home address (optional), school name, school address, teacher's name and teacher's email address (optional). Contact information will only be used to provide information about the contest. For complete contest information go to www.poeticpower.com.

How do I enter?

Enter a poem online at:
www.poeticpower.com
or
Mail your poem to:
Poetry Contest
PO Box 303
Smithfield, UT 84335

Enter an essay online at:
www.poeticpower.com
or
Mail your essay to:
Essay Contest
PO Box 303
Smithfield, UT 84335

When is the deadline?
Poetry contest deadlines are August 19th, December 5th and April 16th. Essay contest deadlines are July 15th, October 15th and February 17th. Students can enter one poem and one essay for each spring, summer, and fall contest deadline.

Are there benefits for my teacher?
Yes. Teachers with five or more students published receive a free anthology that includes their students' writing. Teachers may also earn points in our Classroom Rewards program to use towards supplies in their classroom.

For more information please go to our website at **www.poeticpower.com**, email us at editor@poeticpower.com or call 435-713-4411.

TABLE OF CONTENTS

POETIC ACHIEVEMENT HONOR SCHOOLS	1
LANGUAGE ARTS GRANT RECIPIENTS	7
TOP TEN WINNERS	9
GRADES 4-5-6 HIGH MERIT POEMS	17
GRADES K-1-2-3 HIGH MERIT POEMS	161
INDEX BY AUTHOR	185
INDEX BY SCHOOL	195

STATES INCLUDED IN THIS EDITION:

Connecticut
Delaware
District of Columbia
Maine
Maryland
Massachusetts
New Hampshire
New Jersey
New York
Ohio
Pennsylvania
Rhode Island
Vermont
Virginia

Fall 2013 Poetic Achievement Honor Schools

Teachers who had fifteen or more poets accepted to be published

The following schools are recognized as receiving a "Poetic Achievement Award." This award is given to schools who have a large number of entries of which over fifty percent are accepted for publication. With hundreds of schools entering our contest, only a small percent of these schools are honored with this award. The purpose of this award is to recognize schools with excellent Language Arts programs. This award qualifies these schools to receive a complimentary copy of this anthology.

Aston Elementary School
Aston, PA
Vivienne F. Cameron*

Bartle Elementary School
Highland Park, NJ
Janet Garnett*

Birches Elementary School
Turnersville, NJ
Roseanne Guerrini
Bettiann Young*

Birchwood School
Cleveland, OH
Helene Debelak*
Judith Little

Blackrock School
Coventry, RI
Michaela L. Keenan*

Boonsboro Elementary School
Boonsboro, MD
Suzanne Sullivan*

Boyce Middle School
Upper St Clair, PA
Diane Ecker*

Burgettstown Elementary Center
Burgettstown, PA
Lorraine MacFarlane*

Caroline G Atkinson School
Freeport, NY
Carrie Frederick-Muchnick
Wendy Jackson*

Catherine A Dwyer Elementary School
Wharton, NJ
Nancy Reeves
Sandra Struble
Mrs. Webster

Chickahominy Middle School
Mechanicsville, VA
Holly Angelidis
Shannon Floyd*
Kimberly Harrell*
Melissa Ingram-Crouch
Leigh Rooke
Paulette Scott

Clover Hill Elementary School
Midlothian, VA
Carole Marable*

Commodore Perry Elementary School
Hadley, PA
Mrs. Greathouse*

Dickinson Avenue Elementary School
East Northport, NY
Erin O'Connor
Robert Shertzer
Michele Terranova

Dobbins Elementary School
Poland, OH
Elaine Morlan*

Eagle's Nest Christian School
Milton, DE
Mrs. Hague*

Ettrick Elementary School
Ettrick, VA
Maria MacLaughlin*

Foster Elementary School
Pittsburgh, PA
Nicci Giehll*
Mrs. McGinnis*

GATE-Central Academy
Middletown, OH
Cheryl Ames*
Dani Ortega*

Hammarskjold Middle School
East Brunswick, NJ
Jane Dougherty
Michele Green*

Holy Family School
Flushing, NY
Jennifer Browne*
Linda Corrigan

Hurley Elementary/Middle School
Hurley, VA
Charlotte Ashby*

Interboro GATE Program
Prospect Park, PA
Kelly DiLullo*
Joyce Faragasso*

Jack Jackter Intermediate School
Colchester, CT
Leslie Cicilline
Linda Kurczy*

Jefferson Middle School
Pittsburgh, PA
Georgia Beckas
Sue Carris*
Jamie Siegel

Licking Valley Primary/Intermediate School
Newark, OH
Erin Fee*

Lincoln Elementary School
Pittsburgh, PA
Stacy Maehling
Kelly Pascarella*
Brooke Takoch

Marie Curie Institute
Amsterdam, NY
Jerilynn Einarsson*
Diana L. Giardino*
Jennifer Satas
Linda Sawicki*

Marion Elementary School
Belle Vernon, PA
Carol Aten Frow*

Mary Walter Elementary School
Bealeton, VA
Patricia Baker*

Poetic Achievement Honor Schools

Medway Middle School
Medway, ME
Pauline Hanley*

Miller City-New Cleveland School
Miller City, OH
Gina Schnipke*

Moravian Academy Middle School
Bethlehem, PA
Cindy Siegfried*

Mystic Middle School
Mystic, CT
Heather Harris*

Nazareth Area Intermediate School
Nazareth, PA
Karen Kammerdiener
Lynn Post*

Nether Providence Elementary School
Wallingford, PA
Mark Rosenberg*

New York Institute for Special Ed
Bronx, NY
Edward Flynn
Jill Klein
Nicole Korn*
David Nora-Jimenez

Norman J Levy Lakeside School
Merrick, NY
Susan Molloy*

Oak Ridge Elementary School
Harleysville, PA
Ross Pollack*

Oakdale-Bohemia Middle School
Oakdale, NY
Kay O'Rourke*

Our Lady of Good Counsel School
Staten Island, NY
Tracy Cunningham*

Our Lady of Hope School
Middle Village, NY
Mr. Demonte
Martha Madri*
Donna Zaffuto

Pemberton Elementary School
Henrico, VA
Ann M. Ballinger
Katie Schmid*

Pennridge North Middle School
Perkasie, PA
Petie Ritchie*

Pocopson Elementary School
West Chester, PA
David Lichter*

Public School 235 Lenox
Brooklyn, NY
Jennifer Moerler*
Mrs. Vernon

Riverside Middle School
Riverside, NJ
Lori Wareham*

Roosevelt Elementary School
Rahway, NJ
Natalie Polanin
Deborah Prakapas*

Sacred Heart School
Oxford, PA
Cara Grebner*

St Anselm Elementary School
Philadelphia, PA
Regina Dunn*
Ruth McIntyre
Freda M. Tait*
Miss Wolfe

St Bartholomew School
    Bethesda, MD
        Sr. Nena Larocco*

St Brigid School
    Portland, ME
        Mr. Healy
        Lorilee A. Newman*

St Hilary of Poitiers School
    Rydal, PA
        Patricia Sermarini*

St James School
    Sewickley, PA
        Karen Scully*

St Joseph Montessori School
    Columbus, OH
        William M. Reed*

St Joseph School-Fullerton
    Baltimore, MD
        Kathy Albergo*
        Connie Barnes
        J. Delores Keefer*
        Peggy Radziminski*

Village School
    Marblehead, MA
        Adam Angelopolus*
        Stephanie Trainor-Madigan*

Westgate Alternative Elementary School
    Columbus, OH
        Tracey Graham*

William M Meredith School
    Philadelphia, PA
        Deborah Coy*

Wooster Christian School
    Wooster, OH
        Karen Masowich*

Language Arts Grant Recipients 2013-2014

For over 20 years, we've offered language arts grants and are proud that we have provided over $100,000 to schools across the United States and Canada. After receiving a "Poetic Achievement Award" schools were encouraged to apply for a Creative Communication Language Arts Grant. The following is a list of schools who received a two hundred and fifty dollar grant for the 2013-2014 school year.

A F Maloney Elementary School, Blackstone, MA
Allegan High School, Allegan, MI
Benet Academy, Lisle, IL
Birchwood School, Cleveland, OH
Blessed Sacrament Catholic School, Seminole, FL
Boyce Middle School, Upper St Clair, PA
Brookville Intermediate School, Brookville, OH
Durant High School, Durant, IA
Elbridge Gale Elementary School, Wellington, FL
Holy Cross High School, Delran, NJ
Li's Academy, Arcadia, CA
Our Lady Star of the Sea School, Grosse Pointe Woods, MI
Outley Elementary School, Houston TX
Parkway Christian School, Sterling Heights, MI
Pleasant View Middle School, Grove City, OH
Ramsay School, Ramsay, MT
Rochelle Middle School, Rochelle, IL
St Stanislaus School, Meriden, CT
Stevensville Middle School, Stevensville, MD
Thomasville Primary School, Thomasville, NC
Troy Intermediate School, Troy, PA
Vacaville Christian Schools, Vacaville, CA
Valley Academy Charter School, Hurricane, UT
Wattsburg Area Middle School, Erie, PA

Please note, effective Fall 2013, our grants program has now been replaced by Classroom Rewards. This new program allows any teacher to be eligible to earn points towards much needed classroom supplies. There is no limit on eligibility and there are no purchases required for a teacher to earn rewards. Any teacher with students accepted and published in our contests or who refers another teacher to our contest will receive points.

Top Ten Winners

List of Top Ten Winners for Fall 2013; listed alphabetically

Tuesday Grace Minghui Blobaum	Grade 2	Sarah Rawson Smith Elementary School	GA
Chandler Blackwell	Grade 6	Rolling Hills Country Day School	CA
Meghan Dahm	Grade 3	Erin Elementary School	WI
Anusha Deshpande	Grade 5	Willa Cather Elementary School	NE
David Ernst	Grade 3	Pleasant Lake Elementary School	IN
Cally Eskew	Grade 5	Foothill Elementary School	CO
Haile Goodings	Grade 2	Edward L Bouie Sr Elementary School	GA
Kellen Hill	Grade 6	Overbrook School	TN
Niko Keddy	Grade 6	Oakdale-Bohemia Middle School	NY
Christina Lafkas	Grade 6	Norman J Levy Lakeside School	NY
Myla O'Dell	Grade 3	Homeschool	NB
Sarina Patel	Grade 6	Williams Middle Magnet School	FL
Cierra Peterson	Grade 3	Valley Academy Charter School	UT
D'yanni Rhyne	Grade 3	S Ray Lowder Elementary School	NC
Kendall Sisler	Grade 4	Boonsboro Elementary School	MD
Grace Tallman	Grade 6	Headwaters Academy	MT
Ella Ticknor	Grade 1	Interboro GATE Program	PA
Victoria Wagner	Grade 3	Elmont Elementary School	KS
Lasarina Hope Webster	Grade 3	Kathleen H Ryerson Elementary School	CT
Sophie Yang	Grade 6	Bala Cynwyd Middle School	PA

All Top Ten Winners may also be seen at www.poeticpower.com

Autumn

When the autumn sky intrudes into your summer
When the wind starts to speak
When storm surges invade your area
And the air is crisp and cool
It's sweater wearing time.

As school days beckon
And the sky says an earlier goodnight
The drizzles of rain lullaby you to sleep
When green leaves turn gold and red
When the trees are void of leaves
White ghosts of clouds
Flounder above the town

As autumn trips into winter
People begin to cough and sneeze
I wonder…
Where did all the green go?

Christina Lafkas, Grade 6

My Sweet Slice of Sky

So transfixed was I by the swath of nutmeg morning sky,
The pearly shaft savored slowly by my tongue,
That I stopped to stare; drinking in the gorgeous scenery.
Pleasure spouted like a bountiful fountain,
My every hungering glory satisfied,
By this luminous planetary wonder,
Unraveled before my eyes.
A smudge of glossy pre-dawn was tentatively and shyly shown,
The graphite-gray and plum-colored hues appetizing,
To those with a dreamier palette.
And for those with an affinity for the refined warm colors;
A streak of glowing peachy amber.
There is a piece of the gigantic sky,
Like a slice of a large pie,
For everyone to enjoy and revel in its sprightly magnificence.

Sarina Patel, Grade 6

Nature

The sunshine on the evergreen at dawn
the birds are starting to sing in the trees
the rays upon their wings have fed their song
as the sun hits red rocks softly
as it skips
as it shimmers
like a portrait in the pines
silhouetted by an azure blue
a big gust of wind moves the feathered birds
like a symphony of joy taking flight
the birds seem delighted to look up and see the cloudless sky
they do their dance
they sing their songs
all nature knows summer is here

Cally Eskew, Grade 5

Seasons

The year dances like children
Flowers grow, the sun comes out
Leaves begin to fall, the snow fills the whole city

In spring, the whole world brightens up,
The rain waters our flowers that bring joy to the world

During summer, the sun shows itself clearly,
Children come out to go to the pool on a sunny day

When autumn occurs, it signals the coming of the end of the year,
The leaves are leaving the tree

Winter comes as a holy season with so many holidays
The snow trickles down to show a white blanket

The end of the year comes and cycles again,
This time with a different form of weather

The year dances like children,
Flowers grow, the sun comes out
Leaves begin to fall, the snow fills the whole city

Anusha Deshpande, Grade 5

Music

Music in my ears is like
Honey dripping from the clarinet.
Music in my ears is like
A baby bird chirping from a violin.
Music in my ears is like
Bells ringing out of the trumpet.
Music in my ears is like
A cello boasting because it is so beautiful.
Music in my ears is like
A trombone claiming a celebration.
Music in my ears is like
A viola loving to be the older twin of the violin.

Music to my ears is
A voice I have never heard;
Calling me to Him,
The creator of me;
The one who gives me a great feeling of belonging
In the world.

Kendall Sisler, Grade 4

Leaves

We are walking through the autumn cold
Wintry flecks swirl through my hair
The pull from the dog
At the end of the leash
Is eager, expectant
Ahead, I see leaves.

The leaves cover the sidewalk ahead
They are deep, deeper than Kipper
For she has legs like meatballs
And a body like a sausage
Yet that does not deter her
She leaps, twists, bounds
The leaves like liquid sand
Parting, only to fall back.

I trudge towards her, laughing
She snorts, and a leaf spirals off her nose
Like a snowflake
Everything seems more friendly
The street, the house, the tree
We walk to the park, leaving only a path
Where we waded in the leaves.
Grace Tallman, Grade 6

That Feeling

I feel something like the world
   Is smiling at me
Like I never have to say anything
   And people hear my plea

I feel content and hopeful
   Like a bird with a new song
As if everyone decided
   That they should get along

The obstacles are still here
   For nothing can be perfect
But this feeling I am feeling
   Makes all of it so worth it

This joy will go away someday
   But now it resides with me
For there are few better things in this world
   Than this feeling of joy and glee
Kellen Hill, Grade 6

The Sunflower

As I walk in the field, I see Mr. Sunflower.

It stares back at me like a mirror.
As the wind blows it sways back, forth, side to side.

Even though it's very tall, I still see his brightness.

It shows soon the joy of the sunflower,
Will be spread for miles as it sews its seeds.

It smiles at me; as years pass it gets smaller, but I get bigger and older.
Together we know we'll be gone soon.

My sunflower grins as it loses a petal.
When it loses its last petal, I feel its love for life fade.
But its seeds are sewn and life's legacy of laughter parades,
Across the field, undaunted in its pride.
Chandler Blackwell, Grade 6

Thanksgiving

Thank you
for all my eyes can see,
vibrantly colored leaves in the trees and on the ground
the car of family members in the driveway
reminiscing over past Thanksgivings

Thank you
for all my ears can hear,
the jubilant, loud laughter at the dinner table
energetic footfalls of younger children constant
grandma saying, "It's almost done" or, "It'll be out soon!" almost all day

Thank you
for all my tongue can taste,
mouthwatering, scrumptious turkey, elegantly prepared
pumpkin pie reaching out and grabbing you at dessert
everyone is stuffed, and are food-filled pillows after our delicious meal
Niko Keddy, Grade 6

Magic of the Moment

The magic of the moment is my mommy kissing me,
   she gives lots of hugs and sings sweet melodies.
The magic of the moment is my brother making pancakes,
   I wait and I wait but he tells me it's not time to take.
The magic of the moment is my daddy tickling my feet,
   I laugh and I laugh then I hide under the sheet.
The magic of the moment is my grandfather buying treats,
   I ask can we go to the store because they're yummy and sweet.
The magic of the moment is my grandmother buying me pink lip gloss,
   when I get it, I'm so excited and I wipe it from cross to cross.
The magic of the moment is my lovely family,
   giving kisses, hugs, treats and love ALL to me!
Haile Goodings, Grade 2

Autumn

A heatless torch upon a thick branch, a thickening carpet of false fire.
Flakes are dancing to the ground, will the wind never tire?
A splattered canvas of colors, oranges, reds and yellow.
A speckle of brown and green, not all hues and dyes mellow.
Little sweet bulbs swinging on trees, ripening to the full.
Many farms are kept busy, how could life be dull?
A furry head emerges, followed by two or three.
The seeds and fruit are disappearing, and hunters full of glee.
The air bites and stings, yet the sky's still tranquil and clear.
Tremendous white scoops float in the vast calm, none of which are near.
An ensemble of wind blows, now more than a mere breeze.
Tree branches quiver, for their leaves are being teased.
The sun shines radiantly, warding off the frost.
It can't keep on forever, an annual war, lost.
The days are shorter now, scarce is becoming the light.
The cold is visiting, a prelude to a snowy night.

Sophie Yang, Grade 6

The Thankful Lion

King of the jungle with a great big roar,
When predators hear it, I am ready for war.
I have a big, fluffy mane when I get into a fight,
It protects my neck from a dangerous bite.
I walk through the jungle with the smell of zebras, rhinos, and other food,
All of these things put me in a good mood!
I have a beautiful, gold coat to keep me cool or warm,
Hanging rocks keep me sheltered from a storm.
I am a lion and there is no need to hide,
Because I am thankful to live with a family, my pride.

Ella Ticknor, Grade 1

Carry Me Home

White holds me in his quiet, warm arms
Red is the color who kisses my check on a sad lonely day
Yellow is the color that fills my heart with love, a color which brightens my day
But blue is the color that carries me home

Black keeps a family together, but at the same time unweaves the line
Purple picks plum ripe berries and hushes a baby's cry
Green is mother nature a nice soft bed of leaves
But blue is the color that carries me home

Orange is small, like a tangerine seed but can grow into something bigger
Pink is a Haiku flower, a quiet sprinkling of peace
But blue is the color that carries me home

Blue, yes blue. The river is a world of blue
Forever and forever flowing
But blue, yes blue, is the one color
Who carries me home

Lasarina Hope Webster, Grade 3

I Ask Myself to Clean My Room

I ask myself to clean my room,
'Cause this is something I hate to do.
Vacuuming, dusting, making the bed,
I'd rather watch TV or play a game instead.

I never like to clean my room,
I don't like mops, dust rags or brooms.
It takes too long and it's boring you see,
I'd rather have someone clean it for me.

There are toys and clothes all over the floor,
Shoes around the bed and trash in front of the door.
No place to sit, no place to walk,
It looks like a crime scene but there's no chalk.

I ask myself to clean my room,
Someone needs to help me quick.
Because if I do not clean this room,
The smell is going to make me sick.

D'yanni Rhyne, Grade 3

Who Am I ?

Who am I?

Am I the breeze that blows through the wind?
Am I a peaceful sunset?
Am I the music that inspires you?

Am I peaceful? Am I brave? Am I strong?
I am powerful, strong, unique, beautiful, generous, caring, helpful

In my soul I see a deep loving heart…I see a big smile….
I see music dancing around me…
I see that I am lifting peoples' spirits. I see gold dancing…
I see flowers starting to burst open with their beauty and grace.
I see the colors of the rainbow and sunsets…they are beauty…

I hope…I wonder…
I believe, I dream and I am inspired.

Tuesday Grace Minghui Blobaum, Grade 2

Snow

A white blanket covers the Earth and
B reaks silence all around.
C hildren go out to play, covering themselves in white all
D ay. Children go outside
E ven though it's super cold.
F rost covers everything and kids
G ather ice to make a fort,
H eaving ice over their head and stacking it on top of a mound.
"**I** ncoming!" shouts someone as they throw a ball of ice.
"**J** olly, it's a white Christmas!" Parents say as they watch their
K ids playing happily together.
     Snow has broken loose.

Victoria Wagner, Grade 3

Autumn's Last Surprise

You might think that in fall the world is lifeless.
The birds have headed south.
The bears are starting to hibernate,
and other animals have moved on.

Fall is far from lifeless.
The grass is a beautiful green
soaking up the sun.
The golden leaves on the maple trees
are dancing in the breeze.
The sky is an amazing shade of blue.
The red apples dangle from the apple tree
sparkling in the sun.
The long brown pine cones look like ice cream cones
hanging from the pine tree.

The sounds of autumn are many.
A flock of geese honking overhead as they move south
In hopes of a warmer winter.
Chickadees are singing their lovely fall songs.
Blue jays are warning everyone they are still here.

The air smells so sweet this time of the year.
Fall is far from lifeless.

Myla O'Dell, Grade 3

Writer's Walk

I feel

the warm sun shining on my back
with a little heat on me
clean air is breathing
through my nose

I see

yellow, orange and red leaves
trees wherever I go
red apples hanging on apple trees
red leaves on a branch, looking sad

I hear

birds singing a beautiful melody
honking geese flying south for the cold winter
crows squawking for their property

I feel

cold fall air touching me
fall and winter are talking and whistling

Meghan Dahm, Grade 3

Me

When I'm by myself
and I close my eyes
I am a snowman with a strawberry nose.
I'm juicy apples that fall down in the fall.
I'm a bird that flies around in the sky.
I'm a bowling ball that makes strikes every time.
I'm a nerd that loves math.
I'm a trampoline that makes people
jump really high.
I'm a volleyball player that
outscores the other team.
I'm a dog eating my homework.
I'm as kind as a kitten.
And when I open my eyes
what I care to be is me.

Cierra Peterson, Grade 3

Mother Nature

Mother Nature is delighted
She provides
Cherries, berries and strawberries
She comes forth in the
Rising sun till day is done
She makes shelter with her leaves

Some day everyone will be pleased
She provides plants for food
If she didn't, there would be no life cycle
Then with a touch of a tender hand
she puts to sleep
Sea and land.

David Ernst, Grade 3

Grades 4-5-6
High Merit Poems

Playing Baseball with the Best Dad Ever
My dad and I sprint onto
the cleat tormented dirt
we play as the shadows rise
like a bear waking up from
a long
winter sleep
we play under the blueness
of the sky
as the ball runs into the wind
and it sings of freedom in the air
under the great spring sun
we play with the might
of 100 oxen
we play with the
cold icy ball
until we're under the twinkling stars
and my dad and I sprint off
the cleat tormented dirt
Jack Graboski, Grade 4

Dreams
Dreams are pearly pink
like the clouds that streak the sky at sunset
Dreams are silver
like the moon on a clear night in the country.
Dreams are light blue
like the ocean on a sunny day.
Dreams are white
like fresh, crisp snowflakes swirling in the winter air,
Dreams are field green
like the dewy grass that tickles my feet in the springtime

Dreams are never black
like ink seeping into a sheet of paper,
draining its life,
Or red like glowing eyes
in the dark.
Dreams are happy and sweet.
Dreams are a beautiful rainbow.
Miranda Dobkin, Grade 5

War
War is something that you do
Even though a bullet might hit you.
Bullets fly through the smoky sky
And sometimes hit their allies.
As the enemies' defense was
No match for our bombardment.
As the Dreadnoughts fought,
As fighters dotted across the sky
As many men died, and some tried to bide it.
As transport ships stop at their ports,
They drop off tanks to take down enemy forts.
War is something that might make you take cover,
But with God's power, the war will be over.
Matthew Nichols, Grade 5

The Dancing Words
It's the words that twirl,
They spin and leap,
I jump to them,
I flex them and I kick them,
I express them,
I point them,
I contract them,
I love words so much!
The emotional ones,
The ones I stretch and split,
And the ones that balance on their tippy toes until they drop,
Tap I love,
Heel drops and toe stands, it's music to my ears,
I slide after certain words,
They are so crisp I want to fit them all into my dance,
I catch them in mid pick up as they shuffle past me,
I turn to them,
And they roll to the ground,
They are my special words and always will be.
Sara Rosenthal, Grade 5

Illustrations
Illustrations in the book,
Oh how much I envy when I look.
Colors of rainbows, every kind,
There is so much I would love to find.

Abstracts and pictures that are beautiful,
Even though sometimes they are very unusual,
Amazing textures and patterns are so clear,
I can almost listen to the picture with a close ear.

Glossy and glowing figures that describe so much of the story,
Some written about love and some written about glory,
Illustrations tell so much about life,
Sometimes it shows struggle or strife.

Some stories can be happy and some can be very sad,
That is why the illustrations tell the readers to not feel bad.
The author can have an exceptional talent of being artistic,
Find the one for you that is idealistic.
Haley Hamilton, Grade 6

Yellow
Leisurely and happily yellow floats above,
As it should be held in your priorities,
Never cold or grudge holding,
Your jubilation fuels yellow,
Disloyalty and harshness aren't part of its functions,
Yellow has clear motives,
You needn't be afraid,
  Careless,
    Coherent,
      Content,
Is yellow
Katie McCurrie, Grade 6

Indian Rama, Ravana, and Kanuman

Ravana, Lord of the Demons
With evil servants at his side, ten-headed Ravana needed no help.
But when good Tama came astride
Ravana could scarcely yelp.
His kingdom was built in the middle of the ocean
When sailors passed it by they got that strange notion
Then Kanuman set the kingdom on fire
and Ravana had but one desire
He tried to stop Hanuman with seven great lashes
but Hanuman burned the lashes to ashes
Then Kanuman escaped as quick as a sparrow
and Rama shot Ravana down with a great arrow.
Benjamin Miron, Grade 5 and Jaden Fluet, Grade 6

Soaring Eagle

Fly to the top of the highest mountain and feel proud
Let the wind guide you to a brand new life, a brand new experience
Feel your wings and feet skim the cold river water
Decide which way to go without second thoughts
Touch the clouds but remember that the sky is not the limit
Stay true to yourself and believe in happy moments
Discover something new and exciting every day
Keep living your life how you want to, don't let people change you
Stand up for yourself, friends, and family
Don't let your beauty fade away
Forget the pain and tears, all the bad times
You are a Soaring Eagle
Ashley Phillips, Grade 4

Ode of Cheesecake

Cheesecake you are my favorite
You have to be because you are yummy
And you hold so many good toppings and different flavors
What do you think about that?
Your are sweet; you are creamy
And you are the one I worship day and night, cheesecake
Because you're cold, creamy, sweet, tangy, wet-feeling delicious
Even if you're not around I love you
So always will I know
Can you be get even better or will you stay the same?
Because I don't car what flavor or what kind
I love you!
Haleigh Cook-Hayes, Grade 4

A Chipmunk

It is early morning, late fall
Walking through the woods
I hear the wind blowing the trees
And squirrels rustling the leaves
I smell the watery dew and the sweet smell of flowers
It's breezy but I have a warm feeling
I see red, orange, and yellow leaves
Dark green grass and dark brown trees
Then I see a chipmunk eating grass
Should I get back for breakfast?
Abbey Finn, Grade 4

Those Amazing Rays

Colorful flashes flee across the sky,
Some almost too fast for the human eye.
The misty spirals are unknown shapes,
That cover the sky with large, bold scrapes.
I look at the sky, beautiful and tie-dyed,
The Northern Lights reaching forty-miles high.
They make me dizzy and I'm in awe,
Looking at the sky, cut open by a rainbow chainsaw.
Aurora Borealis is an amazing sight,
Making people want to soar up and take flight.
I want to see them in person someday,
Maybe I will see those amazing rays.
Zoe Wolfus, Grade 4

Winter

Winter snow rolled into a ball.
Winter is the best season of all.
The cold breeze against my head
makes me want to stay in bed.
Leggings, wool socks, and a thick sweater
makes everything feel better.
Winter holiday is a time to play
when cousins, uncles, and aunts come to stay.
Crunch, crunch, crunch of the frosty snow
off to sledding we must go.
Winter is the best season of them all
Family and friends make it a ball.
Elise Kohnke, Grade 5

Colors Are in My Dream

Blue is in my dream because it is the
color of the sky which protects us
Yellow is in my dream because it is the
color of the sun that gives us light
Purple is in my dream because it is my
favorite color, it makes me feel calm or relaxed
Green is in my dream because it is a
natural color, like a blade of grass.
Black and white are in my dream
because they are neutral colors and they
balance my dream
My dream is a whole new life!
Ellie Sweeney Benzon, Grade 5

I Remember Halloween

I remember trick or treating on Halloween
I remember playing tricks on friends and family
I remember sorting my candy at home
And taking my sister's candy
I remember getting clubbed by toilet paper
I remember running from my parents when it was time to go home
I remember getting on a hay ride
Even though I didn't want to
I remember that cold, starry night with my friends
But my favorite memory's yet to come.
Blake Miller, Grade 5

Rachel Louise Carson

Rachel Carson was born on May 27th 1908,
57 years later she was sent to heaven.
She never had a child,
Yet she had cancer for a while.
She never got married or had a wedding ring,
But she spent her time writing books like *Silent Spring*.
She graduated from John Hopkins University in 1932,
And studying the sea was something she loved to do.
She wrote a book called *The Sea Around Us* in 1951.
The US National Book Award is something special she won.
Some things I wonder are when she wrote her books
If she sat in her room in a quiet cozy nook.
If there was an nice aroma, or what she used to become inspired,
If she had a hearth in her room, or would kindle a fire.
Would she get hot and get nervous or seep out sweat,
Writing her books was really hard I bet.

Dayjanea Gordon, Grade 4

World Filled with Peace

There was smoke that filled the air,
every place you looked, it was everywhere.
The sounds were like thunder,
which made me wonder.
What if we could have peace,
and make everything that sounded like thunder cease?
What if we could all just agree
on one little thing that everybody is fighting for?
It takes a lot of strength
to keep on going the length.
It takes a lot of courage to see a friend in pain.
It must be difficult not to go insane.
You feel horrible and terrible,
you just don't know what to do or even where to move.
What if just once, maybe, we could have thunder cease,
And a world filled with peace?

Jacob DiFranco, Grade 6

Purple

I can see my lovely lavender dress.
It's beautiful, I must confess.
The purple on my sweatshirt, too.
My schoolbag has a hint of violet-blue.
I can hear the zipper. Zip, zip, zip!
From my purple jacket. Rip, rip, rip!
As I taste my grape lollipop.
Lickety lick from the top.
I feel my purple teddy bear.
So soft and cuddly with violet hair.
To smell the lilacs from the vine.
The sweet aroma of a happy time.
Some say purple makes you sad.
I don't get it, that thought makes me feel bad.
Sit back and enjoy God's beautiful sky.
I thank God for purple. My, my, my!

Katelyn Morrissy, Grade 5

Baseball

My adrenaline rushes as I come up to bat.
I step to the plate and dig my heels in.
The pitcher winds up; I get ready to swing.
First pitch is a strike, but I still have two more.
The next pitch comes and I swing hard.
CRACK!
I hear the fans cheer as I run to first.
I step on first base and the ump calls, "Safe!"
There's nothing like playing baseball.

Max Cavada, Grade 4

Football

Football is fun.
Off the snap, I try to block my person
To make the quarterback fumble.
The ball is an oval shape.
All the players go for the football.
The piece of ground is one hundred yards,
Launch off the snap of the football and fight
For victory.

Isaac Cory, Grade 4

Farm

In autumn farmers harvest their crops
They have worked so hard to grow them
They're planted in straight rows
The leaves on the trees are colorful
Their beauty is great as they lay on the farm
When the horse tramples over them
They crunch like a potato chip
On the farm

Riley Muller, Grade 5

Halloween Scares

With their green skin, brooms, and transparent heads
I feel they're watching me from under my bed.
Goblins, witches, and ghosts
Oh no, I think they're close!
I open my eyes to take a peek
They're standing right in front of me so I squeak
So my mother comes in to check on me
When she does, all the monsters flee!

Jacob Depinet, Grade 6

A Night Sky and a Long Voyage

Crash, waves hitting the ship
In inky blackness, stars are twinkling everywhere
Nothing but ocean, thousands of stars
Can't take it anymore
Everyone is restless, tired of the sea
But, not me
The sky keeps me going
I hope the night never ends

Ben Whitt, Grade 4

Deer Hunting

I put my rifle in the back of my papa's truck,
I hope to shoot a 14-point buck.

My Winchester 243
Has always been lucky for me.

I hope the buck is standing broadside,
That would really make me smile.

Through the sight it looks closer,
Slowly I squeeze the trigger.

Venison for the winter,
Life couldn't be better.

Jordan Harding, Grade 6

Hate

Hate is all that Hitler was
He didn't care at all
Children crying, shotguns firing
That's all the people saw

Other people watching by
Hiding in the shadows
Too afraid to speak or cry
Because they were afraid to die

Love is just a simple word that really means a lot
People believed that hate was the answer, but it was not
Hate is all that Hitler was
All he was, was hate

Catarina Rodrigues, Grade 6

Mellow Yellow

Yellow is brightness in someone's face,
When they've just run to third base.
Yellow is sour lemons with a bite,
My face scrunched up in the candlelight.
Yellow is a lollipop making someone really happy,
It could even be my old pappy.
Yellow is an angel looking down on me,
Oh, I wonder where she could be.
Yellow is bananas on a tropical island blue,
Even I know that they grow there too.
Yellow is the color of the sunrise,
Even when the clouds give it a disguise.
Yellow is a great sight to see,
When it's buzzing like a bumblebee.

Sorrell Long, Grade 6

Grandparents Are

People who care about you.
People who tell embarrassing stories about your parents
People who give you treats sometimes
People who love you.

Sage Hillier, Grade 6

Summer

Summer is here, so it is time for fun
We are all ready to play in the sun.

No more school to be stressed out
We are all excited to scream and shout!

Swimming in the pool is always fun
All the joy has just begun!

Seeing the fireflies twinkle at night
Makes me love that bright sight!

The warmth of the sun during the day
Is great to go outside and play.

The smell of the barbecue is always great
We are stuffed because of the burgers we ate!

Summer time is always cool
So please don't send me back to school!

Natalie O'Connor, Grade 6

Boxing Ring

I approach the empty room
I take in the sweat and pain
And fast like a viper, blood pumps in my vein

My hands wrapped up
To protect my soft skin
As I start to punch, my mind screams to win

I repeatedly hit hard
With thunder in my fist
I remember all my family and friends
So many on that list

I swing my fist in anger
"Bam, Bam" goes the bag
I go on and don't stop
I continue and don't lag

I sit down to breathe and I look around
The only bag hanging is now about to go back down

James Boyle, Grade 6

Gold

Settle down, stay a while, take your shoes off.
Take a taste of a life only a fool would froth.
Enjoy the view and pick a few of your most treasured parts.
Health of heart
Wealth of knowledge
Will not angrily deceive
Good of heart
Great of passion
Going where you please

Dylan Jenny, Grade 6

The Ride
I lean back
Hearing the wind
Whisper in my ear
As I canter across the open fields
My mind wanders
As I stare forward at the trees before me
And we lead over a stream
The horse responds
Before I make the signal to go on
As if we are one
Mind connected
On this ride
Anna Wiza, Grade 6

Thanksgiving
T urkey plump and juicy,
H am hot and tasty,
A ll the joys of fall,
N ever seem to fail,
K ids play in the leaves,
S printing as they please,
G od truly blessed this day,
I n every single way,
V ivid images of pumpkin pie appear
I n my empty plate,
N o one ever, ever fails to
G ive thanks on Thanksgiving day.
Jon Dotson, Grade 6

Gingerbread Man
Run, run as fast as you can,
You can't catch me
I'm the gingerbread man
You would only catch me
If you dipped me in milk,
But if you do
Please don't dip me in "Silk"
for I would dissolve
like acid on a frank
Fine
You can catch me,
Hank.
Perrin Petell, Grade 5

Nature
With the sun shining so bright
It's a wondrous sight
The trees blow
While the breezes flow
With seasons all around
And so much that hasn't been found
With animals near
The woods are beautiful all year
On Earth it stands
While being discovered by man
Veronica Nickerson, Grade 5

My Poodle
My poodle is like my shadow
she's always following me around
when at night behind her cell door
she sings
Bark! Bark! Bark!
In the morning she runs
and springs up like life depended on it
and she puts her black nose
in the air filled sky
she puts her eyes up
and stares at me
as her eyes remind me
of the first day her jewels locked on me
and put cupid's arrow in my heart
Dekai Averett, Grade 4

Change the World
Help your fellow peers
Be kind to others and
Fill the world with cheer
Recycle your trash
Don't be harsh
Life goes by in a flash
Stop the bullying
It's not funny
Find your life's meaning
Stand up and be strong
Never give up on yourself
Fill the world with colors
And
CHANGE THE WORLD
Azza Ahmed, Grade 6

I Give Thanks
Thank you, God, for all you've done.
You should feel like number one.

You have given me a new day.
I know that you're not far away.

I am thankful for my new house,
It's even better than a lighthouse.

I am thankful for all you did,
There is nothing that you overdid.

I will love you, forever and ever
Because you can do whatever, whenever.
Jacob Gardner, Grade 4

Volcanoes
I see the mountains in the landscape
They crave to erupt
The water battling fiercely
Washing lava to stone at shore
Abhirup Chakrabarti, Grade 5

What Is Fun?
Fun is not something
you get from a store
Fun is something you do
that you really adore.

If fun had a price
it would be free
because it is so special
to you and to me.

Fun has no shortcuts
fun has no cheat codes
fun has no easy, medium
or hard modes.

So what is fun?
Well, I have the answer, thankfully.
Fun is spending time
with your friends and family.
Ramil Hirsawa, Grade 5

The Panthyr
Panthyr, Panthyr, sleek and black
How do you mount your vicious attack?
What do you think? What do you feel?
Why is your fur as cold as steel?

Why is your realm so bleak like a pyre?
Were you created in a dark fire?
Why the loneliness? Why the scowl?
Why do you seem (to me) so foul?

Am I right to say, you are alone?
Or do you share your mighty throne?
Is thy heart black? Or art thou soft?
What lies above in thy sinister loft?

Panthyr, Panthyr, sleek and black
How do you mount your vicious attack?
What do you think? What do you feel?
Why is your fur as cold as steel?
Sam Miller, Grade 5

The Ocean
Crashing waves,
Shades of blue and green.
Sparkling golden sands,
Shimmering in the sunlight.
The endless blue sky,
Stretches out before us.
There are squeals from above,
The seagulls are soaring.
In the sky, so free.
The ocean is alive,
And full of secrets.
Guanyi Cao, Grade 5

Away

In the beautiful breeze I feel my heart let go, of the troubles that refuse to leave me alone.
No words of evil may creep in my ears, for the sweet singing birds are all I can hear.
Weather it be shade or light, day or night, I'd rather be here, away from the fright.
Nobody to tell me what to do, here it's my path and I shall chose.
No heavy burden to carry upon my back, for here there is no work to take you off track.
No harsh screaming storms to twist me around, only perfect skies to lift my feet off the ground.
No opinions to take, no yes or no, here you're in charge and only what you say goes.
In the away, yes this perfect place, there are no dreams to chase.
Because here your dreams have already come true, and nobody here matters but…you!

Jessica Gray, Grade 6

Hosanna

I remember the real meaning of Easter.
I remember old Peter Cottontail visiting my house.
I remember going to church to celebrate the resurrection of Jesus Christ.
I remember listening to the church choir shout, Hosanna up into the heavens.
I remember opening the resurrection eggs in Sunday school.
I remember hunting for treat-filled Easter eggs at my house.
I remember focusing on what the Easter Bunny left behind for us, even though that's not why we celebrate Easter.
I remember the thrill of the Messiah rising out of the ashes.
But my favorite memory's yet to come…

Joshua Crihfield, Grade 5

What It's Like to Be Cake

I hate the way people say "YUM" when they see me.
I also don't like the expression "that was a piece of cake."

One example is you can never have any people friends because you know they're going to eat you.
And, does anyone even cares that it really tickles when you put frosting on me?

But, someday I will get my revenge.
You're next to be baked into cakes.
Watch your backs.

Ivy Grosk, Grade 4

Winter

Snowflakes falling down to the soft bed of snow that blankets us in a frosty world of sledding and ice skating.
Life wouldn't be the same without that ice glow that makes wintertime special in every way possible.
The snow spreads from city to city making the trees' leaves stop growing and freezes in icy dresses.
I love hot chocolate in front of the fire as little lace woven snowflakes and snow angels fall to the ground.
The wind whistles with holiday carols and merry tunes as well as smells of Christmas dinner on the stove.
If you're lucky you might even hear the feet of tiny reindeer on the top of your house.
So, winter is my favorite time of year with everything from snow to hot chocolate.
Winter will always bring surprises.

Lowrie Woodside, Grade 5

Football

I am from charging down the sideline and scoring to sprinting down the sideline to get the ball carrier.
I am from chasing and wrecking the ball carrier to trucking to keep running.
I am from hurting people when I tackle them to them hurting me when they tackle me.
I am from running the ball to trying to get the ball.
I am from getting dirty to getting clean.
I am from annoying my brother to him annoying me.
I am from eating candy to eating fruit.
And best of all I am from the best parents ever.

Ryan Mikolajczak, Grade 5

It's About
It's about lines and lines of code.
Making sure it won't overload.
While processing a truckload.

It's about microchips and robots.
Remote controlled robot pots.
Lots and lots of little bots.

It's about old computers made brand new.
Broken TV's work again.
Creating the good out of what was brand new.

It's about experimenting, testing and collaborating.
Making things that could do good.
But still are probably all no-good.

It's about having fun and fiddling around.
Bolts and parts on the ground.
Soldering things that way 10 pounds.

It's about what I do that is so cool.
Sebastian Tucker, Grade 5

It's About…
It's about balls soaring
The crowd roaring
Because this sport isn't boring

It's about a home run being hit
The pitcher slams his mitt
while the other team has a fit

It's about catching a fly ball
Hoping that your team wins it all
Though umpires make bad calls

It's about the excitement of the sport
People wearing players on their shirts
With the player that they support

It's about people drinking Coke
A bat being broke
Everyone laughing as if it was a joke

It's about the most exciting sport in the world
Ashley Torrey, Grade 5

I'm Sleeping
I'm sleeping in a tree.
I wake up to the sound of wind whistling through the leaves.
When I woke up I smelled dead deer.
So I ran and ran and ran through the dark green forest.
It was so hot in the summer, the hot breeze was hitting my face.
So I took a rest.
Should I keep running or sleep?
Connor Becker, Grade 4

Dogs
Those sneaky slobbery dogs that eat my shoes and socks
They're as wild as an infant but worse
They eat my homework as a treat
They make a mess with their feet
Their tail is like a tornado going round and round
They make mud in the house like a rat
Dogs are crazy
Matthew Weaver, Grade 5

The Soccer Game
S occer is the sport I love
O n the field I run
C an I
C an I
E ven if I try
R un, kick in the goalie the ball flies
Like a bird flying into the net swift we win the game!
Isaiah Garcia, Grade 5

Veterans
V eteran's fought for us
E veryone has freedom
T he army fought for our freedom
E very man and women fought for our liberty and justice
R eally courageous and brave to fight for our freedom
A ny soldier is strong and brave
N ow veterans can say "I fought for you"
Kristopher Burns, Grade 4

Sick
Sneezy, wheezy, and sick as can be.
My runny nose lets out a big sneeze.
Cold, but hot, and it's not too thick,
The snot out of my nose goes drip, drip, drip
Down my face and on my chin. The pain runs all through my skin.
A kiss from my Mom wipes the pain away.
Or was it the fact that Daddy told me to go outside and play?
Gabriela Gant, Grade 4

Grandma Is
The joy in my heart when I think about her.
The cookies and tasty treats.
The beautiful pearl earrings sitting on the dresser.
The laughter coming from the kitchen.
The games filled with fun and togetherness.
The smell of fluorescent roses.
The warm cushiony pillow to rest your head upon.
Elysse Abraham, Grade 6

Nana Is
Always there when I need help.
Her backpack with patches from around the world.
Trying to be with me whenever she can.
A wonderful, caring, and loving person.
The best grandma I could wish for.
Liam Brolly, Grade 6

High Merit Poems – Grades 4, 5, and 6

Sunflowers
Living, colorful
Calm, loving, growing
Makes me think of peace
Nature
David Roscoe, Grade 4

My Mom
My Mom has a baby.
My Mom likes to shop.
She is very cool.
My friends know it too.
Keyontae Lewis, Grade 4

Long Ago
Long ago, in a little house,
There lived a little mouse.
It was a bread house,
But it was just right for a mouse.
Raelynn Eakins, Grade 4

The Sky
Bright, dark
Rains, snows, clears up
The galaxy is very dark
Air
Carson O'Connell, Grade 4

Peace
Lovely, beautiful
Kind, respectful, friendship
Paz is a quiet thing
Calm
Marcus Madiedo, Grade 4

Snowy Wonderland
Ride down a hill on a great big sled,
Walk into a nice warm shed,
Drink hot cocoa in a big cup,
Fall asleep with a small white pup!
Isabelle Stoehr, Grade 5

Sniff
Fluffy, cuddly
Nibbling, sniffing, hiding
He is so cute
Guinea pig
Abby Jones, Grade 5

Flower
Smooth, pretty, color
Grows, blooms, wilts
Makes me think of spring
Plant
Priya Patel, Grade 4

Birthday Wishes*
Wishes I keep to myself:

Wish I could play the drums as well as my brother
because I could be in the school band

Wish my brother would not be so annoying
because he always follows me around and copies everything I do

Wish I could win my second USTA tournament
and get another trophy to get a higher ranking

Wish I could be taller so the kids at school
would not tease about it anymore and ask me anymore

Wish I could have another brother the same age and skill level as me
so I would not have to play easy with him

Wish my cousins lived closer
because I love to go to our lake house with them to swim and play all day

Wish that my brother could come to Fenn with me and be in the same singing group as me
so we could be in concerts together

Wish my dad didn't have to work so much
so I would be able to see him ore and play catch

Wish I could be an Astronaut so I could be the first man on Mars
William Okurowski, Grade 5
*Inspired by the novel "Inside Out and Back Again"

Gym Class
Running around, I sing the blues
I really do hate gym class
Running around, I sing the blues
I really do hate gym class
why do I have to run, I really am not that fast

I asked my dad for help
He took me and we trained all day
I asked my dad for help
He took me and we trained all day
I asked my dad for help
He took me and we trained all day
I think it might have worked, it brought to mind for me to say

Sometimes I look like a bird
When I try really hard
sometimes I look like a bird
When I try really hard
I might need to work out, maybe I should consider a Y card

Running around, I sing the blues
I really do hate gym class
Running around, I sing the blues
I really do hate gym class, thank goodness I'm almost done with this class
Alex Dragas, Grade 6

Thankful

I am thankful for
My mom and grandma's hearts
Multiplied by two
I'm also thankful for
My mom's vegetable stew
Hot and spicy
Just how I like it
Nice and flavory
I can't wait until she gets it out of the bucket
I am thankful for
Clay and Conner
Sticking up for me
So I don't scream in horror
I am also thankful for Ryan
Because he doesn't scream like a lion
I love to swim in the bay
I am also thankful
To be here today

Madison Meadows, Grade 4

Hate

All of this started with that 4-letter word, HATE
Hate
Why did Hitler have to use that word?
Hate
Does it matter which religion or race?
Why did he kill the Jews and other races?
Hate
Why did it have to be this way?
Couldn't we live freely as normal people?
Hate
This is how it was. Kids under 15 will be killed right away.
Not even sent to concentration camps.
Others were put in gas chambers to be killed.
Hate
Nazis stole the Jew's valuables.
Some people stayed alive from this horrible day.
Hate
That's how it started just from Hate.

Cecelia Rought, Grade 6

The Jewish...

With David's Star pinned to their chests,
 the Jews were hoping to be blessed.
The Nazi army was on patrol,
 to kill every Jewish soul.
When the Jews were sent away to die,
 parents sacrificed their lives,
 to protect their children and close their eyes.
But as the Nazi's got more coarse,
 the Jewish people's hope got worse.
And right as the Jews were about to get killed,
 the U.S. Army gave them a thrill.
They had been saved,
 and they shall always be remembered and praised.

Chiara Dooley, Grade 6

Memories

A memory is a wonderful thing
Good times and bad times.
Happy times and sad times.
Some that you wish you never had
And some you wish you could hold on to forever.

The best ones are always with the people you love
And the worst ones are the ones without them.
A memory is something irreplaceable.
One cannot be bought or sold.
A great memory is priceless.

You can never get rid of a memory.
No matter how awful they are.
They will always be there through thick and thin.
Like the devil and angel on your shoulder.
Supporting you or pushing you back.

They record everything you do like a diary in your mind.

Matthew Kilmurray, Grade 6

Dance

Dance is a bubble
No one can pop it
It always ends when the dance finishes
And all you want is for it to come back

Dance is a mountain
High altitude when you succeed to reach the top
Sometimes you just slide down
But when you try, reaching the top is easy

Dance is oxygen
You breathe it in
It soothes your life
And people can't live without it

Dance is a dream
A pinch wakes you up
But it is always there
Inside your life, impacting you forever

Margaret Sandler, Grade 6

Those Last Words

The last words my grandfather said to me just before he died,
Those words told me this job wasn't going to be as easy as pie!
I thought about them day and night,
What should I do?
To find someone to share his spirit I had to find someone soon!
After all, when I was little he called me his little straw of hay!
But I soon found my answer the very next day.
When I woke up I called for my little friend and he came trotting
All blonde and fluffy with his sweet little eyes
And I hugged him,
My sweet golden little puppy.

Jordan Cavender, Grade 5

High Merit Poems – Grades 4, 5, and 6

Green

Green…
Brilliantly blooming at a great pace.
Spreading color all over the place.
It continuously springs,
And it beautifully sings.
Enveloping everything wherever it goes.
Speeding along, it rarely slows.
Full of life with little despair.
Energy flowing from everywhere.

Teeming,
  Teaching,
Teetering,
  Teasing.
Jealousy makes many things dull.
It's the exact opposite of a lull.
Clear and true,
Green, the energetic hue.
Ben Nelson, Grade 6

Green

Green is a willow tree
An evergreen for Christmas
Green is the grass in my yard
A lush forest
Green makes me feel great!

An avocado plant
A tasty apple
A pistachio nut
Green is a leafy fern
The malachite in a palace

Green is money
It looks like an emerald
It smells like lime
It is mint in tea
Green is the sound of the wind
Green is the sea
George Corfias, Grade 4

Winter Leaves

W ind is blowing
I nside avoiding snow
N o flowers
T rees are bare
E very year it comes
R ain turns to snow

L ong icicles on my roof
E ve of Christmas
A nimals hibernating
V ery cold
E mpty hearts
S pring will come soon
Margaux Walz, Grade 5

My Dog

S urprisingly handsome.
H appy all the time.
A lways chewing on something.
D eadly cute.
O utstandingly fun.
W onderful!
Kaleb Brown, Grade 4

Ashes

Ashes, ashes, dancing in the sky
Making everybody say, "Oh, my!"
Their mother is fire, she is big and bright
She is nature's beautiful light.
Their father is wood, he is Earth's child
I sit there and watch the ashes go wild.
Hannah Oswald, Grade 4

Rain

Stop, rain,
Stop coming down.
Even if I do like your sound.
Sky, stop.
Stop your rain.
Rain, stop giving playful kids pain.
Marli Harris, Grade 5

Snow

Glittering flakes falling from the sky
Covering the ground like a blanket
Trees with frosting on them
Marshmallows fill the land
Sparkling the atmosphere
Oh, beautiful snow days!
Rachel Christensen, Grade 5

Merry Christmas

All the birds are going south
Because this town is now Christmas Town.
Christmas is coming up and
Scary days are going down.
Gifts are under the tree.
It's a merry Christmas!
Carl Slate, Grade 4

Spring

I love to hear the birds and bees.
I love the smell of apple trees.
I love to eat the honey
And look at cute white bunnies.
I love hearing the birds sing.
Oh how I love spring!
Kylie Bowe, Grade 4

Ocean

Running into the water
Straight to paradise
Ocean Blue

Salty waves fierce and feisty
Big bold and brave
Crashing down on the sand

Perfect waves
For boogie boarding
Finally calming down
At ends day

As the sun descends
The sand at dusk still warm
The moon and stars
Come out to play
Kira Poliviou, Grade 6

Shining Bright

The stars are gleaming
Strong and bright
They sing a song
And say goodnight
They dance they sway
Across the sky
They linger there
As time goes by
Shining through the milky way
Still aglow for me today
Over the moon
They wander free
Chasing the darkness above the sea
The stars are gleaming
Strong and bright
They sing a song…
And say goodnight
Lily Amadio, Grade 6

Just Think

One person was full of hate
Full of greed
And that one person
Started it all
— Just think —
11 million Jews died
Dead, not here anymore
Gone forever
Never to be seen again
— Just think —
12 years of this
12 years of
Concentration camps
Death, and mourning
— Just think —
Raquelle Roesch, Grade 6

It's All About...
It's about paddle ball being played
No one sitting in the shade
Staying hydrated, drinking kool aid

It's about getting a tan everywhere you look there is sand
It is so hot you need a fan

It's about going to the boardwalk
Licking melting ice cream
Shopping 'til you wipe every store clean

It's about being relaxed eating salty snacks
Watching the kayaks

It's about splashing in the water so hazy
Lifeguards whistling like crazy
Teenagers being lazy

It's about breathing the cool air having the time of your life there
Not having a care

It's about watching the advertisement planes fly by
Looking at the beautiful sky
Eating delicious boardwalk French fries
Shannon Garvey, Grade 5

The Tiger
The brown, black striped creature
Pink, tough tongue slurping its paw as if it was a Popsicle
Rough, firm stone pads gripping to the ground
Its wide eyes, its flicking ears, its twitching tail
It's purring like a deep velvety growl
Swish! Swoosh! Go the trees gently blowing around the tiger
Scurry! Scurry! Scurry!
The tiger hears the mouse
Tiptoe! Tiptoe! Goes the tiger
He slowly walks like a turtle
He waits and… POUNCE!
He gobbles up the mouse
And takes a nice long nap

Natalie Haugen, Grade 4

Celebrate Thanksgiving
Thanksgiving is a time to praise,
A time to let your happiness raise.
A time to sit at a table and eat,
With your family and your friends to greet.
Thanksgiving is a time to be glad,
With your siblings, your mom, and your dad.
Thanksgiving is a time to feast,
On corn, potatoes, and turkey at least.
Thanksgiving is in the season of fall,
With wind, dry leaves, and pumpkins for all.
I like Thanksgiving. It's pretty fun,
It's a time to celebrate with everyone.
Jessie Yahner, Grade 4

Fall
Morning dew catches my eye,
as fading clouds move away from the sky.
Soft sand covers the ground,
as things in it wait to be found.
Rocks and acorns cover the floor,
in these wonderful sights, I would like to see more.
Now instead of down, lets look up,
where water is being held, not in a cup.
The sun is up there, bright as can be,
there are more beautiful sights to see.
The shaking trees make clean air,
as the wind blowing, runs through my hair.
Birds and crickets chirping loudly,
as squirrels sitting in their homes proudly.
Leaves changing colors ready to fall–this is a great sight for all.
Green grass moving all around,
as we listen to natures lovely sound.
Take a look, so many sights to see,
Earth is a great place to be.
Say goodbye to summer, it will now be gone,
say hello to fall, let's bring it on.
Anika Melkote, Grade 4

Rain
Absorbed into the air
Heavy rain transforming into silver-lined drops
Like little crystals in the air
Descend from the round-edged clouds
Which drop on the ground and instantly disappear
Round after round they each take turns
Coming back down
To sing a song
Of pitter-patter
C
 a
  s
   c
    a
     d
      i
       n
        g
off glass windows and cars
Eventually ending
Giving to a brighter day
Jaclyn Schuman, Grade 6

Baton
Baton is my favorite thing to do!
It makes you feel independent and free.
When you're performing in front of the crowd,
it's like the spot light is on you.
Feeling the baton twirling between your
fingers is like nothing else in the world.
Baton is my escape.
Victoria Moore, Grade 6

Blue
Blue is the early morning sky
The rushing ocean
And bubbles gently floating in the air
Blue is quiet like a library
Where I like to read a book
Or in a movie theater
Before the start of the show
Blue tastes like yummy apple pie
Delicious red velvet cheesecake
And steaming hot chocolate
Blue feels soft like my hair
Fluffy like my pillow
And comfy like my clothes
Blue can really sing!
Elizabeth Barthelus, Grade 4

Red
Red is the color of Santa's suit
A lacy Valentine heart
And a tasty strawberry pie
Red sounds like a loud gun shot
That makes everyone run
At the Jamaican Parade
It tastes saucy
Like a juicy meatball
And refreshing like fruit punch
On a hot day
Red feels warm
Like a crackling fire
Taking away the chill
Red can light up your world!
Clive Campbell, Grade 4

Flying Pests
Get out you stupid birds
Stop eating my mother's corn
You're just some giant turds
You're making me feel forlorn
My mother told me to watch out
But now I've let her down
I'm gonna be in trouble without a doubt
And when I am, her face will turn brown
Oh wait, I know what to do
I'll need some cloth and fabric of course
But at least it will get rid of you
And I won't sit in the corner by force
Here we are, here comes the show
I've just built a scarecrow!
Ryan Vuillemot, Grade 5

Animals and People
Animals are just like you
They bark, you talk
They run and play in the park
While you swing on the monkey bars
Alaina Lewis, Grade 5

I Am
I am awesome!
I'm very curious.
I play video games.
I play sports.
I am awesome!

I pretend I'm a soldier.
I run and jump to everything.
I feel no pain but my own.
I help others.
I am awesome!

I care for others.
I save people in danger.
I get very sleepy.
I try and try and never give up.
I am awesome!
Spencer Mann, Grade 6

Fire Spell
I know a spell,
of which I yell,
over mountains and hills.
It would give some people chills,
which doesn't make sense,
because it misrepresents,
what the spell actually does.
The spell goes like this:
"All the forces of nature collide,
all from mother nature's pride,
but I would only like the one,
of all the forces you could meet,
fire's the one I'd like to greet."
What it would do,
is set me ablaze,
and amaze,
everyone around me.
Bailey Coon, Grade 5

Pink
Compassion
 Love
  Joy
Warmly welcoming the wanderer's soul
Happily inviting them in from the cold
Helping kindly
Whomever it can
Helping
 Happy
  Joyful
   Glad
Gently touching
With loving hand
It is in all of us
Pink can understand
Claire Fennell, Grade 6

Purple
Is the color of a crayon
Smooth purple grapes
And my beautiful purple dress
It's a volcano erupting,
A table falling
And fireworks booming
It tastes like creamy ice cream,
Cheesy pizza,
And red, ripe strawberries
It is a massaging chair,
And a comfy, soft bed
Purple changes your world!
Marlynn Dorielan, Grade 4

My Great Day
T urkey day is great
H am is always on the table
A ll the family came
N ice and neat
K itchen was clean
S ongs were sung
G ood food
I ce was in the pop
V arieties of food
I ate too much
N o food was left
G reat joy
Logan Hurley, Grade 6

One Person
One person started it all
One person made them fall
One person could've stopped it
One person stood and watched it
One person was in the camp
One person thought he was champ
One person stayed in a house
One person tried to stay quiet as a mouse
One person thought he would win
One person was plucked with a pin
One person was very lost
But several people remember the Holocaust
Eliza Burgoyne, Grade 6

Dancing
D ancing is just a work of art
A nd it can be fierce or graceful
N ever think that you can't
C ause in dancing can't is not a word
I 've always lived up to doing it
N ever regretting my thoughts
G o on now
Try it on your own
The only way to succeeding
Is knowing that you tried
Emma McDonald, Grade 5

Rose

The sky unfolds
The sun awakens from a nightly slumber
The bright green, knee-high grasses of a meadow bask in the sun's amber rays
The forest tumbles out, spreading cool patches of shade onto a sun-warmed meadow
The clearest of brooks trickles through the forest and the meadow
The brook continuously babbles its unmistakable song, so beautiful and sweet, just like its waters
Wild roses unfurl their fragrant petals, so delicate and fragile, protected only by their merciless thorns
Just like the rose, even through the beauty of a mild summer day, not everything is perfect.
The sky can be dark and menacing
The sun may be concealed
The meadow's grasses could go limp
The forest can frighten the bravest to enter
The clearest of brooks might become murky, can cease to sing a song, could be pungent and stagnant
A rose can lose a soft grip on moistureless petals
A smell so sweet can turn acrid
Thorns would be razor-edged and extended
But, never think of imperfections.
There is one in everything.
Think of the Rose.

Evelina West, Grade 6

Imagine a World

Imagine a world where the golden sun meets the diamond-like moon
Where steaming molten lava clashes with clear sapphire water

Imagine a world where shadowy silhouettes stride through the thick coal-black fiery mist near the erupted volcano
Where spirits roam the large wondrous mountains and leave to find its true self in the valleys of heaven

Imagine a world where all your questions could be answered and fear does not exist
Where you see no poor or homeless families stroll through never-ending periods of poverty

Imagine a world where creatures play with the clouds and sea animals go through the coral of the Lost City of Atlantis
Where plants could be free from the roots that imprison them in dirty brown soil

Imagine a world where you can fly; where your imagination takes you
Be who you want to be in this world.

No one is stopping you

Noah Giglietti, Grade 6

My Sports

Soccer is an action movie in fast forward
the fast paced game runs on and on
when your eyes meet the scoreboard your, face turns pale
and the game feels as if it will never end.
A goal is an award at the Grammys
when you hear the ball scrape the back of the net
when the game is tied and you are so proud
when you are running back to midfield, you have that look on your face.
Football is a wave
the score is intense
you know that you have a chance to win
when the ball is in midair for the last play of the game.
A touchdown is a homerun in the world series
when you know that you have made a difference in the game and people now know your name.

Connor Skowron, Grade 6

I Am

I am a strong gymnast.
I wonder if I will be in the Olympics.
I hear people cheering.
I see my family in the bleachers.
I want to become a professional gymnast.

I am a strong gymnast.
I pretend I am Gabby Douglas.
I feel like I can do it.
I touch my pillow and dream big.
I worry that I am going to get hurt.
I cry when people die.

I am a strong gymnast.
I understand when other girls win at competitions.
I say I am ready.
I dream that I can do a full back twist off the beam.
I hope I do great.
I am a strong gymnast.

Alyssa Kazanjian, Grade 5

Winter

Fall, fall, fall is leaving, winters coming all the way
leaves are falling, snow is calling, shout hooray!
slipping and sliding, it's all you do
winter's fun for me and you

breath in the air
take a good sniff
all that winter wear
is making you stiff

get your hot cocoa
take a big sip
ow, that hurt
it burnt your lip

so say hello to all that snow
and say goodbye to all the leaves
brr it's cold, that's why it's time
for winters coming all the way

Kira Safferstein, Grade 5

Mutant Petting Zoo

Have you ever visited a Mutant Petting Zoo?
I did and I got to
feed the zpeng,
pet the monkbird,
wave to the redbear,
pet the spider monkey,
laugh at the lophin,
and hold the zilia.

It was so much fun!
I think everyone should go see the Mutant Petting Zoo!

Kerstin Hamman, Grade 5

I See Fall

I am a young man who loves fall.
I wonder if the bright leaves crumble.
I hear laughter of children having fun in the fall
breeze playing in the colorful leaf piles.
I see beautiful fall colors in the tall oak trees.
I want fluffy colorful leave piles to jump in with my friend.
I am a young man who loves fall.

I pretend to swim in the soft leaf pile.
I feel happy and excited about fall because autumn
is an exciting, wonderful season.
I touch leaves, trees and branches.
I worry about the wet rain pouring and strong
winds blowing.
I am a young man who loves fall.

I understand that kids play in leaf piles.
I say jokes to my friends.
I dream of building fun leaf piles.
I try enjoying outdoors and nature.
I hope I go outside for fun in the fall air.
I am a young man who loves fall.

Jacob Pimentel, Grade 5

Frogs

Frogs are green.
They are the color of a green bean.
They sometimes can't be seen.
Some are new.
There might be a few.
Some might be out of sight.
Maybe they do not like light.
But maybe it is because they don't want to die.
Maybe they hide so they can catch flies.
I like frogs
Because they are not as big as a hog.
They can hop on logs.
And they can pop out of the fog.
I like when they swim.
I would like to call one Jim.
When they jump,
I never hear one thump.
Maybe because they are sleek.
Or they might just be meek.
But the greatest part of the frog
Is that they were made from God.

Mary Angela Pinci, Grade 5

Hitler

H is for hate an evil four letter word
I is for inequality for the Jews
T is for terrorism of what the Nazi's were doing
L is for leave which the Jews wanted to do
E is for equality which the Jews should have
R is for racists that the Nazi's were

Trent Federico, Grade 6

Ode to My Family
Oh, I love my mom
Oh, I love my dad
When sad, I get comfort
From Mommy and Dad.

Nana and Grandpa
I fall in love with kisses and cuddles
We go to the movies
To see Judy Moody.

Mimi and cousins:
Noah, Brady, Jonah
We all play football
Uh-oh, here comes the ball!

Oh family, oh family!
I love you so
You love me as much as the whole wide world
Oh family, oh family!, I love you so dear
I'll love you forever far and near.
Arissa Riley, Grade 4

Strike Three! You're Out!
I am a fearless, left-handed softball player
I wonder if I will get better
I hear the sound of silence when I'm about to pitch the big, round, hard, yellow ball
I see my parents in the crowd cheering me on
I want to play on the world famous U.S. women's softball team
I am a fearless, left-handed softball player

I pretend I am the coach when players need help
I feel the seams on the ball when I am about to pitch it
I touch the heavy, metal bat
I worry that I am not good enough for professional leagues
I am a fearless, left-handed softball player

I understand all my dreams won't come true
I say I know I can
I dream of being a world champion
I try to do my best
I hope I will always be able to play softball, forever
I am a fearless, left-handed softball player
Olivia Gilbert, Grade 5

Yiming Su
Y iming is a good name for me.
I 'm living in Mt. Lebanon.
M cGinnis is my home room teacher's name.
I n school, my favorite class is art.
N ame is important to me.
G o to the school Monday to Friday.

S mart at playing Legos
U sually sometimes like to go outside
Yiming Su, Grade 5

Swimming
It's about…
Stepping up to the diving block
You're watching the clock

It's about…
Flying of the diving block
Streamlining to the flags

It's about…
You're hands following the same flowing pattern
your mind acting from memory

It's about…
Turning on the wall
You know you are half way through

It's about…
That moment that you touch the wall
The feeling that floods through your body

It's about…
Asking your coach how much time you dropped
And if you qualify for districts, states, or nationals

It's about…
My favorite sport
Manav Gundecha, Grade 5

Christmas
Christmas is coming and I just can't wait
Santa loads our tree with gifts that are great.

He very carefully picks out the things I really like
Last time I got a laptop, Xbox and a dirt bike.

I try every year to stay up late enough to see
How in the world he gets down our little chimney.

He goes through a lot to get it all into place
Up and down 100 times as if it was a race.

Not a scratch on the floor or a nick on the door
Just presents everywhere spread out on the floor.

One year I really saw a bunch of reindeer tracks
I knew he was there because he ate all the snacks.

We leave Santa his favorite cookies, chunky chocolate chip
The carrots are for the reindeer, they like them with ranch dip!

As my father said, "I better think twice"
To listen to him and take his advice

To be a good boy and stick to my goal
Make good decisions or I'll get lumps of coal!
Donny Brewster, Grade 5

Thanksgiving

Thanksgiving is a wonderful season.
I can think of a lot of good reasons.

Life is what God gave to me,
I am as free as I want to be.

Thanksgiving is a good time to pray,
I don't even bother to play.

I am going to eat all of the turkey,
I just hope it isn't jerky.

I am going to pray all day,
Just do what I do, and you'll have a great day.
Joshua Beblar, Grade 4

Winter

When I see the white snow all over the ground,
I know that winter's making its way around.
I can smell the hot chocolate and marshmallows galore.
It is almost time for some fun outdoors.

When I slip on my winter attire,
I feel nice and warm like I am standing by the fire.
When I step outside and touch the cold snow,
I suddenly feel the strong wind starting to blow.

I grab my red sled and start sprinting up the hill,
I am suddenly filled with a joyful thrill.
I realize that this may be,
The best winter it could possibly be.
Brenna Glance, Grade 6

The Beauty of Rain

It's sunrise after rain in spring.
I can hear other birds chirping and raindrops dripping off the trees.
The rain feels very damp on my feathers.
The stacks of hay and the rotting fence's stench fill the air.
The rainbow in the sky is purple, blue, yellow and orange.
I look around and see the beautiful kaleidoscope.
I'm drying my wet feathers from the rain.
I love the relaxed feeling of the rainbow.
Will this peace ever end?
Kaitlyn, Grade 4

Christmas Morning

Wake up to see all the presents under the tree,
All the cookies have disappeared
What has happened?
Who has been here?
We ask Mom and Dad,
They say it was the jolly fat man
Also known as Santa Claus
I look at my sister to see the look on her face,
We all are amazed.
Autumn Forte, Grade 6

Hermit Crab

I reach for a shell on the beach's wet sand.
The waves crash and I force it into my hand.
I look inside the tiny blue shell.
I saw a hermit crab and it didn't look so well.
It looked frightened of a human being.
For the first time it is seeing.
If scared, a pinch of its claws could put me in tears.
But hey, it's the beach and crabs have ears.
So I don't want to whine and make the crab upset.
Plus, I'm standing in water and getting very wet.
I become hotter and hotter from the rays of the sun.
So I place the crab in the water and no harm done.
I race home as my feet burn.
Maybe next time I'll bring a bucket, there's something to learn.
Aidan Duffy, Grade 5

Thank You

Thank you for the stable roof over my head,
That protects me from wind, rain, and frigid snow.

Thank you for the delicious food on my plate,
As people in Haiti starve.

Thank you for my loving family,
Mom, Dad, and sisters.

Thank you for the clothes on my back,
The ones that keep me warm and the ones that fit just right.

But most of all, thank you for your love and happiness,
Because I wouldn't be able to live without it!
Shannon Hickey, Grade 5

Innocence Lost

I will never forget the day,
When over three thousand people passed away.
People were crying on the city street,
Praying that the towers would not meet.

As the second plane crashed,
The firefighters dashed.
Up the long stairwell our firefighters went,
Smelling that horrible smoky scent.

Children lost their parents that day,
All they really could do was pray.
Twelve years later their memories live on,
Forever that day our innocence was gone.
Lauren Guy, Grade 6

Horses of Above

I can hear the horses galloping in a storm,
I can hear the horses during the day,
I can hear the horses during the night,
I can her the horses whenever I want because they are in my soul
Emily Hart, Grade 6

I Will Heal
I am intelligent and Athletic
I wonder why people die
I hear fans calling my name, "Isaiah!"
I see myself, what's inside me
I want a Galaxy S4 because of the movies
I am intelligent and athletic

I pretend to be a doctor who saves kids
I feel sad about me closing my eyes forever
I touch Zeus, the god of the sky
I worry I am going to die
I cry when I think of my godmother
I am intelligent and athletic

I understand my grandfather
I say there is only one God
I dream that I will be the best doctor
I try to be the best football player
I hope that I will be a famous wide receiver
I am intelligent and athletic
Isaiah Rush, Grade 5

The New Puppy
It was a warm July day
you came to visit
and get a puppy
I was hoping it would be me
I wanted a forever home
some of my brothers and sister had died
but I was lucky
you didn't notice me I was very shy
I was scared to come out
but then you picked me
you caught lightning bugs
and put them next to me
you had tummy troubles and so did I
you just didn't know yet
now you do and now I know
you love me you brush me water me
and take me to trick or treat
you give me Smarties because you
know they are safe for you and me
I love you lots your puppy
Elizabeth Erin Selfe, Grade 4

Halloween
H ey it's Halloween
A ll the kids
L ove Halloween
L ittle to big
O h! We just love Halloween
W e love to get candy and
E at it 'til it runs out
E very parent hopes
N o cavities with all of that candy
Daeviana Blount, Grade 5

Colorful Dreams
Dreams are blue
for the ocean or sea
Dreams are white
for clouds making pictures in the sky
Dreams are gray
for a stormy day
Dreams are black
empty because you have none
Dreams are green
for plants, trees and money making us rich
Dreams are brown
for chocolate satisfying my sweet tooth
Dreams are yellow
for the sun that warms the earth
Dreams are red
for roses on dates
Dreams are a rainbow
that gives us company
Rimervi Mendez, Grade 5

Pink
Pink is the love
And warmth you
Feel inside
Pink is the heart
You should never hide
Warm and soft
As the sunset sky
Pink are the bows
In a child's hair
Folded and tightened in
A mother's care
Pink is the smell of
The tulips planted
By a grandmother
With a voice as pink
Pink goes la, la, la
Pink is the puppy
Barking for you
Isabella Capaldi, Grade 5

Blue
Is the sky on a nice day
Violets that are in my yard
And bright new shoes
I hear someone blue
And the big wave that hits the ocean
Or a screeching blue chair
It's the taste of blueberries
And the sticky cotton candy
With a great sweet taste of a lollipop
The feeling when my father yells at me
Being blue feels like being blown away
Blue feels like a winter day
This color helps you get past the day.
Miles DeJesus, Grade 4

The Ocean
Continuous waves
Breaking down
The ocean floor
Becoming deeper and deeper
As I swim past the waves
They seem not to disappear
And go on forever.
The ocean is vast
In a distance
Far away
I see
People playing on the beach
I inhale,
The saltiness.
Massive waves thrashing
As ice cold, refreshing water
Startles me
Frightened,
I quickly swim to shore
Joshua Abramovich, Grade 6

Hunting
My clothes are laid out,
and my alarm is set.
I'm anxiously awaiting,
for the best hunting day yet.

I have a hard time sleeping;
I want the morning to get here.
All I can think about
is a big huge deer!

Finally I hear the alarm,
and it's time to go.
I hope it's a good day
and some deer show.

Even if they don't,
it will still be great.
Any time I get a chance to be in the woods,
I never hesitate.
Bryce Jones, Grade 6

Trees
Trees are so pretty
With all their leaves and branches
They sway in the breeze

Nice, beautiful trees
Birch, oak, pine, and hickory
All the awesome kinds

Oh, majestic trees
Rising into the blue sky
My, how I love them
Jack Adase, Grade 6

Painting

When I'm painting I feel free like a winter breeze,
When I'm painting I can smell the paint as sea breeze
When I'm painting I hear the bristles prickling across the page and everything else spills away,
When I'm painting I can touch the brush and build an archway.

When I'm painting I can taste the success with everything I sketch,
When I'm painting it is my mind I do stretch
When I'm painting it's an escape into Norway,
When I'm painting it can take me far away.

When I'm painting I can see over the seas,
When I'm painting I do it with such ease,
When I'm painting I can often hear the bay,
When I'm painting all my cares just go away.

Julia Susie, Grade 6

Christmas

I remember the thrill of finally pulling out the list from that year and showing and explaining everything to my mom in great detail.
I remember the night before the big day and just dreaming about everything on that list.
I remember the thrill of not sleeping that whole night and just looking at the clock.
And then, finally falling asleep.
I remember the morning of Christmas going into my sister's room and saying "GET UP" a million times until she gets up.
I remember when we got downstairs we each took turns opening presents.
I remember that night we would go to my grandparents' house where our whole family went every Christmas ever since I was a baby.
I remember that night eating almost the whole pumpkin pie and then driving home super late and falling right asleep in the back of my mom's car.

Chloe Streckfus, Grade 5

Clouds on the Blue Canvas

A shining blue canvas stained with the morning light and white pastel lay over the big earth like it is a child in his cradle.
Pink and orange paints spill among the remaining stars and black emptiness. The once plain blue is now thriving with wonderful color like fireworks in the night.
This sky is truly a work of art.
The sun is now visible in the air, floating on a string of invisible, thin silk it is.
The sun rises over the mountains and shines out and adds the finishing touch.
Sun rays rush like a busy highway on Monday all around.
The sun kisses the cheeks of small children staring at the marvelous display before them.
The clouds shine as bright as the sun itself.
The sun sinks below the mountains.
The canvas and bursting colors fade into the shadows of the empty space and will come again tomorrow.

Fiona Riegert, Grade 5

Lime

On the outside, you look like the skin of a lizard in the form of a ball
You feel like the roughness of a lizard skin when you pet it
When I peel you, you sound like when someone is trying to rip a piece of paper without tearing it.
When I slice you, you sound like a phone on vibrate when someone is trying to call you
Inside, you look like a scrunched piece of green paper
You feel like the baggy skin of an elephant
You smell like the very strong and sour perfume
You taste like sour patch kids when you chew them
Tell me, why is your smell very, very, sour and strong?

Gabriela Fuller, Grade 5

Soccer
Soccer
Amazing, fantastic
Passing, dribbling, kicking
A lot of hustling
Sport
Luka Berkovic, Grade 5

Water
Water
Liquid, H20
Moving, splashing, flowing
Going, down a waterfall
Aqua
Nathen Hynes, Grade 6

Roberto Clemente
Roberto Clemente
Small, fast
Catching, diving, throwing
Always throws to home
Legend
John Andrew Brown, Grade 5

Snowy Days
Christmas
Fun, exciting
Laughing, skiing, loving
Giving love to family
Holiday
Gia Capristo, Grade 5

Ms. Giehll
Ms Giehll
Thin, nice
Teaching, helping, smiling
Her actions are amazing
Teacher
Nina Paliouras, Grade 5

Katniss
Katniss
Volunteer, tribute
Fighting, surviving, winning
The girl on fire
Mocking jay
Caitie Brooks, Grade 5

Jack-o-lantern
Jack-o-lantern
Spooky, orange
Glowing, frightening, scaring
He's round and orange
Pumpkin
Logan Schermerhorn, Grade 5

Leaves Are Falling
Crunch, crunch, snap, crunch the leaves crunch.
under my feet. The cold breeze stings my face.
I can smell fall and the lady bugs and the leaves.

I can see my breath in the air.
I can see the scary jack o lanterns glowing in their scary ways.
I can hear the birds in the trees and hear the creek and screams.

I can see the leaves falling everywhere and the mini tornados made with leaves.
I can hear the acorns fall on the roofs bang, tink, bom, tink, tink.
Mackenzie Larimer, Grade 6

Brave
Brave is the sight of a golden sword.
Brave is the sight of the savior of a lord.
Brave is the sight of the grass in the wind thrashing and bashing not able to win.
Brave is the sight of the golden heart.
Brave is the sight of a plane in the air silently cruising without a care.
Brave is the sight of the light that shines all the time.
Brave is the sight of lightning in the sky and stars in the night.
Brave is anything whether it be continuing, losing, winning, or even fighting.
Brave is not measured in any way, for braveness itself is here to stay.
So tell me, are you brave?
Ashley Mariani, Grade 5

Beautiful Bohemia
My neighborhood is the buzzing of people racing to get the greasy,
delicious pizza for Friday night parties
My neighborhood is cars inching down Belver Dr. and 7th St. to get to
the high school when the sky is still dull
My neighborhood is birds chirping in the trees like Mozart conducting his orchestra
And it is a sweet scent drifting through the air when our neighbors
are having a scrumptious barbecue
And it is as joyful as cute little children laughing and yelling while
playing when the sun is at its highest point.
Kelly Romandi, Grade 6

Grapefruit
On the outside, you look like a big, yellow, ball
You feel like a soft baby's cheek
When I peel you, you sound like the sound of branch's breaking in the wind
When I slice you, it sounds like a person carving wood
Inside, you look like a pink table cloth with tiny lumps
You feel like a bumpy, rough, road
You smell like a ripe orange
You taste like sour pink lemonade
Tell me, why do you have the same color as the sun?
Charlize Tejeda, Grade 5

Thanksgiving
Turkey hatchlings peeking out of their eggs.
Pumpkin pie made at home from dough and love.
Farms, pumpkins, apples, squash, and animals to have fun.
Colored leaves crumbling on the ground as the birds are flying south.
Thanksgiving, a time for family love.
Natalie Quintino, Grade 4

High Merit Poems – Grades 4, 5, and 6

Scared
Scared is black
It sounds like screams
It smells like fear
It tastes like two-week old pie
It looks like the devil
Scared is like stepping on a shard of glass
Olivia Parker, Grade 5

Love in Jesus and Angels
A round the world
N ever will I forget
G ive and peace
E verything is for him
L oving and soft, for the
S on of God
Micah Blankenship, Grade 6

Happiness
Happiness is like white fluffy clouds
It sounds like laughter
It smells like fresh-cut grass
It tastes like chocolate fudge
It looks like a sunflower
Happiness feels like 100%
Jessica Lacava, Grade 5

Fall Is Nice
Fall is all these things and more...
Fun jumping in piles of leaves,
Apple picking time,
Longer nights are upon us.
Look as the wind blows.
Fall is my favorite season. Is it yours?
Jenna Raczka, Grade 4

Ink
Why
Do calligraphy pens
Get ink
All over
Our
Hands?
Zhen Suda, Grade 5

Furious
It looks like black
It sounds like crackling fire
It smells like vinegar
It tastes like jalepenos
It looks like lightning
Furious feels like yelling
Connor Woodward, Grade 5

Birthday Wishes*
Wishes I keep to myself:

Wish my parents
would let me play
tackle football for Fenn

Wish I could play a professional
sport and make a living
doing something I love

Wish I could beat my siblings

Wish mother would let
me play basketball instead
of skiing every weekend

Wish I could persuade Fenn into letting 5th graders
play a sport for Fenn and be on
one of Fenn's sport teams this year

Wish father would let me stay up later
and have my bedtime be 10:00 instead of 9:30
and have them quit babying me and playing the youngest game with me

Mostly, I wish that I will be drafted
into Lexington Little League Majors this season
instead of having to play in AAA and wait 'til next year
until I can play with the older kids.
Stuart McCallum, Grade 5
*Inspired by "Inside Out and Back Again"

Fabulous Autumn Weeks
Light jackets come out, the temperature starts to get a little colder
An enormous amount of wind blows by, leaves drift to the ground
Bright, vivid colors of the changing leaves, orange, red, amber, brown
The crunchy leaves scrunching

Plump pumpkins being carved
Jack-o-lanterns glowing in the darkness

The doorbell is a trumpet, ringing so loudly
Family is pouring in like a big wave
Sweet buttery corn being eaten
Cinnamon apple cider being poured, the mug breathes scorching hot steam
Pleasant warm, fluffy, buttery mashed potatoes
Terrific tender turkeys, splendid steaming stuffing
Delicious cinnamon apple fritters

Wake up time, birds chirping abundantly
Wonderful music to my ears
Shiny apples glow like a crystal ball

A crisp breeze brushes my face gently
Goodbye light jackets, hello heavy jackets, scarfs, and hats
Katie Postel, Grade 6

Goal!
On the field
towards the goal
around players
past people
near the net
across the field
against a hard player
down the whole field
near the goal takes a shot
above the goalie's head
without a doubt…Goal!
Cristina D'Amato, Grade 5

Beautiful Birds
A beautiful bird sings a beautiful song.
I wish I could listen to it all day long.
Some birds, like owls, stay up all night.
For some critters, that can be a fright.
For if they are seen, to the owl they belong.

Speaking of amazing birds of prey,
I watch them from my window every day.
There is a nest of hawks in my tree,
With fluffy tales, as red as can be.
Then Niko barks, and they all fly away.
Krista Polanofsky, Grade 4

Autumn
The leaves crunch beneath my feet,
The sun is at my back.

The fields are bright with autumn light,
The moon a harvest glow.

Pumpkins, apples, wheat fields around me,
Autumn really glows.

The stars shine down on me,
And I know why Autumn is a favorite.
Sarah Bjornstad, Grade 5

Halloween Night
On Halloween night,
There shall be a great fright.

Goblins, ghosts roaming the streets,
Trying to find the best treats.

If I get scared to death,
I will have to take a deep breath.

Too bad it's over, I am very sad,
But maybe next year I won't be so bad.
Christian Penkrat, Grade 6

The Beauty of Art
It's about drawing with pastels
as hard as shells

It's about going to
art class walking into
the dream world of beauty

It's about learning art
Getting smart
Turning into art

It's about getting better
pictures getting bigger
drawing harder pictures

It's about a different
way to show
my feelings

It's about how
I like to
express myself

It's about what I like to do!
Hannah Zhou, Grade 5

Nature Is My Home
The birds drift by,
Delicate and shy.
Bright colors all around me.
I even see a bumblebee.

Nature is my home,
Its cares for me so dearly.
Like a mother,
Caring for a child.

The luscious grass will be my bed.
Oh! The fun will never end!
The sparkling blue ponds are my showers.
The outdoors gives me super powers!

It seems, oh my!
I can understand the animals!
I can hear whistles and barks.
Look! There are some skylarks!

Nature is my home,
It cares for me so dearly.
Like a mother,
Caring for a child.
Erin Sudbey, Grade 5

What Is a Book?
What is a book?
A pathway to a new place
A perfect way to escape
My best friend in a time of need
A bandage when I bleed
Full of sunshine on a rainy day
I can run away and play
Full of adventures new and old
Stories ready to be told
That is a book
Sydney Schauwecker, Grade 6

Outer Space
Sun, moon, and stars,
Venus and Mars,
Mercury and Jupiter too.
There's Saturn's icy rings,
And Uranus' beautiful color.
Then there's Neptune, near the
Coldest dwarf, used to be a planet,
Pluto, named by Venetian Phair,
The planets will never be too near,
To our loved planet Earth's atmosphere.
Ellie Butcher, Grade 4

Soccer Balls
Onto the field
Off their feet
In the air
Above their heads
Down to the ground
Around his feet
Past the player
Up in the air
Past the goalie
Into the goal!
Erik Andersen, Grade 5

Ode to Pizza
Ah, yes, pizza
How you taste so great
With cheese, meat, anything!
Yes, I love you so dear
I could eat you all day and night
I cannot put you down
Even would not think of dropping you
I'll love you all my life
And when I die and I'm in the afterlife
I'll still love you until the end of time.
Ryan Carey, Grade 4

Winter
See the drifting snow
Quiet as can be falling
Peaceful and serene
Isabella Bracco, Grade 5

High Merit Poems – Grades 4, 5, and 6

Out of Sight
Deep in the forest
In the trees
Rustling the leaves
Was a bird
Max Saltzer, Grade 4

Snow
S ledding down a hill
N ight time comes, then more snow
O utside flakes of ice are falling
W hoosh a snowball is thrown
Lucas Cusick, Grade 5

Dogs
Loud, crazy, wild, playful.
They are cute and fluffy.
You could snuggle and cuddle and play.
Just remember — they are fun!
Nicole Geres, Grade 5

Scary Skeleton
The skeleton has lots of bones
That move and play many tones
The children are out on the town
He should be buried in the ground.
Nicholas Schumacher, Grade 6

Earthquake
All land is quiet
Animals are preparing
The land is shaking
Dylan Monaghan, Grade 5

Blissful Julia
Julia is a petal on a flower.
She is as pink as a ballet slipper.
She likes dancing, painting, and swimming.
Julia Carvalho, Grade 6

Pouner
Miranda is a panther.
She is as quiet as a shadow.
She likes running, playing, and pouncing.
Miranda Goerlich, Grade 6

LEGO Man Aaron
Aaron is a LEGO man.
He is as sly as a ninja.
He likes sparring, gaming, and building.
Aaron Massey, Grade 6

In the Mountains
Over the mountain
In the grassy meadows swept
Tree leaves go away
Bethany Stacy, Grade 6

Preeminent Autumn
The elegant blue pool when it is being closed marks the end of summer
A frosty breeze flies as I put on my jacket for the first time
In mid-September you start to feel the glacial chill on your face as you wait for the bus
The crunching of leaves brittle leaves
As you jog along
Tasting the warm, fluffy mashed potatoes in my mouth
Hearing the eerie silence of fall is like seeing a beaver with no teeth
October comes as you smell the aroma of hot chocolate and cookies
Trick or treaters get ready for Halloween by picking out a ghastly costume
The awaited holiday is finally here as
Children roam the formidable streets
The first days of November roll around
As heaters almost instantly turn on
Thanksgiving times comes around and the family gathers
After the appetizers, its time to eat
The turkey tasted so good it was a gourmet meal
After days of not eating
As fall turns to winter the overwhelming scent of smoke form chimneys rise
Soon the gold red and brown disappear in a depressing shock
December comes and it gets cold
Here comes winter!
Ethan Forberg, Grade 6

Snow
They gently float down
From the sky proclaiming the end of fall
So very many fly from above
You can't count them all
Open your mouth
Stick out your tongue
Eat the snowy flakes
Make a snowman, a jolly snowman
No matter how long it takes
They glisten and gleam
In the night sky all together
They float around and fly
The ground is unable to be seen anymore
Go grab your sled and run out the door
A snowball fight is calling my name
I challenge you to this awesome game
My mittens are wet my hat on the ground
Everyone is gone, there is not a single sound I look up at the frosty air
Noticing no one anywhere
Me alone in my winter wonderland
This occasion deserves a marching band
Alexandra Amico, Grade 6

Autumn
Autumn to me includes the aroma of hot apple cider steaming in the kettle.
As I step outside the brisk breeze sweeps across my face.
When I step further I feel as if I'm in a world of color,
trees with shades of orange, yellow, and red leaves
slowly descending into the ever so growing rainbow of color
blanketing the ground as if protecting the grass from the harsh wind.
That is what autumn is to me.
Jack Kollmar, Grade 6

Flower
Flowers
Beautiful, colorful
Standing, shining, flowing
My flower stands in the yard
Stem
Allison Foos, Grade 5

My Puppy
Stella
Silly, curious
Biting, barking, teasing stink bugs
Scared of the vacuum
Puppy
Elle McQuaide, Grade 5

Star
Star
Cute, weird
Meowing, licking, playing
Is the cutest cat
Kitty
Maia Anderson, Grade 5

Dolphin
Dolphin
Wet, wonderful
Playing, swimming, jumping
Diving in the water
Mammal
Briana Robinson, Grade 5

Dragon
Dragon
Scary, fierce
Flying, roaring, fire-breathing
He has giant wings
Smaug
Miguel Nankishore, Grade 5

Up Here
It is very cold up in the clouds,
Everything echoes, it's very loud.
You think it's hot?
Oh, certainly not!
Up here where there is no crowd.
Erin Lutz, Grade 5

Baseball
Baseball
Small, round
Hitting, throwing, catching
Coaches will help you
Sport
Andrew Wells, Grade 5

Victory
Victory is saving your comrades life
On the ground and not responding
Saving them from seeing the light
Letting them live another day in the physical world

Victory is surviving the war
Dodging every pellet aimed at you
Taking down everyone who would harm you
Fighting through every wound you suffer

Victory is winning the war after many brutal years
Having gold draped around your neck
Pulling through all the cynical times that are not worth every minute
Trying to relive the many years that are now all a blur

Victory is seeing your spouse again
To hold them in your arms
Sobbing on your shoulders
Exclaiming how much they love you
Maddy Billows, Grade 6

My Dog Scout
He has hair as yellow as a golden nugget.
He has white patches as white as snow.
He has sparkling eyes that shine like a diamond.
He has soft fur that's silky smooth when I hug him.

I love him because he watches over me.
I love him because he protects me like a bear watching over its cub.
I love him because he is always by my side like glue stuck to paper.
I love him because he never stops loving me.

He likes to run like a cheetah after its prey.
He likes to swim like a fish in the ocean.
He likes to dive for oysters by putting his head fully under water.
He likes to have long mile walks with his tongue hanging out at the end.

He loves me like parents loving a child.
He snuggles me with his head on my lap.
He is kind to me but not other dogs.
He is my dog Scout and he is the best dog in the world.
Ian Senz, Grade 6

The Mineshaft
It was 10pm on a rainy night. Minecraft, I was playing with all my might.
It was dark outside and kind of creepy. We went mining. We were not sleepy.
We went exploring and found a mineshaft. I found a note. Not uncommon in Minecraft.
It read: "Beware the Herobrine is near." We were all in fantastic fear!
We crept slowly heading towards the exit. We really did not want to vex it!
An eerie shriek we suddenly heard. We were really quite disturbed!
It has glowing white eyes. It had taken us by surprise!
At the moment I realized it was him! The scary, creepy Herobrine!
I was about to quit the game. Hoping the fear I could contain.
Right before I turned off the TV, I heard a screaming not coming from me!
So, remember if you go mining, the Herobrine there might be dining.
Kyleigh Gianfrancesco, Grade 4

High Merit Poems – Grades 4, 5, and 6

Snow
Glittery white blanket
Covering the world
Marshmallows on fences
And frosting on trees and bushes
Sparkles in the moonlight
Looking like tiny clouds
Soaring through the sky
So fun to play in
I love snow
Sarah Culkin, Grade 5

Halloween
H airy, scary monsters.
A wesome costumes
L augh a lot!
L ate at night.
O dd costumes.
W alk to tons of houses!
E at a lot of candy!
E ek!
N ever enough scares!
Aubry G. Krivak, Grade 4

Trick-or-Treat
During trick-or-treat
Kids have much fun
Dressing up differently
As something or someone.

Children have a lot of fun
Running up and down the streets
Knocking on each door they see
Getting more and more sugary treats!
Sky Giovannetti, Grade 6

Hermit Crab
I was from the land of mist
in freedom
rocked by the waves
to find treasure in the ocean
madness gone
never forget the time in the ocean
my goal was lost
but I got a new family
to take care of me
Joey Monti, Grade 4

Guess
I see prizes
I hear laughter
I taste popcorn
I feel the cool air
I smell hot dogs
I am at the…
Carnival
Kelly Wei, Grade 5

Alone
It's dark.
I hear bombs going off.
No one is there to help me.
I'm all Alone!

I realize I'm in the war!
I'm horrified and trembling with fear.
I hear screams and guns go off.
No one is there to help me.
I'm all Alone!

I hear someone coming.
I'm about to run, but then I see light.
It's the people fighting for our country.
They take me to their camp.
I see my brother!
Someone is there for me.
I'm not Alone!
Sydney Ryan, Grade 5

Horseback Riding
It's about a helmet,
pads, uniform, and
a horse.

Get on a horse,
sit on the saddle,
grab the reins,
tap with your
ankles, and
ride the horse

It's about walking,
trotting, and running

It's about having fun,
loving the horse
exercise, and learning
how to ride.
Lilly Strogach, Grade 4

Anticipation
Three smooth
Eggs in a nest
Blue as the sea,
Round as the earth
Smooth, still,
Baby blue
About to POP!
And give
Three pink, fluffy,
Robins to the earth,
Any
Minute
Now!
Talia Bloom, Grade 4

Summer Is Here Again
Summer is here; hot sun, hot dogs
swimming at the pool

Light breeze, summer leaves
Fall is here

Fall breeze, fall leaves, fall festivals
Thanksgiving, Halloween, leaves are falling

Cold breeze, fall leaves
winter is here

Snow play all day; hot cocoa
Warm fire, happy ways to spend holidays
Snow days, snow falls, cold winter evenings

Cool breeze, winter leaves
spring is here

Pretty flowers, bloom every hour
rain falls, animal babies, Easter

Warm breeze, spring leaves
summer is here again
Lydia Walter, Grade 5

Winter
The last leaves come down from fall
When winter takes all
Skating across the icy pond
Building a snowman in your front yard
Despite the numbing cold

Hot cocoa mornings
And
Under the covers nights

Mittens
Jackets
Pants
Long sleeves
Scarves
Hats
And boots
Are the order of the season

Dusk arrives
And you crunch your way back home
Following your frozen footprints

An arctic vacation
Aaron Stern, Grade 6

Fall
I saw some red leaves.
That came off a bright green tree.
I screamed it is fall!
Logan Ashby, Grade 6

The Sound of Fall
It was in the fall
You can hear the crunch of leaves
Then you see a deer
Jonathan Hurley, Grade 6

The Stream
Look down at the stream
watch the beautiful current
the fish will flow down.
Cody Stacy, Grade 6

My Favorite Shirt
Turquoise, shiny
Wrinkles, waves, washes
Makes me think of lipstick
Francesca Belgiorno, Grade 4

Winter
My yard in a frost
No leaves falling from the trees
Fall has come winter
Spencer Wireman, Grade 6

Silent Night
On a silent night.
When the animals arrive.
The night has awoke.
Jackson Slone, Grade 6

Rainbow
The seven colors,
Making the colorful bridge,
Across the blue sky.
Lucy Shao, Grade 5

Snow
Chilly, icy, snow
Piling, chilling, wonderland
Fluttering below
Haleigh Dively, Grade 5

Bugs
Bugs are interesting
Some bugs look awesome but gross
Bugs act very weird
Ryan Cavanagh, Grade 5

The Small Oval Green Fruit
On the outside, you look like a small green apple
You feel like a piece of rubber
When I peel you, you sound like when someone is ripping a piece of paper
When I slice you, you sound like you are squirting water
Inside, you look like a lot of flower petals
You feel like a bubble inside
You smell like a Lemon Head candy
You taste like a Cry Baby candy
Tell me, why are you small, green, sour, and sweet?
Stephanie Ortiz, Grade 5

Eight Turtles
Eight turtles got tired of staying where they were, so
one turtle went to the middle of the road and sat in the hot sun…splat!
The next turtle went to see an alligator…chomp!
The third turtle went to visit the desert…sizzle.
The next turtle went to catch a wave…swoosh!
The fifth turtle slept on a log…splash!
The next turtle met a predator…gulp!
The seventh one met up with a bear…roar!
The last turtle tried to catch lightning…BOOM!
Jalyn Monfort, Grade 5

Holocaust
H itler, an evil man who killed millions
O nly one man who made a huge difference in so many people's lives
L iving or non-living everyone despised Hitler but people were too scared to speak up
O utburst of violence caused by Hitler
C aring people took in the Jews and cared for them
A cross the world many people stood by and watched as these horrible things happened
U ncontrollable fear spread through all of the Jews
S ome people helped and showed so much care while others turned away
T ill this day NEVER forget the holocaust!
Tasmir Gregorie, Grade 6

Christmas
The smell of the pines when the kids are putting up the tree.
And the ringing of the chimes for our family and me

My older brother and I make some colorful yummy cookies
and put them in the oven to bake
The cookies are popping and sizzling and the smell is just to hard to take

We stir the cocoa and put it on the table and make a label that says "Santa Claus"
My brother and I hop in our beds and say goodnight to Ziggy our dog
Ava Gruss, Grade 5

Home
I belonged at home, home where my friends and I chased each other,
Where I got to jump on the trampoline.
Home where I got to swing on the playscape and play in the woods,
Home where the swings swung back and forward.
Where the trampoline's net shook and shook,
Where the coyotes and wolves howled in the woods.
I belonged at home.
Sydney Mikalonis, Grade 5

Halloween

Halloween is a good holiday
You run around the streets.
Getting candy plus dressing up.
And making jack-o-lanterns.
Plus going to a haunted house.
Gabe Kelley, Grade 5

My Companion

Dogs
Cute, furry
Sniffing, barking, playing
I love my dog
Companion
Dante Impastato, Grade 5

Stars

S himmering light
T he starry night
A rtwork in the sky
R each high above the ground
S tars are beautiful.
Gwen Burrows, Grade 6

The Headless Horseman

It is a thing with no head
It has come back from the dead
It lived in a grave
Now that is quite brave
And now it just cut off your head
Gavin Stamps, Grade 6

Pumpkins

There was a big pumpkin patch
Something was crawling in the batch.
The pumpkin was round,
And it weighed a pound.
Pick one without a scratch.
Nicholas Schildtknecht, Grade 4

Bullet

Bullet
Big, fast
Warming, tiring, daring
He has fluffy fur
Pet
Connor Berg, Grade 5

Jack

Jack
Horseless, short
Nonscaring, nonfrightening, jesting
A huge big head
Horselessheadsman
Erik Nies, Grade 5

The Best Day of My Life

The sky streaked with purple and blue watercolors
My fingers were stained with the ink of the blueberries from the field
The air tingles with the distant scent of the fresh Maine sea salt and newly cut grass
The birds chirped along with the melodic tune of the crickets buzz
My hair brushed against my sunburned face
I had never felt so calm
The day had been spent eating Doritos under the cotton ball clouds
We drove the tractor through the wood and explored muddy trails
We went to play on the swing in the barn
And lit the oil lanterns for nighttime
Then late in the afternoon,
We watched the parents cook the lobster for dinner
We went to pick blueberries in the far meadow for many hours
We had a late supper together
And watched the sunset fade to black
Annabel Everett, Grade 5

the waterfall

the waterfall
it is king, dominator, ruler of the land

it is a sifter
splitting water currents apart
letting them recollect into pools just to break them again

it is a diving board
thousands of little water droplets launching 80 feet into the smooth cool pool

it is an oasis
giver of life
a reward
for conquering mt. haystack
William Skelly, Grade 5

The Continents

Seven continents
Calling my name
Traveling the world
Like an explorer
Seeing everything this world has to offer
That would be amazing

My Grammy has done it
Been to all seven
Europe, Asia, Africa, North America, South America, Australia, and Antarctica
Then there's me
Never even been out of the county
But I've got life to live
So I'd better get started early
Henry Shifflett, Grade 6

The Rock

He is a Metamorphic rock.
He is as strong as a Quartzite rock.
Quincey likes spending time with family, swimming, and playing sports.
Quincey Matthews, Grade 6

Into the Heavenly
cloud so fluffy
cloud so puffy
just like a bed
for a sleepy head
as it rises
into the heavenly
people on the ground
tell a tale
about two people
who judge the living
and the dead
they say
no matter what
they will stay
on your side
and they'll help you
survive the days
ahead
William Clark, Grade 4

Holocaust Horror
There were horrible screams
Of people who once had dreams
In the Holocaust

Hearts were broken
We will never forget
How the Jews got upset In the Holocaust

Nobody tried to help
They all were bystanders
Even though the Jews yelped
For safety
In the Holocaust

Terror and horror for so much time
The Jews cried and cried
Adolf Hitler thought it was right
In the Holocaust
Jason Huggler, Grade 6

Cold Blooded Gusts of Wind
The bottom of my sneakers,
Pounding down on top of dry leaves,
Makes the sound of crunching crackers,
The month of "La Dance Macabre,"
Sends a shiver up my spine,
Running my fingers,
On the smooth curved edges of a pumpkin,
Is far from the feeling,
Of snow melting in the palms of my hand.
The first frost is soon to come,
Closer than you may think,
But let's live this moment now,
Enjoy it while we can.
Vanessa Isbrandt, Grade 6

Color of the Leaves
With a colorful surprise
And trees big and wide
A pile of leaves
Is down at my side

I look up in the sky
All pink and white
With puffy clouds
What a wonderful sight

As I look through my window
The winter breeze blows
Good bye fall
Hello snow
Sadie Mink, Grade 6

Orange
Orange is copper,
It is also a pumpkin.
If you listen, you can hear it shining.
Orange is a flame.
It makes me feel warm and toasty.
Orange feels rough like sand.
It smells like a flower.
It is warm like the summer breeze.
A cat is orange.
My chips are orange too.
My paper is even orange.
Goldfish are orange also.
My subtraction holey card is orange.
Orange is my favorite color.
Kylie Commons, Grade 4

Winter Is Here
W hite snow covers the ground,
I ce as soft as the clouds.
N ature so peaceful in sound,
T ime to snuggle away from the crowd.
E njoying family around.
R acing sled going down.

I ce skating and
S now tubing are in town.

H oliday is here.
E very family and friends
R eunite to hear the
E xciting season of the year.
Keara Malazarte, Grade 4

Homework
Here I am late at night
Thinking of what I should write
Homework can be a very big fright
But its time to say goodnight
Brenden Koykka, Grade 4

Raspberry Mom
Her hair is brown her eyes are blue
Kind but strong
She is sweeter than a peach

As we sit outside
The sun beating on our faces
I hear childhood memories
As we sit and read books

Sweet but seedy
Pretty but scratchy
As red as a tomato
Small but juicy

Smooth as silk
Sweet but delicious
Soft but strong
Bitter but sweet

Pretty like a bouquet of flowers
Strong but delicate
Healthy like an apple
That is my Raspberry Mom
Brycen Boyle, Grade 5

It's About…
It's about words everywhere
Taking them in
Drinking them like lemonade

It's about musical ones
Guiding your fingers
Filling you with song

It's about directional ones
Telling you what to do
Putting you on the right path

It's about adventure
Taking you to wherever you are going
Never wanting to close it up

It's about pages and pages
In orderly fashion
Keeping your excitement organized

It's about happy endings
They all live happily ever after
The perfect place to stop
Ellie Barrickman, Grade 5

Winter Has Arrived
Beautiful dark night
Snowflakes falling from the sky
Winter has now arrived
Alexander Higginbotham, Grade 6

I Fought for You
You were very brave.
Some lives you gave.
You didn't think twice.
You made the sacrifice.

It broke our hearts.
When we were apart.
You fought for us.
So in God we trust.
Ella Ford, Grade 5

Weather
W et ground
E arthquake shaking
A ir masses cold and warm
  Big and small
T hunderstorms booming
H urricane crazy
  Blowing all around
E ar-aching thunder
R ain across the world
Emily Thompson, Grade 6

Segregation
Apart
Apart from them
The "different" ones
Us in shacks
They in mansions
We are trash to them
They think they are royalty
We are no different
We are all people
Naomi Meininger, Grade 5

Nature and People
Shiny day.
Sunny day.
Dog and cat.
Grease monkey.
Children.
Lightning and storms.
Insects.
North Carolina.
Princess, prince and king.
Ayrienna Allen, Grade 4

Let It Snow
Let it snow let it snow
gather around it's about to snow.
gather around let your tree lights glow,
here comes Christmas!
here comes Christmas!
lets get gifts like baby dolls and toy cars
I love the winter.
Kaytlee Clark, Grade 5

Halloween in Hanover
kids are walking to houses
kids knocking on doors
hoping to get a treat
it's cold and dark outside
orange pumpkins by houses and on porches
people sitting out giving out candy
fake red blood on peoples' costumes
high screams from girls
witches are doing their cackle
I see the darkness
I hit the best few houses
I go home
I eat some yummy candy
time for bed
Cole Porter, Grade 4

Summer
Hot fun days at the pool
As I jump into the water it feels so cool.

Playing with friends in the sand
Hoping that this day would never end.

Jumping, running, having fun
Getting burned by the blazing sun.

Friday nights are so cool,
Especially when you're in the pool.

These are the days I never doubt
This is what summer is all about.
Adam, Grade 5

The American Girl Experience
Dolls, outfits, shoes, if you like
You could even get a bike
Historical, modern, any style
Girls and moms searching for a while

Girls bring dolls to change their look
In the hair salon nook
Updos, facials, and fancy nails
Buns, braids, and ponytails

Finally, when the day is done
Girls and dolls go out for fun
Food, drinks, candy galore
Balloons, streamers, and so much more
Isabela Wilson, Grade 4

The Dragonfly at the Pond
I was at the pond
A dragonfly flew across my face
I didn't want it to do anything to me
So I stayed silent
Jason Stone, Grade 5

Pink
Pink is a flower you can smell
A bracelet you can wear
And a dress that goes with purple
It's the sound of a flamingo
The flap of a butterfly's wing
And the shimmer of pink glitter
Pink tastes yummy like strawberries
Refreshing cough drops
And sweet cotton candy
It feels like delicate flowers
Sweet cherries
And the tip of a pink marker
Pink can give you candy
And smiles.
Judy Nguyen, Grade 4

Phillies
There once was a man named Chase.
He was a very bad batter.
And he never even stole a base.
He became sadder and sadder.
He made an error.
So he hid in his locker,
And hits became rarer and rarer.
Now he wants to play soccer.
Now Chase will practice alone.
He'll train.
He'll break a bone,
And feel a lot of pain.
Chase worked on his pace
So he got a career-high of one stolen base.
Arkasha Rakach, Grade 5

Stars
Black, dull, boring night,
look up, what a sight.
Little suns light the night,
twinkling over our heads.

I can see a constellation,
connection of stars far away.
Making the sky twinkle and light up,
shining bright with light.

Look! One is flying,
soaring across the sky.
Beautiful radiant stars,
shooting in the new-lit night.
Belinda Henry, Grade 6

Snow
Snow falls like graceful ballerinas.
It dances in the sky.
They are all unique in different ways.
Not one has the same shape.
Christina DiMaggio, Grade 5

Rainbow
Beautiful and truly cool
Flies soars and watches over us
Leads the way to a pot of gold
A colorful arch in the sky
Ends in the nucleus of the sea
William Chew, Grade 4

Sandi
Sandi
Furry, skinny
Digging, chewing, sleeping
She is very adorable
Dog
Allison Ceccio, Grade 5

Angry Birds
Angry birds
Fun, addicting
Throwing, flying, hitting
Pigs stole the eggs
Squawk!
Tobias Hall, Grade 6

Puppy
Puppy
Soft, cute
Running, jumping, fetching
My puppy is energetic
Frisco
Billy Zittle, Grade 5

Leaf
My name is Ridgid
A huge tree is where I live
I hang on a limb
I have a lot of brothers
I'm tiny, I am a leaf
Estella Griffin, Grade 5

Wind Chimes
Music
Long and delicate
Swaying and clinking
Found outside and usually hanging
Wind Chimes
Caitlin DeStefano, Grade 5

Sugar Maple Leaf
I'm a stunning leaf!
My fringes are so jagged!
We descend from trees.
I'm a leaf on a journey.
We are exceptional, too!
Lianna Rieser, Grade 5

That Dreadful Event
The terror and hurt in the people's eyes, the scared cries
To think the Jews were happy there, until Hitler came and brought despair
He, that dreadful man full of hate, brought many Jews to their fate
He thought he'd be a hero, but he ended a zero
But to think during this dreadful event, people watched through their vents
They saw it happen, but did nothing when they could've done something
They could've stopped it, but they chose to watch it
The bystanders just as bad, while they should've been mad
While the Jews stayed in camps to die, it all started with one guy
He killed many and wanted them all dead, Hitler was sick in the head
Now we remember the people lost, those that were in the Holocaust
We pray day and night for those who forgot what it was like to fly a kite.
Julia Daley, Grade 6

Thank You God
T hank you God you
H ave
A lways been there for me
N ever have you let me down
K nowing you are there for me
S aying you love me and
G iving me everything you can
I love you and always will
V ery, very blessed
I am
N ever will he let you down
G od will always be there for you and me through the rough time, through the good.
Savannah Dotson, Grade 6

The Shy Kid
You know that new shy kid that always sits in the corner,
Never talks to anybody but that one kid who's really nice.
It's not that unnatural, but I don't know why.
It's just that really shy kid makes you wonder why,
Why is he or maybe even she's so, so shy.
Even though it's been very quiet in the class,
Just go outside with them they might be very interesting.
They might just make you laugh.
They might or they might not agree on everything you say.
But so what, they're the new kid, of course they're not, it's not like they've known you for years and years, they might just become your next best friend, just wait a couple of years.
Francisco Ramirez, Grade 6

Fourth of July
I remember 4th of July 3 years ago
I remember throwing fire crackers
I remember jumping in the pool every time a mortar went off on the diving board
And fishing
I remember going on a boat ride
I remember catching a snake
I remember going in the hot tub
Even mom enjoyed it
I remember playing with my dog
But my favorite memory is yet to come…
Ian Boecker, Grade 5

Fall

Orchards of apples being picked
Some being made into cider
Some being made into pies
The smell of apples and cinnamon fill the air

Red leaves, green leaves
Rust leaves, yellow leaves
Crunching under foot

Vibrant
Golden colors
Rainy
Earthy
Grass and leaves

Breezy
Chilly
Fall is ending
Preparing us for winter

Chipmunks gathering acorns
To hibernate

Trees getting bare
Winter's almost here.

Lara Reiss, Grade 6

The Holocaust

People did not care
Lots of victims lost their hair
Why did Hitler find this fair
There is so much hate in the world
There was lots of fear
There was no cheer
Only lots of tears
There is so much hate in the world
Each day people got sent to camps
Then got numbers in their arms like stamps
There is so much hate in the world

Ashley Potope, Grade 6

Halloween

Halloween is fun but scary
A bully summons Bloody-Mary.

I try to run but my costume is too tight
So I turn around and put up a fight.

She tries to hit me but I run
I then see a zipper of fun.

My brother comes out of the closet, laughs, and video tapes
I turn around and I give him the sad face.

Kennedy Goremusandu, Grade 6

Who Am I?

I am your constant guide.
Train me, strengthen me, and I will lead you to success.
Ignore me, deem me unimportant, and I will destroy you.

I'm your child.
What I become depends on you.
I can become vast and powerful,
Or pitiful and weak.
I serve all great individuals,
And all failures as well.
Those who are kings, I make kings.
Those who are beggars, I make beggars.

I am not a machine, although I work like one,
With the same precision and perception.
You can run me for profit,
Or run me for ruin.
To me, it does not matter.

Take me, train me, and the world shall kneel before you.
If not, than you shall kneel before the world.

Who am I?

I am Knowledge.

Ogaga Obrimah, Grade 6

Waves

Wish wash
Wish wash
The waves come rolling in
Splish splash
Splish splash
I feel like jumping in
Cur-plump
Cur-plump
And then
I am falling
In

Charlotte Dockery and Megan Keller, Grade 6

Snow and Me

Snow, Snow, beautiful snow
When there is snow, I don't mow
I usually stay at home watching
my father who is frantically notching
sticks to count the winter days
I know and show there are so many ways
to spend the long and cold winter days.
But usually you will always see
me indoors with a warm cup of tea.
Even though the beautiful snow is God's pride
I'm most comfortable staying inside.

Christiana Tsai Hubbard, Grade 5

A Fun Christmas
Christmas is very fun.
Kids are very joyful.
Kids play in the snow.
All are ready to hear Santa say Ho Ho Ho!
Everybody hopes there will be snow for the snowman.
After Christmas dinner everybody will be full.
I love Christmas.
Christmas is cool.
Hayden Baron, Grade 6

Books About Captain Hook
I love reading books
I like stories about Captain Hook
He is the best
The books never make me want to take a rest.
I can never stop reading
With his crew he has a meeting.
He tries to get Peter Pan
While doing that a crocodile eats his hand.
Nina Gillingham, Grade 6

Fire
Fire starts with wood and a flame
And then I hear it calling my name
Maezee, Maezee, come over here
It gets bigger and bigger as I get near
Its flames are dancing all about
The flames were phenomenal, there's no doubt
It gets brighter, but it's almost dawn
And now it is dawn and the fire is gone
Maezee Brown, Grade 4

Christmas
There is a lot of cheer in the air.
Snow began to fall.
Families come together near and far.
They celebrate this wonderful holiday with love and laughter.
There is a tree in the living room with lots of ornaments.
Children are excited for Santa to come.
On December 25, they are playing with their toys.
Later, they gather together for Christmas dinner.
Kristen Tetil, Grade 6

Orange of Fall
Orange is a peach so sweet.
And like the water,
When it reflects the color of the leaves
Like the orange foliage under my feet,
The cool pumpkin faces that are so neat.
Orange is my favorite color of Gatorade,
And like the vest you wear while hunting.
Orange is my favorite color, next to black and white.
Austin Swartley, Grade 6

It's About Football
It's about crunching pads and some brutal tackles
Quarterback sacks and dropping back in the pocket
Throwing down field bombs just like a sky rocket

It's about Sunday, Monday, and Thursday
Players giving it their all on every single play
Never hanging their heads in dismay

It's about helmets crashing and receivers dashing
Touchdown dances
Three point stances

It's about fans roaring
Spirits soaring
Guts and glory

It's about coaches screaming
Banners streaming
Trophies gleaming

It's about men as big as trucks
Quarterbacks giving the ball a chuck
Trying to find a last little bit of luck

It's about the game I love
Cal Walsh, Grade 5

My Best Friend Called Hope
You're the Ivy to my bean
You're the actor to my scene
You're the Peanut to my Jam
You're the one that holds my hand

Despite the aches and pain we break
We bring joy and laughter and love
We bring you friendship not a fake
We work together when push comes to shove

You're the house to my light
You're the angel when there's fright
You're the shadow in the night
You're the beauty in the sight

You'd be the dream to come
You'll bring hope for everyone
You're the one that shows the signs
I could be yours, you could be mine

When they say don't get your hopes up
I don't put my hopes down
Hope is a wonderful thing
If you realize, it's all around
Joellen Allah-Mensah, Grade 6

The Dream About Basketball
Swoosh…
Right into the basket it goes.
Right out of the hands Of big strong Moes.
That was a 3 pointer he said,
Now can I,
Please go to bed!
Lydia Simone, Grade 5

Fall
Fall has got it all
with leaf piles growing very tall,
When leaf piles aren't in sight,
I am in a fright
Fall is so great,
I *can* wait for it to go away.
Zach Bianco, Grade 5

The Lonely Tortoise
On a misty beach far away
Lives a tortoise, all alone
He has never seen a human
Or another tortoise.
Only the birds above him
Ignoring him, just like the rest of the world.
Tommy Shenefield, Grade 6

Basketball
3 pointers 2 pointers 1 pointer
They are all helpful
Shooting, dribbling, passing
That's the skills you will need
And they all come together
to win the game
Dilan Piscatello, Grade 5

The Wonderful Moon
The night can be bright
If you look to the light
It shimmers on the lake.
However, you cannot take
The wonderful moon
That shines into your room.
Kevin Slotterbeck, Grade 4

Happy Birthday
Happy Birthday to you.
I hope you have fun, yes it is true.
It is a very special day.
I sure would like to say.
Happy birthday to my amazing friend.
Come on let's make this a trend.
Hadiyah Coates, Grade 5

5th Grade Jitters
Will my teacher be nice?
Or as angry as a 350 pound gorilla after he just got woken up.

Will the classroom be neat and tidy?
Or will it be as messy as an art room after a dirty project.

Will my friends still like me?
Or will they be with another group of people and act like I'm invisible.

Will my locker keep all my supplies safe?
Or eat it when I'm not looking.

Will my lunch be gourmet?
Or will it be like a plop of disgusting muck.

It's like my first day jitters will never go away.
Abby Burke, Grade 5

Nightmares
Walking, walking,
Out of my house, through the woods, crossing the river.
Thinking, thinking,
Of how my family never loved me, how they made me work, sweat, cry.
Climbing, climbing,
A tree to escape from the danger below.
Wondering, wondering
If my family will miss me, if they'll see that I'm gone.
Hearing, hearing,
The creatures lurking in the darkness.
Wandering, wandering
And finding a cave that seems so lonely.
Screaming, screaming
As darkness swallows me.
I wake up in my nice, little bed
And wonder what was going on in my head.
Megan Reading, Grade 5

I'm Bored
I'm bored.
My leg is very sore,
And it's from walking all day.
In a way,
I want to play outside,
Even though I'm in playing video games all day, and the fields are very wide.
But the power's out,
So I'm out.
So I'll just read a book,
The one with the cover I always look,
But my dog ripped out all the pages,
And hung it on a hook.
But I guess I'll play outside,
'cause there's nothing to deny,
And it actually worked all right,
And the best part — it didn't take all night.
Brittany Hronich, Grade 5

The Life of Daniel
He was kidnapped as a boy
never returned home
But very close to God
lived with wicked people
thrown in a lions' den
always faithful
always merciful
His friends thrown into a fiery furnace
But miraculously no harm
No smell
No singes
these people and Daniel always with God.
Michael Lamitola, Grade 5

What Is a Dragon?
What is a dragon?
Has silver claws with spikes on them.
Likes blueberry pie with tea.
Is blue and pink with bright blue eyes.
Has big rainbow wings,
With neon green spikes on its back.
Bit teeth that are super white,
A tail that changes colors.
Super strong.
Blows rainbow fire.
Amazing,
That is a dragon!
Eliya Sanchez, Grade 4

What I See in a Winter Wonderland
Icicles everywhere
the smell of hot chocolate in the air
Having a snowball fight
watching snow fall on a cold winter night
Santa coming to town
happiness all around
Decorating a tree with family
watch a Christmas movie
Bears hibernating
butterflies migrating
Presents under the tree
now what do you see?
Mikaela Benchimol, Grade 5

I Want My Team to Win
I want my team to win a football game
my mind exploded with possibilities
my whole team is scattered all over the field
A runner passes by
I dive to tackle him
I got him…but he got away
that really hurt, I think to myself
football really hurts
Now I am at middle line backer
This is a game of my childhood
Tommy Ball, Grade 4

Holocaust
Hitler did terrible things
On his mind was killing Jews
Left to die in terrible ways
Orderly methods of genocide
Chambers of gas killed many
America and others came
United the Holocaust ended
Shot himself, Hitler did
The terrible things will never be forgotten
Joshua Richter, Grade 6

Holocaust
H itler
O ne by one they were sent to camps.
L ittle by little they survived.
O h my! What a tragic time!
C hildren dying
A dults dying
U ndeniable punishment
S o bad
T hen finally they were freed by America.
Jordan Sensenig, Grade 6

Hitler Is
H orrendous
O utrageous
L oathsome
O ffensive
C ruel
A ssassin
U napologetic
S inister
T errorizing
Brionna Hynes, Grade 6

Holocaust
H itler
O ccupied Northern Europe
L iving in institutional settings
O utbreak of war
C oncentration camps
A uthorities forced-labor camps
U nconditionally surrendered to Allies.
S tarvation
T rains moved camp inmates
Vito Mastromonaco, Grade 6

Fall
The cool chill of the morning breeze
Taking out the sweaters and jackets
A blanket of falling leaves
Red, orange, yellow
What does it mean?
It means that soon
There will be a new blanket of white
Erin Libby, Grade 6

Fun
Joy
Joy is something important in my life.
Like my family
I like spending time with them.
Friends, they are funny and awesome.
Children, they are cute and funny.
Teachers, funny and kind.
My TA, sweet and understanding.
Special someone, caring and wonderful.
These people give me joy.
Ashley De La Cruz, Grade 6

Animals in the Barn
So many animals that live in the barn
The cat's favorite toy is a bundle of yarn
Everyone loves the white horse
But he always seems to put up a course
I can only hear the dogs
They are louder than the hogs
The chickens are crazy
The goats are lazy
As soon as I saw the little white mouse
I ran right to the house
Morgan Cline, Grade 6

Snow
Snow is so inviting,
It invites kids to play,
It shimmers and glitters
in the sun.
It dances in the sky,
but gravity pulls it down.
When snow works together
it makes a blanket.
Without snow the environment
would not be complete.
Maggie Loughran, Grade 5

I Just Want to Be Loved
I called to the birds
And they chirped
On my branches
Nested eggs
Grew and flew
Away!
I'm alone now
I want to be loved
I hope to live
For one hundred years!
Matthew Piechocki, Grade 5

Wild Wolf
Giovanni is a Black wolf.
He is as strong as a brick wall.
He loved hunting, eating meat and playing.
Giovanni Andrus, Grade 6

The Ballerina

The ballerina poses and waits.
The song begins and a low applause rumbles in the crowd.
Her toe taps, getting into position.
She leaps and lands like a butterfly.
Her dress flows as she pirouettes.
The audience chants, "Ooh Ahh!"
She feels refreshed as she makes a grand lift.
She lands in an arabesque,
then she turns on her toes so gracefully.

Her ocean blue silk dress flutters with her body.
The sleek blackberry bracelet and neck band indent her peach skin.
The rose petal pink toe shoes move to the beat.
Her amethyst jewel eyes shine in the spotlight.
Wavy chestnut brown hair flows around her shoulders.
Her berry lips frame pearl white teeth.
She poses and the dance ends.
The best recital for the ballerina.

Haley Himes, Grade 4

Your Best Friend

You can hide your secrets deep in the forest,
Where the eagles soar and the lions roar.
Nobody will ever find out,
but don't hide your secrets from me!
Even though I have no leaves,
I still stand tall, and I am stronger than a tree.
So don't keep your secrets from me!
I'm always there to help, so don't hide!
I am your support, I am your guide,
the clouds, the stars, the moon, the sun,
I'm brighter than the sky, or anyone!
I'm loving, I'm caring, kind like a sister,
Not a hater, an enemy, nor a trickster.
If you need help, then I lend a hand,
and there's only one of me, unlike a hundred grains of sand.
So can you guess who I am?
If you can't guess, or comprehend, then here's the answer:
I am your best friend

Cecilia Fu, Grade 6

Fall

September blows cool air in the sky,
September's leaves change to red, orange, and yellow,
Then they start to sprinkle down like summer rain.
September fades the rest of the flowers from summer;
It squeezes what's left of summer's heat.
September picks the last apple from the orchard.
October's red-orange, yellow leaves
Sprinkle down on us from the trees.
October leaves flutter: bright butterflies
Against the brilliant, blue, sky,
October has a chill in the air; when witches unlock
Spirits from the dead on Halloween,
October lights up the night with the moon shining
On the bright, black, sky
November gets ready for winter's snow.
November huddles together to stay warm;
It hibernates in cold, wet dens for the winter.
November's trees are lit by the moon,

Madison Fili, Grade 4

My Blue Dreams

My dreams are blue.
My dreams are blue like the ocean after
Sunset with light waves.
My dreams are blue like the beautiful sky with
Blue birds chirping in the morning.

My dreams are blue like cookie monster laughing
Full of enthusiasm with his blue fur.
My dreams are blue like the sweetness coming
From blue berries on a hot summer day.

My dreams are blue like a sapphire in a silver ring.
My dreams are blue like the indigo color of my jeans.
My dreams are blue like the color of my favorite candy, Airheads.
My dreams are blue like the color of dolphins
Clicking and jumping out of the water in delight.

My dreams are blue, what's yours?

Hephzibah Emmanuel, Grade 5

Crutches

Crutches hold you up
Without them, you would fall hard on the ground
Thump, smack, bump.
You would never be able to walk, without crutches.
You wouldn't be able to eat, without crutches.
You would never be able to write, without crutches.
You wouldn't be able to touch, without crutches.
You would never be able to breathe, without crutches.
Put it this way,
You wouldn't be able to live, without crutches.
Everything in your life is held by crutches.
So, make sure you think about your crutches
For if you don't your crutches might as well disappear.

Kailyn Bielecki, Grade 6

Throwing the Ball for My Dog Rusty

When I pitch the ball Rusty darts to get it like a golden jet
he makes the hushed October wild
his barks of excitement fill my heart with happiness
he's so quick, his lazy little shadow trails behind him
it can't catch up, it won't catch up
Rusty moves gracefully and speedily
there's no end to his panting there will never be
he's so speedy, it's incredible!
with every stride he takes, his collar jingles
he comes back to me and licks me
his licks are like 1,000 cold icy kisses
the fuzzy little fellow laps around our yard
his running may never come to an end

Jamie Alderfer, Grade 4

Mother's Day
Mom
My mom is caring, and understanding,
She's like sugar, she is sweet.
My mom is the nicest person ever,
She can't eat bread unless it's whole wheat.

My mom loves her siblings, even though they got her in trouble,
She was full of energy, she was crazy.
My mom was a class clown,
If she looks back on all her years, it's kind of hazy.

My mom was very funny,
She was also very bad.
My mom soon learned to change her ways,
She is sorry for letting me grow up without a dad.

My mom is a nice "young" woman,
She used to be very wild.
My mom is a caring, beautiful person,
She is now only mild.

Mom, if I didn't have you, I would be lost,
If I didn't have you my life would be dust.
I hope you like my poem I made you,
If I didn't know you I'd say it's a must.

Breonna Morrison, Grade 6

Ode To Football
Oh football, How much I love you.
When You get kicked, I feel your pain.

When you're spiraling
All through the air,
I can feel the wind
Come right against you.

When I sleep with you
I can see your dream.
That probably means
We like the same teams.

When I lose you I look all over earth to find you.
You are so playful, You are never hateful.

You make me happy
Just like a simple taffy.
When I'm on the field
You're right next to me.

When you're not in motion
I can look more at you.
And that's all I have to say
About you and my emotions.

Noah Locke, Grade 4

My Thanksgiving
As I pull into my hotel
I know I will have a story to tell
Because it has a water park
Bigger than the mansion of Tony Stark
When I go to the dinner buffet
I forget everything I did today
Yummy turkey and cornbread
Or maybe just a taco instead
After I eat my humongous dinner
I play a big game and try to be a winner
"Magiquest" is quite fun
From the third to fourth floor I do run
I go to bed, really quite tired
This truly is a place to be admired
After the experience, here's what I say
Go to "Great Wolf Lodge" for a fabulous stay.

Colton Friesen, Grade 5

Thanksgiving
Leaves erupt all around me
The aroma of Thanksgiving turkey fills the air
The Macy's parade begins
The smell of cranberry sauce whirls around me
The aroma of Thanksgiving turkey fills the air
The kitchen is a wonderland of smells
The smell of cranberry sauce whirls around me
My sister sits beside me, relaxing
The kitchen is a wonderland of smells
We dig into the Thanksgiving feast
My sister sits beside me, relaxing
We eat until we can't eat anymore
We dig into the Thanksgiving feast
The Macy's parade begins
We eat until we can't eat anymore
Leaves erupt all around me

Molly Doherty, Grade 4

My Room Is Haunted
I'm pretty sure that my room
Is haunted!
Creepy,
Crawly,
Things running around.
When I leave my room it is clean,
When I come back it's a mess!
I'm pretty sure that my room
Is haunted
With a ghost.
I'm pretty sure that it's a girl
Named Mary.
I'm not quite sure but, maybe she died on the 25th of a month,
Because each month on that day I hear
Her scream.

Sophie Dunlap, Grade 5

High Merit Poems – Grades 4, 5, and 6

Soccer
Soccer
Amazing, wonderful
Kicking, scoring, passing
Soccer is the best
Goals
Fernando Coronado, Grade 6

Christmas
Christmas
Jolly, joyful
Loving, playing, cooking
Family is always over
Cookies
Ja'kiya Elrod, Grade 6

Basketball
Basketball
Fun, exciting
Dunking, helping, winning
Favorite game to play
Sport
Joseph Cassinera, Grade 6

Halloween
Halloween
Awesome, mischievous
Scaring, tricking, begging
Trick or treat fun
Holiday
Jason Ogbolu, Grade 5

Dragons
Dragons
Dangerous, colorful
Crazy, moving, continuing
They are very fireproof
Lizard
Josiah Tucker, Grade 6

Candy
Candy
Tasty, sweet
Eating, chewing, tasting
Has lots of sugar
Great
Ashley Jaquez, Grade 6

Friends
Friends
Fun, active
Playing, shopping, running
I love them a lot
Careful
Ashley Portillo, Grade 6

Blue
Blue is the ocean waving on the horizon.
The salty scent of seashells…
It can be silently still…
Or as LOUD as a blue whale.
The largest mammal our eyes can see…
Majestic.
Roar!!
A crayon skillfully sketching the skies —
The color of both my peeping eyes…
Blue is the taste of the ice cube at the start.
Seeing some butterflies soaring in the sky…
Blue wings fluttering, fleeing by…
The sweet smell of an Iris fills my nose…
It's the color I feel when my heart has troubles…
The flapping fins of my pet fish named Bubbles.
A patriotic part of our American flag…
Blue is the flavor of freedom when married to red stripes and white stars…
We fly free through this color among the clouds…
Madison McGuire, Grade 5

Thanksgiving
Thank you for all my ears can hear
The startling sound of the oven…
BEEP! BEEP! BEEP!
When it goes off we are ready for the roasted turkey
My family and friends laughing at old memories
Thanksgiving birds being selected for the next repast
Those turkeys are extremely loud

Thank you for all that my mouth can taste
The juicy mouthwatering flavors on this special day
The soon to be done hot cocoa and the cold refreshing cider quenching my thirst
My sweet tooth is arriving
Time for some dessert

Thank you for all my body can feel
The warm enlightening fire making me smile
My jacket as soft as a baby's bottom rubbing my skin
The gracious hugs making me feel loved and happy
Elizabeth Blizzard, Grade 6

Spring
March reveals spring from where it was hidden.
Its breath is a joyful voice.
Its drizzles sound like an orchestra in the wood.
A March breeze welcomes everything into a new beginning.
April's crystal clean waters sparkle like diamonds.
The sky reminds April of shiny blue sapphires.
The cardinal's feathers are ruby red and stand out
against the emerald green of willow trees.
April is a month of beautiful colors.
May watches spring babies as if she were their mother.
The grass is green and soft.
The sun shines brightly and looks as though it is watching the babies, too.
The blossoms on the tree float helplessly down until they finally reach the ground.
Madison Oreski, Grade 4

Basketball

In practice, my coach makes us touch the ground,
And he's not kidding around.
We work at shooting balls all practice long,
And I do my best to follow along.
We could dribble all day because it's fun to play,
But we have to leave at the end of the day.
Kevin Young, Grade 4

Moonshadows

Moonshadows casting shadows down to the dew drops
gleaming on the plants
Like sunlight piercing through a prism

Except it is not sunlight it is shadows from the moon…
Moonshadows that cannot be seen.
William Dunlop, Grade 5

Knight

K illing and ruthless, fighting for freedom
N oble and loyal to their king
I n full armor, charging on horseback down the battlefield
G oing in to war to protect the king and his land
H onorable and living by the life of chivalry
T rustworthy and doing good deeds for the people of the kingdom.
John Schmenk, Grade 4

Christmas

Oh, how beautiful the Christmas tree
Filled with ornaments and lights
The sparkling white snow
How splendid the presents
Santa sleighs in at night with all your delights
Christmas is not a day, it's a season of joy
Martina Agak, Grade 5

Sun and Moon

From the sun in the day that shines so bright,
to the moon that sparkles in the darkened night.
The sun and moon they are best friends.
Their fun together never ends.
They take turns like best friends do,
one at night and morning too.
Alexandra Abood, Grade 5

My Sister

She is the heart of the house
As great as the sun
She loves me no matter what
Our blood says we're sisters, I say we're b.f.f.'s
She's a golden thread to the meaning of life
I love my sister!
Allyson Mahoney, Grade 4

Spring

May snuggles the little babies,
Tiny cheerful babies,
Cuteness fills the air.
Animals start to open their eyes,
looking at their mom and dad.
My birthday is in MAY!
June open its heart and lets the sun come out.
Kids run and laugh all day. Adults sit back and
Drink lemonade. At night, kids jump in
the air and catch fireflies.
July says happy 4th of July.
Bright colors fill the sky
When fireworks pop in the air.
Red, white, and blue flags pop out.
Have a good spring!
Jacklyn Bradley, Grade 4

Do I Feel the Winter?

I walk outside with my clothes buckled to my skin,
I feel the ice cold air whip out my mouth as I breath,
the sound of my clicking and chattering teeth catch my attention
as it is the only sound in my hushed neighborhood.

The swift movement of air takes my attention off the white sugar
and onto the whispering air that tickles my nose.

I lick my chapped lips only to feel the cold overtake my lips again,
as I walk down the snowy pathway,
I hear the crunching under my feet.

I halted to a stop to look up at the sprinkling sky,
only to be greeted by a lump of snow,
realizing it was just the tree I was okay.
Lauryn Winn, Grade 5

An Ordinary Tree

I am an ordinary tree.
My leaves are my hair.
My hair turns different colors four times a year.
Children try to pick my fruit.
My body is my trunk.
Small birds come to visit with me,
Once in a while.
I am an ordinary tree.

I am an ordinary tree.
My apples fall to the dirty, dusty ground,
during a wild wind storm.
Little kids bite my juicy apples.
Crunch, crunch, crunch
I am an ordinary tree.
Julia Eich, Grade 4

High Merit Poems – Grades 4, 5, and 6

Black
Lying in the darkness
Forming a horrible scheme
I am evil but not sure how to use it
Being very empty
    Lacking myriads ingenious
    Cause of crime
    King of emptiness
I am very depressed
A.J. Daley, Grade 6

Softball
S creaming cheers all day long
O ut in one, two, three
F laming hits down the line
T hey want to see the ball fly
B unting is my specialty
A ll I want is to hit a home run
L aughing and giggling
L ove playing this game
Kyleigh Waugh, Grade 5

Good vs Evil
Good
Nice, kind
Helping, caring, sharing
Heart, heaven, detention, prison
Fighting, hurting, lying
Bad, reckless
Evil
Giovanni Martinez, Grade 6

Clouds
Fluffy pieces of cotton.
They make different shapes in the sky.
They remain at day and in the starry night.
I love to look at the things they create.
This time a bunny, next time a mouse.
I love to watch them.
These for certain are clouds.
Hannah Wagner, Grade 6

Joseph
Joseph
Trouble, brother
Playing, thinking, loving
Always making a mess
Running, reading, falling
Jumps, crawls
Troublemaker
Michaela Jackson, Grade 5

Bamboo
Bamboo is a plant
Strong forests of giant stalks
It is very tall
Giovanni Rapposelli, Grade 5

The Hunt
It's early afternoon
In the middle of winter.
I hear the snow crunching beneath me.
I smell the prey wondering around this Arctic desert.
The air is freezing with a slight breeze.
The only thing I see is the bright white snow suddenly I see an animal.
I sprint after it. But finally I catch the prey.
Should I save the meat or not?
Will Douglas, Grade 4

Bigfoot
Bigfoot is an amazing creature.
It can grow up to 11 feet tall.
They can be very strong.
They all try to hid themselves.
Some people don't believe in Bigfoot.
He is real; I know it.
They communicate to each other by howls, whistles, and wood knocks.
I think Bigfoot is failing because there are so many sightings.
Colby Hamer, Grade 6

Medway Huskies
We have a Medway husky, Shadow is his name.
He walks around the Medway halls, never any shame.
Shadow is a good dog, you'll find him on the Medway blog.
He posts real cool things, he's always got a smile.
You'll never catch him with a frown, not even for a while.
Our Medway husky is real cool. He is proud of our Medway school.
Cheers for teams, makes winning goals, he's really good in a basket throw.
So I'll tell you now that Shadow's cool, and we're proud to have him at our Medway school.
Austyn Fox, Grade 6

Knocked Out
I remember me taking my first punch
I remember me getting 17 shots per day
I remember me getting back up when I was injured and I was glad about that
I remember my first day of boxing
I remember my first boxing title
I remember my highest overall even if it wasn't as good as a couple of people
I remember my dad pushing me and pushing me
But my favorite memory's yet to come.
Zakiy Gasparovic, Grade 5

The Most Important Thing about Halloween
The most important thing about Halloween is carving a pumpkin.
Pumpkins grow on a vine in a pumpkin patch.
Big, plump, and orange.
Eat their seeds; they're delicious.
Carve it silly, sad, or angry.
Give it a glow.
You can even put it on your front porch.
But, the most important thing about Halloween is carving a pumpkin.
Luke Weimer, Grade 4

Basketball

B ig ball
A gile players
S coring points
K eeping positive
E nding overtimes
T rying to get a slam dunk
B uzzer beaters
A mazing shots
L ayups made to win
L oud crowds
Turner Lehman, Grade 5

The Holocaust

Hitler was an evil man.
Hitler had an evil plan.
"Kill all Jews," Hitler said.
For their race must be dead.
In the camps, is where they stayed.
For one's death was never delayed.
Hitler's hate was awfully bad.
The Holocaust was very sad.
Sadness rains on this event.
To the gods their souls are sent.
Jacob Gould, Grade 6

Fall Is Here

Golden and red trees
With a soft breeze
As it whispers, "Winter is coming"
For this is the time for Fall

Goodbye beautiful flowers
Through cold Fall hours
We'll miss you so
We don't want to let you go
For this is the time for Fall
Brooke Ryan, Grade 6

Veteran's Day

Those soldiers fought for us
Celebrated on November 11th
Once called Armistice Day
In 1919 when Wilson was president
It is a sad, serious day
Remembering many people who died
Even children
The world was destroyed
Eisenhower signed the bill into law
Now a day dedicated to world peace
Joey Iberis, Grade 4

Anaconda

Moving beside me
Wrapping in my arms right now
Getting warmed up quick!
Aamin Rahman, Grade 4

I Am

I am a dancer and a singer
I wonder what my future will be
I hear the birds chirping
I see pretty flowers
I want there to be less fighting in war
I am a dancer and a singer

I pretend I am famous
I feel the sun on my back
I touch the clouds
I worry about tornados and earthquakes
I cry for the hunger to stop
I am a dancer and a singer

I understand that everything isn't fair
I say that everyone is who they are
I dream that I will be a millionaire
I try to do my best
I hope to be a professional dancer
I am a dancer and a singer
Madison Birt, Grade 6

I Am

I am young and foolish
I wonder where all the wolves went?
I hear the wind whistle
I see the waves lap the shore
I want Minecraft
I am young and foolish

I pretend to fall asleep
I feel unwanted
I touch the sky
I worry about myself
I cry about nothing
I am young and foolish

I understand people are my enemy
I say, "Stay motivated"
I dream of nothing
I try to convince my enemies to stop
I hope they will
I am young and foolish
Daniel Cote, Grade 6

Winter

Leaves falling,
Snow swaying,
My feet begin to freeze
As the ice crumbles beneath me.
Carolers caroling,
Cookies baking,
The oven is warm.
It's the only thing that is
In the December storm.
McKenna Merriman, Grade 5

Red

Red is a bird I can see.
Red is a scrape when I fall
On my knee.
Red is a ripe raspberry I can eat.
Red is an apple
Made to be sweet.
Red is as warm
As a fire at night.
Red is the smell
Of a burning light.
Red is a cardinal
Landing on my head.
Red is a sentence
That is read, read, read!
Read is a heart
Thumping so keen.
Red gets angry
When someone is mean.
Red yells, "Ow, ow, ow!"
Red reminds me of
The one word "wow!"
Joachim McElroy, Grade 5

Blue

Blue is a raindrop
With a quiet ring
Blue is what people sing
It's the water on
The beach
Blue is softer than
A feather
Blue is the
Month of September
Blue is like a hug
It's also sugar
In a coffee mug
Blue goes swosh, swosh, swosh
In a new tube
Of glue
Blue is the shine
Of a windowsill
Blue are the stars
On the flag
Blue is the color
That makes you glad
Puneet Gupta, Grade 6

Breaking Bonds

Far away in the night a scream cut
Through like a knife.
How gray the time is,
Misery and hate.
Then suddenly a bond is broken,
And there is a gleaming sun instead.
Then all there is is love and care.
Casper Mika, Grade 5

My Little Nittany Lion

My little Nittany Lion
is as fierce as a thunderstorm.
He is a soft kitty
and is quite warm.

My little Nittany Lion
sleeps most of the day.
He rarely wakes up to eat
and really hates to play.

My little Nittany Lion
hasn't a single fear.
When he gets bothered by the dog
there's not a scared meow to hear.

My little Nittany Lion
is as brave as a knight.
He runs out an open door
without a yelp of fright.
Kaelea Hayes, Grade 5

Artemis the Archer

The arrow pulled back
My heart beating
Leaves crunching
And clapping in awe
The whispers say shoot
I take a breath
The cold shivers at the thought of Artemis
I let go
The arrow turns and turns
Bull's eye!
Black, blue, red
Yellow! In the middle
The crack of the arrow
Splitting between the target
The rain pours in celebration
The thunder pounds in amazement
The lightning flashes in jealousy
Jealousy
Of Artemis
Ava Selby, Grade 4

School

So much depends on
A building

With classrooms
And teachers in them

With desks
And chairs

With books
And children
Haley Lewis, Grade 4

Fall Falls

Whish, whoosh
Brur, brun
Crinkle, crackle
Hin, hun

Leaves whispering
Critters out
Cold comes
Winter shouts

Whish, whoosh
Brur, brun
Crinkle, crackle
Hin, hun

Fall is gone
Winter triumphs
Warmth is taken
Ice awakens

Whish, whoosh
Brur, brun
Crinkle, crackle
Hin, hun
Elizabeth Schaefer, Grade 5

Halloween

H orrifying spirits
A wesome costumes
L eaves galore
L ooks much too lovely
O utstanding every time
W onderful treats
E ndless fun
E ating candy
N othing can beat Halloween
Kelly Cincotta, Grade 4

Thanksgiving

A delicious pumpkin pie scent in the air
Such a big and juicy turkey
Uncle Billy is here
Yes we scored a touchdown
Where is the turkey?
Pass the gravy Jim
Who took all the pumpkin pie?
Where is the turkey?
Pass the gravy Jim
Who took all the pumpkin pie?
Where is the turkey
I lost my plate
Who took all the pumpkin pie?
Uncle Billy is here
I lost my plate
A delicious pumpkin pie scent in the air
Carlos Guillen, Grade 4

My Mom

Today I'm writing about my mom.
She's kind,
She works very hard,
She knows what is good for me,
She's fun.

But when I get home,
Or in the car,
She gives me hugs and kisses,
She is the best mom I will ever have.

Her name is Karen.
We go shopping.
She supports me in soccer.

When I was a little baby,
I was scared of the dark,
She sang me a song.

When she got me,
she said God chose me.
That's all.
Michael Burks, Grade 6

Volleyball and Basketball

Can serve, bump, spike, and set
You can also use a net
Knee pads are so strong
Are good for a game so long
6 players, 2 games, and 3 hits
Players don't throw any fits
To not miss a ball you must be shouting
If you miss a ball there's no pouting

When a player is shooting
The crowd is hooting
Foul shots make people shiver
Might also make them quiver
Dribbling, passing, and running
Helping you win which is stunning
5 players wear jerseys as you can see
They work together as a team

Both a sport
Use a court
Both use a ball
Both active after all
Cayla Troyer, Grade 6

My Kitten

Within my heart, lies a bold little beauty
that shows a symbol of life
She's a message from the glowing heavens
A lazy little shadow, with a golden face,
and my love
Lizzy Bywaters, Grade 4

Spring Beauties
Perrywinkle dewdrops
Glimmer in the gold during dawn
Golden flowers elevate
Delicate as crystal
Bunny rabbits
Nibble the clover around dandelions
That glow like sun
Big sunrise
Pink, orange, blue
Shines its rays down to the world below
Trickling water runs through streams
As green frogs bounce across banks
Trees elevate with golden maple sap
and beautiful blossoms form perfectly pink
Pink petals float down gently
In the soft, refreshing breeze
Onto grass blades
Fireflies shine against the
Night's translucent stars
Crickets chirp in the moonlight
As dawn comes again
Tegan Poerio, Grade 5

White
White is a baby
Playing in the snow,
White is a snowflake
On your nose,
White is the clouds
That are ever so high,
White is also a
Snowman which wishes
He will never die,
It's also a bunny
Hopping around in
The bushes where
He would never
Be found,
White is a baseball
Sitting on the mound,
White are the lights
On a Christmas tree,
White is the rose
Someone gave to me,
White is also a wonder of the world.
Reagan T. Keane, Grade 6

Panda vs Turtle
Panda
White, chubby
Crawling, sleeping, hugging
Zoo, jungle, beach, island
Crawling, wading, eating
Green, round
Turtle
Zachary Coslove, Grade 6

Dictionary
D ictionaries are
I ncredibly smart
C an be boring because, they are
T oo big to read, they are
I n your house
O n your bookshelf, and
N ow they give
A nswers for words
R ight definitions, so
Y ou now know more about dictionaries
Sara Menand, Grade 5

My Robot
I have a robot that
rubs my feet,
cleans the dishes,
picks up my room,
cleans my closet,
makes my bed,
scratches my head,
does my homework,
makes my food,
writes my poems...
Isaiah Radcliff, Grade 5

Marblehead
M assachusetts
A historic place
R ocky shoreline
B eautiful
L ovely
E ssex county
H arbor
E xtraordinary
A wesome
D elightful
Bryn Burton, Grade 6

Ice Cream
Ice cream is very sweet.
It is also my favorite treat.
You can serve it hot or cold.
The ice cream flavors are very bold.
You can find it at the beach.
My favorite kind is peach.
Ice cream melts fast.
I wish it would last.
I love ice cream.
When I eat it I scream.
Chloe Sheridan, Grade 5

Lightning
Lightning is a strike of panic
Lightning is a fast runner
Lightning is a flash of beauty.
Dilan Patel, Grade 5

Pink
Pink is sweet
Pink is nice
Pink is the
Tail of mice
A lollipop
After a boo-boo
Tying a pink lace
Of a brand new shoe
The granddaughter
Of purple
The sister
Of red
The color you
See before bed
The lipstick of ladies
The winks of men
Pink is like
A clicking pen
Pink is so clever
Pink is the friendship
That will last forever
Grace Comas, Grade 6

The Glass That Holds Me In
Windows
that's what they're called

The glass that holds me in

The weirdness of it
It looking at me
Me looking at it

The glass that holds me in

Showing off
Saying, look at me, I'm see-through

The glass that holds me in

The brilliant look at sunrise and sunset
Like a thousand stars

The glass that holds me in
Taja Wilkins, Grade 6

Winter
Crisp freezing feeling, winter is here!
Perfect time to put on snow gear.
Play all day.
And come back to say I sure had fun today.
Winter is my favorite time of year.
People have so much cheer.
Snowflakes fall like confetti.
Santa's coming and I'm ready.
Dylan Bolling, Grade 6

Turkey Bandit

No forks nor knives
for our Thanksgiving Feast.
We were sad to find we had a turkey thief.
Shane, the turkey was our bandit,
His mission was to leave us empty handed.
Brenden Rostucher, Grade 4

Patches You Came to Us

Patches, you came to us on Christmas Day.
From Kansas, it was far away.
I was so happy when you jumped on me.
You filled my heart with glee.
I love you to the moonlight and back again.
Sarah Greco, Grade 4

Popcorn

Pop pop
Sizzle sizzle
Pop sizzle
Pop pop
Mmm popcorn
Walden Hart, Grade 5

There Once Was…

There once was a boy named Harry Potter,
Who Voldemort always tried to slaughter,
Harry beat him every time,
Until Voldemort would resign,
And Harry was filled with glory and honor.
Hailey Hoffman, Grade 6

Grandparents Are…

Always there to help.
Fun to talk and play with.
Willing to do, and give anything for us.
Taking us to many, enjoyable places.
Always making our day.
Isha Kaza, Grade 6

Grandparents Are…

Always there to help you.
Creative and kind.
Willing to help you build projects.
Constantly teaching you things.
Great to have around.
Maya Ettle, Grade 6

My Grandparents Are

Sweet just like a lollipop.
Loving and caring for me.
Happy and joyful about all good things.
Open to the world around them.
Understanding and thoughtful of others.
Conner Thierry, Grade 6

Football

I am a strong boy who loves football
I wonder if our team will win
I hear my coaches yell and the cheerleaders cheer as I get another epic touchdown
I see the quarterback throw the ball directly at me
I want my team to win the final game in overtime
I am a strong boy who loves football

I pretend I am always in the game playing
I feel the football going into my hand and me rolling into the end zone
I touch the yellow goal post
I worry about getting tackled really hard by a line backer
I am a strong boy who loves football

I understand all the very confusing, hard plays
I say watch the line backer
I dream of being in a championship
I try to catch every ball
I hope that our team will win every game we play
I am a strong boy who loves football
Brett Silva, Grade 5

The Beautiful Outdoors

I am a girl who loves the outdoors
I wonder when I will see spring again
I hear the winds whistle through the trees as if squirrels were having a hard hitting race
I see chipmunks stuffing their cheeks preparing for hibernation
I want pollution to cease to exist so the world stays beautiful
I am a girl who loves the outdoors

I pretend I'm a flower blooming through the frost
I feel the chill air hit against my face as if mother-nature were mad
I touch the freezing white frost
I worry about hurricanes destroying the very beautiful nature around us
I am a girl who loves the outdoors

I understand if something destroys the beautiful nature
I say how wonderful nature is
I dream of nature never being polluted
I try keeping the outdoors clean
I hope for peace in every single country through every nation
I am a girl who loves the outdoors
Mackenna Croft, Grade 5

The Wondrous Fruit

On the outside, you look like a beautiful polished art canvas.
You feel like the smooth skin of a glass baby.
When I peel you, you sound like a light body puncturing still water.
When I slice you, you sound like a quick and sudden zip, then silence.
Inside, you look like a yellow-white covered wheel on a bike with many spokes.
You feel like a road made of speed bumps.
You smell like a fresh load of laundry from the dryer.
You taste like a tangy and sweet burst of flavor.
Tell me tangerine, what are your other wonders?
Kailey Beckford, Grade 5

White

White is a pearl in the sea,
It tastes like a gooey marshmallow;
White is cream and frosty,
It smells like ivory.
White's sound is milk,
Dripping into a cup,
Or paste spreading on paper.
White feels like a pillow,
So soft, soft, soft
It is bleach and bloodless,
White is fair and pure.
That's what white is to me.
Ellie Brogan, Grade 4

The Storm!

Crack! Bang!
The crisp breeze blows
the rain as a raspy noise
Zap! the power goes out

Grab the lantern
bright as the sun
Crack! Bang!
that gave me quite a fright

The clean smell of rain
reassured me it was all right
George Reed, Grade 6

What Red Means to Me

The charging bull's eyes,
as the matador's cape flies.
Santa's present sack,
some tomato on a Big Mac.
My red crisp apples,
the caps on Snapples.
The crunchy fall leaves,
falling down from the trees.
The name of my favorite movie,
which to me is pretty groovy.;
To me, red is a mad color,
but to you it might be a not-so-bad color.
Ryan Schurr, Grade 6

The Power of Rings

I wear a tux
I walk down the aisle
I give rings
I walk with a flower girl
I stand around
I watch them get married
I eat yummy food
I have fun
I am a ring bearer
Wish me luck
Reese Lees, Grade 4

Spring

March makes wind,
blows all of the trees.
It is cool and warm.
Plants grow all over,
It's as green as can be.
Cool and calm with a gentle breeze,
birds tweet and
talk with sayings of nature
for all to hear
as creatures come out of hiding.
April is shining as bright as a diamond.
The Easter bunny gives candy
And sun.
Love is in the air as families get
Together and have a feast for Easter.
and have a fun time
May is sunny and filled with
Color and gives summer its hot and
cool weather.
Hannah Moore, Grade 4

Softball

It's about the sweating times
The players running and sliding
Trying to go big time
It's about the swing of the bat
The ball
The bases
It's about the grand slams
Intense parents in the stands
Anxious coaches waving their hands
It's about the fielders
The pitchers
The batters
It's about being alert
The yellow balls
The smell of the dirt
It's about the black pants
The red jerseys
Chanting and cheers
It's about the best sport ever
Rebecca Boorse, Grade 5

Grady Brown

G reatly loved
R eally nice
A lways friendly
D evilishly cunning
Y outhfully joyful

B rilliantly witty
R eally nice person
O ngoing spirit
W onderfully inventive
N ever stops improving
Grady Brown, Grade 5

Life

Life is a dandelion
Long and fragile
Beautiful and unique
Weak yet powerful
Dull and colorful

Life is moving on
Letting the special things go
Forgetting the bad
Remembering the good
Refreshing your mind

Life is a wrecking ball
Knocking you down
Banishing the evil
Creating devastation

Life is a piece of glass
Crumbling to the cold, hard ground
Shattering into millions of pieces
Tearing you apart
Delaney Stewart, Grade 6

Bravery

Bravery is a star
Shining throughout the night
The light may go out
Once it is gone, it is gone forever
Until you regain it.

Bravery is a pencil
The tip will break
Into many pieces
But you can always sharpen it.

Bravery is a sailboat
Bobbing up and down
Dancing in the clear, blue waters
You never know what waves
Will come your way.

Bravery is a trophy
Only you cannot see it
It is a trophy in your heart
That you can never forget.
Maria Scricco, Grade 6

Halloween

Halloween
Scary, haunted
Screaming, eating, scaring
Pumpkin, witch, Santa, elf
Screeching, playing, opening
Joyful, happiness
Christmas
Samantha Rom, Grade 5

High Merit Poems – Grades 4, 5, and 6

The Fall Leaves
Fall leaves are falling
Jumping in the leaf piles
All the leaves on me
Cristina Noelle Guanio, Grade 5

Ocean
Waves of the ocean
Makes me want to shout and sing
The sun is rising
Kaylee Granados-Martinez, Grade 5

Moon
Lighting up the night
Sometimes full and sometimes new
But leaves when day comes
Maya Jones, Grade 5

Night
The moon is shining
The wolves are howling loudly
They're ready to hunt!
Kobe Guo, Grade 5

Giraffe
It eats from big trees
It has prints that others don't
It has a long neck!
Gianna Shearer, Grade 4

Beautiful Spring Time!
Beautiful roses sprouting
They come in many different colors
They are very pretty
Alicia Carr, Grade 6

Winter
winter is coming
lots of snowflakes falling down
playing in the snow
Caroline Woodward, Grade 5

Me
As fun as can be
No one can change who I am
I am a great me!
Madeline Groves, Grade 4

I'm a Blue Jay
Gabriella is a Blue Jay.
She is as blue as the sky
She enjoys flying, singing, and dancing.
Gabriella Hayden, Grade 6

Fall
Leaves begin to fall from trees, just as the temperature starts to fall

Down… Down…Down…

The colorful leaves lying on the grass
Soon scooped up and made into clusters,
Then jumped on countless times
Till the darkness of night falls.

Sweet pumpkin pie lies on a table,
Prepared to be topped with whipped cream.

At night bowls of candy are placed on doorsteps,
Kids run about from house to house,
Collecting handfuls of candy,
As night starts to slip away for a new day.

Open ovens signal the start of the fall feasts of Thanksgiving.
The table is being set with gravy, mashed potatoes, stuffing, pumpkin pie,
And finally, the turkey.

Plates are being filled,
Second helpings have been served,
Desserts have been devoured after yet another a fantastic Thanksgiving Feast.
All the leaves have fallen, leaving the trees bare.

Toys and other merchandise are sold at stores all around for it is Black Friday.
Days have gone by and snow has just shown that fall has just come to an end.
Nicholas Currier, Grade 6

Skyrim
I love you Skyrim.
You are my favorite game. I love to play with you.

When I play you, I have the best time.
I feel mad when I don't see you.

With you I can fight dragons and giants, humongous spiders and trolls.
Kill monsters and tyrants.

When I play I can fight and build, or join the Dark Brotherhood.
And the Thieves Guild.

When I play I can build up my skills, or do quests for money.
And do close up kills.

I can join different places. I can help people.
I can become a Thane in many places.

When I play I have to wait a long time.
I can fight Bandits or Thalmore, go to jail after committing a crime.

I love you Skyrim
I am level 13
You are my best game.
Emma Martin, Grade 4

Homework

Would you look outside?
It's such a nice day.
The flowers are blooming
The sunlight is booming
It's to bad I'm stuck
inside my big house
doing my homework
which is hard for me.
Valery Charland, Grade 5

Halloween

On Halloween I like to trick or treat.
Sometimes the candy is very sweet.

On Halloween I really don't care
That's not something that I fear.

On Halloween I get lots of candy.
I spend a lot of time with my family.
Brandon Jones, Grade 6

My Mind

Go inside a mind,
See its levers working like a clock.
Perhaps you'll find glinting gears working–
As hard as a calculator.
Perhaps you'll find chains moving and
Thoughts being made.
Or perhaps you'll find something
Special about to be shown to the world.
Rachel Novick, Grade 5

Christmas

I love the presents under the tree,
What a wonderful Christmas it will be!
I run up to them and start to scream,
I love Christmas even more than ice cream!
I really hope I get an iPod,
My sister looks at me and starts to nod.
I get my iPod and I say, "Yippee!"
And then I play until half past three!
Autumn Allen, Grade 4

Cafeteria Food

The cafeteria ladies toss a paper tray,
With a frown as a hello,
Old sauce of crusted pizza,
Nasty, clumpy, yellow Jell-O.
Crumbly rotted ravioli
Rubbery blubbery macaroni.
Spoiled milk anyone?
You shall eat until you're done!
Sara Caligiuri, Grade 6

Lemon War

A lemon is a delicacy,
It's sourness only compares to its sweetness.
In heart it is sweet,
But in reality it's cold and sour.
Nothing says it's good or bad.
In the end it is brighter than the sun
But nothing is forgotten.
Memories never go away.
Sean Larkin, Grade 5

Thanksgiving

I open the door to my grandmother's house
and heave a great big sigh.
The smell of apple pie shoots up my nose
with turkey close behind.
I hear the pots and pans clatter
as Grandpa stuffs the goose.
I watch as Caramel the family pup
barks and greets the guests.
Amelia Caron, Grade 5

Football

F antastic
O utstanding
O ffense
T ouchdown
B est sport
A wesome
L inebacker
L oud fans
Jackson Fellows, Grade 5

Fire vs Water

Fire
Hot, white,
Burning, scorching, charring,
Forests, camps
Oceans, springs
Running, cooling, falling,
Chilling, aqua,
Water
Elijah Brown, Grade 6

Winter

Winter is frigid
Winter brings snow
Snow so beautiful
Fluttering down
Icicles dangling from balconies and cars
Snowy and icy trees sparkle
When the sun beams down
What a beautiful winter sight!
Gregory Lewis, Grade 5

Tessa and Collin

Tessa is short
Tessa is sweet
She is 10
She is an artist
Tessa is great
She makes huge mansions
But she will always be
My number 1 friend

Collin is tall
Collin is epic
He is 11
He is a great imaginer
Collin is awesome
He always makes shacks
But I will always be
Her number 1 friend

We always play
But we always disagree
But that is how
It's supposed to be.
Collin Oedy, Grade 6

The Silent Night

Christmas night is on its way
The lights glow
The holly hangs
The Christmas spirit is in the air
Christmas night is on its way.

But Christmas isn't about presents or food
The food is good
The presents are great
But Christmas isn't about presents or food.

Christmas is a time to love
A time to sing
A time for family
A time to worship Christ together
Christmas is a time to love.

Christmas is here and will soon pass
The presents are opened
The food is eaten
And Jesus has been born
Christmas is here and will soon pass.
Joseph Bradley, Grade 5

Rejection

Discouraged and down,
Audition you didn't pass,
Tears fall to the ground,
Just proudly hold your head high,
There is always a next time.
Marrianna Vitelli, Grade 6

Courage

C ourage was a dog,
O ut on the street,
U nder a box,
R escued by a woman,
A bandoned no longer,
G iven another chance to shine,
E scaped his old destiny.
Nathan Schindler, Grade 5

Sun

The sun is so bright
It shares its light
With its beautiful colors
It rises in the morning
That lights up the day
And it sets in the evening
The sun is so wonderful.
Charlie Triandafilou, Grade 5

Snow

It falls all day
So white and beautiful
They are different shapes and sizes
They come from the sky
We play in it all day
Were ever you go it's there
Snow all around
Gavin Chesen, Grade 5

Fall

Not too hot
Not too cold
Jumping in the fallen leaves
Dropped by beautiful trees
So colorful
A beautiful season
Oh, so wonderful!
Emma Christensen, Grade 5

Spider X

SpiderX
Sneaky, fast
Running, jumping, daring
An amazing super hero character
Dodging, fighting, falling
Smart brave
Arachnid
Raiden Portzline, Grade 5

Man's Best Friend

What is man's best friend?
Dog, one of many creatures,
No two are the same,
Running as fast as leopards,
Barking as loud as loud as lions.
Abby Tzanakis, Grade 6

The Lonely Pumpkin

Here I sit, the lonely pumpkin
waiting for my turn to be picked.
I hope, I hope I get a great carver
so I can be displayed to sit on the porch
on Halloween night.
I love seeing nice Trick-or-Treaters waiting
for their yummy candy.
I hope that the family that picked and carved me,
plant my seeds and I can once again be in the lovely pumpkin patch.
I hope they also use my pulp so they can make pumpkin pie on Thanksgiving.
I really hope this will all happen again next Autumn.
Autumn Zeak, Grade 4

A Great Christmas

I remember the night before Christmas and being so hyper.
I remember that I never wanted go to bed.
I remember that we must get cookies for Santa.
And we needed milk and Santa's favorite, coke.
I remember that my mom had to force us to go to bed.
I remember that I was in bed, but wouldn't fall asleep.
I remember lying in bed and trying to see a glance of him.
Even though it was so late I would not go to bed.
I remember waking up on Christmas morning and being so happy for presents.
But my favorite memory is still to come.
Jack Lord, Grade 5

Christmas Eve

I remember Christmas Eve.
I remember staring at my clock all night long.
I remember thinking about all the things I want for Christmas
and which gifts I will get and the ones I won't.
I remember closing my eyes and trying to go to bed
I remember jumping out of bed at 5:00 and running to the Christmas tree.
I remember seeing all of my cool gifts
even though I did not get everything I wanted.
I remember hugging my parents.
But my favorite memory's yet to come.
Samantha Sarubin, Grade 5

Why?

Why did Hitler hate the Jewish people?
Why were other races different from Jewish?
Why did the Jewish people have to sleep in holes just to stay alive one more night?
Why did Hitler kill them all?
Why would other German citizens not help?
Why would the Nazi's take them to Ghettos and gas them to death?
Why did the Holocaust ever happen?
Why can't someone tell us?
Maci Herman, Grade 6

Thanksgiving

My favorite thing on Thanksgiving is to gather around the table and have turkey.
My family and I have a lot of fun eating turkey together.
I also like to say "Happy Thanksgiving" to everyone around the world.
Mikael Jones, Grade 5

Friends

A friend is a very special person
In another person's life.
A friend is an almost-perfect person
Who helps to relieve strife.
Some friends
Are people you see just for a while;
But my friend is a person
Who makes me smile.
My friend is a person
Who's full of love and care,
And I know when I need her
She will always be there.
So as we walk together
Down the street and laugh,
I think that you're the best friend
A girl could ever have.
Jamie Roballo, Grade 5

Open Your Eyes

Open your eyes
Don't watch the people die
Open your eyes
Help the children who cry
Open your eyes
Can't you see Hitler's lies
Open your eyes
Stop watching the sad sights
Open your eyes
People sneak out for food to buy
Open your eyes
Stop the stomping boots through the night
Open your eyes
Help people that never see the light
Open your eyes
Please, open your eyes
Sarah Givone, Grade 6

By the Rocks

The Rocks'
Reflection glistening in the water,
Pink and orange from the setting sun.

So perfect,
Water sparkles, sun gleams, rocks shimmer,
My heart catches in my lungs.

Stand up, seagulls quiet,
Look out, the day is nearly done.

Run, hair flying, take a jump,
So captivating here with no one.

Soft splash, water ripples,
My heart beats for the ocean: We are one.
Halina Dreger, Grade 6

Are You

Are you awesome?
Are you cool?
Are you cute?
Are you fantastic?
Are you a dancer?
Smart and a singer?
Are you out of this world?
But are you yourself?
Sabrina Karimova, Grade 5

Wolf in Me

There is a wolf in me
With sharp pointy teeth,
Like 100 needles and claws.
Like tiny silver blades; it howls
Like a man getting stitches; it sprints
Like a bullet through the night.
It lives in my brain and makes
Me want to play.
Andrew Schwed, Grade 5

The Shark

The shark went to swim in the water,
but then he ran into an otter
I'm sure he'll regret it,
and I'm sure he'll forget it
He wished he had a pet,
he wouldn't break a sweat
The shark took the otter home,
then he let it go so it can roam.
Mark Prioleau, Grade 5

Halloween

Halloween is a fun, scary holiday.
We all love to go out and play.

Halloween makes my brother scared.
It's time to make a friendly dare.

Halloween will make you run.
It is time to have some fun.
Jadyn Andre, Grade 6

Harriet

My name is Harriet
I always save the day.
I look up at the North Star
I know I'll find a way.
I look down at my feet
and hobble on one foot.
I hide in the chimneys of safe houses
getting covered in ashes and soot.
Tristan Jones, Grade 5

Thanksgiving

Thanksgiving feast, mmm
Our mouths are stuffed with cornbread
I watch the Macy's parade go on
We see a big fat Kermit balloon
Our mouths are stuffed with cornbread
We eat mashed potatoes with gravy
We see a big fat Kermit balloon
While we watch, turkey is ready
We eat mashed potatoes with gravy
I watch Charlie Brown Thanksgiving
While we watch, turkey is ready
Pie finished cooking
I watch Charlie Brown Thanksgiving
I watch the Macy's parade go on
Pie finished cooking
Thanksgiving feast, mmm
Chase Crandall, Grade 4

Summer

Hot blistering sun
Sweltering sidewalks
Hot enough to cook an egg
Salty ocean air
Roams the area
Waves ripping like endless dominos
Days as long as years
Fireball sunsets descending into the ocean
At night,
Crackling campfires
Toasted marshmallows
And melted chocolate…
Gritty sand still suck between your toes
Waiting to be sprinkled throughout your
House
As you return
Sammy Loew, Grade 6

Final Win

The game
fouling tied game
back and forth
back and forth
scoreboard changing
fans cheering
shoes squeaking
last seconds
open court
on a pursuit
nervous sweating
jump
shot
swish
victory
we won 56-54.
Kelby George, Grade 4

High Merit Poems – Grades 4, 5, and 6

Thanksgiving

Today is Thanksgiving
The day we offer thanks
Presents sitting in front of me
I can't believe that Hanukkah is so early
The day we offer thanks
Turkey, stuffing, cranberry sauce, what to choose
I can't believe that Hanukkah is so early
Watching the Macy's parade, eating doughnuts with a drink
Turkey, stuffing, cranberry sauce, what to choose
I love when the whole family is together
Watching the Macy's parade, eating doughnuts with a drink
Just an amazing holiday
I love when the whole family is together
Presents sitting in front of me
Just an amazing holiday
Today is Thanksgiving

Benjamin Levine, Grade 4

The Changing of the Seasons

As summer became a memory in the past,
Winter came unexpectedly and fast.
It came with delights and complaints
And delicious foods on special plates!
Thanksgiving comes and goes
And leaves us with a red nose and cold toes.
Now the plates are stacked high with cookies to adore,
But soon we are begging our Grandma for more.
We save some for Santa along with some milk,
In hopes he'll fill our stockings, specially made of red silk.
Then, Christmas arrives and fills us with glee
As we find gifts under the illuminated tree.
Not only food and gifts galore,
But snow's covering the Earth's floor!
It's Jack Frost's gift of a winter wonderland,
But God, the wonderful man, lent a helping hand.

Raelyn Horne, Grade 6

Violence in My Neighborhood

P olice patrol my neighborhood
R espect your neighbors
E ach and every person should do good
V iolence is not the answer
E veryone deserves peace
N ever fight so we won't be put in a bad situation
T each children to respect mankind.

V iolence kills people and hurts people, too
I nclude people in your community to look out for each other
O ffer to help someone in times of need
L ove and peace
E veryone deserves friendship and kindness
N egative actions bring violence into your community
C hanging your community is important
E veryone deserves to be free from violence.

Rodneyka Thompson, Grade 5

Grandpa

Grandpa Egedy moved in with us four years ago
So what's so funny about that, you would like to know?
He sits with us at dinner time every night
And his funny stories are such a delight.
He tells us silly jokes and we crack up
Sometimes he falls asleep holding his coffee cup.
Stories about his ship when he was a Navy boy
Snoring bunk mates, awful food, these tales bring us such joy.
Grandpa used to be deaf and we would have to scream
Yesterday he got hearing aids and that was always his dream.
He loves to sing the old gospel hymns
Standing in our kitchen exercising his limbs.
FOX News is always on with the volume oh so loud
No other TV station would ever be allowed!
Come to my house and my grandpa will make you smile
He will tell you funny stories, so plan to stay awhile.

Andrew Egedy, Grade 5

June Welcomes Summer

June welcomes summer into life:
the sweet sound of children laughing and playing
in the crisp, late evening June sun,
their mothers calling for them to come in before darkness comes.
Later, in the dark, people and families
join in the fun of roasting marshmallows over the open fire.
July adds color to the dull skies,
letting colors of fireworks bloom
with happiness and the freedom of America.
Red, white, and blue light up the sky,
children running side to side to see the lights with color in the sky.
August brings the heat to people outdoors,
making the last of the summer berries ripe for harvest treats,
mothers baking,
boys and girls taking water bottles from the cold freezers
to the warm August outdoors.

Rebekah Nilles, Grade 4

Old Man Winter

Old man winter,
I hear him grumble
As the leaves turn
From crisp greens to subtle oranges and reds

As the trees lose their leaves,
It looks as if they lost their clothes

Now I walk outside, I see my breath
My cheeks turn pink like cherry blossoms
If I stay out long enough,
They turn red as roses

As old man winter
Rumbles and grumbles,
My favorite season comes around

Erin Schnupp, Grade 6

Disruptive Students
students
sometimes
have numerous ideas
sometimes
make teachers furious

paper airplanes thrown
a million questions asked
time wasted
insults made
loud noises erupt
students
sometimes
make a teacher's head explode
Michael Luna, Grade 6

Blue
Blue is a flying blue jay
A pretty flower
And the color of my favorite jeans
It is the glistening ocean
A flashing lightning bolt
And the flag of our nation
Blue tastes refreshing
Like Gatorade on a hot day
And juicy blue berries
Blue feels like rain
Dripping down your neck
It feels happy
Like swimming in the ocean
Blue can make your day!
Isaiah Leach, Grade 4

A Thanksgiving Dinner
Take a turkey, stuff it fat.
Some of this and some of that.
Get some turnips, peel them well,
Cook a big squash in its shell.

Now potatoes, big and white.
Mash until they're soft and light.
Cranberries tart and sweet,
With the turkey, we must eat.

Pickles, yes, and then oh my!
For a dessert, a pumpkin pie!
Golden brown and spicy sweet,
That a fine Thanksgiving treat!
Wyatt Bobbey, Grade 4

Christmas
Joyful, jolly
Giving, getting, celebrating
It's green and red
Christ
Michael Cejpek, Grade 5

Sports
Sports are fun
they help you keep fit.
Basketball, baseball, rugby,
lacrosse, football, soccer,
and many more.
You can play them
and maybe make
a score.
Edward Cannon, Grade 5

Devin He
D evin likes Doctor Who
E ragon is a favorite book of mine
V ery, very funny
I LOVE READING
N ever stops playing

H e likes sports
E lectronics are fun
Devin He, Grade 5

Baseball
B aseball is fun
A t bat watch the ball
S wing the bat
E ven have a good time playing baseball
B aseball is confidence
A t fielding do your best
L ove the sport
L ove baseball
Vincent Capria, Grade 5

November
N ever-ending fun.
O verstuffed am I.
V egetables galore!
E veryone is together.
M other and I prepare the food.
B efore we eat, we pray.
E xactly what I thought it would be.
R eally looking forward to Christmas.
Isabella Vescera, Grade 5

Holocaust
Hitler, hateful, killing, cruel,
No one should like the Nazi rule.
Killing Jews and other races,
One by one at fast paces.
Children hurt and others crying,
Races poisoned and most dying.
Many families living in fear,
A sad story of which to hear.
Owen Kern, Grade 6

It's About
It's about…
Big pads and fat gloves
Thick shoulder pads

It's about…
slap shots, wrist shots
and snap shots

It's about…
slippery ice and big skates
getting the puck from your opponents

It's about…
skating fast
and winning the race to the puck

It's about…
precise passes
and breakaways

It's about
teamwork
and working hard
Jack Boas, Grade 5

Paper
A piece of paper
Nothing on it
Right in front of me
I cannot write
With nothing to know about
Nothing to write about

I could write about ships
I could write about sharks
When the teacher says
Ready, set, write!

A blank page sits in front of me.
What are you writing about?
The teacher says
Nothing! I yell.
My brain is on delay.
Well, write what your heart tells you
Or just jot something down.

A piece of paper
Right in front of me
The whole page filled up.
Graham Schaefer, Grade 5

Deer
Moves lightly through trees
Hears you coming, runs away
Treat them with respect.
Danny Renzetti, Grade 4

High Merit Poems – Grades 4, 5, and 6

Skyrim
Through the woods, I ran.
Hiding from the dragon I was.
"It saw me" I thought.
It landed in front of me then breathed fire,
I shouted at it and then ran.
I thought I outran it until it was above me.
I ran into Whiterun, a city.
The dragon left then never cam back.
Mitchell Jennewine, Grade 6

My Dog
My dogs name is Daisy.
She is black and white.
Even though she is seven.
She still is very small.
Also she is very active.
She also has two sisters.
They both look like her.
I can't wait to see her grow.
Chelsey Nutt, Grade 6

My Friends
Friends are nice
They are kind
Should be helpful
They aren't mean
We always have friends to turn to
Friends are always there for you
I have many friends
My friends could be family
Holly Weightman, Grade 6

Winter Time
Winter so nice and bright
Snow so right
What a wonderful sight,
Everything is amazingly white
Coat zipped up so tight,
Wish you could fly a kite
When you go to bed at night,
You wake up at a beautiful daylight.
Robbie Pendleton II, Grade 6

Winter
It's a cold season,
There's no doubt to reason.
What's in the air?
No one has a care.
I am the only one who can see
What the future is going to be.
Kids are happy to greet Santa Claus.
So, be watchful—school will take a pause.
Kyle Jackson, Grade 6

What Should Be in the Poem
There I was with a pen in my hand
Thinking up things that were just bland
Wondering of things to write
Clenching my fists tight

Scanning for what to do
And wondering what, when, and who
Wondering of things to change
Finding my words to be strange

Starting to really worry
Definitely need to hurry
What should be in the poem
Thinking about it at home
Tyler Yup, Grade 5

Dreams Sense
Dreams, dreams, dreams
They sound like life yet
Have no sound,

Dreams feel cozy and safe,

They taste like fresh warm
Air in your imagination and they
Look like amazing
Angels in the sky,

Dreams, dreams, dreams
Dreams are really
The best of all
Max Roesener, Grade 5

Hurricane Sandy
I was watching TV
When a bee flew in
So I ran to the living room
Trying to get away from it
And that is when
The power went out!

That was when
My mother told me
About Hurricane Sandy
Then it got darker
As my mother kept talking
Telling me about
The horrible storm.
Cassandra Rose Landaverde, Grade 4

The Dark
Upon us the dark awaits.
To grab us, pull us, draw us near,
Shadows lurking deep within us.
I am your worst fear.
Sydney Brick, Grade 5

Lightning
My color white,
Big and bold,
I zap the ground
with my powerful hold.

I come when there are storms,
Rain awaits me to the shower,
Remember that I come past an
   hour!
Tsampica Mitchell, Grade 5

Volcano
Magma booming out,
Rising over surrounding terrain.
Demolition, fire, and ash.
No longer is the land a prosperous green,

But it is a field of glowing embers.
This annihilation of the senescence
Was an act of innovation
For a makeshift Earth.
Henry Leopold, Grade 6

The Wind
The wind is daring
The wind is caring
Oh please, please
Rescue me
I may blow you over
I am heading to Dover
Goodbye for now
I'll be back
Somehow
Madison Wallace, Grade 5

Holocaust
H itler
O ffensive
L ousy
O ppressive
C razy
A wful
U nfortunate
S ad
T errible
Sarah Smith, Grade 6

Arctic Fox
Late sunrise
early cold winter.
The winds rubbing against me.
The cool winter's air is cool and moist.
I'm hunting for my family.
I feel lonely without them.
Will I find food on the way back?
Cole Chiapperino, Grade 4

Autumn Glory

Autumn is a mystery,
As magical as it is beautiful,
No one knows how it happens,
Yet when it does,
The wind sends the leaves into swirling spirals,
And bewitches your eyes,
Autumn is a cloak,
One day it is off,
But suddenly it is on,
Surrounding the Earth with its brightly coloured leaves,
Cool climates,
And abundant harvests,
Autumn is all of the above,
Until a dark, frosty winter,
Pounces onto the world,
And transforms everything,
Into frost, snow and cold,
Autumn vanishes,
And says goodbye,
And sets off down the path,
To next year...

Anne-Emilie Rouffiac, Grade 6

The Whuubermoppey

If you see the frog mellow,
Beware the bumbling bog below,
Beware the Whuubermoppey, my friend.
With teeth and claws and tearing paws,
You'll surely have a great mirage, about the Whuubermoppey,
My friend. So don't go near the frogs below.
Said Hickery Sickery Dippary Den.
I do not ken, he said right then, and off away he strode.
He took his sword in hand and said I am Tarzan.
He found the frogs, and fell in to the bog, to find the human hog.
He saw the Whuubermoppey,
With tearing paws and horrible claws;
It soon would be upon him.
He stood with a large gait,
And felt like a small piece of bait,
With bravery he stood,
He saw a lot of soot,
And he lunged at it with super strength, and swept it at its eyes.
It yowled and howled and thrashed about,
But his sword went snicker-snack,
And the Whuubermoppey was no more.

Coyote Fisher, Grade 5

Green

Green is the best
It's better than all the rest,
Green is great
It's a color I will never hate,
Green is the smell of a fresh cut field,
Green is the smell of a lime that is peeled,
Green is the taste of string beans and my favorite ice cream,
Green is the color of the Celtics basketball,
Green is the color of the leaves on a tree that is tall,
Green is the sound of a party on St. Patty's Day,
Green is the sound at the park where kids play,
Green is the feel of my Notre Dame sweatshirt,
Green is the feel when I fall in the dirt,
Green is the color of me being Irish,
Green is cool, green is right,
Green goes fight, fight fight!
Green is the color of everyone's Christmas,
Green is the color of lights on the tree,
Green is the color of my favorite car,
Green is the color of my new guitar,
I love green!

Martin Keane, Grade 6

I Am

I am a wonderful person who loves basketball
I wonder why some girls like basketball
I hear the water bottles wobble and the coaches
screaming, go left, go right, and people cheering
I see people screaming, go team go, and players scoring
I want to score at least five three-pointers in one game
I am a wonderful person who loves basketball
I pretend that I am the best player ever
I feel that I get better and better every
game I play every year
I touch the ball and shoot
I worry that I might break my arm blocking someone
I am a wonderful person who loves basketball
I understand to watch out for other players
I say that basketball is fun
I dream of winning a championship game yearly
I try to do my best
I hope we win our games yearly
I am a wonderful person who loves basketball

Julianna Landi, Grade 5

A Great Thanksgiving

As the food cooked, the kids played, and
Mom laid the plates on the table.
Our hearts felt with pride.
Then finally, the guest came inside.
We ate turkey, ham, and drunk punch.
Then, our plates were empty and everyone left.
We had a great Thanksgiving.

Emily Cline, Grade 6

Seashell

A dark night with a glowing moon.
In my hands–
Saved from the sand.
The bumpy waves on its back–
I listen.
The smooth surface of the ocean treasure touches me.
I let it go.

Maggie Hannis, Grade 5

High Merit Poems – Grades 4, 5, and 6

Through Their Eyes
If I could talk horses' language
I would ask them about their past
I would listen closely and acknowledge them
I would LOVE them for what they are
For their beauty and grace

I would listen closely to learn if there was abuse
Neglect, hurt, or pain

I would help them learn to trust again
To be trusted by people

I can understand what they have been through
They do tell me
They show me flashbacks of what happened in the past

They tell me through their eyes
Emily Bassford, Grade 6

My Life
I love my life;
I feel so bright–
Even when it is night.
Life is a difficult test–
So do your best.
When you get closer to dying,
You have to stop crying.
You have to go to school;
1 through 12, too–
So brace yourself!
In life, time goes by,
So try not to slide.
The good part about life is you get more knowledge,
So you better love your life before it stops
And sadly it will drop.
I love my life. Oh, I live my life!
Even though someday it will stop.
Sheik Conde, Grade 5

Montana
Boom, the shot tears through the air, smash it nails the clay
Zing, the arrow goes as it flies straight at the target.
Bulls eye!

Cast
plop
the fly hits the water

crash
splash
fish on.

Clip clop clip clop my horse waddles up the trail.
Crash, I turn and I gaze at two rams fighting.
Zoom going down the runway towards home.
Peter Napoli, Grade 5

The Water Watcher
I watch the water flow down the river
like a person drinking water
I watch the water go over rocks
like a person pushing someone onto the ground
then…
splash!!!!
it starts to rain
I watch the water flowing down the river still
even though it is raining
I watch the water flowing with out a care that rain is pouring on it
I watch the water be happy
I am the water watcher
Mia Albert, Grade 6

Rainbow Dreams
Dreams are rainbows in the sky,
Sparkling with gold at the ends
Red roses on the top, smelling so sweet
Fall orange leaves glistening with morning dew
Then, a yellow glow as bright as the sun
Lighting up the world making everything look magical!
Green plants next in line, growing, growing
Nourishing the plants is the blue, blue water
Filled with colorful fish
Then comes my favorite purple
All kinds of flowers are displayed on this last stripe
That's my rainbow dream!
Samantha Parelius, Grade 5

Periwinkle
Purple and blue, purple and blue,
A mix of colors; it will do.
A royal color, wealth and fame,
While still independent; in that there's no shame.

Safe
Sensible
Secret
Sacred
Savored

For beauty is a wondrous thing.
Katie Hobart, Grade 6

Dance
Tap, tap, tap!
The heels of my shiny shoes are tap, tap, tapping,
On the wooden dance floor below my feet.
Clap, clap, clap!
My hands are clap, clap, clapping,
To the rhythm of the beat.
Point, point, point!
My toes are pointing to the ground.
Dancing makes me feel
Cozy, safe, and sound.
Caris Worsham, Grade 5

Very Strawberry

On the outside, you look like a dotted heart on a clown's costume
You feel like little pebbles on the road
When I peel you, you sound like a mushy, slushy when I mix it
Inside, you look like red sugar in my cherry fun dip
You feel like a slippery water slide
You smell like my strawberry shampoo I use in my hair
You taste like a nice strawberry smoothie
Mmm, mmm, mmm

Jocelyn Woo, Grade 5

Roads

Roads just keep going,
I see so many.
They have cars and so many people.
They've got two sides, forward and back.
I ride a bike on gigantic roads.
Twists, turns, going this way and that.
Made by cement and rock.
There are so many more, from what I've been told.

Danny Henry, Grade 5

Thanksgiving

Thanksgiving is almost here.
I love Thanksgiving.
I do not think it is weird.
On Thanksgiving, we will have turkey.
I learned that turkeys are dinosaurs.
So, I will say to my mom, 'Please pass the dinosaur.'
When I say that, people will laugh.
Maybe the turkey will say, 'Please don't eat me.'

Elijah Hedgemond, Grade 5

Ode to Milk

Milk is really good,
With all kinds of food like toast, steaks, and spaghetti,
And with the pills that I take every morning.
Every time I drink milk, it reminds me of a vanilla milkshake.
When I drink milk it calls my name,
And when I have food,
I would like some milk with any kind of food.
I can't live without you, milk!

Tristan Barker, Grade 4

Love on Valentine's Day

Heart warming chocolates I send to my love
Flowers and angels all from above
We meet at a kiss and a very big smile
I guess love has been going around for a while
Cupid and flowers everywhere I go
Everything in a peaceful flow
Valentines day is a beautiful sight
And I love it with all my might

Abigail Wilson, Grade 4

Tornado

The clouds were dropping to the ground
They hit the barn like a bomb with a pound

It was a tornado the biggest around
It never went up I saw it only go down

This is a bad day, that's what I see and think
I guess that explains Friday, the thirteenth

Alexander Murphy, Grade 6

The Storm

I can see the clouds rolling in, dark, and scary.
Hear the thunder roar loud and demanding like a lion.

Feel the raindrops fall as the storm is getting worse.
Smell the raindrops mixing with the mud as the hogs roll around.

Taste the raindrops as you open your mouth wide.
Rain, oh, rain what a lovely thing.

Johnathan Buynak, Grade 6

My Strawberry

On the outside, you look like a red heart
You feel like an apple
When I slice you, you sound like a soft banana
Inside, you look like a watermelon
You feel like soft and bumpy
You smell like strawberry candy
You taste like a lime with watermelon
Tell me, why do you have seeds?

Gisell Rodriguez, Grade 5

Dreams

Mystical, delusional, creative
Secrets bestowed within your night adventure
Floating upon a cloud or battling fear itself
Escaping worries and problems
Unpredictable
Capturing you
Destination unknown
Never knowing its final ending

Gianna Lorenzo, Grade 6

The Season of Winter

When I was walking outdoors I was bright eyed
Precipitation of snow that falls by my side
I can grab my sled and glide down a hill
Then fall off the sled and experience a great chill
I would have a snowball fight with neighbors and friends
We will fight and it might never end
I'll make a snowman with happiness and glee
It won't melt away and my life will be worry free

Kameron Saul, Grade 5

High Merit Poems – Grades 4, 5, and 6

Sugar Maple Leaf
Sugar maple leaf
I float towards the ground lightly
Then I'm stepped on "crunch"
I change during the seasons
I can be very ablaze
Kiersten Montag, Grade 5

Basketball
Basketball
Exciting, active
Thrilling, running, scoring
Michael Jordan is awesome
Amazing
Amos Zereoue, Grade 6

The Little Leaf
I am very smooth.
You find me on the street.
I get stuck in trees.
I am orange and I'm red.
I live in a black birch tree.
Kendal Higgins, Grade 5

Dog
Dog
Soft, lovable
Barking, playing, running
They are so cute
Canine
Haya Jokhadar, Grade 5

Blackhawks
Blackhawks
Red, black
Shooting, blocking, diving
They're prodigious at shooting
Hockey
Colin Armentrout, Grade 5

Leo
Dog
Cute, active
Eating, licking, playing
Always tries to escape!
Leo
Katie Hart, Grade 5

Enzo
Enzo
Playful, loving
Cuddling, protecting, barking
He makes me smile
Puppy
Gabriella Morello, Grade 5

The Yo-Yo
I wrap the neon yellow and black string around my finger
I grasp the cobalt blue rims
and thoughtfully wind
the string around the bearing.

I cast.

It spins as it cascades down.
It hums.

I flick my wrist
and it returns to me.

I perform tricks like the bind, the cradle, the bow-tie and splitting the atom.
I've perfect them all.

Some might call me the master of the yo-yo. And I think it's true,
except for the one incident at Fenn involving a window.

Woops.
Riaz Jamal, Grade 5

Stopping in the Trees on a Dark Night*
Whose flowers are these I wonder and think?
Probably thrown away without a blink,
They will not see me scoop them up,
To clutch them in my hand, bright pink.

The forest animals may think it lame,
To pick up flowers that are so plain,
Between two patches of light brown dirt,
The darkness makes my eyes strain.

Then they come walking along,
Singing such a mournful song,
Don't even notice me there,
Running away, my strides long.

The flowers are light in a night that's dark,
Standing out against tree's bark,
And seconds before I have to embark,
And seconds before I have to embark.
Sonali Singh, Grade 6
**Patterned after "Stopping by Woods on a Snowy Evening" by Robert Frost*

The Great Green Lime
On the outside, you look like a green spinning top.
You feel like a small green basketball
When I peel you, you sound like a piece of wood being cut
When I slice you, you sound like little bubbles popping again and again
Inside, you look like someone cut you into small pizza slices
You feel like a rubber orange
You smell like an air freshener
You taste like a sour patch candy
Tell me, why do you have so many different shades of green on you?
Anthony Laferrara, Grade 5

The Start of a New Season

Put away your bathing suits and shorts,
Because it's time to take out your thick pants and warm sweatshirts
Now confused squirrels run into the middle of the road,
As clueless as a newborn baby
As it gets colder you can find the sweet aroma of burning fires
Driving past tons of vast,
Green farmland on your way to a pumpkin patch
Going on rough, bumpy but wonderful hay rides
The sweet caramel on top of a huge
Crisp juicy apple
Leaves being blown by the wind are busy shoppers bustling
Across the streets of NYC
On Thanksgiving there is warm,
Moist pumpkin pie
Also delicious,
Tender turkey
The constant dinging of the oven timer
Let's you know it is time to eat
As it gets colder you known,
That winter is coming soon!

Brooke Lundrigan, Grade 6

The Young Poet

I am a girl who loves writing poetry
I wonder if people like my poetry
I hear soft sounds as the reader is reading
my favorite poem I wrote about my family
I want to be a famous poetry writer when I grow up
I am a girl who loves writing poetry

I pretend I'm reading a poem to a classroom
I feel my hand cramping and my head pounding
in the middle of writing
I touch my pencil and paper
I worry if I will ever become a famous poetry writer
I am a girl who loves writing poetry

I understand some poetry that other people write
I say a lot of rhyming words
I dream about being the best poet
I try my hardest writing smoothly
I hope that I will become the best poetry writer ever
I am a girl who loves writing poetry

Emily Beauchaine, Grade 5

Softball

Standing in the batter's box,
Waiting for the ball.
"Crack!" the ball goes,
Over the heads of third basemen, short stop and left fielder.
Down to the ground it goes, about two feet from the fence.
The left fielder doesn't get it in time,
"Wow! I made it home."
Next inning I'm up 5th
I'm feeling great.
I took the first pitch, I felt the bat connect with the ball.
It went towards right field.
As soon as I look the ball is over the fielder's head
Over the fence and hit the window of a car.
My first slam, awesome.
Now in the 7th inning, losing 17-15.
Two people on base,
I'm up, the pressure is on me.
The first pitch comes in, I swung and missed,
The second pitch came in and I hit another home run.
We won the game!

Emily McGowan, Grade 6

Christmas

Again, it's that time of year.
A time for happiness and cheer.
Deck the halls with holly,
Tis the season to be jolly.
Hang the mistletoe
And hope our Christmas is full of snow.
On the special night, children prepare cookies and milk
Then lie down in their beds soft as silk.
As they're dreaming away about sugar plums
They start to hear awakening hums.
Then down the stairs they rush
Careful not to make a hush.
With their eyes they see
A chubby man in front of the tree.
With a wink of his eye and a tug on his hat
He was gone clear as that.
All that was left you see
Were tightly wrapped presents under the tree.
Then away he flew on his sleigh
Saying Merry Christmas to all, and to all a good day.

Sydney Baciak, Grade 6

The Giant Grapefruit

On the outside, you look like the shining golden sun
You feel like a slithering snake's skin
When I peel you, you sound like bubble wrap popping
When I slice you, it sounds like water rushing down a stream
Inside, you look like a bright pinkish, reddish lemon
You feel like a dog's ear inside
You smell like a flower that just bloomed
You taste like a sour and sweet lime
Tell me, Grapefruit, why are you called a grapefruit?

Julie Schroeder, Grade 5

Kiwi

On the outside, you look like a hairy ball
You feel like a rough road
When I peel you, you sound like a crunching leaf
When I slice you, you sound like ripping paper, slightly
Inside, you look like the sun in the middle
You feel like a smooth table top
You smell like my lime perfume
You taste like a sweet lime
Tell me, why do you look like a tennis ball?

Simone Attles, Grade 5

Video Gamer

I am a professional video gamer anytime.
I wonder if I'll be a professional.
I hear the sounds of walking, jet packs,
water running, and lava boiling and breathing.
I see the beautiful textures and
graphites of the game.
I want to be one of the top gamers in the world.
I am a professional video gamer anytime.

I pretend I am the top gamer on earth.
I feel the plastic controllers on my hands and the
hard plastic of buttons.
I touch the screen when I win.
I worry I won't be a top gamer of the country.
I am a professional video gamer anytime.

I understand I won't be a top gamer.
I say I will be one.
I dream that I will be one.
I try to be the best.
I hope that if I try hard
I will make it.
I am a professional video gamer anytime.
Quintin Moore, Grade 5

Twilight Sled Ride

Bong! Bong!
The clock strikes 6:00
My dog Maxine barks while it rings
I open the door outside
It feels like I am in an ice cube

I grab my sled and glide down a hill
The wind blows through my hair while my cold numb hands
Feel like they are being stung by 1,000 bees
I smell smoke from a nearby house

I can taste the snowflakes that softly fall into my mouth
The purple sky is getting darker
While fixing my gloves I see the bright light of the moon shining

Snap!
Crackle!
Pop!
My sled breaks
I walk up the hill to my house and the ground is an ice skating rink
And it is very slippery.
When I get home I go to get hot cocoa
Fun Twilight Sled Ride
Cadence Krall, Grade 4

Jaydon the Brick Wall

Jaydon is a brick wall because he's unbreakable.
He is as nice as his grandfather and can take tough things too.
He likes bouncing, gaming, and playing outside.
Jaydon Leinheiser, Grade 6

Perfect

There is a place where animals roam free
Where food is everywhere and everything
There's no war, no fighting, no wrong choices to disagree
It's perfect
There's always enough food, enough room, enough shelter,
It's perfect
Nothing is wrong there,
Only right
Nobody yells
Nobody fights
It's perfect

Perfect enough that everyone went there
Soon there wasn't enough room, shelter, and peace
Only fighting, violence, wrong choices, and warfare
So the place shut down
Everyone left
They searched elsewhere for this perfect place all around
They never found it.
Amanda Roberson, Grade 6

Love

Love is a puppy's fur,
Soft as air each and every day
Golden and thick, waving hello to me in the
fresh wind
Strong and tough, growing bigger and lasting longer

Love is a book,
Always evolving and never stopping
Peaceful and mysterious
Never knowing, what good things are soon to come

Love is a kitten,
Soft and furry
Waiting to become bigger, better, stronger
No one can make her feel inferior

Love is a singer's voice,
Soothing, smooth, and delicate
With a steady beat and loving harmony
A conscientious tone of the heart
Nick O'Melia, Grade 6

The Flame

The flame is in my heart
The flame is always lit
The flame dances when you're around
It dies down when you're not
The flame is always lit
I have no power over it
It dances when it wants, making my heart pound
You can't put out the flame,
It's so powerful
Hailee Langenbach, Grade 5

Thanksgiving

Leaves fall, life is good
Fall is Thanksgiving
Kids feast and have fun
Uncles joke, parents laugh
Fall is Thanksgiving
Life is new, tradition is old
Uncles joke, parents laugh
Thanksgiving is going by
Life is new, tradition is old
Family and friends enjoy themselves
Thanksgiving is going by
Life goes on, so do your surroundings
Family and friends enjoy themselves
Kids feast and have fun
Life goes on, so do your surroundings
Leaves fall, life is good
Max Brokaw, Grade 4

Thanksgiving

I like Thanksgiving
I eat with my family
We play football
Mom cooks a delicious turkey
I eat with my family
We have creamy mashed potatoes
Mom cooks a delicious turkey
I watch the parade with my cousins
We have creamy mashed potatoes
Milk, broccoli, and peas too
I watch the parade with my cousins
Fresh pumpkin pie for dessert
Milk, broccoli, and peas too
We play football
Fresh pumpkin pie for dessert
I like Thanksgiving
Emma Bianchi, Grade 4

Thanksgiving

On a cool fall day celebrating Thanksgiving
Spending time with family
Eating pumpkin pie
Jumping in leaves
Spending time with family
Raking leaves
Jumping in leaves
Spending time with cousins
Raking leaves
Watching leaves fall to the ground
Spending time with cousins
Being thankful
Watching leaves fall to the ground
Eating pumpkin pie
Being thankful
On a cool fall day celebrating Thanksgiving
Julia Chung, Grade 4

We Need to Find a Turkey

We need to find a turkey
For Thanksgiving Day.
Let's look in Murkey
And even farther away.

We need to find a turkey!
It's almost sundown!
We already looked in Murkey.
We all wear a frown.

We never found a turkey
For Thanksgiving Day.
I guess we will eat some jerkey
And some plain and gross hay!
Abigail Roth, Grade 5

Downton Abbey

D ramatic
O pulent
W ealthy
N aughty
T raumatizing
O utstanding
N ever poor quality

A mazing
B ritish
B eautiful
E legant
Y earning for next season
Cameron Winch, Grade 6

Children Playing on the Beach

Happiness is rushing
Through the whistling air
Two twins
Sharing and playing
In the golden sand
Plants forming and growing
Like dough in the oven
The fish are jumping
Out of the fresh blue water
While ships are sailing and growling
The children feel free and loved
The twins chatter away as
The blue sky falls over them
Maggie Schmidt, Grade 4

The Bird

This bird has wings, but
it can be loud,
it caws all day and most of the night,
when it finally goes to bed,
it wakes up
upside down!
Madison Francis, Grade 5

Lifetime

a tree growing
every day

growing
higher and higher
taller and taller
getting stronger each day

then
it falls
dies silently

one thing remaining
it's a stub

a memory of its greatness
Tyler McAlister, Grade 6

Rainy Day

Pitter-Patter
the rain goes by
The wind blows gently
as the rain falls.

The rain intensifies
the ground becomes moist.
Looking out the window
I see big puddles

The rain weakens
to a soft drizzle.
The rainy day soon ends

I went out to jump in puddles.
When I saw a rainbow.
Felix Mo, Grade 6

Peace

Why can't the
Hatred stop
Fighting cease
Wars come to a halt?

The suffering begone
Jails be forgotten
Bad locked up in vaults.

Everyone be friends
Enemies are no more
The bad be no one's fault.

Why can't it just all stop?

Tolerance to all.
Taylor Bates, Grade 6

Winter

Winter is white
Winter is fun
Grab your gloves
Bye-bye, sun

Tie your boots
Grab the sled
Put on your hat
Make sure it's red

Big snowman
Long orange nose
Black hat
A plastic rose

Addison Danforth, Grade 5

Holocaust

Hitler was filled with hate,
The Jews didn't know their fate,
Nazis came and took them away,
There they would all stay,
To camps to let them die,
There they would all cry,
They went to showers to get clean,
But, it was just something mean,
They all got gassed,
Hundreds of people passed,
They all had different deaths,
They all had to take their last breaths,
The Jews thought all hope was lost,
Hitler created the Holocaust.

Carson Pieper, Grade 6

The Best Halloween

Meow
Said the cat
With the neon yellow hat
Boo
Said the ghost
With a very weird boast
Trick or Treat
Said the people
On the street

It is 10:00
The fun is done.
Until next year
Run

Ellie Miller, Grade 5

God

In the sky it is beautiful.
God loves the world with all his heart.
The dove is a symbol of his love.
The wire of his love is unbreakable.

Bryce Cammarotta, Grade 5

Soccer

I want to go to soccer,
My mom says I can go,
I'll hurry to get ready,
We have to go to Bow.

I have to get a mouthguard,
And a couple pairs of socks,
I have to get a uniform
We have to check the clocks!

Just a couple things to go,
I can only find one cleat,
I found one old stinky one,
It's not exactly neat!

We have to get something to drink,
Some gatorade will do,
put it in a knapsack,
that's not exactly new!

So now we are at soccer,
It should start a two,
But we arrived at three o'clock
And now the game is through.

Elliot Harne, Grade 4

Christmas Eve

Layers of snow,
falling from the sky.
Sipping hot chocolate
with a slice of apple pie.

Family members laughing,
huddled around the fire.
The Christmas tree glistening
bringing holiday spirits higher.

Humming Christmas carols,
they're stuck in my head.
I put out the fire
and wait for Santa in my cozy bed.

I hear sleigh bells ringing
and a thump on the roof.
A swoosh down the chimney
and a small little POOF!

I go downstairs,
and look at the tree.
When I look at the bottom,
I see piles of presents just for me!

Tyler Tran, Grade 6

Leaves

Leaves, leaves
Are so high,
Filling up,
the autumn sky.
Leaves, leaves,
Everywhere,
Filling up,
The autumn air.
Leaves, leaves,
on the ground,
Going 'round,
And 'round,
All around!

Laurel Ralph, Grade 5

Brady Elswick

B right ideas
R eally tall
A rchery
D ynamic
Y earn for world peace

E arning good grades
L earning in school
S ledding in the wintertime
W eird
I nto photography
C ats
K ickball is my favorite sport

Brady Elswick, Grade 5

The Hunting Grounds

Me and Daddy
Sat on some leaves
I thought…this is boring
Daddy, did you hear that?
No, what?
Give me the gun!
Soon, four deer went across the creek.
I shot a doe.
I dragged it.
I butchered it.
I cooked it.
I seasoned it.
I ate it.

Olivia Stidham, Grade 4

White Rose

The white rose is my blank canvas.
The layers start forming like a ballgown.
How?
Just the touch of my finger,
The white rose will shatter.
I feel the smooth rose —
And white snowflakes fall.

Julia Roos, Grade 5

Nachos
Nachos
Cheesy, creamy
Tasting, eating, dipping
Tasty, meaty, spicy
Awesome!
Marcos Sanchez, Grade 5

Bunnies
Bunnies
Cute, adorable
Loving, caring, hugging
I love bunny rabbits
Fluffy pants
Isabella Habicht, Grade 5

Dragons
Dragons
Fire breathing
Shiny, scaly, colorful
Flapping wings, sharp talons
Mighty
Alex Dumminger, Grade 5

Fishes
Fish
Colorful, bright
Swimming, splashing, speeding
Through the big blue ocean
Amazing.
Drew Frederick, Grade 5

Friend
Clem
Is awesome
He is cool
He is good at
Kickball
Andrew Provonsha, Grade 5

Good Night
Sleeping
Is amazing
Full of dreams and laughing
Sometimes you will have a nightmare
Snoring
Adalia Pasch, Grade 5

Tacos
Tacos
Spicy, messy
Satisfying, crunching, chewing
In my stomach
Delicious
Clemens Foos, Grade 5

Blue
Blue is the color when I look up into the sky.
I see flashes of blue when bluebirds fly by.
I hear blue waves when they crash on the sand.
I hear blue icicles when they crash land.
The taste of blueberries reminds me of summer fun.
I'd like to eat bluefish but I never caught one.
I touched the fancy blue car like it was solid gold.
I bet if I touched a blue whale it would feel cold.
Blue cheese has a smell like no other, but some people like it, especially my mother.
Some flowers smell good that are blue. My mother likes those, too.
Blue is how I feel when I'm sad and down.
But blue can be the hottest fire around.
I like all the shades of blue.
There is one for everyone. How about you?

Kristian Azzarano, Grade 5

Why Do People Chew Gum
I hate being chewed.
Maybe I should get frozen so your jaw would hurt.
Why do you blow me up like a balloon I look like a fat sumo wrestler?
I feel slimy and wet.
All I hear is the sound of chewing.
I see pitch black and then I see light…
pitch black…
light…
pitch black…
light…
pitch black…
light…
The worst part is when you blow me up so big I…
BLOW UP!!!

Dylan Starner, Grade 4

Why You Should Live Your Life
There are a voluminous amount of reasons for you to live life
The reason you're born is to live
You may even love your wife
And help people who need it most and give

Don't give up on your life, just think about the ones you love
And know what the repercussion is then decide it's better to be with them
Think about a lively thing like a dove
And say "you should still live your life, it's valuable like a gem"

Just because something's not the way you want
Something may constrict your life but that doesn't mean your life is done
Don't end your life, repress yourself and say "it's more dangerous than a stunt"
You will still have good times and a wellspring of fun

Kyle Gieder, Grade 6

Happiness
I love my friends and family, because they bring so much happiness and laughter to me.
I enjoy being very happy all day.
I am very thankful to have all my friends and family and all of my helpful teachers.
They all bring such happiness to me.

Eileen Suriel, Grade 5

High Merit Poems – Grades 4, 5, and 6

Rose

Hear the crunch of Autumn's crisp leaves,
The sky is black, on this midnight's stroll.
Every breath I take, I feel my chest heave,
Yet, I still get a feeling there's a warm, comforting soul.

Feeling cold, not safe or warm,
I heard a large tree snap.
During a fall thunderstorm,
I shot up as I heard a loud thunderclap.

I can see lights through my black and white vision,
Suddenly I realized I was right.
I ran up to the house with a little confusion,
On this scary, dark, autumn night.

Feeling scared, at an unfamiliar place,
Although I know the road I chose.
Suddenly, I saw a familiar face,
Then she called out my name, Rose.

Leslie George, Grade 6

Strength

Strength is a cloud,
Sometimes mellow, soft, puffy,
Sometimes harsh, brutal, and windy,
Floating above watching, waiting.

Strength is letting go when a loved one dies,
But never forgetting how it happened,
Going to war to save our lives,
Then being injured in action.

Strength is gaining trust from somebody,
Then being stabbed in the back the next day,
Saving many lives,
Loving each and every one.

Strength is when you break your arm,
When playing a sport but not giving up,
Loving the sport,
Keep on playing while dreaming.

Jamie Lessing, Grade 6

My Poem

I had to write a poem one day.
I grabbed my supplies and started right away.

I struggled and struggled thinking what to write,
it was then that my teacher started a fight.

"They should write a poem because they're so bright."
"I know they know them, they should show me what's right."

The next day all the way into the night,
we had to write poems to show her she's right.

Nathan Hafer, Grade 5

The Beach

Shiny, golden sand squishes in my toes,
My hair whips across my face as the strong wind blows.
Cold, sparkling water tickles my feet,
As I walk along the sand I see something neat.

Round and small sitting in the sand,
I pick it up and hold it in my hand.
A tiny little seashell sad and alone,
I bring it with me and take it home.

I've had that shell to this day,
It makes me smile in a special way.
That memory of the beach always in my mind,
That little seashell is one of a kind.

Francesca Taylor, Grade 6

Halloween

T he spirits are scary!
R owdy trick-or-treaters!
I mpulsive ghosts haunt you!
C andy-finding!
K indly giving treats!

O utstanding amounts of candy!
R unning from house to house

T he time is almost midnight!
R adical costumes;
E very house has a jack-o-lantern!
"A re the goblins coming?" is a question I ask.
T ime to have fun!

Connor Beckett, Grade 4

My Birthday

I remember when I got my iPod touch.
I remember when I got a skate board.
I remember getting new shoes,
And wore them all day long.
I remember bringing in donuts for my class.
I remember getting treats after that
Even though I shared.
I remember getting home and eating my donuts.
But, there is still more to come for the adventure in my life.

Michael Heil, Grade 5

Bystanders

Forced to live in a crowded space
Nobody remember any face
Had anyone known where they were going?
They could have prevented this time from showing?

People saw what they have done
Everybody watched and held their tongue
Lots of people knew what Hitler did
What could we have done for it to be prevented?

Hannah Hoch, Grade 6

Care for Animals
Animals need food,
Many have trouble living,
All of them need homes,
It is dangerous for them,
Some may live with their mothers.
Kara Rieker, Grade 6

Friendly Feathers
Give thanks
Thankful for food
Stuffing yourself with food
I love family on Thanksgiving
Yummy
Caroline Cote, Grade 4

Thanksgiving Turkey
Turkey
Red head, feathers
Runs away, hastily
Down the sky touching mountain cliff
Quickly
Ronnie Percival, Grade 4

I Love
H elpful is for making things easy
O bedient is listening to you
R estless is for messing around
S uperb is awesome
E nergy lots of energy to canter and go nuts
Amaya Hughes, Grade 5

The Big Fat Turkey
Turkey
Big, fat, feathers
Yum, juicy, delicious
Yummy fat delicious turkey
Give thanks
Jakob Stutmann, Grade 4

Ethan
E xcited
T houghtful
H appy
A mazing
N atural
Ethan Rashkind, Grade 5

Gobbler
Turkeys
Gobbling in fear
Trying to run away
Feathers as brown as a tree trunk
Gobbling
Andrew Gomez, Grade 4

The Amusement Park
I am a girl who loves thrill rides.
I wonder what the future will have.
I hear the sound of rides moving,
people screaming, people talking, people laughing,
I hear games playing.
I see lots of people waiting to go on rides.
I want to go to the amusement park to have fun every day.
I am a girl who loves thrill rides.

I pretend that I'm on a fast roller coaster.
I feel the wind of the roller coaster rustling past us while we're in line.
I touch the air on rides.
I worry that I will get lost in the amusement park.
I am a girl who loves thrill rides.

I understand sometimes the rides can have difficulties.
I say they're fun and exciting.
I dream I'm on the fastest ride.
I try to have great times.
I hope I go to the amusement park again next year.
I am a girl who loves thrill rides.
Laura Jencks, Grade 5

Green
Up
Up
Up
I go, feeling wonderful.
I could climb a mountain,
Jump from a cliff and land on my feet,
Swim forever.
Of all the others,
I'm the most natural of course.
Thought eh others may think they're better, I, alone, know they're not.
I'm not just appeasing, but can be,
Will be full of spirit.
I am,
    Fantastic
    Fair, free
    Flowing
    Full
    Fun
    Fast
Unlike others who can be dangerous and brave,
But I will never change, oh never!
Emmeline Wetzel, Grade 6

Stone
I feel the cold, hard, stone as I am being pulled away
From the nice, warm, sunny place
From the place I spent all those summers
Playing and having fun.
Now, as the warm chill the breeze makes turns into a shiver from the stone,
I take on last glance at the place,
I am losing it forever.
Jack Heaphy, Grade 6

High Merit Poems – Grades 4, 5, and 6

Ayanna

Ayanna.
It means shy, kind, and funny.
It is 20.
It is like a plum.
Having a barbecue.
My mom, she loves me,
and she taught me to be patient and helpful.
She helps me with math homework.
My name is Ayanna.
It means I do hard work and never give up!

Ayanna York, Grade 6

All About Me

Kayanna White
quiet, smart, caring
sister of Precious
who feels grateful about sisters
who needs friends, food, family
who gives high fives, handshakes and smiles
who'd like to see Miss Jay
who dreams of happy places
A student of Mrs. Tadlock's class
Kayanna White

Kayanna White, Grade 5

September!

Leaves are falling off trees.
September is gathering leaves and jumping in them.
September is playing soccer.
September is lots of sports.
September is riding bikes.
Leaves are turning different colors.
September is starting to get colder,
school is back in.
Reading all day.
September is really fun.

Luke Smith, Grade 4

Soccer

Running, running, sprinting!
In out, in, out, as I breathe heavily,
Guarding the ball as I carry it,
Then here is my chance, break away!
As I line up for my shot, I look up, magnificent, I think to myself.
As my foot sweeps the ball,
The keeper sets up.
Shot, and GOAL!

Melissa Sicinski, Grade 6

Grandparents Are…

The nice feeling you get inside when you see them.
Always making you laugh at their jokes.
Making you feel full with the food that they make for you.
Willing to play any game you want with them.
Like your best friend.

Taylor Busch, Grade 6

Christmas

People decorate trees, and sing songs,
Finally it's Christmas, after I've waited so long!
Everywhere I look, there are Christmas lights,
And Santa rides his sleigh and brings joy through the night!
Children open presents, on their face a wide smile,
As carolers sing songs, their voices heard for miles!
Kids play with their gifts, as adults prepare the food,
And all the happy spirit has everyone in a good mood!
On Christmas day, after spreading all this cheer,
The children climb into their beds, ready for next year!

Lydia Podvorec, Grade 6

Giraffe

On the savanna, a giraffe drinks.
Above her head, birds sing gleefully.
By her side stands a friendly gazelle.
Being shy, the giraffe walks away.
After a few steps, she stops, turns around, and yells to the gazelle.
Except gazelle has found a new friend.
Despite feeling sad, she feels happy too, and heads home.
Before she gets home, she sees the gazelle with his friend.
Behind them is a herd of giraffes.
In the night air, they dance and are happy.

Elizabeth Breckenridge, Grade 6

The World

So many cultures
Spanish, English, Chinese
So many different lands
High grass, wetlands, tundra, jungle, desert, forest
So many animals
Camels, tigers, elephants, snakes and kangaroos
Seven different continents
Asia, Europe, Australia, Antarctica
Africa, North America and South America
Which one is home to you?

Teddy Pearson, Grade 4

Different

Why? Why do you look at me like that?
With hatred and disgust filled inside your eyes.
Why? Why do you treat me like that?
Sending me and my family to camps.
Why? Why do you speak to me like that?
You call me a filthy pig but for what reason?
Why? I ask my mama, why do they do these things to us?
And she simply answers because we are different.

Ruheen Sidhu, Grade 6

Halloween

Halloween is horrifying and fun
Children run for candy until it's done

Halloween is haunted and scary
Some monsters are ordinary, some are hairy

Emoni Wise, Grade 6

Midnight Spark

I had decided to take a little walk,
to come out of my bed for I was as stiff as a rock.
It was almost dawn the sky a shade of pink,
And while I walked I began to think.
Who was lurking in the shadows over there?
As a cat jumped out I sighed, it had given me quite a scare.
Suddenly out of the corner of my eye I saw,
A spark fly out of building one hundred four.
I froze in my tracks and stared up at the sky
Another and another, they came up very high.
I knew they weren't fireworks, that was for sure
So I ran back to my building and opened the door,
"There's a fire, a fire down the block someone call a fire truck!"
It came wailing breaking the silence of the night
And as it stopped a man jumped out of the door on the right.
He ran into house wearing gear and all,
and jumped through the window on the second to last floor.
It ended up being that the people were all right,
and nobody asked where I was on that fateful night.

Rivka Bella Rabaev, Grade 6

I Am

I am funny and social
I wonder if people will find a cure for cancer
I hear the ocean
I see my family at a movie
I want my cousin back
I am funny and social

I pretend I am a singer
I feel the winter coming
I touch the snow
I cry for the people in the army
I am funny and social

I understand why I have Turner Syndrome
I say if you're happy, I'm happy
I dream about happiness around the world
I try to get good grades
I hope I see my nana and papa in Florida
I am funny and social

Jordan Southwick, Grade 6

Dark and Creepy Cave

I walk by a dark and creepy cave
it has nothing I can see
as my friends and I walk by
I say, "let's go in."
We have flashlights and we look around
we see spiders, bats, and snakes
then we find an ancient lab
spooky stuff is all around,
orbs and ghosts and monster making machines,
we ran out
never to return!

Stephen Reed, Grade 5

Basketball

I am a big basketball fan and player.
I wonder which team will pick me.
I hear the silence of the crowd as my
team tries to get the game winning shot.
I see my future of being a great
basketball player.
I want to make the game winning shot
in the championship game.
I am a big basketball fan and player.

I pretend that I am playing on my driveway.
I feel the rubber of the basketball as I
shoot the game winning shot.
I touch the golden championship trophy.
I worry that my team will not win the big game.
I am a big basketball fan and player.

I understand we might not win the game.
I say try harder to win.
I dream that I win ten championships.
I try to win many games.
I hope I win as many games as I possibly can.
I am a big basketball fan and player.

Benson Thacher, Grade 5

My Christmas Hope

My Mom went for a Christmas tree.
I wanted it to be small.
But when she returned,
It was very tall.
She said it was more special than a berry.
When I woke up the next morning the tree was merry.
I went to bed with sugar plums dancing in my head.
I also heard a sled.
The pitter patter of a hoof
Made my dog go "Woof."
The next morning I saw all the gifts and
The little note said,
"Merry Christmas to all!"

Chloe Purcell, Grade 4

Grandpa and I

The picture hanging on my bedroom wall
Memories of my past
I look at it as a missing piece to my life's puzzle
The background with pink and purple flowers and butterflies
Represented my love at age three

"Grandpa loves you"
Is the key to the hidden door hidden in my sad memories
I miss him so much
It's been hard without him
I know he watches over me and my family every day
Missing our family just as much as I miss him
He is my guardian angel

Hannah Woodford, Grade 6

There's a Fly in My Tea
There is a black spot in my tea.
I take a closer look.
It's a fly
Lying on a sugar cube.
What should I do?
I hear a slurping sound.
It's drinking my tea!
Maybe I should swat at it, I thought.
I grab the fly swatter, and 'shoo' at it.
It flies away.
I sigh in relief.
When I look back at my tea,
I swear he grinned at me!
Paige Cabrera, Grade 4

Sharks Are Beautiful
As I went out to the dock
Shadows fall
but I see a big dim one
and it's all alone
as it flows downstream
with beautiful skin and fins
It waves, then I wave back,
then I remember what I was looking for,
I was looking for a shark
and I wonder where it is
I wait and wait till I hear crickets
    yet nothing
then I see its big shadow
Justin May, Grade 4

Banana Split Sunrise
Strawberry ice-cream
Making the clouds
Pretty pink
Chocolate-chip-cookie-dough
Making it dark
Vanilla ice-cream
Lighting the clouds
Purple sprinkles on top
With
A cherry
And caramel
Making
The sun
Elizabeth Happel, Grade 4

Sponge vs Patrick
SpongeBob
Yellow, sponge
Laughing, singing, jumping.
Pacific, sink, Atlantic, beach.
Smiling, annoying, eating.
Star, pink.
Patrick
Pricila Espinoza, Grade 6

My Pet
He is big and nice.
Furry as a sheep,
He loves to eat a lot.
You might think he's a dog but he is not.
His name is Peanut Butter.
My guinea Pig.
He is fun to play with.
And that is why I love him.
Alyssa Roberts, Grade 6

Summer Memories
When colorful flowers
are history,
When green leaves
are just a myth,
And wet ground is
just a legend,
Snow is all
you can sift.
Amelia Evans, Grade 5

I Am a Chef!
I am a chef
I work all day
My cakes are excellent
My bakings are good too
I work in a five star restaurant
People come hungry and leave happy
Oh, how I love to cook!
I love being a chef!
Mazey Smaciarz, Grade 6

Christmas
Putting up the tree,
With ornaments,
Santa comes,
Leaving presents,
Opening gifts,
Playing with them too,
A wonderful day,
A wonderful holiday.
Sofia Morra, Grade 5

The Howl of the Wind
A misery rose from the air
The cry of a thousand wolves
It yowled and scratched at the trees
Its claws open and sharper than glass
The pain of its moans never ceased
While in tantrum it threw out its tears
And I listened with chills as the laments
Of the wind and the rain never eased
Sylvia Nica, Grade 6

Why?
My friend asks me:
Why?
Why am I bullied?
Why am I treated like a doormat?
Why?
Why do I feel hated?
Why are only a couple of my friends nice?
Why?
Do I deserve this?
I will make friends
I can make friends
This year will be different
Makayla Thorpe, Grade 4

My Fish Is Gone
My fish was blue,
my fish was huge,
but now it lays
still and cold.

My fish no more
will splish and splash,
my fish has clogged
my toilet…

but finally my fish is
flushed.
Alexxus Phifer, Grade 5

Substitute Teacher
Our teacher didn't come one day,
She's sick in bed
That's not okay!
We wonder who
Our substitute teacher will be
Will she give us detention
Or hand out tests that she sees?
Finally she walks right in with no delay
Let's play a game she manages to say.
What! What! What did we hear?
I wish this teacher could stay
For the whole year!
Lena Simone, Grade 5

Basketball
B ank shots
A thletes
S lam dunk
K nicks
E pic match ups
T eamwork
B askets
A thletic ability
L ayups
L akers
Spencer VanGils, Grade 5

A Celebration of Poets – East Grades K-6 Fall 2013

Senses of Dreams

A dream sounds like a nice
day at the beach, because the ocean sounds beautiful
A dream feels like an inspiration
because it sets you out to do anything you want
A dream tastes like Skittles
because all dreams are sweet
A dream looks like a lemonade fountain never ending
A dream smells like fresh chocolate chip cookies
waiting to be eaten
Dreams can have a lot of senses
and these are the one I imagine

Alana Wilson, Grade 5

A Dream about Winter

It is a cold, windy, winter day.
The snow is blowing so hard.
I am excited for it to stop so I can go outside.
I dream about being outside.... The snow has stopped!
I grab my sled and head for the door. I am about to have some fun.
I run over to the sledding hill and I jump straight down it.
I feel the snow touch my sled and I keep going.
I am going so fast, now. I am about to crash into a tree!
But before I hit it, I suddenly stop.
I realize I am back in my room and I just woke up.
And then I think it was probably a dream and I go downstairs.

Thomas Hohmann, Grade 4

My Family

My love for my family is like glowing heaven
life is a garden path to heaven
our souls grow strong together
the wind is a warm hug for my family
love is overflowing my heart
we lay on my bed looking at the sky
when I got up, my family was still asleep
my parents lay in the sun
my dad and my mom are the heart of the house
my sister is brighter than a shooting star
my family's hope is so lovely

Monica Gergies, Grade 4

Electricity

Enchanting yellow
Lights, making the
Entire room bright.
Can be made with wind or water, sometimes its
Temperature is hotter than the sun.
Running through lots of power lines,
It creates self-starting
Cars.
It powers
Televisions,
Youch! If you get shocked.

Braeden Singleton, Grade 5

Rhyming About Wickersham's Garden

Look outside it's so
Bright like my bike
So clean and green.
The radishes are red
Like my bed and
The spinach is green
Like my green beans.
The tomatoes are round high off the ground.
Some peppers are yellow
Like my Jell-O.
My garden is like my den as beautiful as a baby hen

Fabian Beauchamp, Grade 5

The 5 Senses of Autumn

When it is Autumn I see leaves changing colors
From green to yellow to red to brown
I see them Fall to the ground
I smell apple pie and apple cider
And smoke from peoples' chimneys
I feel chilly breezes on my face and through my hair
I hear the sound of leaves crunching beneath my feet
And the wind whistling as it blows
I taste sweet apples green and red
And the yummy taste of candies
Autumn!

Jordan Neale, Grade 5

Patience is a Snail

Patience is a snail,
who creeps slowly through his life
and lurks.

He takes caution in every hesitant movement he makes,
and lingers over the past
in apprehension of the future.

The meandering snail of patience
leaves trails of his presence
glowing slimily behind him.

Madison Jones, Grade 6

Things Justin Does for Fun

I like watching my favorite football team win and
feeling the thrill of a roller coaster riding in the wind.
Making shots in basketball and
roller skating without a fall.
I feel confident as I peddle the boat.
Even though I surf in the water, I sometimes float.

Beating someone in paintball and winning
All these things I like doing.
Also, playing with the sand at the beach and
spending time playing with family can be so sweet.

Justin Bryant, Grade 6

High Merit Poems – Grades 4, 5, and 6

Thanksgiving

Thank you for my hands to hold
Shiny, red, juicy apples
Picked fresh from the trees
Corn on the cob so ripe and sweet
and my Thanksgiving dinner plate
Stacked miles high with delicious food

Thank you for my eyes to see
Bright, colorful, crisp leaves
The beautiful cornucopia
Stuffed with squash, pumpkins, apples, and corn
And the Macy's Thanksgiving Day Parade

Thank you for my tongue to taste
Tender turkey that is a firework
Exploding with flavor in my mouth
The smooth cranberry sauce
And the fluffy, salty mashed potatoes
Brooke Zecchini, Grade 6

Artist by Night

I am a tree hugger and an artist.
I wonder if trees can understand how I feel about them.
I hear the pencils and colors speak to me and wanting me to create.
I see the trees be partners of dance with the wind,
I want to paint the night sky,
I am a tree hugger and an artist.
I pretend I am painting in a tree by moonlight,
I feel the rainbows kissing my artwork,
I touch the sky with a paint brush as the colors explode,
I worry I will lose my artistic vision,
I cry for the trees that are cut down.
I am a tree hugger and an artist.
I understand that people don't believe in special trees.
I say that leaves fly around me,
I dream of colors swirling about,
I try to remember the art that I want to draw.
I hope the leaves will still follow me without constraint.
I am a tree hugger and an artist.
Natalie Getchey, Grade 6

The Tale of Mr. Dupwhikum

Mr. Dupwhikum is big and tall
He never likes to go to the mall
Mr. Dupwhikum lives on a farm
It has a lot of charm
He is very busy
He has a wife named Lizzy
Mr. Dupwhikum is a funny man
He has two left hands
Mr. Dupwhikum likes to eat candy
And he is really handy
He is all right. Sometimes he is uptight
Mr. Dupwhikum is somewhat hefty
The best thing about him is they call him "Lefty"
Julia Viscuso, Grade 5

Thanksgiving

It was Thanksgiving before you even knew it
We ate pumpkin pie for breakfast
Then I sat on the couch
I was watching the parade
We ate pumpkin pie for breakfast
For dinner we had turkey and light food
I was watching the parade
"Mom Ben's here!" said Jack
For dinner we had turkey and other food
My favorite colors are yellow, orange and brown
"Mom, Ben's here" said Jack.
At last we played football, "I won" said Jack
My favorite colors are yellow, orange, and brown
I sat on the couch
At last we played football "I won" said Jack
It was Thanksgiving before you even knew it.
Jack Wilke, Grade 4

Autumn

Leaves crunch
as we walk down the narrow path
shades of yellow, red, and green
glisten in the afternoon sun
the narrow path gets shorter
as we walk further and further

Down the road we see a light
Could this be the end?
It seems so close
but we feel so far

We see a man at the end
Is he real?
Or just a shadow of the leaves
blowing in the fall wind?
Iffath Ahmed-Syed and Jada Ward, Grade 5

Loving God

Every day I wake up with a smile on my face
Because I know our God above is protecting the human race
I turn on the news and see stories about heroes
Fighting to bring all the bad to a zero
These people are performing good acts on earth
For some it was a calling at birth
God works to find the good in all of us
So everyday life doesn't become such a fuss
There's no time to hate or think bad thoughts
Our goal should be peace, not battles fought
Dig deep inside and know you're not alone
One day you'll come face to face with your God on the throne
So wake up, be happy and live right
Go to bed with a clear conscious at night
It's all about doing the right thing
And enjoying all that life has to bring
Lexy Owens, Grade 5

Holocaust
Those days were full of sacrifice,
They'll be gone forever,
This went on for days,
Just like always.

The memories are scarce,
The thoughts are harsh,
What did they do?
If only we knew.

The sadness is horrible,
The children were dead,
Their parents were next to die,
Just please tell us why.

We need to keep hope.
Just keep the strength,
No matter the Holocaust's length
Amanda Wriker, Grade 6

Strength
Strength is a voice
Projecting through difficult challenges
Showing trust and courage.

Strength is a friend
Pulling you through rough decisions
Patting you on the back
When you accomplish something.

Strength is you
Making your own decisions
Standing up to obstacles ahead
Growing bigger and bolder.

Strength is a flame
Incinerating through the crisp twigs
Keeping you warm
Throwing hate away.
Christian Jensen, Grade 6

Friends Are Forever
Friends are forever,
they are there all the time,
sometimes opposites,
like lemons and limes
Friends are forever,
they are always together,
never leaving each others side,
they will separate never
Friends are forever,
like the sky above,
their relationship is simple,
like a peaceful dove
Friends are forever.
Madyson Scott, Grade 6

Fall Leaves
Sometimes I think to myself
as I see the bare trees,
Can life be as fragile as the
falling fall leaves?
With the wisps of white frost
falling from the blue skies,
with the strength of the snow drops
weighing above my eyes.
The colors of leaves like blurs of
orange and yellow
Red for the bricks of the fire
so mellow,
and I think as the dusk forms
like flames in the night,
No more leaves in the trees, they
fall free in the sky.
Sometimes I think to myself
as I see the bare trees,
Can life be as fragile as the falling
fall leaves?
Lucy Turner, Grade 5

Rain
I see the rain
outside my window
drip drop drip drop.

Boom! Bang! Flash!
Thunder and lightning
as scary as Friday the 13th.

I see the rain and lightning
as bright as the sun
and as clear as glass.

I feel the rain
as wet as a waterfall
as cold as snow.

I hear the rain
drop pitter patter pitter patter
and the thunder boom crash
crash boom pitter patter.
Riley Harnett, Grade 6

I Like That Stuff
I like that stuff
Football
Quarterbacks slashing,
Runningbacks bashing,

Runningbacks bleeding,
Quarterbacks cheating,
I like that stuff
Football
Hardy Burns, Grade 5

Scary Night
There's always the night
That gives you a fright
You go Trick-or-Treat
Under the moon light.

You walk in the dark
As the stars shine bright
But the monsters are out
On Halloween night.

As the witches cheered
The Trick-or-Treaters feared
The ghosts are out
Everyone ran about.

Trick-or-Treaters scram in terror
Scariness is everywhere
Ghouls and goblins what a sight
And all is found on Halloween night.
Chayla Herner, Grade 6

A True Friend
Someone always there for you
A person by your side
Someone who is true
A forgiver

Someone to tell a secret to
A person to talk to
Someone to get you out of the blue
A smile maker

Someone who looks after you
A care taker
Someone who knows you
Like a sibling

Someone you can't do anything without
A necessity
Someone who does anything for you
A true friend
Aasjot Siani, Grade 6

My Fishy Moments
When I get home from school
I rush upstairs
To my room
I get in my blanket
And do my homework
It keeps me happy
Because when my great grandma died
I wanted to get my blanket
When I'm sad it just calls my name
I still love my blanket when I'm happy
My blanket will never stop being loved
Ellie Lange, Grade 4

High Merit Poems – Grades 4, 5, and 6

Sphere of Season

First is summer, where you can smell the shore.
Vacations, I want more.
Then comes fall when you can feel the breeze,
And see the carpet of leaves.
Third is winter where the snow whooshes around.
And you wish it would last all year 'round.
Finally, spring with its flowers,
They will become radiant with April showers.
I have four reasons to enjoy the seasons!
Michelle-Ann Lavallée Harris, Grade 6

Halloween Night

H aunted houses
A ll ghosts creep around
L ightning strikes
L ights flicker on and off
O h, what a scary night!
W ebs on the wall
E lephant costumes
E aster bunny costumes
N ights like this I will never go trick-or-treating
Macy Brown, Grade 4

The British Are Coming

This is the time, the time is here
Oh no, oh no, the British are near
Here they come, two lights do shine
When this is done, I hope freedom is mine
Before the dawn, I hope they'll be gone
Marching, marching over the ridge
We will head them off at the bridge
Here we are ready to fire, the first shot will ring
Onward to freedom our voices sing.
Nolan Brewster, Grade 4

I Am From…

I am from having Thanksgiving as a family.
I am from the scaly lizards in their cages.
I am from jumping the waves at Misquamicut Beach.
I am from backyard picnics and blazing camp fires.
I am from sneakers, jogging pants, and character T-shirts.
I am from loving pizza and washing it down with milk.
I am from Santa, Easter Bunny, and Goblins.
I am from shooting hoops and tag.
I am from the best moments I could ever have.
Augustin Michaud, Grade 5

Time

The infinite idea, the answer
Can never be controlled by man
Past turns to present, present turns to future
A minute to a decade
A moment so pure
So confusing no man or god could find the answer
One act, word, or movement can change it all
David Romero, Grade 5

The Old Man

In a somber village lived an old man
Who had a ragged hat and a helpful pan
Benevolent was the guy next door
The guy gave him the pan and also more
In the old man's house there was an audible sound
So when the guy came in the man was prostrate on the ground
When the man got up and thanked the guy
He saw a profuse number of people really close by
So the man thanked everyone and closed the door
He locked it really so no one sees him anymore.
Adeeba Kareem, Grade 5

Love

Love is a sweet kind of tone,
that doesn't make people alone.
Love is everywhere you just don't know.
Love is hidden inside of you,
you just don't believe it's the truth.
Don't get lost because love will guide you the way there.
You had better watch and be aware,
because love is a sweet kind of tone,
that doesn't make people alone.
Nylah Jordan, Grade 6

Holocaust

H ostages being taken, tortured, and killed
O ne person starting it all, the bad things happening
L oved ones being killed and tortured
O ther countries being bystanders, not doing anything
C lever people trying to save themselves
A llies that finally helped the war against Nazi Germany
U nknown places the Jews were going
S ouls being demolished and ruined
T housands of Jews were massacred
Kevin Pierson, Grade 6

Forest

Trees blocking the sun
Leaves covering the ground
Streams pattering on rocks
Berry bushes, black and red
Caves with bats and bears
Scary things all around
No light, no light at all
As you go on the trail
You will see deer and laugh as they frolic along
Caroline Freese, Grade 5

Spring

S unlight fills the world
P retty young flowers sprout from the ground
R ipples appear in newly formed puddles
I nstead of sitting inside we frolic and play
N ew life pops up all around us
G ardens grow ripe and fresh
Emilee Brooks, Grade 5

Football

I am a fearless boy who likes football
I wonder what is in the future
I hear my favorite football team, the Patriots, just won a game
and versed the Dolphins
I see that they are never going to lose again
I want to be on the Patriots and be their wide receiver
I am a fearless boy who likes football

I pretend I am a quarterback on the Patriots
I feel in the future, I am going to be the best quarterback ever
I touch my own signed football
I worry that I might get a concussion from playing football
I am a fearless boy who likes football

I understand that I'm not old enough yet
I say I must play football
I dream that I am a star
I try to be a quarterback
I hope I am a quarterback on a great football team
I am a fearless boy who likes football

Anthony Amaral, Grade 5

Brown

Brown,
The person that takes care of family,
Even if he's low on money.
he tries to achieve everybody's needs,
And always get lauded because of his good deeds.

Brown,
A person that can be independent,
And still live life to the fullest extent.
He is not afraid to stand up for what he believes in,
Even if his chance of being right is slim.

Brown,
A person that lets everyone shine,
And will never say, "The spotlight is all mine."
He is not that famous,
Even though his actions are never aimless.

Brown,
The color of responsibility

Vivek Babu, Grade 6

Winter

December shuns the birds.
Making them fly south, so their flock may survive.
Snow falls and lands on my nose.
I see squirrels and chipmunks scattering to find food for the winter,
and I can no longer hear the pitter patter of the deer,
So I know winter is finally here.
January welcomes the New Year.
The excitement of waiting for 12:00,
People having parties, children laughing, and finally,
just for a moment,
silence goes thought the house,
then "3, 2, 1..." The ball drops,
Clink, clank, clink, clank!
Go the pots and pans, banging together.
February loves handing out candy in your class.
My dad gives me a rose,
Mom gives me chocolate,
and my sister gives me the best gift of all:
a hug and a card
that states "I love you."

Evelyn Spayd, Grade 4

Red

Red looks like fire, so beautiful, so bright
It makes us feel safe, all through the night
Red tastes like a cherry, so juicy as a snack
Going to a picnic
Cherries you must pack
Red smells like a rose, gentle, sometimes sad
Seeing one can make you feel loved or mad
Red sounds like a singing cardinal
Hearing it will make you say "Wow!"
but don't get too happy, the cat will strike, "Pow!"
Red feels like anger building up inside of you
And when it's too full, it'll burst through
Red is a sunset
Red is a bird
Just waiting, waiting, waiting to be heard
Red is a tomato used for many things
Like sauce and ketchup
Who knows what red can bring!
Red is a phoenix, one who can fly
And know it is flying throughout the sky

Gabriella Calderon, Grade 4

July 2nd

Today I had my birthday
It was the best day ever
There was cake
More ice cream then you can imagine
I got so many gifts I didn't know what to do with
July 2nd is my favorite day of the year
When I got the things I asked for
I didn't have to do one chore
My birthday—July 2nd.

Kendra Reed, Grade 6

A Terrible Storm

Last year the storm blew hard
Trees fell upon our yard
The dogs were barking
The wind was blowing
The people were calling, "Look out, Look out!"
Power lines crashed with a mighty boom
A tree almost fell upon my room
I am happy I survived
That very bad, awful storm.

Kevin Quain, Grade 4

Green

Grass is green
Leaves are green
Bushes are green
Airborne leaves sound like green
Crunchy lutes sound green
The cash register sounds green
Green apples taste green
Pears taste green
Lutes taste green
Grass tastes green
Leaves feel green
A green shirt feels green
Green can bring you air.
Jonathan Velsor, Grade 4

Green

Is long skinny grass
Round, seedless green grapes
And leaves on a tree in the summer
It's a quiet baby sleeping
A soundless classroom
On a peaceful day
It tastes like sweet grapes
Yummy broccoli
And long string beans
It's smooth like a flat rock
Soft like a blanket
And hard like a table
Green can change the world!
Saoirse O'Hara, Grade 4

Wolves

I wonder about wolves,
Beautiful majestic creatures.

I wonder about wolves,
The alpha male and female,
Like king and queen.

I wonder about wolves,
So big and so bold,
Protecting their pups like
Mother and Father.

I wonder about wolves.
Payton Spearin, Grade 6

Football

I like a sport named football
I even like to get tackled
Boom! A tackle from number 64.
I like to win, but also have a challenge.
Sack! Down goes the QB.
Up goes the crowd as loud as they can
We won the game 24-7!
Jovanni Acosta, Grade 5

Time for Hurricane Sandy

It was time to get ready
For the big storm
So we packed our bags
To go to my aunt's house.

Trees were falling
All around
I even saw a
A tree going down.

Finally the wind stopped
And it started to rain
I was glad it was over
That day was insane!
Kristy Fleurmont, Grade 4

My Birthday

I get a lot of gifts
And maybe a poster of Taylor Swift

It's a special day
I'm going to grow up and go my own way

I wear special clothes
But I make sure it has no holes

People will stare
But it's only because they care

I will turn a new age
And start a new page
Cynthia Torres, Grade 6

Hunting

My dad and I get up so quietly,
So silently.
We go into the woods,
With all of our goods.
We sit under a tree,
And then we see a turkey.
It's hiding behind the brier,
I aim and fire.
I hope and hope it will hit,
I can't sit even one little bit.
It goes down,
Without a sound.
We go back home,
Under our nice, warm dome.
Aaron Cole, Grade 4

The Snowman

The snowman is
as dressed up like he is going to church
as packed like a suitcase
as tall and handsome like me.
Andrew Cooke, Grade 5

Spaghetti

Boxes
of spaghetti,
boiling in the water
Boiling in the steaming,
bubbling,
firing, hot water

Hard sticks
turn into
long, squirmy,
delicious,
spaghetti strands

You put it
on the plate,
with, yummy, shredded cheese

The most delicious
part of it…
the meatball

lava,
red sauce

You have a fork…
Then shove it down your throat.
Tommy Fitzsimmons, Grade 5

It's about Colorful Candy Corn

People eat it on Halloween
It has the colors and everything

It's sweet and yummy to eat
It beats all the other treats

It is has the spirit for Halloween.
Orange, Yellow, and White

Don't take mine
Because they're too divine

Because they're yummy for me
For me to eat

When I see them
I just eat them

Sometimes I say why can't they be pink?
It makes my heart sink:-(

If you don't like them
Then leave them, FOR ME!

It's about the candy I love.
Colorful Candy Corn
Caroline Schneble, Grade 5

Birthday Wishes*
Wishes I keep to myself:

Wish I could be the world's
best lacrosse
player.

Wish I could
be a
billionaire

Wish I could play professional
lacrosse for the Denver
Outlaws.

Wish I could go to Duke
to play lacrosse for the
Blue Devils

Wish I could go all over the
world for
one year.

Most of all I wish I could see my Grandma
and Grandpa for the
first time ever
Will Potter, Grade 5
*Inspired by "Inside Out and Back Again"

All About Piano
It's about swift fingers
flowing and gliding
drifting over white and black hills

It's about keeping the rhythm
tapping your foot
the crowd giving lots of input

It's about wrapping yourself in the music
flying over keys
melting over the white and black sea

It's about sudden movements
being dramatic
showing that you're fantastic

It's about showing off
bowing low
stepping off the stage, way to go!

It's about pats on the back
going to dinner
thinking you're a winner

It's about what I love most!
Kaeli Kaymak-Loveless, Grade 5

Thanksgiving
T urkey
H am
A pple pie
N ew colors on the trees
K icking the football in the front yard
S weet potatoes on my plate
G oing to my Aunt's for dessert
I ce cream
V isiting my family
I nvitation to Thanksgiving
N uts and Rolos — my mom's special treat
G oing to my dad's house to hang out
Bryan Fusaro, Grade 5

The Joy of Winter
Winter is the best time of year
With all the people and all the cheer
The rides in the sleigh
Make for a wonderful day
We ride through the snow
As we feel the cold winds blow
As Jack Frost comes around
Signs of summer are nowhere found
Hot cocoa and marshmallows by the fire
Family and friends tell tales I admire
I give thanks to the Lord above
For all He grants, especially love
Landon Shank, Grade 6

Thanksgiving
T hankful
H aving fun!!!!
A utumn
N ice food to eat
K eep the pie going!
S pending time with family
G iving food
I like turkey
V acation
I ncredible stuffing
N ever wanting the day to end
G od's Thanksgiving
Jake Simonds, Grade 5

The Car
We all plopped in the car,
everyone was excited but me.

I was scared,
I always had experiences
of dogs jumping on me,
and I didn't like that.
The house appeared.
We heard loud big barks
we pulled in and knocked on the door —
Connor Monahan, Grade 5

Eleven
I am eleven
Getting older
Too many responsibilities
Big brother
To an annoying sibling
Younger brother
To a wise older brother
Dad, Mom
They both expect more
But I am still eleven
I'm still too young
I can't be any more
then what I am
Yet each day
I edge closer
To a stronger new me
Wasif Zaman, Grade 6

Fall
As I rush through town,
The leaves as beautiful as a rose,
The air sweet-scented with pumpkins,
The fall breeze blowing on my face.

As I rush through town,
There are scary people and tons of candy,
I honor the veterans, who fought in wars,
And I smell a turkey feast.

As I rush through town,
It is as crisp as frost,
The leaves are twirling with delight,
The moonlight gleaming in my eyes.

How could you not like fall?
Avan Shah, Grade 4

Dreamy Material
Dreams? What are they made of?
No one knows. Maybe powders;
How about tea?
Or are they caught by the BFG?
Made by wizards?
Or from Santaphrax?
What about pillows
Do they make dreams?
How do I know that they are there?
Can you find them,
Does the night make them
And give them away?
We can see them in the night,
When we sleep, we have a vision,
It's very interesting, do say!
Dreams are so peculiar
Katerina Smondyrev, Grade 5

High Merit Poems – Grades 4, 5, and 6

Cotton Wood
Fell from a tall tree
Through the fall I turn bright shades
Traveled far and wide
Stays green through spring and summer
I'm unique in my own way
Anthony Mongeluzi, Grade 5

Adventure Leaf
I am a green leaf
I flew off my tree last night
I saw many things
I traveled to tons of roofs
They all welcomed me with wind
Anna Michnik, Grade 5

European Birch Leaf
I'm short and fragile
I soar in the crisp, cold air
I explore all year
I'm a European Birch
I lose my leaves in the fall
Dana Moser, Grade 5

Kelsey
Kelsey
Great, sweet
Laughing, helping, dancing
She is very kind
Friend
Vianca Pineda, Grade 5

Green
Green is
  the greenest grass
  a neon light
  a scaly snake
  a sour apple
Jackson Morgan, Grade 5

My White Oak Leaf
I soar like the wind
I come from a White Oak tree
Acorns grow with me
I fall off my tree again
My journey is not over
Gia Judge, Grade 5

European Birch
I am very clever
I'm a European Birch
I like exploring
People find me in late fall
My adventure will end soon
Deanna Moser, Grade 5

The Mourning
The dreary day covers the Earth like snow
But I don't care
I see you
Salty tears run down my face
But I don't care
I hear you
Love has been washed away in the wind
But I don't care
Because I know it's with you
I can feel sadness in my soul
But I don't care
Because I can also feel you
The Earth is isolated and I feel empty
But I don't care because not only can I feel your warmth yet I know you're there
I lay down in the snow opening my mouth ready to say "You changed me"
Which I know I don't need to say
Because I love you
Not only your face but your harmony
I don't need to say rest in peace
Because why wouldn't you be?
Juliana Feit, Grade 6

A Place Called Home
Small and wet, also called Holland
Covered in grain windmills and tulips
Surrounded by water on two sides and canals running all the way through
The king and queen lead their country to happiness
Citizens enjoy a slice of Gouda on wheat
Children ride their bicycles all around
Passing old farmers walking on wooden shoes
Families bond over soccer games wearing only orange
Four times Holland's size and dry most days is Ohio
Covered by wheat and corn fields
The Governor guides the state to loyalty
Citizens enjoy hamburgers and hotdogs
Children stay active on the wii
The Amish work with their horse and buggies
Families cheer when the Buckeyes play
With a six-hour time difference but season the same
Winter, spring, summer, and fall
Friendship and love from Dutch and Americans
That is why I call them my homelands
Sofie Van Wezel, Grade 6

I Remember Red Zone
I remember getting 15,000 tickets at red zone.
I remember winning some game that I didn't know how to play.
I remember getting candy.
And I felt amazed that I won.
I remember going back and losing.
I remember trying and trying.
I remember my last token and I used it for a fishing game and I won 1,000 tickets.
Even though I won 16,000 tickets of all of the games I played,
I remember the lady at red zone saying "Wow!"
But my favorite memories are yet to come.
Parker Barta, Grade 5

Costume
Oh, what costume should I be?
There's so many to choose from, you see.
I could be a mermaid, an ape
Or Batman with a cape.
But I think I will be
Wizard of Oz's Dorothy!
Mikayla Yarish, Grade 6

Summer
S wimming all day long
U nique summer beauty
M agnificent hot days
M osquitos swarming all around
E njoying no school
R elaxing in the sunlight.
Sydney Alloco, Grade 6

Soccer
S core a goal
O n the goalie. Teammates
C heering your name.
C atch the ball. Get rid of it!
E ven though we're losing
R ight now we're having fun!
Matthew Nock, Grade 5

Red
Red is the color of the leaves in the fall,
It can be the color of a rose with it all
Red can be like madness,
It can be a fire of calmness
Red can be a ladybug shining in the sun,
It can be a tomato, ripe and done
Ashley Hronich, Grade 4

Candy
Candy, candy, so sweet and yummy
A source of joy, a source of energy
Fun to eat, rainy or sunny
Broccoli is nothing compared to candy
And I do not care if I get a cavity
I just really love candy
Yasmine Skalli, Grade 5

Tornado
Rattling against the houses.
Tackling down the trees.
Sweeping up litter.
Taking the hives of bees.
Dust in the air.
Giving people nightmares.
Brendan Fulginiti, Grade 5

Astonishing Autumn
Packing away shorts, tank tops, thin tees, and flip-flops
because summer is ending…and autumn is here!

No more bright bathing suits and soft, warm sand in my toes,
because now its autumn and its cold!
Crisp, red, ripe, round, and delicious apples
Smooth, plump, and ready to carve pumpkins for yummy, outstanding pumpkin pie!

Colorful, beautiful, perfect, leaves drifting down from the gigantic trees.
Enjoyable football games on TV, with your family!

Enthusiastic trick-or-treaters at your door.
MMMMM…it's candy galore!

It's getting cold outside.
It is Antarctica out there!
Although it's cold, kids are still outside!
Crunching, scrunching, leaves as kids run.
WOW! It looks like they are having fun!
WHAT A PHENOMENAL TIME OF YEAR!

Tender, juicy, enormous, turkey.
It is as big as a devastating tsunami!
Fresh aroma of scrumptious, sweet, delicious, apple pie for dessert.

Fall is ending. Taking out, fluffy, cozy, and puffy jackets.
WINTER HERE I COME!
Adriana Giangrasso, Grade 6

It's About…
It's about the snowy months
November, December,
and January

It's about snow balls
Throwing them and turning it into a free-for-all!
Rolling them bigger still, and piling them on top of each-other

It's about dressing up snowmen
Grabbing scarves, carrots,
Mittens, and buttons

It's about sledding with friends
sliding down the slippery slopes
Whooping with laughter

It's about going inside and having a refreshing hot-chocolate drink
Plunking marshmallows into the chocolatey brew
Swirling the hot liquid with a spoon
Then drinking it up, warming my insides

It's about my favorite time of the year!
Emilia Endara, Grade 5

I Fought for You

You were brave,
Many lives you saved.

You were as tough as a lion,
When all those bullets were flyin'.

When you went away,
We went to church to pray.

You fought for liberty,
And you earned a victory.

"I fought for you,
And so did my crew," I heard you say.

Some paid a price,
But all of you made the sacrifice.
Michael Eckenrode, Grade 5

I Was the Wind

I was looking out the car window
At the fall scenery
When all of a sudden,
I could feel
The wind calling to me.
It tugged my hair and whipped past me,
And carried me away,
And took me to a far off place
Where children laugh all day.
I was the wind, soaring through the sky
Gliding swiftly as a deer–
I zoomed past rainbow colored forests
And heard young children cheer.
But soon, the wind brought me back
To my parents, and then I spent
The rest of the day remembering
The place where I went.
Trisha Lahiry, Grade 5

Purple

POWER and WEALTH purple rules you
Buying your life
Ruling your family
Runs on your MONEY
Raising taxes
Wearing robes
Power
 People
  Reigning
   Rumble
    Potent
     Almighty
      Forceful
       Vigorous
        Strong
Cal Sollie, Grade 6

Crash

Driving in your car just a normal day.
Maybe a peek at that text,
I'm sure that its ok.
You lose control then hit a car.
Spinning, spinning, like a top on a jar.

You stop and think what have you done?
I can tell you it is not fun…

I hear the roaring sirens blare,
I look to see the driver pale.

I try to move but am not able,
This was just a normal day…
Andrew Melita, Grade 6

Beach

I see seagulls swooping down,
And snatching people's food.

I hear the waves crash when,
They try to suck me in.

I taste the salty water,
As I swim deep into the ocean.

I feel the hot sun,
Beaming down on me like a laser.

I smell the freshness,
Of Oceans City's air all around me.
Brandon Cotter, Grade 5

Green

Green is the color of grass
My favorite sweater
And a pair of pants
It's the crunchy sound
Of granny eating an apple
Under a tree
Green tastes nutritious like a salad
A crisp apple
Or some salty pistachios
It feels soft
Like a delicate caterpillar
And stretchy
Like rubber bands that are green
Green makes the world grow!
Imayla Russell, Grade 4

The Song

A song is like a bird tweeting in the wind
and the wind howls like a wolf in the night
while the tree rustling in the wind
and Beethoven playing the piano.
Matthew Graf, Grade 6

Gymnastics

Nervously, I wait,
I'm ready to salute,
Wondering…what will be my fate?

I've been waiting for this day,
I've practiced so much,
But what if I fall, then what would I say?

I'm in my pose,
I'm ready to go,
The music is about to play.

I take a deep breath,
Plaster a smile on my face,
Feeling like I'm about to meet my death.

I'm soaring through the air,
Jumping, tumbling, and sprinting,
Doing what others wouldn't dare.

Sitting on the sideline,
Waiting to be called,
Will the medal be mine?

That is my name being called out so loudly,
I don't know why I was worried,
I marched up to the podium so proudly!
Anabelle Bergeron, Grade 6

Mom versus Son

My mother claims,
 it will rot my brains,
  and make me insane, them video games!

I don't mind if they rot,
 because this game is hot.
  I line up my next shot.

I play hour after hour,
 until my mom cuts the power,
  because I'm not in the shower.
   Then my mood gets sour.

There is a pain in my neck
 and my room is a wreck.
  I hope mom forgets
   about my homework check.

My eyes are so red.
 I feel like I'm dead,
  and there's a pain in my head!

My mom might be right,
 but I'll stick to the fight,
  that video games are tight!
David Dokos, Grade 6

Flowers
Bloom in the spring
So beautiful
All different colors and sizes
They smell like fresh honey
and gingersnaps
Each one tells its own special story
Flowers fill the Earth with joy
Julia Grisius, Grade 5

Dogs
Dogs
Cute, cuddly
Running, playing, jumping
Plays in the backyard
Barking, loving, eating
Nice, adorable
Cutiepie
Chloe Burhans, Grade 5

Snowflakes
Snowflakes are like children,
Playing in the winter air.
Twirling, swirling, spinning,
And dancing in a pair.
As they float down to earth.
They say a small reason.
Why they love the holiday season.
Codie Brown, Grade 5

Tomato Sky
Both are full of light,
In some cases dark.
Every seed is like a star,
Bright and shiny, they are.
And that is why they are alike,
Even though they are far.
They will never be apart.
Emma Kramer, Grade 5

My Life Story
My Mom and Dad are sweet.
I love my family and friends.
I love my sister and brother
And they come from another mother.
I love my cousins too.
I love my family and friends.
I will love them to the end.
Destiny Porter, Grade 4

Spiders
Spiders have eight legs,
They're in all different shapes,
The foods are insects,
Webs are attached everywhere,
Spiders lay eggs in their webs.
Jenna D'Amico, Grade 6

Red
Red is the color
Of a juicy apple
The blood from a cut
Like a darker shade of pink
It sounds like Kool-Aid
Being poured in a cup
And a loud crash
When a glass shatters
On the floor
Red tastes juicy
Like round grapes
And sweet like a ripe apple
It feels sad
When someone gets in trouble
And their face turns red
Red can bring a tear to your eye.
Domonic Innocent, Grade 4

Thanksgiving
What a nice autumn day
Stuffing my mouth with stuffing
Yummy
Watching the Macy's parade
Stuffing my mouth with stuffing
More mashed potatoes please
Watching the Macy's parade
Looking at this feast
More mashed potatoes please
Eating delectable pumpkin pie
Looking at this feast
Family around the table
Eating delectable pumpkin pie
Yummy
Family around the table
What a nice autumn day
Megan Sharon, Grade 4

Peace
Peace means
No war
No drugs
Freedom
Peace means
No noisy arguments
No murder
Life
If there were world peace
Loved ones would still be alive
There would not be any crisis
People would be happier
If there were peace
World peace
Or any kind of peace
The world would be a lot better
Jason Yan, Grade 6

Dream
In dreams you can have everything,

In dreams you can be on your
bed eating popcorn.

In dreams you can smell everything
from chocolate to dirt.

In dreams you can be crying and
wake up with tears streaming
down your face.

In dreams you can have anything
from candy to money.

In dreams you can be a doctor
helping out a patient.

In dreams the world is open to you.
Torgyn Hart, Grade 5

Ode to Sweet Cake
Sweet cake
Sweet, soft
Love you on
My birthday
Ice-cream
Makes me
Happy
Love chocolate
Strawberry, cherry
Filled with
Colors, smells
Like joy
Makes everyone
Joyful it's
So warm
Makes me
Full with
Happiness
Sweet cake
Alexis Williams, Grade 4

Cheetah
Cheetah, cheetah,
Cat with spots,
Such a skinny cat with dots…
Fastest runner,
On the Earth,
When it races,
Hooray, hooray!
Burst of speed,
Quite a blast,
Cheetah runs,
Really fast!
Carlos Almanzar, Grade 5

My Baby Brother
My baby brother is 1 year old.
He is so sweet.
He loves to cuddle with me.
He has fat cheeks.
He loves to sleep.
I love my baby brother.
Laniyah Dennis, Grade 4

1000 Years Ago
1000 years ago no humans were alive,
So did spiders rule Earth?
Did volcanoes spit out juice?
Did cave men ride on dinosaurs?
How do we know what life was like
1000 years ago?
Dakota Clontz, Grade 4

Cold Fall Day
Many leaves falling,
The cold wind is blustering,
Full of cold crisp air,
Birds fly south for the winter,
A tree is stripped of its leaves.
Danny Bransfield, Grade 6

Deer Through the Night Fields
Dark, cold, quiet night,
Light shines off of the deer's eyes,
Staring down at me,
Their furs' faint color shows through,
As they dash into darkness.
Ashley Jones, Grade 6

Thanksgiving Feast
Dinner
Conversation
Eating delicious food
Being with family and friends
A meal
Jessica Matthew, Grade 4

Holding Hands
Holding your hands
Walking through the field,
Loving, warming hands,
Thinking, believing, dreaming,
Dragging your feet on the ground.
Jeana Calibey, Grade 6

Main Dish
Turkey
Yummy hungry
Boring eating watching
Delicious bird wishing bone
Wishbone
Rashad Jabbar, Grade 4

Our Mother
Sometimes I sit and stare for a while
At her beautiful smile, her perfect profile

Our Mother
Her rich brown eyes, like two precious gold mines
Her emerald-green skin, dotted with pines
She garbs herself only in a frock made of ivory snow
And a necklace of rivers, already in flow

Our Mother
Who cries like the rain, laughs like a rainbow, and smiles like the sun
She likes to cause thunderstorms, it's her ideal way of fun
She is everyone's friend, and we are her children

Our Mother
She is alive, but not living
She is Mother Nature.
Sharon Lee, Grade 5

The Sun Rises Again
The Sun is very important
It is the first thing in the bright morning
And the last thing before dawn
Most of your best and worst moments happen from it
Helping bring beautiful moments
Bringing me dreams of gold
Happy and beautiful moments fill my mind
Reminds me I shall live on
It reminds me that great is the Sun
Because of it my soul has grown stronger
And every one can sing of freedom
And say we're not scared of the sting of the bee
We're not scared of when the dark comes
Because of the sun, my darkest enemies will never rise before me again
Never again my trembling step
When I look up beautiful moments fill my mind
The Sun reminds me I still have a life of dreams upon me
Molly Hendricks, Grade 4

The Dark Chest
In a dark forest there is a legend about many deaths.
It all started with a beautiful and poised young girl named Beth;
Who had a wily love, whose name was Dan.
But their love was forbidden so they ran,
When they ran Dan disappeared.
So Beth peered,
Into a cavernous house that hid a secret.
No one knows that secret.
Until now, that secret was a very dark chest.
In that chest there was a nest,
That held a voluminous crystal egg.
And that crystal egg
Held a deranged dark power.
And that power can make the bravest cower.
So beware for that dark power still exists, in a young girl named Beth.
Sammy Kitchen, Grade 6

The Hardest Thing

Because lifetimes hurt like broken glass
Because evenings burn out all too fast
Because it was a typical story, waiting for a twist
Because I was still waiting on that goodnight kiss
Because buttercups don't bloom when you need
Because we knew we had ten mouths to feed
Because magic is heard, but never said
Because there are movies everywhere, but Hollywood's dead
Because your missile missed its frightful aim
Because none of my English teachers remembered my name
Because daddy always forgot to listen
Because a squirt of Windex only makes the window glisten
Because I was so caught up in the play I forgot my role
Because Santa wouldn't take me back to the north pole
Because I cried for more time when I lost my first tooth
Because Grandma died before she told me the truth
Because God taught me, that I'm always the guest
Because hey, everyone's just trying their best
Because he makes me feel like the world's oldest kid
I said it, because "I love you," is the hardest thing I ever did.

Abigail Sylvor Greenberg, Grade 6

Dance

Dance is a tear
An expression of the emotions inside of you
A drop of water that means much more
Something that happens when someone is deeply touched
Dance is a bird
Flying with joy
Will sometimes get stunned
But will always recover
Dance is a window
It allows you to see what's inside
Makes everything visible
Shows the true, free person
Dance is a balloon
Floats when filled
But only when filled with soul of a dancer
Can you watch the dancer leave earth
Dance is a gate
A gate into something mysterious
Something unimaginable and
Something indescribable

Eva Moore, Grade 6

Christmas

C hristmas carols
H o ho ho! Santa calls
R ocking around the Christmas tree with my family
I t is a winter wonderland outside
S now falling on the trees in my backyard
T he smell of pine rushing through my nose
M aking a list, checking it twice
A s Santa's coming down the chimney
S itting by the fire, drinking hot cocoa

Hanna Gwiazdowski, Grade 5

Seasons

Winter is?
Bitter, cold, windy blizzards
Animals hibernating, away from the icy snow
Ice skating, sledding, skiing, tubing

Spring is?
Not too hot, not too cold, perfect weather I suppose
Bees buzzing and birds chirping
Flowers in hues of purple and blues

Summer is?
Long, sunny, blazing days
Bees and wasps out stinging
Swimming, diving, cook-outs, vacationing

Fall is?
Leaves changing, school in session
Apple-picking, pumpkin-picking, trick-or-treating
Animals migrating and getting ready to hibernate

Madyson Haas, Grade 6

Don't Quit

I'll never quit
never quit trying to swish 3-pointers
or perfect my ball handling

Never stop trying to pitch perfectly
or hit home runs into the pond
or even trying to be the first girl to play in the MLB

I'll never stop running, to keep my endurance up
I won't stop kicking soccer balls either
because if I do, I'll never start again

I won't stop studying
no matter how hard it is
because I'll be rewarded with great grades

I can't stop being myself
because if I do,
Who am I?

Caitlin Kennedy-Jensen, Grade 6

Words

It's the words that soar out of bounds…
I run them down, I save them…
The blocked ones…
The ones I catch in mid flight as they soar past…
The rebounds I wait for greedily or stalk until,
Suddenly, they drop…
Strategies are so great that I want to fit them all
Into one game like stalactites blocking the way
Words,
Words,
Words.

Brandon Kauffman, Grade 5

My Ode to Leo

You loved to play and run around,
You were always so, so glad.
You loved to always make some sounds,
I always saw a face that wasn't sad.

I hope we aren't apart for such a long time,
Right now I'm just a rootless seed.
Being away from you is a taste of lemon lime,
Right now you're the dog I need.

I know that you are not human like me,
But you will always be like my brother.
Of course you will always look and see,
That I'll never choose another!

T. Sabrina Schmidt, Grade 4

Braces

I just got these silvery braces.
What will people say at school?
I hope I won't get stared at by millions of faces.
I'm sure they'll think I'm uncool.
What will I do,
When my friends see my face?
I'll just stay under covers and write in my diary too.
If they see me they'll say, "Look at ugly Delaney Grace!"
Instead of staying under the covers all day long,
I'll arrive at school proudly,
With my head up and I'll stay strong,
Trying not to feel drowsy.
Will people like me? It all depends.
Calm down, here come my friends.

Delaney Driscoll, Grade 5

Summer

I see…
yellow sun making the flowers smell like honey.
I feel…
the wind as it blows my hair back.
I see…
the birds singing their little song.
I see…
the sun like a beautiful sun flower. It glistens off the beautiful sun.
I feel…
the fresh breeze in my nose.
I feel…
the warm grass in between my toes.
I feel…
the warm rays of the sun in my hair.

Hannah Jones, Grade 6

Red

Awe red. Bravery and courage are always threaded with red.
You wear red to be proud of what you have, not to brag.
It is to be bold, not to be cold.
Red is red and that is how it is.

Tyler Berger, Grade 6

Fall

Summer has ended
School has started
Report cards are almost out
Leaves fall from all of the trees
In pretty shades of red, orange, and yellow
Days are getting shorter
Even if we've just changed our clocks
The candy is almost gone
And the smell of turkey is in all of the houses
And people are lined up in the dark
The day after
Soon snow is falling on the ground
Christmas decorations are everywhere
Ending fall

Brian Phung, Grade 6

Christmas Eve

The family is over, we are having fun,
Dancing, prancing, eating a ton,
When the feast is over the presents come,
Then we open them one by one.

After presents the family goes home,
We take showers, and baths with lots of bubbly foam,
Mom sits down to read us our favorite holiday tome,
But thinking about presents causes my mind to roam.

Next I get into bed to go to sleep,
Tossing, turning, counting sheep,
Waiting for Santa, not making a peep,
I fall asleep to the sound of jingling bells.

Ivy Newman, Grade 5

Pomegranate Safari

Pomegranate safari can be healthy
It can be dangerous too
Let me bring you on this beautiful adventure
Trust me it isn't sour—it'll surprise you

Pomegranates are fruit of the gods
It is really quite so cool
Safaris are good adventures
They're a time to be out of school

Pomegranates and safaris are good in spring
They are good in summer too
They can be very frontierful for me
Why won't they be for you?

Josiah Brown, Grade 5

Snow

So beautiful on the ground.
Reminds us of Christmastime.
Bringing the school kids two hour delays and cancellations.
Wonderful and playful snow.

Chase Walker, Grade 6

Blankets

the soft
warm
and fuzzy blankets
books and teddy bears
get thrown onto them
as you read
or sleep
in winter or fall
or when you believe something is inside
of your closet
you curl up in the warmth of a blanket
when they get ripped
torn
or dirty
you wash them in the washer and dry them
in the dryer
at first
they are just thread
so now they sew them
into soft warm and fuzzy
blankets

Rachel Lee, Grade 4

Bright Summer Days

Feel the summer breeze
Whiz through the air
The bright light reflects off the sand
The waves crash on shore
On a great summer day
I lay out on the sand
Shades on
Just waiting for that butterfly
To land on my nose
Or on my toes
As I sit on the glistening sand
The next think I know
I've been wiped out by a wave
I see many kites fly up in the sky
Just as the seagulls glide in the wind
The smell of sunscreen fills the air
I see dogs
Happily making way to the waves
The baby sea turtle finally hatches
The amazing life on the beach
Is so relaxing

Makala Ingegni, Grade 5

The Battle of the Games

Video game
Medium, gray
Amazing, entertaining, interesting
Gamestop, Walmart, Target, Monopoly
Playing, selling, moving
Big, rainbow
Board game

Alejandro Peralta, Grade 6

My Playful Puppy

My puppy never stops playing
She chases me, she's blasting towards me
My puppy makes my heart burst
Sometimes she amazes me
My puppy is free outside
She always wants to go outside to play
I chuck her toy, she goes and gets it
And brings it back to me
My puppy is amazing
She is a wonderful puppy

Kyle Krader, Grade 4

Autumn

The leaves are falling, falling, falling
gently to the yellowed autumn grass below.
The wind tosses the orange and brown
leaves to and fro.
The air has a crisp smell of cold as
it prepares for winter.
Squirrels gather acorns and run all about.
The days grow shorter as the sun glows
against the evening clouds.
Oh, how I wish autumn could stay.

Katherine Nigro, Grade 4

What Is Autumn?

Fall is brown, yellow and red
I look out the window next to the bed.
I see bare trees,
and honeybees.
The fireplace is going,
and the animals are sleeping.
Turkey on the table,
I will eat all of it if I'm able.
This is fall,
Having a ball

Olivia Donahue, Grade 5

Halloween

Halloween is a scary thing.
It always makes you want to scream!
There are witches who frighten
And goblins who like fighting.
Ghosts give you
A scare
As werewolves
Cast a glare.
Monsters own the night,
But the treats make it all right.

Julie Prestigiacomo, Grade 5

Summer Chores

Green grass and sunshine
Water produces the life
Lawnmower kills it

Erin Starke, Grade 6

The Scared Storm

The gushing wind comes at me
the air gets cold
bad memories come to my mind
I want to cry
darkness covers my soul
bitter twisted lies
shadows fall
my heart scattered into pieces
a dark grave in my soul
my memory fades
darkness is everywhere
the world twisted and turned
I am frightened
I called for help
nothing was working
my heart was beating like a lightning bolt
what will happen to me
I thought that it was the end of the world
but it wasn't
it was bad part of my dream
so I went outside and played

Devang Bhandari, Grade 4

The Life of Daniel

from Jerusalem
to Babylon
made a wise man
sent to the court room
to interpret a dream
dream interpreted
back for food
can't eat meat
only eat veggies
new king
a Persian king
can't pray
but still does
consequences happen
then comes the lions' den
lions come
Daniel prays
the praying does help (really it does)
then angel shut up the lions
God saves
Jesus does too!

Cormac Murtagh, Grade 5

Fire and Water

Water
Cold, all around
Drifting, nonstopping, flooding
Soft, blue, red, yellow
Burning, spreading, crackling
Hot, loud
Fire

Daniel Meade, Grade 5

Black and White

Black is
Powerful
  Empty
    Controlling
Hidden and mysterious
Strong and protective
Black is the midnight sky and the dull black luster of coal

Shrouded in mystery, hiding something inside, revealing no emotion
Never lying, simple and straightforward, perfect and pure

White is
Complete
  Whole
    Just
Peaceful and innocent
Isolated and plain
White is the soft clouds and the color of milky quartz

Claire Chen, Grade 6

Irish Dance Hard Shoes

In a box, tucked in storage
Slowly attracting dust and mildew
Hears the sound of the door opening
Gets carried out of its tomb
It hears trebles, tips and bangs as it travels
It reminds it of its glory days
To the studio
A new hopeful, a girl
Tries on all my friends
They don't fit, finally her last hope, me.
Before she has to buy those snooty new shoes.
But she takes me over to the studio
Dances, dances like no one else
Will she bring me back to my glory days?
After practice ends, I hold my breath
But, she cradles me under her arms
And takes me back to my glory days.

Catie Summers, Grade 5

My Favorite Holiday

Christmas is my favorite holiday
All snowy and white,
Along with the colors green and red.
We set up the beautiful Christmas tree,
With lights and ornaments on every branch.
We go to bed,
And wake up in the morning excited.
We run to the living room
As fast as we can,
To find gifts beneath the tree.
We excitedly open them
To find exactly what we wanted.
Now I wait until next year,
For my favorite holiday to come again.

Baileigh Horan, Grade 6

Summer Vacation

As I enter, I wonder if this is better,
roller coasters great and tall, I hope when I'm up there I don't fall.
Kings Dominion, the best place to ride,
the wind makes you feel like you're in the tide.
Rolling wildly on a steel bar,
way faster than a car.
Then you'll feel the sensation,
of being on summer vacation.

Rayce Robins, Grade 6

The Prayer of the Wolf

In the untouched woodland
that is ruled by the wolves,
we shall pray for more deer and moose;
we do not want to be on the side of the Hunter,
Hunting only for trophies and glory,
but for us to live,
something else has to die.

Mark M. Baron, Grade 5

Snow Days

I love school but, I enjoy snow days more!
Sledding down the hill in my backyard is exciting!
Until I hit a tree stump and fall face first in the snow.
After sledding we build snowmen, in my case, snow-mermaids.
Snowball fights and igloos are some other things we do in the snow.
By the time we finish our activities we are VERY cold!
So I go inside and drink a warm cup of cocoa.

Joelle Kennedy, Grade 6

Fall

Whoosh, whoosh, whoosh
I feel the wind on my face.
I see the leaves falling like the apples on the trees.
The leaves are like chips
crunch, crunch, crunch.
Pumpkins being carved
bring the fright of Halloween

Noah Scott, Grade 6

Happy

Happy is light blue
It sounds like laughter
It smells like fresh-baked cookies
It tastes like ice cream in the summer
It looks like a puppy getting a new home
Happy feels like hugs from your grandparents

Ashton Wiseley, Grade 5

Ellen the Horse Gets Attacked

H er mane flows in the wind,
O nward she goes, her scent travels downwind.
R ustling in the bushes is a puma with an ear-to-ear grin.
S he shakes and bucks, luckily she's thick skinned.
E llen fights, even though she's pinned!

Elaineah Brown, Grade 4

Winter

W e love to frolic in the fields of white
I n the snow we stick out our tongues and catch the snowflakes
N othing more delightful than drinking warm hot cocoa
T he laughter of kids echoes in the snow
E xcitement in the air
R eally, we are happy

Gabriel White, Grade 6

Hitler

H is for hate against all the Jews
I is for Iratainn Hitler gave the Jews
T is for tons of Jews dying in the poison showers
L is for lots of Jews going into camps
E is for entering the Jews houses and taking the men
R is for Nazis rioting and killing Jews

Eric Stevenson, Grade 6

Christmas

The big bright lights all around the Christmas tree
Hung all nice and bright
As we put ornaments on the tree
We stand around having fun
Listening to Christmas songs on the radio
Hoping to get presents and my stocking filled high

Ashley Severns, Grade 5

I Am

I am a wolf, waiting for prey,
I am the sun, shining like a million stars,
I am Thanksgiving, feeding the hungry,
I am love, putting compassion into every soul,
I am white, filling your mind with something, yet nothing,
I am the light.

Olivia Stann, Grade 4

The Pumpkin

One day I carved a pumpkin as scary as can be,
And then it came alive, and then it screamed, "Yippee!"
I cuddled with my pumpkin, all throughout the night.
I woke up in the morning, my pumpkin out of sight.
I went into the kitchen, and knew that he had died,
'Cause sitting on the table was a fresh-baked pumpkin pie.

Simon Squires, Grade 5

Christmas

Christmas is fun and full of joys,
And I get a lot of toys.
On Christmas I have a feast,
Since I'm with my family, I can eat like a beast.
On Christmas Eve I play in the snow,
The next day I hear ho-ho-ho.

Travell White, Grade 6

Picture Day

It's picture day, oh boy, oh boy,
I'll cheese and I'll smile,
I may be hungry in awhile.
What should I eat?
Cheese cheese, it is not messy or wild!

Yeah, well I smile for my picture and then I scream,
"Oh no!"
When I smile and say cheese,
the photographer sees…
cheese!
All in my braces!

Why did I choose cheese?
When I said I would say cheese, I did not mean with cheese!

Mercedes Bernal, Grade 5

Party In The Northern Sky

Shimmering in the black of night,
Are strange colorful, and blazing lights.
Have no fear! Now listen here!
Do you wonder what's going on in the North up there?
A mix of green, pink, violet, and white,
These wonders are having a party tonight!
Blue is bopping, there's no stopping
The northern lights from partying tonight!
Crimson, like an eagle with vibrant wings.
White, like a diamond with sorts of things.
Green is the most beautiful thing you've seen.
This party's sparkle is getting keen!
Magenta is zipping, indigo is zapping,
Silver and gold waltz with the light.
The party's fired up for tonight!

Ethan Nguyen, Grade 4

Football

Team
Coach, play book
Quarterback, pass, throw
Receiver, run, catch, linebacker
Referee, clock, whistle, yellow flag,
Clipping, holding, penalty, 10 yards, huddle,
Call the play, block, first down, move those chains,
Hard tackle, on side kick, spin, offense, defense,
Field goal, interception, end zone, touchdown,
Score, extra point, half-time, band stadium,
Cheerleaders, fans, rivals, overtime,
Small town Friday Nights,
Championship,
Let's Go,
WIN!

Gavin Cox, Grade 5

Slithering Sneaking Stalking Slimy Snakes
They slither, they stare
They stalk you, the trees and the air

You shiver, you shake
When you see the sight of a snake

It hisses, its eyes filled with hate
I realize I am their bait

They come from the dungeon
Blind as a bat
What do they think, I am a rat?

Their sight is slight
But their fangs are big and burly
They're slimy and scary
Their skin's so pearly

I burst into a dash
Snakes twist and turn
My feet ache and feel like
They are about to burn
One almost bit me
I thought I bled
I'm on the run
They have not been fed.
Katie Olson, Grade 5

My Favorite Show of the Year
It's about grace and movement,
Dress up in costumes and make up
In the theater

It's about being on time
Going to every practice
Cannot wait until show time

It's about the parts,
Clara and Fritz
Mice and Soldiers
Mother Ginger's Children and Snowflakes

It's about dress rehearsals going over the time limit
Costumes being the perfect fit
Never quitting your practice

It's about the props
Mother's big dress and those decorated pointe shoes
The huge Christmas tree and Grandma's butt, that will amuse

It's about the show
The applause and the flowers
The stars and the bowers

It's about my favorite show of the year
Annie Scott, Grade 5

Flowers
Vibrant colors
pink, yellow, blue, red sometime maroon
make me happy,
Make me peaceful
and make my eyes itch

Flowers say
congratulations,
sorry for your loss,
happy birthday,
I love you

The sweet scent calls to the bees
inviting them to sip the nectar
as they carry away the seeds form the flower

Flowers straying seeds as they
float in the wind
Earth's beautiful creations
Clarissa Granados, Grade 6

Pier
The wind blows as you walk
You walk alone
You walk down the long abandoned pier
The broken stilts wobble
Still Something pulls you farther on the pier
The old windmill blades spin slowly on the pin
The smell of dead sea and hurt memory fill the air
A storm brews; a voice still calls you at the end of the pier
But now something pulls you back
You stop, dead, frozen
The lightning strikes right on the pier
You turn to run, then
A wave takes you under
The suffocating depth pulls you in
You push, but something is yanking like a magnet
You gasp for air, but soon there is none
You feel something reach for you
Still you try to pull on
Your strength is gone
Baylee Peperak, Grade 4

The Wonderful World of Heaven
I cry looking at his casket
I lay my card right next to him
I start to hug everyone then I grasp them tightly
I feel my tears running down my face
I can't hear his voice anymore
I cry instead
I hug grandma tight because it is her dad
I am happy for grandpa
but sad he is not here
Knowing he is in a better place
I feel better.
Olivia Conley, Grade 4

Thanksgiving

Thanksgiving started with
The Pilgrims from the Mayflower
But first they had to get along with
The Indians that had all the power.

The Pilgrims needed help because
Many people were dying
So the Indians helped them grow crops and gave them medicine
Which stopped all the crying.

The Pilgrims were so grateful
So they threw a big feast
Since both groups got together there were
One-hundred people at the least.

Nowadays, Thanksgiving is the same
We give thanks and appreciate the good things in life
You should be glad you have a family, big or small
Even if you only have just a husband or just a wife.

I love my family
They are the best
They love and care for me so
In my eyes they are better than the rest!

Mykayla Askew, Grade 6

Snow

I get dressed to leave
I get on some clothes
I also get a jacket and gloves
And a scarf and a hat

The snow is falling from the sky
So soft and so white
I feel like I'm in bed
Laying down to go to sleep

I can make snowballs
I can have snowball fights.
We make forts and throw snowballs at each other
So much you can do in the snow

I lay in the snow
Moving my hands and my feet
Up and down as they go
That is how I make snow angels

So much fun in the snow
Look at all you can do
I know I like the snow
Do you like it too?

Oluwafemi Olosunde, Grade 5

At a Funeral

At a funeral, I sing the blues
for someone who is never coming home to me
sobbing hard, I sing the blues
for someone who is never coming home to me
empty chairs around the table, what more could happen to me?

My heart, sings the blues when I look at the empty chair
my heart sings the blues when I think how is this fair
I fall apart over and over again
my aching heart will never again share.

The emptiness, sings the blues
pointing out he is not here with me
the emptiness sings the blues
making me realize they will never be here for me to see
empty, empty, empty
but they will never be gone to me

At a funeral I sing, the blues
for someone never coming home to me
sobbing hard, I sing the blues
for someone never coming home to me
to many empty chairs around chairs around the tables
what more could happen to me?

Zenna Eaton, Grade 6

Papa

He was the man with many expressions,
He was a man whom people left with great impressions.
I saw him sick for years in bed,
How he would lie there on that comfy bedspread.

I was four-years-old when he sadly passed away,
I still remember that day as if it were yesterday.
I ran up to his room only to find him not there in bed,
I was scared, sad, but then I knew that he was dead.

He was my buddy, my mate, my friend,
I felt heartbroken as if this were the end.
I thought about all the good times we had shared,
After I had thought of him for a while I got scared.

My heart was touched that day,
As he went away.
Although I was little I felt like I had known him for a whole lifetime,
All I wish was that I had a little more time.

That day I had tasted great defeat,
I get a little sad now when I pass his old street.
I remember us having loads of fun,
He was a good man and will live eternally in heaven.

Helen Rothfus, Grade 6

I Am

I am happy and quiet
I wonder if there are more planets in space
I hear ringing
I see dots
I want college money
I am happy and quiet

I am happy and quiet
I pretend the game's up
I feel happy
I touch the wind when it comes by
I worry that my dad and mom are going to die
I cry if I get hurt
I am happy and quiet

I am happy and quiet
I understand math
I say that new stuff will be invented
I dream about me and my dad
I try to do new stuff
I hope I'll be a mechanic
I am happy and quiet

Brandon Tower, Grade 5

Sad

I am sad because my baby brother died
yesterday morning when I was at school.
We went to go see my brother and my mommy
and then I held him in my arms.
Then I gave him a kiss on the head.
I wish he was alive so I could see him and hug him;
but I can't because he is not alive.

If he was alive, I would be so happy;
but he's not here, so I am so sad because
I miss him so much.
I am so sad because I will never see him again
after the funeral.
I will be sad if we buried him in the ground.
I will be depressed if I don't see him alive; but
I will be happy to keep his ashes.

I love you Kingston.

Love,
Kailah
10/10/13

Kailah Kinney, Grade 6

Winter

Winter is a wonder waiting to be found.
It's like a blanket of white.
It is a magnificent thing.
Only for a month, it has Christmas, laughing and joy.
That is winter.

Isaiah Costa, Grade 5

Aging

What is aging?
Aging is getting older.
Starting out small and getting bigger.
Getting a car, having a job,
Freedom,
Your own house, a family of your own,
And more respect.
Many don't like aging, 'cause it makes you look like a prune.
There is more responsibility like,
Taxes, payments, mouths to feed,
No one to rely on.
You can't control aging,
It just comes.
Marked with numbers.
Kids love it.
Adults don't.
Aging.

Maya Hammond, Grade 6

My Big Sister

My sister is annoying to me,
I don't know how to stop it,
She looks like a donkey and smells like a monkey,
If I got her eyeliner I would chop it.

She tries to make me frown,
I try giving her kicks,
She tries to put me down,
I chop up her lipsticks.

If I actually ignored,
She would be so frustrated,
She would be so bored,
She would not be there as if she faded.

I solved the problem now I'm good,
Everything turned out how it should.

Natasha Curimbaba, Grade 5

Hate

Why must it be around
Hate
It separates people into groups against each other
Hate
Bringing sadness to the world
Hate
Letting tears fill the eyes
Hate
Yet it might be the start of hope

Remember all the hate,
Not on a specific date.
Bystanders don't help,
Rescuers never have to hear another yelp.
Hate

Jamila Cobrinik, Grade 6

Snowman Party

Once a sneaky snowman crept
Up onto his friend's step.
For tonight the snowman would
Have a party in the woods.
All the snowmen danced and sang
Until the jolly school bell rang.
Then they slid into their place
Maybe next they'd have a race!
Nora Betts, Grade 4

Football

Cold, sweet, juice,
Sliding down the cup,
Into my dry throat.
Running down the warm steps,
Onto the dried grass. Energized.
Ready. Then the football races toward me.
Jumping. Feeling the force of the ball
Hitting me.
Patrick Howell, Grade 5

A New Land

Forests, trees; touching the sky
Indians, bows on their backs
Spearing salmon in the rolling water
Eagles soaring very high
Hold on tight to your father
Prickly thorns, hurting my thigh
It is a new land, a wonderland
Made just for me to explore!
Taylor Sherry, Grade 4

Moon

I am flying
Overhead, up high.
I see the tops of
Plum trees, I smell
The saltwater. Then…
The heavy weight
Of the moon —
Pushes me to sleep.
Sophie Kramer, Grade 5

Christmas

Christmas is my favorite holiday.
No, it's not Memorial Day!
I love the joy of celebrating with others
Dads, Moms, Sisters, and Brothers.
We are happy
Jesus was born
Only on Good Friday,
we mourn.
Kieran P. Santos, Grade 5

Brave as the Man on the Moon

The moon was a white ghost,
Slithering through the night sky.
Glowing like a shaded lamp,
Going "Ooh."
I noticed the "Oohs"
Were really the wind.
Now that I know,
And I am not scared,
I'm as brave as the man
Who lives there alone.
I noticed the man
On the moon wasn't really a person,
Just shadows and craters.
So I can't compare myself
To him, either.
I guess
I'll just say
I'm as brave as
Neil Armstrong —
He's real,
and he *did* go there.
Alexandra Pereira, Grade 5

Change

The ocean is a landscape
Illustrated to perfection
The turquoise waves ripple
Fringed with white foam
The sun is a volcano
Pouring out its fiery heat
Baking the people below
Warming the white, powdery sand
The clouds are shaped angels
Floating high above
In its own ocean of blue
White and fluffy
Or thin and wispy
The sunset is a watercolor masterpiece.
Cherry red streaks of twilight
Appear and fade as the rosy sun dips
Below the mountain peaks
The sky turns into blankets of navy
The stars are sprinkles
One by one dots of silver
Began to appear
Madina Shabazz, Grade 6

Royal Blue

Joyful is royal blue
It sounds like a crowd cheering
It smells like fresh blueberries
It tastes like a fresh pie
It looks like a king's crown
It feels like when you win a
championship soccer game.
Jacob Minnick, Grade 5

If Only Monday Was a Person

If only Monday was a person
I'd put a curse on that person

May its place in the week disappear
May a new fun day appear!

May it be Friday please, oh please
May it be Friday now please, please
GEEZE LOUISE!!

If only Monday was a person
I'd put a curse on that person!!
Belle Woodward, Grade 6

The Fight Between Twins

One wrong word
he gives me the evil eye
One wrong move
he mocks me
A silver blade of anger pierces me
A fiery anger blazes between us
he showers his rage upon me
I dart away
he dashes after me
I seek out my mother
he doesn't dare pursue me
the fight is not over…only paused
Ian Martin, Grade 4

Tornado

It twirls and whirls
Over vast Kansas plains,
Causing terrifying winds and rains.

Strong as a bull,
Travels hundreds of miles an hour,
Graceful as a swan,
Tall as a tower.

Destruction as far as the eye can see,
Tornados,
Not much help to you and me.
Annie Butcher, Grade 5

Thanksgiving Day

Thanksgiving is a good season,
I like it for a reason.
I go to my grandma's house to eat,
Grandma makes delicious corn and meat.
I like the stuffing and the turkey,
But my sister likes beef jerky.
I am thankful for my family,
And that we live in the land of the free.
Thanksgiving is a time to pray.
You should celebrate this day.
Ian Ragno, Grade 4

High Merit Poems – Grades 4, 5, and 6

Tornado
Outside the winds are howling,
yearning to tear the world to shreds,
to hear the mournful calling,
across the skies are hues of reds.

The tornado's danger is impending,
a whirling mass of air and cloud,
a premonition that the world is ending,
the currents of air are blowing loud.

A star of white shines through,
the tornado may be passing,
the doves let out a gentle coo,
the tornado must be going if they sing.

The world is alive once more,
the tornado is gone evermore.
Maya Legersky, Grade 5

I Was Here
I was here
breathing
thinking
feeling.
I was here
but now
I am reduced
to bones and dust.
I was here
but the only sign
of my life
is my name
in a gravestone.
Was I remembered?
Forgotten?
I cannot be sure
But I was here.
Sarah Kogan, Grade 5

Where I'm From
I come from crunchy tacos,
smooth fudge and
cheesy nachos with a lot of cheese.
I come from nice people,
helping me and
me helping people.
I come from a lot of talent,
good looks and
being nice to everyone.
I come from a nice family and friends
they're here for me when I need them.
I come from a lot of places and
going to see a lot of places.
I come from a lot of videogames
and a lot of texting my friends.
Nick Foley, Grade 6

Halloween
H alloween is finally here!
A wesome costumes,
L eaves change colors.
L eaves fall off the trees.
O utside playing with friends.
W ith your family celebrating;
E veryone is trick-or-treating.
E veryone is carving pumpkins.
N ovember is just around the corner.
Grace Michaels, Grade 4

Feelings
There is an emotion
I cannot name, for
Fear of letting
All it's ingredients
Out in the open
For there are several, but
The name of this
Mysterious emotion is
Feelings
Mykayla Brown, Grade 5

Blue Shadow
The mirror cast its eye upon
a shadow in the corner,
hiding from the breath of dawn,
a solemn daylight mourner.

The shadow exhaled a dreary sigh
and slunk further from the hues.
The mirror sought to wonder why
the shadow felt such blues.
Ella Miller, Grade 6

The Lovely Princess
A young prince rides up to a tower
And cries, with zeal, through the door:
"Thou art a princess, my lovely flower,
All ladies and men would adore.

Yea, thy skin is smoother than cream.
Thine eyes are as bright as the moon.
Thy hair cannot truly be what it seems.
Your voice carries the loveliest tune!"
John Young, Grade 4

Easter vs Christmas
Easter
Pink, purple
Egg hunts, praying, seeking
Candy, bunnies, toys, clothes
Wrapping, buying, singing
Red, green
Christmas
Larissa Combs, Grade 6

Monster Menu
Soup
needle soup, good for your taste buds,
with hot fillings and with no TNT waste

Appetizer
salted worms in pickle dips with
fried cut up mouse chips

Dinner
a good spider salted and webbed or
arms of an iguana stewed in slime

Dessert
rat a la mode and
insect tea (termite free)

Enjoy!
Trisha Caldwell, Grade 5

I'd Like To
Go to the ballet
Invite Taylor Swift for a stay

Be a florist
Find a magic forest

Meet a snake that isn't mean
Go see a king and queen

Walk on sunshine
Drive a combine

Drop my brothers at the zoo
Tell my parents what to do

Learn to play the piano
Make a house from strawberry jello
Justice Reckner, Grade 4

Music
It speaks to me,
Touches my soul

It is a way for me to hesitate,
To escape the reality,
The problems

Thoughts about plans, work,
Fade away
When I listen.

The rhythm
Sound
Voice
Meaning
Kristina Matkevich, Grade 6

Dad
Dad
Funny, nice
Loving, giving, laughing
He loves me a lot
Father
Jack Austin, Grade 5

Beach
Buoys jumping out of the water
gentle wind whistling against the sand
the sweet ice cream melting in my mouth
the salty breeze blowing across my face
the smooth insides of all the glorious shells
Nathien Valeri, Grade 5

Swimming
Swimming
Exhausting, exciting
Kicking, hydrating, sleeping
Coaches who motivate you
Sport
Elizabeth Ramoy, Grade 5

Soccer
Soccer
Fun, exciting
Running, kicking, throwing
It is good exercise
Football
Clarisse Dapul, Grade 5

Basketball
I see the ball go in the net
I hear the swish when I score
I taste the sweat in my mouth
I feel the breeze while running
I smell the rubber on the ball
Robert Piontkowski III, Grade 5

Knight
Knight
Brave, strong
Saving, helping, fighting
They are very loyal
Hero
Nathan Ellis, Grade 5

Jesus
Jesus
Faithful, gifted
Loving, caring, appreciating
A blessing in disguise
God
Kaylee Copenspire, Grade 5

The Sands of Gore
It's been 77 days waiting here, and across the sands that are not near,
The dusty, blowing sands of Gore, is my trusting loyal friend Paveer.

What happened to my nearest pal? Did he go in search to find a gal?
Or get captured by a carnivorous pack, of the fuzzy pepper-speckled baral?

Did he get poisoned by the fruit "balloo?" Maybe fell into a palpanjoo;
The wide mouthed plant of the aging forest, to be slurped down through the stamen too?

Perhaps he crossed into a different world, with pictures turning and being swirled.
Like turning pages in a great book, with pictures turning and being swirled.

Or perhaps he went to find his peace, in a wonderful realm full of stress release.
Where he and his body and mind could rest. Where worries and troubles and woes all cease.

It's been 77 days waiting here, and across the sands that are not near,
The dusty, blowing sands of Gores, lays, my peaceful, loving friend, Paveer.
Kendall Wienecke, Grade 6

Grapefruit Daddy
I like his black hair and his eyes are stern
He has strong arms that could wrestle a mule, they are dark too
He's somewhat heavy set in his old shirts and hats
He slips on his shoes and puts on a smile, "We're ready to go," he says

We walk through the park while he tells me stories, "Oh look, we're almost
to the tree"
The sun is so hot we pick faster
Even though it's hot we pick all day

On our way back we try not to fall over the sticks
We find a rotten grapefruit and my daddy picks it up and throws it behind us
We get to the car and sit there for a while counting what we got

We go home and make lots of food
My dad is real picky, but I know him, he can be sour, he can be sweet
Hey, kind of like a grapefruit
Graclynn Lewis, Grade 5

Locked Out of the House
I watch children so happy, they practically glow
They are farmers, and laughter's what they grow,
As I observe through the cold window.

I wish I could join them; they won't let me in,
I'm usually treated like their own kin,
Wagging my tail sadly, I watch dinner begin.

But wait! The back door is open a bit,
I ram into it and it flies after one hit,
I sneak into the dining room (but not before shredding the oven mitts).

I stole the turkey, quick as a mouse,
And managed to demolish Auntie's new blouse,
Maybe that's why I, poor Sparky, am locked out of the house.
Lauren Paynton, Grade 6

Dreams

Dreams smell like delicious Hershey's chocolate
sitting on a table tempting you to eat it.

Dreams taste like a juicy peach
just gushing when you bite.

Dreams look like a caramel waterfall
gliding down.

Dreams sound like young robins
chirping, making the morning peaceful

Dreams feel like a massage
after a hard day.

Robert Lambert, Grade 5

Winter Time

At this time of the year snow falls
Look outside you just want to go play in it
The snow lays on the ground inch by inch
Dress in warm clothes
Snow boots on your feet
Heavy winter jacket over top
I went outside the front door it was a winter wonderland
A snowman is made with a carrot nose
and two eyes made out of coal
Snowball fights with your best friend
Time to go back inside after hours of fun
Drink hot chocolate to keep warm.

Jaelynn Clegg, Grade 6

Winter

Snow falls in blissful silence
Their pointed tips are exquisitely unique.
Snow brings enjoyment and glee to all children
The hills are covered with vivid colors speeding down the hill.
The air outside is frigid
Even the scorching sun cannot melt the bitter ice.
Everything is motionless
Enjoying the picturesque scene before them.
And at night the lights are glowing
While the ice skaters dance.
Nothing can come in place of this delightful scene
God's glory is simply astonishing.

Georgia Pollard, Grade 5

The Football

The white laces,
Gleaming of the dirt brown leather,
In a elliptical shape,
All spiraling through the air,
All finally landing in the receiver's hand,
Then the kapow of the defender into him,
Then the roar of the crowd with a touchdown,
That is football!!!!!!

Nikhil Belgaonkar, Grade 4

Sailing the Sea

Sailing the sea is a hard thing to do,
and Columbus did it with his magnificent crew.
He sailed with three ships from east to west,
He hoped to find land and there he could rest.

There he saw it the great sight of land,
Then he landed ashore on the Bahamas' white sand.
Everyone rejoiced that the world was round,
This is the land that Columbus had found.

Today we learn about Columbus the great,
How he journeyed to America with all of his freight.
We've learned in school that Columbus found this land,
Today I wish I could shake his hand.

John Auth, Grade 6

Bridge to Beauty

I step out the door
Into a land of mist
I see a sparkling shining rainbow
Hanging like a jewel in the sky
A lake of beauty and wonder
A dream
it reminds me of great treasure
it tells that there is really no death
I'm in a whole other world
Great memories soar into my mind
The bright colors sing to me
The stream of glowing color melts and fades away
Leaving nothing but a face in the sun
Tonight I will have new dreams

Carolyn Mowery, Grade 4

Snowy Day

The snow is as soft as cotton balls.
It looks like sugar sprinkled all over the ground.
The frozen lakes look like huge diamonds.
All the animals are warm while hibernating.
The quietness of the day, so peaceful and soothing.
Everything is covered with a light layer of snow.
Not one snowflake is alike.
All of this creates a winter wonderland.

Emily Dongilli, Grade 6

The Love Story

There once was a guy named Bruce
He was as ugly as a moose
He had a girlfriend named Mary
Whose legs where quite hairy
Bruce bought Mary a razor
Then Mary pulled out a tazer
Bruce started pushing and tapping
While Mary kept on zapping
Bruce yelled to Mary, "I didn't mean anything by that"
While Mary yelled back, "don't forget your hat"

John A. Justus, Grade 6

I Am a Confident Dancer

I am a talented young girl who dances
I wonder what dances I will learn
I hear music coming out of speakers, feet moving all over
the dance floor, and people dancing.
I want to be on a famous dance team when I'm older
I am a talented young girl who dances

I pretend that professional dancers are watching me dance
I feel so happy for me and my friends because we dance
I touch accessories I dance with
I worry about me falling during a dance in my recital
I am a talented young girl who dances

I understand that some steps will be hard
I say never ever give up
I dream of being a famous dancer
I try to do my best
I hope my dreams come true about becoming a better dancer
Gabrielle Beaulieu, Grade 5

Thanksgiving

Thank you
For all my tongue can taste
Moist mashed potatoes that are a fluffy blanket in my mouth
The scrumptious leftover Halloween candy
Aunt Sue's warm cookies right from the oven

Thank you
All my nose can smell
The delicious turkey roasting in the oven
The wood burning from the toasty fire
Each delightful dessert that one of us brought

Thank you
All my eyes can see
The terribly terrified turkey gobbling with fright
When everyone was trying to catch it for dinner
The immense feast on the table for us to dig in
Family members hugging as they walk in the door
Mackenzie Waite, Grade 6

My Dreams

My dreams look like a rainbow with many vivid colors,
like fiery orange, mint green, lavender purple
and so many others

My dreams smell sweet, like soft chocolate chip cookies
right out of the oven

They sound like a violin being played, so peaceful and gentle

My dreams feel like a soft, fluffy blanket
keeping me warm at night

They taste sweet, like chocolate melting in your mouth
Olga Pidruchna, Grade 5

Merry Christmas

Christmas is around the corner, it's almost here.
It's time to jump in the air and cheer.

Christmas time is the time to enjoy.
Sit back and play with your new toy.

Putting up your Christmas tree.
Spreading love and lots of glee.

Passing houses, looking at decorations.
Can't wait for Christmas because you have no patients.

Waiting for Santa to come to your house.
You can't catch him; he's as quiet as a mouse.

Playing in the freezing, glistening snow.
Time to turn on your Christmas lights and let them show.

Hearing Santa say, "Merry Christmas to all, and to all a good night."
Then disappear and is out of sight.
Janice Igbinobaro, Grade 6

Love

Love is man's best friend
A dog cuddling on your lap
Licking your nose with small kisses
Warming your heart
Never forgetting he understands "better than a human"

Love is a warm chocolate chip cookie
Straight from the oven
It keeps you feeling so loved
Holding a smile on your face

Love is a warm hug
On a cold day
A smile that will not go away
A safe place to run

Love is a fuzzy blanket
Keeping you warm
Good with hot cocoa
Melting away cold bitterness of the harsh winter
Morgan Bailey, Grade 6

A Bad Hair Day

I was walking down the street and my rubber band POPPED
My hair was so frizzy everybody stopped
To look at me
I said, I broke my rubber band so what am I going to do
I broke my rubber band so can I ask you
I just need some help PLEASE
I'm begging on my knees
So if you ever have a bad hair day
try not to stress and go play
Makira T., Grade 4

Baseball

I am a fearless guy who loves baseball.
I wonder if I will hit the ball.
I hear the crack of the bat and my footsteps
running towards first base, then second base.
I see the ball flying and zooming into the outfield.
I want to run around all the bases and score some runs.
I am a fearless guy who loves baseball.

I pretend that I swing and hit the ball.
I feel nervous when I go up to bat
hoping I will hit the ball.
I touch 1st, 2nd, 3rd, home.
I worry that I will not hit the ball at all.
I am a fearless guy who loves baseball.

I understand my coaches want me to hit.
I say okay, I will hit the ball.
I dream that I will hit it.
I try to swing at it.
I hope that I will hit the ball over the wall.
I am a fearless guy who loves baseball.

Jackson Ciesla, Grade 5

I Wish I Had the Chance

I wish I had the chance
to say I'm sorry
I know it would have meant
so much to you

I wish I had the chance
to dance in the rain
It would have been so beautiful
with the water hitting the ground
and feet tapping

I wish I had the chance
to go back in time
and laughed at that moment we spent together
It would have showed you
how much our friendship meant to me

Sometimes I wish I could have
gone back in time because now
you aren't here

Madyson Beckford, Grade 5

The Baseball Game

I want to be on a card like Roy Halladay.
I hit a home run every day.
When I'm up to the plate people will go wild.
Whack!
As the bat hits the ball into space past the cloud.
Then we win 20 to 6.
Then the ball won't return from space until 8:00 in the morning
while are playing another game.

Christian Velez, Grade 5

Time

Time is like sand
slipping through your outstretched fingers
time goes too fast, and it never seems to linger
time is a mixture of today, yesterday and tomorrow
time is something to grasp
not to fight over
nor to cry over
but to treat like a dolphin, and to adore, to give your soul to.
though you won't ever
ever, ever get it back
You just do it for love.

Are my fingers as slippery as a dolphin's smooth skin
so I can't hold on
to anything
for more than a second
before it falls, through the windows of time?
why does it fall?
can it not stay?
or is that something time will never,
ever, ever do,
even for me?

Mrinalini Wadhwa, Grade 6

Gymnastics

I am a fearless girl who loves gymnastics.
I wonder if I am good enough.
I hear my coaches clapping for me because
I just learned how to do a backhand spring.
I see kids running and jumping on the
spring board.
I want to be good enough to be in the
Olympics one day soon.
I am a fearless girl who loves gymnastics.

I pretend that I am in a higher level.
I feel nervous when I do my backhand spring
on floor.
I touch the big bronze trophy.
I worry about not being good enough to
make the team.
I say I can work harder.
I dream to be in the Olympics.
I try my hardest to improve.
I hope I am strong enough to be on the
team.
I am a fearless girl who loves gymnastics.

Asia McLaughlin, Grade 5

Forest

As I walk, I smell the moist mossy ground,
feel the wind as it blows gently across my face,
and hear the chirp, chirp of the blue birds.
I see trash on the mossy ground, and feel a tear on my cheek.
I walk back through the woods to my cottage.

Alexandria Wells, Grade 5

Birthday Wishes*

Wishes I keep to myself:
Wish I could be like my brother
and be strong as him, and as durable.

Wish I knew my great grandpa
so I could do puzzles with him,
and let him share his wisdom with me.

Wish I could lose my braces.
Wish I could walk away,
when my brothers pick a fight.

Wish my mother would stop
nagging me to make a choice,
when I don't know what to choose

Wish I had a monkey to hug when I'm sad
and climb trees with and be my friend
when no one else will

Wish I could do better in hard situations,
like when I'm bickering with my brothers.
So I could get more things done in less time.

Mostly I wish I could make decisions faster
so Mother can relax with a blanket and read;
she never has time for that.

Max Winneg, Grade 5
*Inspired by the book "Inside Out and Back Again"

Cool Air, Crisp Cider

Long blue pool covers going on as quickly as
Amber and gold leaves
Will soon cover the ground
The leaves drifting calmly
Where peaceful children
In a deep elongated slumber

Families in the cool, crisp air picking
Bright red juicy apples and gently placing them in an
Old, fading, wicker basket
While the family stomps in the
Crackling and crunching leaves

Customers wandering in the pumpkin patches wearing their
Fluffy, puffy coats while sipping there warm, sugary apple cider
And picking out a pumpkin
To turn into an enormous pumpkin, tempting pie

The bumpy, unique feeling and
Odd, creepy, color pallet of ugly shaped gourds
Make me have a spine tingling sensation

The luscious, sticky, tan toned caramel is as thick as
The guts and seeds from a fresh plump, orange pumpkin

Laurel Edwards, Grade 6

Teachers

Teachers are like books
They can open up and give you knowledge

They can entertain
And train your brain
To remember what's important

They give you the best
And you know the rest
They help you bump up your grade

So thank you to the teachers
Who remind me of good books
They provide me with great knowledge
They don't care about my looks
So thank you once again for all you teach to me
If I didn't learn from you
There's no telling where I'd be.

Ava Komasz, Grade 6

Maybe

Just because I smile doesn't mean I'm happy
Just because I laugh doesn't mean I'm carefree
Just because I get up every morning and start afresh
Doesn't mean that I don't sometimes want it to end

But I don't
Because I have
A family that loves me
Friends that care
Lots of people who will always be there
For me

And if I smile, I may not be happy
But maybe I will be
Maybe I'll be the way I want to
Maybe I'll start again
Maybe I'll put everything behind me
Maybe I'll smile because that's who I am

Olivia D'Angelo, Grade 6

The Joyful Boat Ride

The pirate danced daftly
Swaying swiftly to the music
Moving with the clouds
Waving his red hankie
Like he was a professional flamenco dancer

The wind blowing his friend's hair
They could all hear the boat fighting the current of the water

The mountain was speaking to them
"Come and climb me!"
They wouldn't listen
So they kept on having their joyful boat ride

Josh Grubb, Grade 4

What Is Autumn?
A utumn leaves falling down
U nder the leaves you can lounge
T urkey roasting in the oven
U nbelievable ruby reds and lemon yellows
M any families gather around
N othing stops us from greeting the town

T rees are growing from the ground
I nspecting leaves in the town
M any flowers start to grow
E at turkey and beef jerky
Jada Cruz, Grade 5

Energy Now and Forever
Plugs, wires, electricity,
So many sparks fly.
Chemistry lights our world.

Heat made with chemicals,
Electricity in the air,
At houses, schools, and chemistry labs

We run by electricity,
All TVs, computers, and more
Electricity, now and forever!
Makenzy Semelsberger, Grade 5

Hurricane
Whoosh! Splash!
I see a giant funnel cloud
hovering over the ocean
I hear a lightning bolt crack
It was as bright as the sun

I smell the salty sea water
as it rises higher and higher
I feel the humidity rising
I taste the salt as the water splashes
Whoosh! Splash!
Jocelyn Eber, Grade 6

My Golden Retriever
I love my dog
He's the heart of the house
My dog is so pretty
Beautiful moments fill my mind
When you're with him
you feel a spirit run through your body
He has a beautiful golden face
He's glowing heaven as he strikes the earth
He's a little bit of everything to me
He's a dream of brightness
and he's a wonderful little treasure!
Kayla Pike, Grade 4

The Different Types
As I see them dance
I say
One day
I will be just like them
Jazz
As you dance you feel
The beats and go with it
Tap
You hear the sound of the
Metal hit the floor.
Hip-Hop
Jump side to side and shake
Production
A little bit of everything
So get ready to bounce
Lyrical
Quiet, graceful and smooth
Just stay on your toes
Now that's my little bit of
Advice, because I love dance.
Chloe Cooperrider, Grade 4

I Am
I am young and powerful
I wonder why whales are so big
I hear the dolphins chattering
I see the whales coming up to breathe
I want to work with dolphins
I am young and powerful

I pretend to train dolphins
I feel that dolphin hunting should stop
I touch the whales
I worry that dolphins will go extinct
I cry when whales wash up on the beach
I am young and powerful

I understand that people eat dolphin meat
I say that all child abuse should stop
I dream the dolphins will never go extinct
I try to stop all of the child hunger
I hope that all of the wars will end
I am young and powerful
Kaylee Perreault, Grade 6

A Star's Life
The stars wake up on the gloomy nights.
They shine like a glowing moon.
They go to sleep when they see sunlight.
They know they'll be waking soon.

The stars waken bright.
They spy on people's dreams.
They shine with all their might.
That is a star's life scheme.
Sonali Singh, Grade 5

Broccoli Mom
She is sweet, she is kind,
We talk all the time,
Her hair is black,
She is part of a family tree,

She makes delicious food,
She is beautiful inside and out,
She can be mean sometimes,

It's green, it's delicious,
It's small but, grows tall,
It's healthy, it can be smelly,
It can turn into a flower,

I really like both of them
And you would too and this is
About my broccoli mom.
Isabel Fonseca, Grade 5

Fall Has Come
Fall has come
No longer is it warm or sunny
But it is time for school
The weather is cool
And the trees turn bare

It is in fall
That you must roam the halls
Of the school
It isn't time to wear tank tops or shorts
For you are no longer at a resort

The trees are changing
And your classes have been arranged
The weather will be colder
But you can always wait for spring
For fall has come
Leah Homan, Grade 6

When Years Go By
I wonder why when years go by,
Nothing is different,
You do not feel taller,
Nor do you feel shorter,
It feels the same as last year,
There's nothing special
So I wonder why,
Why do years go by,
You feel something has changed,
But think about it,
You will find the sad truth,
Nothing has changed,
Everybody will find this,
Now there can only be one question,
Why do years go by?
Haajar Ahmad Ali, Grade 6

Bear
Bear
Black, white
Caring, sleeping, eating
They look very fluffy
Panda
Olivia Adams, Grade 5

Cobra
Cobra
Long, scaly
Biting, slithering, hiding
Bathing in the sun
Snake
Tyler DellaRocco, Grade 5

Humphrey
Humphrey
Small, nice
Nibbling, squeaking, daring
Brown and white fur
Hamster
Ben Heasley, Grade 5

Softball
Softball
Fun, hard
Throwing, catching, running
Strike the team out
Sport
Brooke Altman, Grade 5

Ray Rice
Ray Rice
Short, fast
Catching, speeding, playing
Raven's running back
Sportsman
Kunaal Mathur, Grade 5

America
America
Industrious, democratic
Protecting, freeing, progressing
A land of liberty
USA
Jakob Taylor, Grade 5

Describing Flowers
Flowers have bloomed,
Some are doomed.
Many wash away,
Picked all day.
Information was consumed.
Christina Adams, Grade 6

Gymnastics
I am a crazy girl who loves gymnastics
I wonder if I will win medals
I hear the crowd cheering for me while I am preparing for my pass at my meet
I see me in the future winning a gold medal
I want to win the Olympic gold medal in gymnastics one day
I am a crazy girl who loves gymnastics

I pretend that I am at the Olympics winning
I feel confident in myself that I will win the Olympic gold medal someday
I touch gold medals in gymnastics
I worry that I will not make it to the Olympics
I am a crazy girl who loves gymnastics

I understand if I cannot make it
I say that I will win
I dream of going to the Olympics
I hope I am a star in gymnastics one day
I am a crazy girl who loves gymnastics
Carly Carroll, Grade 5

Colorful Autumn
No more hot grains of sand under my feet
Now its orange and red leaves from the trees
I see horrific Halloween pumpkins waiting patiently to scare
Frightening kids dressed up in funky costumes dashing from door to door
The aroma of scrumptious pumpkin pie on the window
The sounds of crashing helmets on enjoyable football

Cheerful words of gratitude on Thanksgiving
Crisp, cool breezy winds brushing against my face
Tender juicy turkey with gravy everyone's craving to eat
Thick sticky caramel candy apples waiting to be eaten
Everyone hears loud screaming kids on the crunching leaves
I see bright leaves looking like pumpkins
Cold kids dress in fluffy, puffy cozy jackets to stay warm
Football addicts see football helmets crashing is a tree falling over
Everyone sees bright colored leaves falling off beautiful trees
Come on winter bring it on!!
Michael Shannon, Grade 6

The Wonderful Town of Oakdale
My neighborhood is a quiet place on the bay like a deserted island in the middle of the Atlantic Ocean.

My neighborhood is an interesting town because of the small shops, and restaurants on the water with their tantalizing seafood.

My neighborhood is a haven where everyone is welcomed and can enjoy themselves by swimming, biking, fishing, and having fun.

And it is the perfect place to inhale fresh air and take a brisk bike ride on the bumpy road to Byron Lake Park.

And it is an extraordinary neighborhood where everyone has a fantastic time working, learning, and especially relaxing.
Ryan Kemp, Grade 6

High Merit Poems – Grades 4, 5, and 6

I Am From
I am from a weekend sports to my goal to practice
To be the best that I can do and can't do
To go to the limit
To try my best that I can
I am from my mom, dad and sister helping me
Working at the kitchen table
Working from one place to another
I am from getting respect from my sister
Responsibility from my dad
And courage from my mom
I am from my home
The smells and sounds from the kitchen
The sounds from the living room
The feeling from being in my room
Warm and cold at the same time
I am from my home
Respect from my parents and sister
Working in the kitchen every day
My athletic in sports
This is where I am from
Jonathan Lachman, Grade 6

Moon
The moon an eye watching over the world
Whoosh the wind blows as if it has a spirit
On earth I sit watching the sky taking it in and I wait waiting
Silence is what I hear as if a mute button turned off the world
The world's gentle feeling

Stars seem to become 1 person, the moon like a mountain in the sky
I am I and they are themselves
I wait in my word, feeling the power of a ruler
Stars are my people, the moon is king
The sky was my eye, and the world is my statue
But I am the sky, I am the leader of my world

I tell my thoughts to the sky, wind blows in response
I think a thought over and over again
I am me and they are themselves, I am me and they are themselves
Found in my own world of thoughts, thinking stars are my people
The moon is king, the sky is my eye, and the world is my statue
I am me and they are themselves, pushed away from a sunny day
They are themselves, I am me, free
Hannah Verdun, Grade 6

The Tree
I went to the store to buy a tree.
There was a perfect one in front of me.
It had a letter on it.
Everything got better.
I took it home and put candy canes on it.
It was past my bedtime.
The lights on the tree still shine all night.
Santa will come to bring toys for good people.
Next Christmas I will think twice.
Tyrone Barnes, Grade 4

Volcanoes
Burn everything to a crisp.
Devour things such as trees and rocks.
Shoot out blazing hot magma that slithers slowly
down your side like a snake.
Melt rocks and send trees up into a huge fiery flame.
Don't worry if your magma hardens into a solid rock, remember
you still have much more in your below ground chamber.
Just try your best to avoid water,
It can harden your magma much faster!
Noah Mikkelson, Grade 5

Autumn
Autumn means the sun is getting dull,
The leaves are changing red, yellow
The wind has a bitter twist to it.
The animals are making their homes for winter.
It's time for picking pumpkins
The nights are getting colder
The days are getting shorter
Today is Summer
Tomorrow is autumn.
Jason Catalano, Grade 4

Red Sun Set
It's a red sun set, in early spring.
One red sun set is no big deal to a person.
But to sailors it's a big deal.
A red sun set means the next day would be perfect day for sailing.
You can hear water rustling and fish splashing.
You can smell flowers too.
You can feel the mild wind against your skin.
A beautiful red sun set delights sailors.
So, should I be red or a different color (pink, orange, or purple)?
Lydia Rosiek, Grade 4

Halloween
H orrifying masks
A wesome candy in our bags
L aughing all around
L ots of kids in costumes
O ur family eating candy at the end of the night
W atching toddlers trot in their cute costumes
E veryone is dressed
E ating lots of candy
N ighttime is the time for Halloween
Ashley Davis, Grade 6

Wrestling Is My Life
I put my headgear on
Dreams of greatness go around in my head
I've got a charm
I said, "I can win this"
I said to myself, "when I lose faith, I lose everything"
I wrestle because it's my life, that's why
It's a family tradition
Eric Alderfer, Grade 4

A Celebration of Poets – East Grades K-6 Fall 2013

Summer
S ummer is the best
U nder the water at the beach
M e and my uncle surfing the big waves
M y favorite time of the year
E xcited about eating ice cream in the hot summer sun
R iding my bike down to the lake
Xzayvier Davis, Grade 5

Sad
Sad is dark blue
It sounds like rain drops tapping on the window
It smells like damp air
It tastes like cold meat
It looks like an empty room
Sad feels like a cool breeze
Soraya Reamon, Grade 5

An Apple in the Tree
I sat under a cool and shady tree
As the wind blew by, an apple fell on me.
This apple wasn't big it was red and smooth too.
I just went inside and mom said what did you do.
An apple, an apple, an apple I said,
It really hurt my head.
Stephanie DiMeo, Grade 4

My Grandmother Is:
Great at making sweets like cookies and pies.
Great at telling stories about when she was as young as me.
A wonderful baby-sitter.
A great listener and can keep a secret.
Loving, caring, and a great cook.
Miranda Gibson, Grade 6

I Am
I am creative and fun.
I wonder what I will build out of Legos.
I hear Legos like waves while I am searching.
I see all different Legos.
I want to become a Lego designer.
Gabriel Rosser, Grade 5

Dogs
Dogs bark as loud as someone banging pots and pans together.
Barking, chasing, and jumping.
This is all giving me a headache.
But once you see their sweet face,
It will be all worth it.
Emily Cozzone, Grade 5

Friendship
Friendship is like gold
So never break up
Or your gold will be taken away
So don't make enemies
Shreya Bathula, Grade 5

Grandparents Are…
Full of stories waiting to be told.
The warm feeling in my heart.
Funny and sometimes silly.
Watching the news, wheel of fortune, and jeopardy.
Full of love, endlessly being given.
Leah Shields, Grade 6

Sting Pong
It's about…

Bouncing balls
swinging paddles

It's about…

Sometimes unfair calls
and very deadly battles

It's about…

Friendly brawls
If you lose, you'd better skedaddle

It's about…

Free for all's
If you win, you'll be soaring

It's about…

Hitting plastic balls
Your skin red and stinging

It's about…

A challenge
The most painful paddle game in the world!
Ryan Lenkaitis, Grade 5

Red
Red is a rose,
Gentle and sweet.
Red sounds like a rock song,
Can you hear the beat?
It looks large like a lion,
And as small as a mouse.
Red is the bricks,
Making up a cozy house!
Red is here, there,
And almost anywhere!
Red can be rough and loud,
As a rowdy crowd.
But it can be sweet and soft,
Like the love in your heart!
Red is red!
Emma Celaj, Grade 5

High Merit Poems – Grades 4, 5, and 6

Our World
This is our world
Given to us to share
It won't last
If we don't care
I see blue skies
I see green trees
There are deer in the fields
There are cars in the streets
Now there are plows in the fields
Now there are deer in the streets
Such mistakes we are making
It is not just ours for the taking
We pollute the water
We pollute the air
Please stop
This is not fair
Please care
Please share
Isabella Mohrey, Grade 6

Spring
I see…
rain drops
through the window
drip drop
then I see the bright sun
ya!

I feel…
the wet grass on my feet
slipping while playing tag
with Kate and Sydney.

I hear…
the rain on the roof
drip
drop
Then I hear
boom crash!
Brooke Shrock, Grade 6

Fall
September nudges summer out of the air
Children go back to school
And the peace and quiet will
Begin.
October shakes the trees for leaves to fall
Children run and play trying to catch
The twirling leaves
Beautiful colors gleam
In the sun.
November calls all
Turkeys for Thanksgiving
Everyone is here to celebrate
The Thanksgiving feast.
Emily Kauffeld, Grade 4

Apple Mom
Her hair is brown, her eyes are blue
Her heart is huge; loves the color pink
She has an awesome personality
She has a tasteful style and is always
funny

It's sweet and sour at the same time
Red, yellow, and green, bursting with
Flavor
Juicy and tasteful, delicious and yummy
The best when fresh and ripe

Both very sweet
They both are tasteful in a way
They both are nice
I also love them both
Kendal Blevins, Grade 5

O Christmas Time
The Christmas bulbs o' so round,
Getting the trees right out of the ground.
Ornaments of different shapes,
Giving Santa cookies or crepes.
To me, eggnog tastes bad,
Getting coal is very sad.
The Christmas songs, o' so sweet,
On Christmas, I eat loaves of meat.
Snowflakes, o' so cool,
In Deck the Halls, it tells of the Great Yule.
Two people under mistletoe,
Santa Claus says "Ho, Ho, Ho!"
My mom likes to decorate,
My presents are o' so great.
On my shirt I try not to get a smear,
Thank you all, for a wonderful year!
Bryce Jaworski, Grade 4

I Am
I am pretty and athletic.
I wonder if I will be famous.
I hear bad things happen.
I want to become a singer.
I am pretty and athletic.
I pretend I am a singer.
I feel happy and glad.
I touch the sky sometimes.
I worry about my family.
I cry about my mom and dad.
I am pretty and athletic.
I understand it isn't safe out here.
I say we should stop it.
I dream that I will be famous.
I hope that there will be peace.
I am pretty and athletic.
Camryn Robinson, Grade 5

Dreams Are…
Dreams are
rainbows that make the world colorful
Dreams are
as red as rose petals raining from
above me
Dreams are
as orange as the autumn leaves falling
from the trees
Dreams are
as yellow as the sun on
a bright sunny day
Dreams are
as green as grass when you walk
through the fields
Dreams are
as blue as the sky on a cloudless morning
Dreams are as indigo as
the ocean as you stand there
waiting for a wave to hit your feet
Dreams fill the sky with hope
Justice Jones, Grade 5

Things I See
Collecting pollen, 20-bees
Losing leaves, 19-trees
On some feet, 18-socks
Lined up so neat, 17-rocks
Drinking milk, 16-cats
On a rack, 15-hats
Went flying by, 14-planes
Went rolling by, 13-trains
Writing on paper, 12-pencils
In a shop, 11-utensils
In their coop, 10-hens
On a desk, 9-pens
On a plate, 8-cherries
On a tree, 7-berries
In a bush, 6-grapes
In a jungle, 5-apes
For dessert, 4-pies
Went by, 3-flies
On a road, 2-moose
On a train, 1-caboose
John Fox, Grade 5

My Report
I have a report
that is due tomorrow.
I need an idea
of what to write.
I'm stuck in this room
until I finish.
I am still waiting.
Wait, what's the date?
Oh no! I'm late!
Rachel How, Grade 5

I Am
I am funny and kind
I wonder why people bully
I hear scratches
I want people to stop bullying
I am funny and kind

I pretend to draw well
I feel that people should stop littering
I touch silverware every day
I worry about people littering
I cry when rabbits die
I am funny and kind

I understand money doesn't grow on trees
I say no bullying allowed
I dream of being a teacher when I get older
I try to stop fights from happening
I hope people won't litter someday
I am funny and kind
Kaitlynn Lane, Grade 6

Who She Is
This is the time
You came to life
Age by age you've grown
From a daughter
To a mother
To a grandmother

You are the one
The most caring one
The one who stands out bold
Strong, loving, and beautiful
No one can beat you at all

I see you there for others
Affectionate too
You are the best cook
Just the same way you look
I hope you have a great day
Enjoy 70!
Rhea Iyer, Grade 6

Rainstorm
The loud rain
hitting the ground
while I sit inside

Cold drops smell like mud
coming from dirt
the cold air

Standing in the window
feel the wetness
come to my hands.
Ryder Knierman, Grade 6

It's About Gymnastics
It's about taped ankles
Wrist guards
Grips

It's about tumbling hard
Swinging on the bars
Transforming to a star

It's about going to the Olympics
Winning the gold
Something I will forever hold

It's about trying new drills
Getting better skills
You just have to trust in your coach

It's about hanging with your friends
They will help you get to the end
Working with your team

It's about chasing your dreams
Giving one hundred percent
On every single event

It's about what is in my heart
Meghan Hart, Grade 5

It's About
It's about…
Feeling the sand in between your toes
Making sand castles

It's about…
Diving through the waves
Riding the waves on your boards

It's about …
Having a sand ball fight
Digging the biggest hole ever

It's about…
Having a boat ride
Feeling the water on your face

It's about…
Taking night walks
Pretending you're the lifeguard

It's about…
Tubing on the back of a boat
Trying to get up on the water skis

It's about my favorite vacation ever!
Dani Panati, Grade 5

It's About…
It's about the colors
the splotches of green
and bits of sunbeam

It's about the termites and ants
upon the rain forest's plants
is what they'd call home

It's about poison and leaps
and croaks and creeps
and the little frog's feet

It's about the amphibian I love
Travis Tillman, Grade 5

The Time Has Come
The one bright, yellow, abandoned leaf
Finally ready to leave its home
To go with his family

When the leaf falls and the sun
Is behind it
They blend in
You never knew that the
Bright as the yellow sun leaf fell

All I know about that falling leaf
Is that summer is gone
Fall is here
Jack Chaput, Grade 6

Boston Bruins
B ig and brave
O utrageous and outstanding
S trong and super
T eamwork and chemistry
O ne and only
N ever letting each other down

B east mentality
R ocket speed
U nderestimated
I ncredible toughness
N o one will beat them
S taying strong
Brendan Willett, Grade 6

Shih-Tzu vs Turtle
Shih-Tzu
Small, black
Barking, running, playing
House, shelter, ocean, land
Waddling, tucking, spinning
Green, round
Turtle
Nicholas Davan, Grade 6

High Merit Poems – Grades 4, 5, and 6

Hitler
Opposed to
Letting
Other
Colors, religions,
And
Unharmful people
Stay and live
There in Germany
Haley O'Reilly, Grade 6

Friends
Friends are always there for you
They cheer you up when you're feeling blue
Friends are always on your side
They will never run and hide
Friends will always share their food
They put you in a better mood
Friends can call you on the phone
They will help you feel less alone
Abby Thompson, Grade 5

That Time of Year
The fire is warm,
the gingerbread is sweet,
outside it is cold
with children in the snow.

A train is running on the
track under a tree.
Christmas is here.
Michael Ellis, Grade 4

Purple
Purple is as wise as wise can be.
The wise man wears his purple robe,
Listening silently.
How wise.
Does he know of the dangers coming?
Purple.
The epitome of sagacity.
Royal
Harley Robinson, Grade 6

Chameleon
Your colors can be bright or dark
Depending on your environment.
Whether you're on a log or flower
It's as if you aren't there at all.
You see all predators coming
With your independent eyesight.
Your tongue is like a sticky bullet
For catching flies and other insects.
Noah Hessler-Burdick, Grade 6

The Fire
Two years ago there was a fire.
The fire got higher and higher.
When I took a look
It was brighter than the sun.
Sixty people were in that building.
I knew I had to help.
I called 911.
They came as quickly as they could.
So did the firemen.
But I went out and watched
Because I saved sixty lives.
I was proud.
Jennifer Adu, Grade 4

Ode to Whipped Cream
Oh, whipped cream,
You make my taste buds scream
You are so good,
You put me in a good mood.
When I run out of whipped cream,
It just makes me dream
Of when I used you on pie
But when you're gone it makes me cry.
Who can live without you?
Not me, not even Tru Moo!
This is my ode to whipped cream
And I love you on ice-cream!
Matthew Alfrey, Grade 4

Black
Shadowed and silent, black sneaks in,
Powerful as brown,
Yet sad as blue,
Aggressive as Red,
And sagacious as purple.

Sneaky,
    Sullen,
      Saddened,
        Spying,
Black is an infinite,
Spiral.
Jason Choi, Grade 6

Taking a Walk
I had a fish whose name was Mike
And one day I took him on a hike,
I scooped him up out of the bowl
And then I took him on a stroll,
Around the park we did walk,
With Mike in hand people did gawk,
For them it must have been quite a shock
To see a girl taking a fish for a walk,
Mike and I were just hitting our stride,
When I realized that poor fish had died.
Kelsey Shearon, Grade 6

Halloween
It's Halloween night
Filled with fright
Kids trick or treating
On the ghosts you will be meeting
Pumpkins everywhere
Give a good scare
Sore tummies
dead mummies
Witches will be flying
Ghosts will be crying
Frankenstein awakens
Are you shaken
Happy Halloween!!
Stacia Collins, Grade 5

Cancer Stinks!
The cells increase and sing an angry tune
They punch the body in slow motion
Then you start to realize you feel like junk
That your body is in a commotion

Going to war with yourself
Like Master Chief when his suit is broken
But your ammo doesn't work
Good wishes, just a token

Battles aren't just with guns
Survival is the only way
That's just the resolution.
Ian Cauwenbergh, Grade 6

The Holocaust
The Holocaust made the Jews run
When Hitler once blocked up the sun.
Jews that scream and cry
Making them leave and dye.
Sticking Jews in dirty camps
Camps that was all cold and damp.
Making Jews starve to death
But Jews had hope and one last breath.
Jews huddle together
Hoping the Holocaust wouldn't last forever.
Finally the Holocaust was al set and done
When out came the shining sun.
Melanie Weatherspoon, Grade 6

Cupcakes
C ute
U nbelievably delicious
P erfect
C ake
A mazing
K ind to your taste buds
E xtraordinary
S weet
Alanna Herrey, Grade 6

Hurricane

Reigning from his castle of clouds,
The King of Thunder sends his troops into battle.
With shields of ice,
His first fleet,
Sleet,
Flies to the ground,
Breaking windows,
Denting cars,
Then retreats back to the castle.
Then,
The sinister,
Silent,
Evil Eye stares down on Earth,
Perched high up in his small nest of sky.
Then, giving the King orders,
He commands the sea to rise,
Flooding the Earth,
In destruction and misery,
Until the King of Thunder loses his energy, and finally falls.
Though the mighty King of Thunder has fallen
He bares a scar on Earth that will last a lifetime.

Andrew Brinton, Grade 6

The Beach

warm, soothing sand
crawling between my toes
the gentle breeze

                the sun's blistering heat
              slowly sucking the moisture
                     out of your body

the waves like dominos, tipping on forever
    SPLASH! CRASH!
    SPLASH! CRASH!

                the refreshing sensation
                     of cool water
                     on your skin

spectacular seashells on the ocean floor,
    extraordinary colors, shapes
        and sizes

                     sand castles
                     as high as the sky,
                     limitless

admire the beauty,
   gaze at the spectacle,
      witness the astounding sunset

Kendall Satcowitz, Grade 6

My Hamster

My hamster is soft and adorable
She makes me warm and giggly
At night she is on her very squeaky wheel
She goes crazy on her wheel
When I look at her she quickly changes direction
In the morning she looks worn out
But very peacefully sleeping

Isaac, Grade 4

Dance

I put on my sneakers
Pull up my hair
Run to get my water
Make sure my laces are tied and tight
Out the door I go
Right when I get inside and start to dance
I feel like I can do anything
When the loud music pounds
My passion emerges me
I kick my leg higher than my head
Spinning more than I can count
I spin
Jump
Twirl
And it allows me to be myself
Someone who doesn't care
What other people think
And I know this is what I love to do
When I dance
I don't have to worry if I don't do it right
Because in dance I can be free to express myself

Danielle Wender, Grade 6

The Run

I'm on deck
My friends up
I think
Wouldn't it be awesome if I got a POW
My friend hits it
I'm up — bases loaded — pitcher pitches
I close my eyes for a sec
I open my eyes
I swing, POW, I did it
I get a grand slam, my team is cheering
The announcer says P.N.B. wins 26 to 17
My team comes over and lifts me up
Afterwards the coach says you kids deserve ice cream
The team yells yes!
We all have a drink
The coach says cheers to the undefeated team for 3 years
Cheers, said the team
I say this is the best day of my life
I am happy I got a grand slam and got ice cream
That day I got home and went straight to bed
My mom said time for bed little one

Dillon Schumaker, Grade 4

Santa

This night I'm shaking in fright
that he just might visit me tonight
I think of the years when I was in tears
that he wasn't here to share Christmas cheer
But tonight I can feel that my pain will be healed
that a present will be sealed
for me to unwrap under the Christmas tree

Jonathan Clark, Grade 5

A Grandparent Is…
A wake up hug.
A place to snug.
A big fat kiss.
Something not to miss.
A buncha love.
Rhea Malhotra, Grade 6

Christmas
There were cookies that made me numb
And all that was left was a crumb
And as far as you can see
I am as happy as can be
Now that Christmas has come
Kathrine Yeaw, Grade 6

Vianca
Vianca
Beautiful, kind
Playing, loving, laughing
We always share smiles
Friend
Kelsey Reynolds, Grade 5

Jack
Jack
Creepy, fast
Flying, staring, scaring
He comes out anytime
Ghosts
Samuel Stitz, Grade 5

Moon
The moon shines
bright you can see
it through the
night
Aubrianna Bythrow, Grade 5

Math
Delightful, relaxing
Dividing, adding, subtracting, multiplying
Makes you a lot smarter
Geometry
Braden Ryan, Grade 4

Sad Inside
Whispers are heard
But for he who cries
Is sad inside
Jackson Wilson, Grade 6

Grey Wolf
Cassandra is a lone wolf.
She is as mysterious as the moon.
She likes reading, singing and texting.
Cassandra Arencibia, Grade 6

How Would You Feel?
How would you feel if you were in those death camps?
How would you feel if you were crying for help, being tortured?

How would you feel if you were one of those people,
those screaming and crying?

How would you feel if your friend didn't help you, if they betrayed you?

How would you feel if you were Jewish, and others just stood by,
while you dealt with all that torture, no one wants to help?

How would you feel if you were buying something for your family, but got shot for that?

Do you remember your friends being with you…well, now they are gone.
You should've done something when you had the chance…

How would you feel if you were part of the Nazi Party,
but your family was Jewish and you weren't — would you turn them in?

Do you idolize Adolf Hitler? He killed six million Jews and started the holocaust.
How would you feel if someone killed six million of your people?

How would you feel if you were living there in the year 1933 and you were Jewish?
You probably would've ended up dead… or worse.

How would you feel if you were hiding like Anne Frank
and died in a concentration camp of Typhus, just like she did?

How would you feel if you were hungry, sweaty and tired…
then, finally, the rescuers came — to be happy on that bright, sunny day
when it finally was all over — How would you feel?
Sasha Gabrie, Grade 5

Colors of Fall
Birds no longer chirping, awaking me from my deep sleep,
In their place, rattling leaves and empty bird's nests,
Clinging to trees, as if the ground was hot lava
Putting on a cozy sweater,
So the cool autumn winds can't get to my already shivering body,
Making my way own a cobble path,
Leaves falling ot the ground ever so often,
Making a crunch, crunch, crunch noise under my booths
Thinking about the mouthwatering turkey being served on Thanksgiving,
And remembering the just recently passing Halloween,
While the wind blows my hair over my face,
I look up to see the sun quickly sinking, as if it were in quick sands,
The sky turning a mix of oranges and pinks,
As I start making my way to my house,
Kicking a pebble, and avoiding stepping on the gold, orange, red and brown leaves,
The pebble, a baby's rattle cutting through the silence
The cold breeze continuing, a white crystal dropping here and there, irking certain people,
The serene, calming silence not ending, except for the occasional lone
bird trying to catch up with the rest of the flock,
But then a single white crystal, a snowflake,
Gently drifts down from the sky, landing on my nose
Colleen DiMarzo, Grade 6

Green

Green
Is like the trees
And the growing grass
Parts of the Irish flag are green
The color of my eyes
The tip of my pencil
I feel green right after
A long Halloween
The color of my
Favorite book is green
Some Irish potatoes taste green
Money is green
My art box has a green crayon
My favorite drink and mascot of
The Phillies baseball team
It is the color of a
Nice green tea and
A candle on top of my TV
Mmm, mmm, mmm, nice freshness
Of a green lime
Joseph Scanlon, Grade 5

Red

Red is the lipstick
On a girl's lips.

Red is the soda can
That sometimes you sip.
Red is like the devil
On Halloween night.

Red is your face when
Someone gives you a fright.

Sometimes red is
Like a rose.
Red is flicker, flicker
Like the fire goes.

Red is the stop at
The light, not the start.
Red is the color of my
Ever-beating heart!
Lauren Metro, Grade 5

Summer

Stinging rays of sun
like hot tea
shooting onto my back
and painfully striking my legs.

Suddenly I was on fire.
The hot sun rays
took me by surprise.
I laughed as I looked up.
Hannah Manning, Grade 6

Shimmering Night

Motionless sky
As colorful as a strawberry pie
The sunset has arrived.
Waiting for the stars to arrive
Here it is the diamonds in the sky
Reflecting off one an other
Here it comes
The giant hunk of Swiss cheese
That beautiful moon
Shaped like a crescent
Again
That amazing rainbow sherbet ice cream
Sitting there
In the sky waiting
For the
Giant ball of fire
Goodbye
Night
Natalia Angelis, Grade 5

What Is Happening?

Jews being mistreated
Thrown out of school.
Treated like animals.
Nobody caring about the Jews.

What is happening?
Bystanders just watching.
Jews being picked up by Nazi soldiers.
Sent to death camps.
Hitler giving orders to kill.

What is happening?
Jews dying, but still not losing hope.
Some are sent to death marches.
Some are just left in the ghettos
Jews are afraid and in hiding.
Why is this happening?
What is happening?
Christian Voloshen, Grade 6

Yellow

The hot sun is yellow
So is a smooth banana
And a sour lemon is yellow, too
Yellow is quiet
Like a good book
Or a tiny mouse
Yellow tastes sweet
Like delicious Sunny-D
And sweet like chewy Laffy Taffy
Yellow feels hot like an iron
Or the sun beating down on me
It feels smooth like a napkin in my hand
Yellow can brighten your day!
Beneé Arrington, Grade 4

Rapid Rollercoaster

All the roller-coasters rapidly
Twist and turn
When I get in my senses shiver
My heart is beating like lightning
Feel like I'm going to scream
I'm in a temple of heat
Move like a golden jet
I'm removed from the cart
Struck the earth
Lay in the sun
And rise
Liam Kelly, Grade 4

Angry Elephants

A student sits in class
eight long hours
doing mountains of work
at least a trillion a day

One thing after another
one book after another

When it's time to switch classes
the hallways are like
a big stampede of angry elephants
Ava Fard, Grade 6

Rainforest

Magical beauty
Scorching humidity
The breath of the Earth
The dream life
Home to native tribes

Unique animals
Crystal waters
A dazzling sight
Bountiful fruits
Amazing life
Steven Scanlon, Grade 6

Video Games

V ideo game players
I n my living room
D estroying battle ships
E xploding because of missiles
O ut of the game with my bro

G runts I hear when zombies appear
A ngelius is playing his awesome games
M y life is like a video game
E aster eggs I find that shock my mind
S omething fun to do these days
Angelius Roman, Grade 5

Sing It Loud

I am a courageous girl who loves singing.
I wonder if I will become famous.
I hear the people screaming my name when I
do karaoke at summer camp on the stage.
I see the people in the audience cheering me on.
I want to become a famous singer like my
idol, Taylor Swift.
I am a courageous girl who loves singing.

I pretend I am Selena Gomez singing on stage.
I feel excited to let my feelings out when
I am up on stage.
I touch the shiny black microphone.
I worry I am going to mess up on the stage.
I am a courageous girl who loves singing.

I understand I will mess up sometimes.
I say the breathtaking rhyming lyrics.
I dream I will become a famous singer.
I try my hardest every time.
I hope that people will like my voice when
I sing.
I am a courageous girl who loves singing.

Avery Henley, Grade 5

The World of Wondering Math!

Math facts are basic,
Strategies to problem solve.
Kinds of math problems
word
number
2 digit by 1 digit,
3 digit by 1 digit.
There is a wondering world of math out there.
You know some math problems, some you don't.
Looking for mathematic words to explain.
If you read this, you might be in the math hall of fame.
Math helps make science easier.
Math is needed for many things.

Colby Stough, Grade 4

Black

Black is the color of shadows, hiding behind people.
The color of crows flying over fields.
A color that tastes like smoke and sounds like "Thriller."
A color that feels hard and makes you afraid.
It is the color of the night sky on Halloween.
The color of the lights—turned off.
A color that feels warm and sounds scary.
The color of clouds when a big storm comes.
The color of tires going down the road.
The color of ink on a paper.
A color that sounds like a fire and feels rough.
The color of haunted houses so super scary.
That is black!

Michael Nittoli, Grade 4

Fall Is Here

Fall is here,
It's the best time of year!
Leaves are falling,
Kids are calling!
Raking leaves in a pile,
We'll jump in it in a while!
Scarecrows are being put up,
While pumpkins are being lit up!
Smelling pumpkin cookies in Nanny's house,
While playing with her cat, Mouse!
Kids are getting their costumes on,
And saying, "Let's get the groove on!"
And now it's time to go,
As Mom is saying, "Let's go!"
Getting lots of candy,
Makes me dandy!
When we are done,
I'll say "That was a lot of fun!"
And that is why I love fall,
It's the best season of all!

Madison McDunnah, Grade 5

A Holocaust Child

I was sleeping one night, with fear in my head.
I woke up in a train and heard rumors
That we would all be dead.

My body was half Jewish, and the other half pain.
I was frightened where we'd be taken
On these horrible freight trains.

We arrived at the camps, worried and all.
Every lost soul was thinking, would we survive
Or would we fall?

I held my mother tight, and let loose most of my fright.
As we got separated, I saw a bright light.

I went into a tank, and my beating heart sank.
The kids were running around, as my heart continued to pound.

Then pellets came from the holes up top.
I began to feel my body drop.

Daniel Tripodi, Grade 6

Snowflakes Are

Snowflakes are white raindrops that fall
high from the sky.

Snowflakes are the buckets of paint that top
a mountain's crest.

Snowflakes are the sign that winter is coming.
Snowflakes are the beautiful white puffs that
cover everything.

Ed Clark, Grade 5

The Sea

The sea leaps into the darkness
It wants to touch the sky
Dawn will break soon though
The sun and moon whisper
Remembering the dreams
Sleep will come soon for moon

It cries for light
Sun is what it needs
To see how to reach the sky
Again it tries, again and again

The light is soon to come
Dusk is settling in for rest
The sun shall lull it to sleep
Dusk is no longer listening though
It has gone to sleep for a longer time

The sea leaps
It has succeeded
The sea dances with joy
It can now teach the others
Darrah Young, Grade 5

Emma and I

Emma, two months older than me
Always wears a jacket that is fuzzy
Either tired or crazy
Dirty blond hair that's wavy
Her favorite sport is volleyball
In a toilet she dropped a clay ball
She makes a comment on everything
Emma is an awesome human being

I am not the noisy sort
Soccer is my favorite sport
My favorite colors are light greens
I like to wear comfy jeans
I like to read anywhere
I have light straight blond hair
A teacher is what I want to be
My first name is Kaydee

We are different as well as the same
Through our troubles we share the blame
In our lives there are many bends
Emma and I are best friends
Kaydee Stant, Grade 6

Colorful Leaves

Autumn
Cool scarlet sky
Falling and drifting leaves
Exciting family gatherings
Harvest
Sid Kapoor, Grade 4

What Is This Outside My Window?

What is this outside my window?
All I see is a bird,
But in my heart I feel something different.

What is this outside my window?
A symbol of peace
Calm, content, relaxed.
A sign from God
Showing me I can have peace in my life.

What is this outside my window?
Protecting her young,
Like a fearless warrior.
As the Black Bird attacked
She did not move, she did not stir.
Strong, resilient, steady
— A Lesson.

What is this outside my window?
I will witness the joy of
A New Life.
A fresh start,
a new beginning.
Hope.
Thomas Petrucci, Grade 6

We Remember

As time passes on, we think to ourselves
"Oh what a wonderful life we have!"
Some don't know this life
We remember

Someone thought certain people
Were not good enough
That beliefs were everything
We remember

Hitler believed in a perfect world
That Jews were horrible
That they didn't deserve to live
We remember

11 million people dead
11 million people gone
11 million lives mourned
We remember

People just like you and me
Kids, adults, elders, everyone
Because of one man
We remember
Natalie Meriwether, Grade 6

Cloud Society

People are like clouds.
Different shapes and colors unique.
Constantly moving and changing.
Looks are deceiving.
Moving silently.
Whispering secrets across the sky.

Dreamy or fierce.
Rosy red, swooning sunset
Gloomy gray

Full of anger, happiness, sadness that
Bursts, pops, drops as they glide along.

Moving to places
different jobs to do.
Unexpected down pour,
Golf ball sized hail,
Changing lives forever.

Yet
So graceful
Their own society in the sky
Mikayla Gorelin, Grade 6

Trust

Trust is a secret.
About to burst out of your mouth,
Like a balloon about to hit the ground,
But you keep it up.

Trust is a trophy.
Standing tall,
Like your best friend,
Staying by your side,
Every step of the way,
Giving you a shoulder to cry on,
When her boyfriend breaks up with her.

Trust is a privilege.
Given to you by many,
Leading you into a whole new chapter.

Trust is a pet.
That is loyal and loves you,
The only one you can rely on.
Like a piece of glass,
On a table about to tip and shatter,
All over the rough ground.
Paige Harrison, Grade 6

Squirrel

Scampering up trees,
Grabbing acorns on the way,
Rustling through leaves.
Abby Hrebinko, Grade 5

Shoot, Score, Win!

I run
I jump high with the ball
I throw at my goal
I miss, at least I tried
I run
I block so they can't catch us
I guard so they can't rebound
I miss, at least I tried
I run
I turn to find the ball
I go faster and faster
I score, I can't even say how happy I am
I run
I look at the scoreboard
I see we're doing good
I won I'm happy
I love basketball
Abby Alcott, Grade 4

Nice and Creamy

It's ice cream night
I'm ready to go
I want that
nice creamy
vanilla bar
with a side of sprinkles
man is my mouth drooling
my tail is wagging
they walk
down the steps
let's go
they walk with me in the back
they are out the door
almost there
BANG
they shut the door on me
they better come back with leftovers
Dillan Stewart, Grade 4

Bystander

So
So there
So there I
So there I was
So there I was, watching
So there I was, watching from
So there I was, watching from the
So there I was, watching from the shadows.
Hey!
Hey! He
Hey! He said,
Hey! He said, but
Hey! He said, but I
Hey! He said, but I said
Hey! He said, but I said nothing.
Zachary Clement, Grade 5

Life

Early in the morning
The dew almost dry
In the dawn of the sky
Flowers bloom to die
While dust specks fly by
The calm and quiet
Nothing is chaotic
It is spring
Birds sing
Of course, on a twig
Sun comes up
While animals and flowers wake up
Soon, sun goes down
Moonlight breaks
Water wakes
Days come and go
Like the wind blows
The moon goes low
Day starts again
Let life begin
Paige Merrick, Grade 4

Spring

Ring-a-ding-ding
Spring is knocking on my door
flowers are blooming
snow is melted
spring came as fast as a bee flies

The flowers make me
The flowers make me
Achoo! sneeze
sniff sniff

Can you hear the birds
tweet tweet
with their singing voices

The flowers are beautiful
I love the colors they make me shout
Pink, yellow, orange, blue
Wow I can't believe it's
SPRING
Isabella McCann, Grade 6

Christmas

Merry Christmas!
I like Christmas.
The snow, my family, and songs.
I like to play and get toys.
I am excited.
I love my family.
Merry Christmas to the world.
I like Christmas.
Do you?
Leslie Reyes, Grade 4

Time Vortex

I wish I could walk through time
see what I missed
make things right that were wrong
Step into a contraption
and boom!
Change the past
make the future better…

I am in the vortex of time
Time flashing before my eyes
bright, colors flying everywhere,
Memories traveling through my mind
year
by year
by year
going by
Seeing myself through the windows of time,
A vortex of color…year's…memories…
Time vortex
Randy Toyberman, Grade 6

Rainbow Colors

I love rainbows, they are the best
Hanging higher than a bird's nest
Their colors are sparkle and shine
All seven straight in a line:
RED is like a rose
A sweet scent fills your nose
ORANGE looks like an orange
All juicy and sweet
YELLOW is a lemon, tangy a bit
GREEN is an apple, it has sour power
BLUE is the sky
Where rainbow lives up so high
INDIGO is a stormy sea
That's frightening to you and me
VIOLET is a plum, very soft and round
Which doesn't make a crunchy sound
Rainbows have different meanings
Like fruit and vegetables and stormy seas
They are delightful for you and me!
Amirrah Egoroff, Grade 5

Night Fright

Let's go Trick-or-Treating
after I get dressed up as a witch.
A lady left her candy out for a minute
I took it all, please don't snitch!
Look at that ghost costume
it gives me such a fright!
Why does Trick-or-Treating
have to be at night?
I have 15 pounds of candy
Now let's go home,
my costume is starting to itch!
Sadie McCarrick, Grade 6

The Bay
I see the bay
As it glimmers in the sunlight
I watch the world
Glistening across the shiny lake
As boats glide
Over the smooth water

I absorb the different shades of the water
Many different blues and greens
Mixed with black and white
I love the way the colors spread together
I watch the wonderful background
Including houses, trees and birds
That are just like me

The water is silent
While the cloud passes by
There is no noise
Not even the other seagulls
While I take in the beauty of the bay
Natalie Asbury, Grade 4

I Love the Sound of the Rain!
Trickle,
Trickle…

I hear the rain
Smash! Smash! Smash!

S-P-L-A-T-T-E-R-I-N-G on the ground.

S
  h
    h
      h

Pouring down the pipes

Rain! Rain! Rain!
It has so many sounds!

Trickle, splash, shhh!
I love the sound of the Rain!
Lauren Spinner, Grade 5

Music to My Ears
Hear the drum beat;
Hear the guitar strum;
Makes me move in my seat;
Makes me rat-tat-tat my thumb.

I feel like dancing;
The sounds of claps and cheers;
Hear all the prancing;
Music to my ears.
Cristian Rosario, Grade 4

I Sing the Goalie Blues
I shuffle along and sing the goalie blues
The scratches meant to be
Sliding out, I sing the blues
So many bumps on my knee
It is really fun, but sometimes it can hurt
My jersey and gloves now part of me

I shuffle along, and sing the blues
My wrists hurt a lot today
Parrying balls, I sing the blues
I hope the throbbing goes away
Gloves all sweaty, sticky, gross
It is getting better day by day

I shuffle along, I sing the blues
Look at all my bruises
Punting balls, I sing the blues
As the other team loses
Sitting on the bench resting all my aches
As I sing the goalie blues!
Riley Bak, Grade 4

Dreams
Dreams are like blue blurs,
Streaking across the sky,
Making the finishing touch,
Making my dream pleasant.

Dreams are like green streaks
Of grass on the floor,
Giving an airy and wonderful feeling.

Purple, pink and red start
The right in the night,
As the sun slowly
Abducts into the ground.

The silver globe is high in the sky,
Illuminating the whole dream world
From head to toe.
A new life, a new world, a new me.

This is what I think of a dream.
Chris Lee, Grade 5

Avonworth
A wesome
V aluable
O n a playoff run
N orth in the USA
W est in the world
O n Pennsylvania ground
R ocks!
T he best school
H igh school
Luke Walter, Grade 4

On the Battleship Missouri
the guns pound
all day they are as
loud as 300 whales yawning
the ship shakes a little
the pounding stops
I go up to the main deck
I see I see

a ship sinking
after that I saw
the sunset what a grand sight
but we had to go back down
to our rooms

I sleep on the top bunk
it was crowded in the morning
I got my white coat and pants
it's over
people cheer
Clay Prouty, Grade 4

Valor
Valor is an ocean.
Its waves bob up and down.
sometimes it wants to give up.
Even though it always pulls through.

Valor is a mountain.
Mountains are strong.
People try to bring it down.
But they never seem to fall.

Valor is the wind.
It blows and never stops.
Many obstacles get in its way.
Wind blows until the end.

Valor is the winter.
Winter is clever.
It creeps up behind us.
Suddenly unleashing bitter cold.
Amanda Alegria, Grade 6

Ocean Breeze
It was a warm day
Suits on and ready for play
We jumped in the sea

A breeze blew near me
It was so strong all around
I went to the ground

We swam there that day
As the breeze hit me hard all day
I will come back someday
Niamh Raftery, Grade 6

White Balloon

Floating like a cloud in a crystal blue sky
Almost real, I reach out in front of me
Waiting like a rose ready to be watered
A white clock with black writing, seen by time

Forever forgotten and easily eager to go up
A round circle, a punctual planet
Swaying string, blowing in the whippy wind
A sweet, sugary smell concocts around me

A bow in a little girl's hair
Flowing, in the pink horizon
Trees bow down to their majesty
Waiting for an answer, but it doesn't reply

Sitting in a bird's nest, pampered by all
Being fed by a blue jay
Robins rock it like a baby
Black birds sing to it lovingly

As the white balloon drifts away
On a journey to a new world

Mykala Bledsoe, Grade 4

Earthquakes

Earthquakes are a disaster
Your insides feel like you're in a blender
Earthquakes crack your heart
They destroy your home
They destroy your happiness

The ground looks demented
Fragments everywhere
making the city
look like a war zone
Small buildings have the insides of the stores
messed up
Big buildings have fallen
and caused a blockade
There is shredded glass everywhere
making the city filled
with lots of little mines
A catastrophe that has
Tears flowing
Coming out
and shaking
Ever present

Justin Turkiewicz, Grade 6

Friends

My best friends are brave and bold
They make me warm when I am cold
Friends are more valuable than silver and gold
True friendship can never be sold
I hope we're together until we're old

Harrison Brooks, Grade 5

Fly Free

Fly free, ye creature!
I release thee from your bonds of honor and loyalty

From now thou shall fly high in the skies
Soar through your hopes, desires and dreams

Be selfish for once allow thy vanity
Sing your wishes

Open wide your wings and let love caress ye only
For the first and perhaps the last

Winged creature!
Oh, how thee deserve to fly yet your cage waits
Come and run evade your fate

But no you sing!
"I have flew, lived, sung, feared and lost"
I've had my everlasting freedom

You soar bit longer and fly to thee cage
Of bonds and pressure and love and fight

You sacrifice your time
To ensure thy love to ye kin
Let them fly free
Let them fly free…

Gloria Tsang, Grade 6

All About Me

I have experienced…the taste of saltwater
people cheering the wax on my feet
five foot drop
flying down nature's pillow.

I imagine…flying cars
buses to the moon
anti-gravity
a portal you will need to get to this place
we call this place…

I know…blocks and all the recipes
to kill a monster to craft a sword
to be a hero
to save a village.

I wonder…how to pull the right roper
or gun the rudder
to steer through the bone yard
and to laugh at a hurricane.

I believe…soaring through the clouds
careful of the birds not touching the ground
like a bird and to be free
This is all about me.

Stephen Hanselmann, Grade 5

This School Year

Honor Roll
When you receive your Honor Roll certificate, you're full of joy.
It makes you a smiling girl or boy.
When you celebrate, you have fun and laugh.
It also means you're on the right path.

Teachers
They're fun, and their teaching is never done.
You may think it will be boring, but you'll never be snoring.
From Grades one to two, to three, to six,
To get us to learn, they do some slick tricks.

Sports
What a thrill to watch our sports teams play.
You'd wish you could watch them all day.
We cheer them on,
As they go along.

Graduation
Although it's our final year,
You may turn to tears.
Now that we're moving on,
It's time to say so long.

Kyle Ferguson, Grade 6

Mom

Mom is the friend who is there for you

Mom is the great one who does the little things that make you smile
and the big things that make you celebrate

Mom is the mentor who shows you the world
in a way you would never understand

Mom is the appreciating one who gives thanks for
the accomplishments you make in your life

Mom is the experienced one who you can talk to
and not feel so alone in the world

Mom is the giver who is almost too generous
Mom is the loving one who loves you beyond words

Mom is the worker who when you watch the fireworks,
she makes sure the fun never ends

Now, I don't know if your mom is like this
but this is mine and I will love her 'til the end.

Alex Fratto, Grade 5

Jillian Costello

J ill loves the ocean and likes to body surf.
I n the winter, she likes to hide under blankets and read a book.
L ollipops are what she will eat on Halloween.
L ilies are her favorite flower because they smell beautiful.

Jillian Costello, Grade 6

The Fourth of July

I remember the fourth of July.
I remember the loud fireworks bursting my ears.
I remember ants getting on my snack
And being very hungry after.
I remember finding a four-leaf clover in the grass.
I remember watching the fireworks.
I remember dressing in red, white, and blue
Even that my outfit was not as crazy as others.
I remember the traffic after the show.
But my favorite memory's yet to come.

Emily Traband, Grade 5

Halloween Past

I remember trick or treating on Halloween
I remember getting free candy
I remember jumping on my brother
And running away
I remember dressing up as a zombie
I remember having s'mores on Halloween
I remember going around twice
Even though I didn't get much candy
I remember going with my friends and having fun
But my favorite memory's yet to come

Kyle Engle, Grade 5

The Brilliant Beach

The anxiousness I get as I rub in my sunscreen,
just knowing how good it will feel to jump into
the nice, refreshing ocean.
The hot boiling sand on my feet causing me to vault
right onto the towel,
The radiant sun beating down on my face, making me
feel sweltered.
The enormous waves crashing down along shore,
leaving no evidence they were there except for the white
foam slowly following behind…

Kylie Riveron, Grade 6

Ode to Pizza

Pizza tastes good and pizza tastes nice
With all the different things inside.

Like the crust, and the sauce, the spice, and the cheese
And all of the toppings like the meat and also veggies

So, if it was not here
It would maybe change history for me!

Gabe Penny, Grade 4

Leaves

There once was a funny looking tree,
Who let the leaves free.
It was around the time of fall
There were many different colors of all.
I am glad that God created fall especially for me.

Sophia Thoman, Grade 4

Turtle Tide

They are gracefully flipping their fins,
Like a bird.
The shells look like turquoise gems.
The front fins are sapphire blue.
Their angelic designs find them love.
Love is in the air.

White blue water is slapping the turtles gently.
The lily pads are smooth as silk.
The turtles have scaly heads.
As the turtles are gliding,
They are in a turtle tide.

Abigail Morman, Grade 4

Fall

September's breeze blows the swaying trees
And the leaves begin to rustle.
Smoke out the chimney, coats out the door,
Cold, cold nights await you.
October descends like the falling leaves:
Red, brown, and empty trees.
Leaves disappear like a swarm of bees,
Tumbling down from the tall, tall trees.
November hides behind the clouds of October
And emerges like the sun.
Kids running, parents laughing:
The fun of November begins.

Jake Vickers, Grade 4

The Night Arrives

As I go outside to see the pond
I see the tadpoles swim
The dim light of the sun rises
And I see the rabbits hop
While hearing their squeaking from the top of their lungs
When they are done they shout out
Then they collect carrots to end the day!
The fish hide
The dark blue shouts I'm coming.
It's almost night
The birds go in their nests
And the night arrives.

Keishla Figueroa, Grade 5

Annie the Antelope Moves In

It is sunrise in Africa.
The early spring winds blow freely.
As the winds blow through the trees they make a whistling sound.
It is a perfect day to move in.
All of the beautiful birds are flying freely.
Annie closes her eyes for one second.
When she opens them again, all of the birds come fast towards her.
One of the birds speaks up, "We all want to be friends."
Can Annie trust the birds?
Yes! She can!

Summer Sonricker, Grade 4

Fall

Leaves are falling everywhere!
I run, run, run, jump, and leaves fly everywhere!
I see the squirrels gathering nuts.
There are people walking mutts!
After the leaves have fallen I look at trees.
Now that the flowers have died, I don't see bees.
all the birds are going to migration.
All the bears are ready for hibernation.
All the farmer's hay is cut.
Now it's time to hunt!
So while everybody's at the mall,
I will be outside enjoying the Fall.

Morghan Hampton, Grade 4

My Country I Love

As I look into the mountains I see,
History as if its carved in trees,
It has been here for hundreds of years,
I'm very proud to say I live here,
Warriors have fought high and low,
To save our country from days of old,
We have proved that America will be unstoppable,
A country that is very lovable,
Hearts were broken as people lost loved ones,
They fought with their hearts more than guns,
I would like to take this time to say,
Thank you veterans in any possible way.

Alison Blankenship, Grade 6

Thanksgiving

T urkey
H am,
A pple pie,
N o one has to wear a tie,
K ids waiting patiently,
S tanding in line as far as I can see,
G iving thanks on this day has been a tradition,
I nviting everyone is a new transition,
V ery happy to be a part of this day,
I t is inspiring in every way,
N ow we see a smile on everyone's face,
G od has given us grace.

Caleb Blankenship, Grade 6

The First Thanksgiving

Pilgrims participating in the first Thanksgiving
Three days celebrating
Killing turkeys, feathers everywhere
Baking bread for feasting
Indians joining friends on the first Thanksgiving
Taught the Pilgrims how to hunt
Taught the Pilgrims how to fish
Taught the Pilgrims how to farm
Harvest time
Indian friends, a true part of the holiday!

Ally Corvin, Grade 4

Hate!
H itler — mean and unpleasant
A ll — Jews to be prosecuted
T ime — will come to escape
E xecution — is mean
Michael Fischer, Grade 6

Hate!
H atred of all Jews
A dolf Hitler
T erezin
E xecution of all Jews
Josh Reinhart, Grade 6

Wolf
W hite, brown, gray, and black
O ften hunt
L ike wild dogs
F earless and bold.
Ali Sanchez, Grade 6

Holocaust
H ate
A t all costs
T hat four letter word
E mpty all of the concentration camps
Ryan Roth, Grade 6

Sun
The sun
Gives warmth
To cold creatures
On crisp fall days
Caroline Webb, Grade 5

My Puppy
Cute and lovable.
I love her wet kisses
as she finds her toys
to play with me!
Amber Leininger, Grade 5

Fall
Finally, it's getting cold.
Autumn is upon us.
Leaves falling from the trees.
Let's make a pile and jump in!
Joe Thompson, Grade 5

Fall
Falling leaves
All different colors
Left in the trees
Left on the ground
Dejah Hill, Grade 4

I Am Me
I am…Lorna
I wonder what it would be like to be someone else
I hear lyrics to my favorite song playing in my head
I see the special moments with me and my family in the corners of my eyes
I want to see my family smiling every day

I am me.
I pretend to be a princess
I feel like a dog when he gets a fresh bone
I touch the ridges of the letters on my pencil while I am writing this poem
I worry that tomorrow might not be as good as today
I cry when I am sad, but I just remember…

I am myself.
I understand when I don't get a toy
I say things that might happen in a thousand years
I dream that my future will be bright
I try to make someone's day better than mine
I hope to be the best person I could be, but no matter what…
I am…Lorna.
Lorna Brown, Grade 5

Twilight Sled Ride
BONG! Our cue to ride
Virgo and I launch into the golden, twilight sky
Dancing on the snowflakes
As we land, we create snow white tidal waves
The snowflakes pelting my face as if they were white pellets
I see the sooty black smoke coming from the chimney flues

I glance at the runners of my sled; they are wings of a Pegasus now
I hover just a millimeter off the snowy ground
I hear the wind whistling in my ears
I see the pines and houses flying by like green and white blurs
The winter wind whipping and lashing at my face as if it were a whip

The scent of hot cocoa so strong I can almost taste it
I cry out "Go, Virgo! Go!"
I see our large house looming into view
I see my parents and little brother awaiting my arrival
We are running down our long driveway
I hear the pitter patter of Virgo's paws
We slow down and arrive home
Sean Rinebolt, Grade 4

Green
A green lantern shines on a backpack filled with granny green apples
ready for a picnic in a lush lawn
a deserted silk scarf painted with prickly cacti
marked the spot
next to Crayola markers
stood an Alan Scott comic book
recycle
replenish
green
Maxwell Turnwald, Grade 6

Respect the Earth

Why do people not respect the Earth?
They should recycle, reduce, reuse.

Why do people litter when they should throw their trash away?
It's not so hard to do so but they litter anyway.

Why do people choose not to recycle?
Do they realize what they are doing to the Earth?

Why do people waste gas with their cars and trucks?
They could simply walk, bike, or use a train.

Are you one of these people?
If so, consider changing your ways.

Aidan Walker, Grade 6

The Hearts of the House

My family is
The heart of the house
They are the glowing soul of my heart
They have a faithful heart that relies on me
They are the ones that make me have a golden heart
Without them there is no freedom to me
My great heart will scatter into millions of pieces if they're gone
That will be the time for me to curse and cry
They use all their might to protect me when I'm hurt
Even if they're not there with me
I will always think of them
They are always right next to me
Even if they're not there with me
They are the ones that make me have a smiling face

Devesh Bungatavula, Grade 4

Music

Music is my entire life,
Without it I'd feel like I'm living in a world of strife.
From piano to singing to guitar to drums,
They'll all be useful for when the time comes.

I could be a rock star and hit the charts,
I could be as famous as Da Vinci's arts.
I could busk for money at the shopping mall,
I could join the Cleveland Orchestra and play at Severance Hall.

I could entertain the sick and the people with disabilities,
I could go on forever, so many possibilities.
The instruments I play feel so good to touch.
What I'm trying to say is "I love music so much!".

Lachie West, Grade 6

Flower's Petals

Flowers are a beautiful thing with remarkable scents.
Some flowers can have tons of petals, while others have few.
Petals are soft as a dove's wing and can be as fragile as a sea star.
A flower is a delicate, soft beauty.

Brian Carroll, Grade 5

Fall

What makes fall so special?
All the candy it brings on Halloween
The pumpkin carving or a corn maze
The excitement of the winds blowing
All the leaves 'til it looks like it is snowing
All the costumes
The beautiful sunsets over the lakes
All the cute animals running from the cold
Or the harsh winds blowing your hair 'til it looks
Like you are a tree
Or the knowledge of the approaching winter
The horrible storms that can create falling trees
Or it could be that we say fall in almost every
Sentence
Or that we just love it
Or could it just be maybe that fall is one of
life's greatest mysteries we have yet to know?

Rebecca Michaud, Grade 6

Fright Night

Oh how I love cool October nights
They signal fun and frights

The man on the stilts comes to taunt
When I go to the Halloween Haunt

All the new decorations are fun to see
Roller coasters, rides matched to theme

Fog around! Scary people are hard to see
Cannot feel what is in front of me

Execution man waits by the Scarecrow maze
That guy looks a little crazed

Me, hanging with my brother and Dad, us three
Cannot think of a better way to have fun on Halloween.

Andrew Lawson, Grade 6

Pink

Pink is
A loving pink heart,
A shy blush on my face,
Beautiful pink and red strawberries,
It sounds like soft gentle cherry powder,
Like a piglet oinking,
And even sounds like a flamingo calling me,
Pink tastes like soft cotton candy,
Like sweet juicy raspberries,
And cold, delicious strawberry ice-cream,
It feels like a cute teddy bear,
An adorable pink star,
And like my pink heart,
The bright pink color
Gives me special and sweet delight!

Diya Patel, Grade 4

Joy

Joy is a pair of wings
Lifting their wearer high and soaring with them
Joy is the feeling of cold wind in your hair
Of looking down and knowing that there is no reason to be afraid — you won't fall

Joy is peace
Complete and utter, when everything is right in the world
Joy is the place where your heart can be light
Where you can feel the sunshine, warm on your face

Joy is fragile, a baby
Who came so quickly and fiercely
And who can be damaged and taken just as fast and suddenly
Joy is soft, tender — meant to be handled with great care, but at the same time with abandon

Joy is a ship with her massive sails billowing full
With no specific destination
Just sailing for the pure beauty of it

Joy is the ever-changing ocean
Free, powerful, young, old and
Infinitely vast

Lily Shore, Grade 6

Death (The Afterlife)

As you take your last breath and have your last look at life, as you ease in and everything stops,
Awoken from a seemingly long sleep, blinding lights appear, slowly fade, to reveal a new place.
Images from the past usher in to a new life. Unaware you died yet aware of all else,
You feel that you are not alone as projections of people you knew, people you loved,
Friends, family, and those who changed your life, bring you to open up your senses.
The smell of everything around you is perfect, as is all else, no limits, no worries.
The smell of a rotting tree is disguised by the smell of a rose, as reality escapes your mind.
You hear the light and faint sounds of all things around you.
When you feel things, a familiar yet mysterious memory comes to mind,
Calming, peaceful, and warm feelings become surroundings, as your mind controls all.
The taste of an apple within arm's reach is crisp, juicy, sweet, and perfect.
All of your senses help to hide the fact that everything you do now isn't reality,
Your actions are never received by others,
Yet all actions change your fate.
As everything comes together in your mind, this becomes your new reality, it seems perfect,
The darkness of your death creeps up on you,
But the darkness cannot be defined for you can't feel its presence,
For all you know it's not even there, for your life is being reviewed.
You may say this is purgatory, you may say this is heaven, you may say this is home,
But whatever you think, or whatever you do, it is yours forever
This is the end.

Kevin Stark, Grade 6

When I Am

When I am tired, I am as sleepy as a witch making a death potion, brewing the ingredients together all night in a cauldron
When I am sad, I am like a sad clown that has been fired because of making children scared
When I am annoyed, I am as frustrated as a saber-tooth tiger, not able to eat his dinner
When I am petrified, I am like a cryptic Lochness Monster being scared by anonymous creatures
When I am scared, I am like a pigeon being chased by a blue falcon over a murky pond on my first flight
When I am puzzled, I am like a mouse being bewildered by a cornfield with a sprained ankle

Alex Yeung, Grade 6

Thanksgiving
T hankful for family
H appy times
A lways on Thursday
N ever disappoints
K eeps you awake the night before
S uper sized turkeys
G iving to the ones in need
I nviting friends to Thanksgiving dinner
V anishing hunger
I magining Thanksgiving day football
N ext year is so far away
G iving thanks
Thomas Cassada, Grade 5

Orange of Fall
Orange is the color of fall,
It's the season for football.
It's time for trick-or-treat,
Hear us coming down the street.
It's the time when people try
To be scary and sometimes hairy.
It's the time for light coats,
And longer pants.
It's the time when kids rake the leaves,
Then put them back all over the yard.
ORANGE is the color of fall,
And it brings joy all fall long.
Courtney Nelson, Grade 6

Christmas
Snow
Presents and
Cheer
Santa and
His elves
Work away
Till it's times
To fly away
And deliver joy
To people
All over
The world
Gabrielle Joe, Grade 5

Christmas Time
The snow is cold
It looks like gold
I saw the northern star
It looked pretty far
It becomes Christmas time
The snow will shine
I ate good pumpkin pie
It's the time not to lie
It is the most wonderful time of the year
I hear jingle bells in my ear
Kaylee Justus, Grade 6

Life
Life is a highway
That you are driving on
Movin' along the road

Life is a song
That comes from any place in your heart
You cannot force it; it must come to you

Life is a flower that has not blossomed
It needs some care to open up
then it can be accessed

Life is a roller coaster
It goes up and down
It raises you up to the good times
And drops you down to the bad

Life is one baby
That you cherish with your heart
You only have one
Keep it close to your heart
You can have everything you want
Sammy Vaia, Grade 6

The Beautiful Game
The game that unites us
The fun that returns us
The feeling that let's us

The skills that prove us
The madness that changes us
The greatness that enlightens us

The fun that you have
The rush of adrenaline
A team like your brethren

Whether 11 versus 11
or 4 vs 4
We all love the game

So we return

Back to the Field of the beautiful game…
The game that we love
Soccer
The Beautiful Game
Witt Phillips, Grade 5

My Best Friend
Koda
Playful, loyal
Caring, loving, exciting
He is my brother and my best friend
Canine
Jessica Russell, Grade 6

Hunting in the Leaves of November
Hunting in the leaves of November,
Nothing makes me feel any better,
To come home to a happy feast,
Venison will not be the least.

Listen to the bears patting on the leaves,
Feeling for bees,
Keeping them safe are only the hives,
Protecting their special little lives.

Taking guns off the shelf,
That's not from an elf,
All you need are 1 or 2 bullets,
When you see it, you've got to pull it.

When you sleep, you dream about it,
When you wake up, you live it,
What you need to do
Is start it all over again.
Isaac Adams, Grade 5

I Am a Girl
I am a girl
I wonder where music comes from
I see a piano
I want to succeed
I am a girl

I pretend to be a professional
I feel the stage floor
I touch the piano
I worry I'll play the wrong notes
I cry if I laugh too hard
I am a girl

I understand piano letters
I say music notes
I dream that I'll play forever
I try my best
I hope for peace
I am a girl
Tala Saidi, Grade 4

Sports
I like sports that's what I do.
From cleats to sneakers I lace up my shoes.
I do some tricks.
To score a goal.
'Cause that's how I roll.
I dribble and pass.
Like I'm breaking some glass.
I wear my uniform all-game day.
Till it comes to that time of day
That we need to stop the play
And go home for another day.
Elisabeth Mioduski, Grade 5

Ode to Brownies
You are sweet and gooey
You are very, very chewy
You are mega moist
And you are never bad

I love the chocolate
To me you are the best food
I love the divine taste
I love your brown rectangles
I love you, Brownies!
Troy Spicer, Grade 4

Everyone Is Different
Tall or short
Don't worry
Everyone is different
Skinny or wide
Who cares
You're perfect
Just the way you are
Don't be someone you aren't
Be you!
Everyone is different!
Kylie Rizzotti, Grade 6

My Baby Brother
I have a brand new brother,
he is a brother like no other.
I wish he could start talking,
instead of crying and squawking.
Oh boy, Oh boy, he always has to cry
all the time and I don't know why.
He eats and sleeps all through the day,
I cannot wait until he is big enough to play.
I love my brother and we both love our
Mother.
Christopher Jasinski, Grade 4

The Greatest Pillow
The pillow is

As soft as a
sheep's winter coat

As fluffy as a
cloud in the blue sky

As white as
the sparkling snow in winter
DJ Brandon, Grade 5

Winter
Snow falls to the ground
Birds retreat to the south for winter
Snowmen stand in barren stillness
Elijah Logan, Grade 6

The Colors of My Dreams
I see colors in my dreams
The colors of the rainbow

Red roses blooming brightly
From the soft green grass
Making the garden beautiful

Blue waves from the ocean
Making little kids smile
As they look at the deep blue sky

The yellow sun hangs high above
At dusk the sun sets and
Transforms the sky to
An orange wonderland that
Glues my eyes to it

In my dreams I also see pink
Cotton candy soft and fluffy
In my mouth bringing happiness to me

These are the colors of my dreams
Dasha Telysheva, Grade 5

School
Pencils cracking,
Rulers rapping.
Glue-sticks popping,
Scissors chopping.

Teachers talking,
Students walking.
Sneakers squeaking,
Children peeking.

Bad behavior,
Trouble-maker.
Teachers yelling,
Tears are swelling.

Math is vast,
Reading is fast.
History is old,
Science is bold.

Now it's time to be dismissed,
The first day of school will be missed.
Sahuj Mehta, Grade 6

Turkey Time
Turkey
They taste juicy
It's a relaxing feast
I do like Thanksgiving feasting
Tasty
Sophia Skorupski, Grade 4

Snowflakes
Snowflakes, snowflakes on the ground
Snowflakes, snowflakes all around
Snowflakes, snowflakes on my head
Snowflakes, snowflakes in my bed
Snowflakes, snowflakes here and there
Snowflakes, snowflakes everywhere
Noah Poirier, Grade 4

Hitler
H ateful
I ntolerant
T yrant
L eader
E vil
R uthless
Cristian Bonomo, Grade 6

Hitler
H is for hate that came from Hitler
I is for insane violence to the Jews
T is for talking bad about the Jews
L is for lying about the Jews
E is for exactly what you shouldn't do
R is for not respecting the Jews.
Nick Apruzzi, Grade 6

Audrey
A wesome
U nique
D elightful
R emarkable
E xquisite
Y oung
Audrey, Grade 5

Paul R.
P eople! The British!
A re coming! The British are coming!
U h oh. Something bad is here.
L et's go see.

R edcoats are here!
Sam Kantor, Grade 5

Snow
The moon shines
It twinkles in your eye
Angels were made
There they lay
The white ground crunches
As I walk
Julie Barbier, Grade 5

Chesapeake Bay

The Chesapeake Bay a great place to live and play!
Where the stingrays like to scare us away.

The humming of the boats
With a lazy afternoon on the floats.

Paddle boarding and kayaking are just a few things we do.
And we can't forget about driving the golf cart too!

My dad takes us fishing on the boat.
The person that catches the biggest fish gets to gloat.

Occasionally we get to see the dolphins splish and splash.
That makes us want to smile and laugh.

Soft sand spreads between our toes.
As the waves from the bay flow.

Chesapeake Bay a great place to live and play!
A beautiful sunset ends the day!

Sydney Deringer, Grade 6

The White King

One step at a time
I am powerful for I kill and enlighten the game
I stand tall but I have one place to go
My enemies rise to fight
But it is too late with the protection
My pawns are brave and fearless for they step ahead first
I am proud of my set but I am left to defend myself
In the last position
There are tricks I face for I am the target while others shadow me
I can glisten but I will remain in the dark until I have my kill
I am quite the controller of the game
I am the leader but my queen is powerful
She guards me for her life
She might be taken away but she will be returned when
My fierce young pawn will succeed in bringing her home
I am behind all the tricks to kill once and for all the black king
Once I am gone the game is over
Once I have held my enemy for prisoner the game is over
For I,
Am the White King of Chess.

Aunnesha Bhowmick, Grade 6

The Beach

The rippling of the waves
The wellspring of arrays of beams from the sun
A day at the beach
Is sure a lot of fun
With searching for seashells
A castle in the sand
After a long nonchalant walk
I'll sure have a tan
A dexterous lifeguard on the stand
A Frisbee flying through the crisp air
A day at the beach
Is a day with no care
The receding of the ocean
The crashing of the waves
A day at the beach
Will surely get plenty of raves
Sadly now the day is done
And I am deflated
As a beach ball
A day at the beach exalts me from happy to elated

Sean Serpico, Grade 6

Twilight Sled Ride

Bong! Bong!
The clock strikes 6:00.
I look out the window,
Snow everywhere!
Gabby flew into the twilight sky,
We dart through the pine trees,
Scattering pine needles on the angel dust snow.
The wind feels as crisp and as cold as Jack Frost,

I hear the snow leopards of the mountain,
The wind blows up pine needles in my face,
Two mountain goats leap elegantly across the path,
The twilight moon guides my way.

We're almost there I can smell it,
The sweet, scrumptious smell of hot cocoa,
As we slow down the sled chomps the snow,
The ground is as slippery as ice,
I get inside,
The twilight sled ride is over.

Johnnie Deane, Grade 4

Blank Paper

Staring at a blank piece of paper with only a few lines on it.
The only thought in my head,
In my blank mind…
Was what will I write?
As I stare out the window…
What would I write?
All the ideas were lost like an unknown language.
Waiting to be uncovered and…
Discovered.

Nicole Miranda, Grade 5

I Am a Poem

If I were a poem I would be like,
A rose that is red or a violet that is blue.
I may be five lines or maybe just two.
If I were a poem I could be rhyming, or I could be new
I could be famous or a Haiku.
My friends are Dr. Seuss and Shel Silverstein to name a few.
I could be found on a shelf or even in a pew.
If I were a poem there is a lot I could do.
I would be sad or funny, I could do anything for you.

J.T. Klein, Grade 4

Basketball Game

I am a boy who enjoys playing basketball.
I wonder if I'll win the game.
I hear shoes squeaking, basketballs bouncing, and
the buzzer going off for the win against the Pirates.
I see the basketball in for the big win.
I want to win the championship against
the Panthers on April Nineteenth.
I am a boy who enjoys playing basketball.

I pretend to make a buzzer beater to win.
I feel scared in the championship against the
Panthers because they are very good.
I touch the big, orange basketball.
I worry that I will lose the championship
against the Panthers.
I am a boy who enjoys playing basketball.

I understand it is still okay to lose.
I say we try our best.
I dream of making a three-pointer.
I try to win the game.
I hope that my team will make the championship and win.
I am a boy who enjoys playing basketball.
Joey Weisman, Grade 5

The Shining Sea

The sea shines with glory,
glowing heaven,
sings of freedom,
the sailor's home,
shimmers beneath the sun,
wonders of magical creatures lost in the distance,
magic waves burst with beauty,
as day falls,
the sun sets,
great beauty glitters with passion,
see the sails glowing and gliding,
I wonder if they see,
the magic wonders of the ocean too.
Sophie Rodrique, Grade 4

A Beautiful Sight

It is noon in the summer.
I come outside.
I listen to the sound of water splashing.
I smell the air.
I enjoy it a lot, it feels nice and warm outside
I look up at the sky
I see a beautiful orange, yellow, and purple sunset
I think it's very pretty.
Then I look at my shadow
I admire it because it's green.
I look up again but I'm looking at a tree.
I see a mother robin making a nest and I am amazed.
I wonder what beautiful things I will see next.
Ember Internicola, Grade 4

I Am

I am strong and fast
I wonder if world hunger will stop
I hear the wrongs and try to make them right
I see others suffer from starvation
I want to help
I am strong and fast

I pretend there is peace all over the world
I feel pain like everyone else
I touch people's hearts
I worry for others who can't
I cry for the stopping of hunger
I am strong and fast

I understand frustration
I say we stop fighting
I dream for world peace
I try my hardest
I hope for world peace
I am strong and fast
Mason Smith, Grade 6

Neil Armstrong

Neil Armstrong was the first man to stride on the moon.
And his strenuous space career had just bloomed.
He was born on August 5, 1930.
His secluded childhood was very sturdy.
Neil was fascinated by space.
He soon joined the N.A.S.A. race.
He became a humble astronaut in 1962.
But he was an aviator before from 1949 to 1952.
He was in charge of *Gemini 8* in 1966.
His job and his life depended on this.
His famous quote is one of a kind:
"One small step for man, one giant leap for mankind."
He soon took an escapade on *Apollo 11* to walk on the moon.
The whole entire country was about to swoon.
He passed away on August 25, 2012.
He earned a lot of honor for himself.
We still celebrate the day he walked in space.
And in every picture he has a smiling face.
That means he was happy with his life.
And he's watching our accomplishments day and night.
Abbie Ballak, Grade 5

Orange

The brave, dangerous, courageous red warrior
Comes to the light of yellow, filled with
Happiness, joy, and warmth to form
A unique color that will show the
Bravery and danger on one side
And warmth and joy on the other,
This is the amazing color Orange,
A color with caution and great risk,
But also the great reward when the risk is done
Aleksa Rodic, Grade 6

One-Pound Piggy

My piggy is the cutest
He eats a lot of food
My piggy is the cutest
He has an attitude

He likes to dance around
And never stays put there
He actually weighs a pound
And wanders who knows where

Got a letter through the mail
A cute snout plus four tiny hooves
He's the cutest named "Crazy Tail"
So frightened of packs of wolves!

I ate some bacon
Then found him crying
Said was mistaken
Would he believe my lying?
Kayla Yup, Grade 5

An Ode to Basketball

The sound of bouncing on walls, or floors
Is a sound that no normal person ignore
When you see the orange and black ball
You know it is basketball

You walk into the big gym
And you see the orange rim
If you see it bring joy to all
Then you know it's Basketball

When you see an injured player
It doesn't make the game any greater
If you see someone fall
Then you know it's basketball

Running to the net
Like a really fast jet
If you hear a play being called
Then you know it's Basketball.
Eryce Wilcoxson, Grade 5

Interweave

So much depends
upon
a tiny spider

keeping the
population of insects
down low

making fascinating webs
in the corner
of the kitchen
Leonardo Sanchez, Grade 5

A Man

Taken were the Jews
By the Nazi crews
By Hitler

From all different places
Separated by races
By Hitler

Frightened and chilled
Some were gassed
And were killed
By Hitler

The ones who escaped
Had the luckiest fate
But they were tortured
By Hitler

The Jews dearly paid
For the Holocaust that was made
By Hitler
Jerod Younes, Grade 6

Dream Colors

Dreams are
blue like an ocean
seeping into wet sand

Dreams are
roses flying through
the wind into someone's
bouquet

Dreams are
green money fluttering
through the wind to get
smacked with a $100 bill

Dreams are
a black sigh in the dim
light saying, "speak your last words"

Dreams are
pink fluffy unicorns dancing
on rainbows
Timothy Ruggiero, Grade 5

Green

Green with envy as they say
Is proven to be true
Shifty
Sneaky
Sly
Sad
Jealousy sneaks up on you
Emma Mertz, Grade 6

Summer

The flowers blooming
The birds tweeting
The sun beaming
Kids screaming and playing
Adults sitting and talking
Water from the pool dripping
Sound from the sink running
Sound from the park swing creaking
JaQuez Martin, Grade 6

Winter

The time to drink hot chocolate
Snow falling on the ground
Day time is getting darker
Tons of snow is falling
Putting up lights to see at night
Wearing gloves when going outside
Shoveling all the snow
Building a snowman
Lily Rozik, Grade 6

Snowflakes

Snowflakes are white
They light up the night.
Snowflakes fly majestically in the air
When the trees are bare.
They lay on the ground
And don't make a sound.
Not two snowflakes are alike.
Snowflakes are beautiful.
Kori Kuhns, Grade 6

My New Kitten

Jordan is my new kitten
His paw look like mittens
He always plays with the ball
Until he tumbles and takes a fall
I show him around the town
His signature color is brown
Never bitten, never clawed
He's the greatest kitten I ever saw
Colby McKeta, Grade 6

Football

Tight ends help to make a catch.
The other teams try to give us a match.
You sometimes get hurt, bruises and all.
Quarterbacks have a bad tendency to fall.
Line backers always take big hits.
They are always the ones to blitz.
Kickers make a lot of field goals.
Football touches a lot of souls.
Zade Zadrozny, Grade 6

Rachel Louise Carson

Rachel was born on May 27th 1907,
and had her first book published when
she was only eleven.
She grew up in Springvale PA,
and was always busy with all the
miniature books she made.
Rachel attended college for women in PA,
for writing summit books and
to be a scientist that day.
She was not just a writer and scientist,
she also tried to be a deft ecologist.
One day she was hired by the bureaus of fisheries,
she could finally study ecology.
She was also very humorous and droll,
and when she writes, the pencil
is for her to control.
April 14th 1964, she died
of cancer and all the days before
she died, all cuddled in a nook
and everyone just asked why.

Elaine Droxler, Grade 4

Once

He was once a man.
A strong content man.
He could feel the soft breezes,
See far beyond the horizon,
Hear the echo of silence,
Taste berries dance on his tongue,
And smell the warmth of the grass and the sky.
He once was a man.
Until his once perfect heart shriveled into ash,
And his playful warmth drained as a chill slunk in.
Until the cheerful boy left in him stormed off and wept,
And his feelings became as useless as cracked toys in the attic,
And the dreams kept so hopeful in him sizzled and boiled away,
And his soul lost the lust for
The feel of soft breezes
The view past the horizon
The echo of silence
The taste of the berries
And the smell of the warmth of the grass on the sky.
He once was a man. Not anymore.

Abigail C. Auden, Grade 5

The Stillness of Night

I sat on the grass
Listening to the stillness of night
When the peace was interrupted with a voice
It was my mother's
Calling me for supper
But I didn't move
I liked the quietness
But then I smelled my favorite food
So I ran home

Anna Fonarov, Grade 5

The Leedleboot

Once there was a leedleboot
It made the sound of leedleloot,
Every day it liked to cuddle
With a yellow muddlefuddle,
The muddlefuddle was very voluminously big
And liked to ungainly eat some fruit bar figs.
The leedleboot wasn't big, it was small
But wide like a round red bouncy ball,
The leedleboot likes to eat ice cream
While dancing under the boogie beam,
He had fuzzy silver deranged fur
When he talked it came out like a slur,
The leedleboot liked to tell jokes
To his best friend the mingaloxe,
The mingaloxe was very, very red
That he'll get the red all over his bed,
The leedleboot glows in the cavernous dark
But only when he's nonchalantly asleep at the park

Julia Cavalieri, Grade 6

The Stream

Spongy banks with
silver ferns and
crisp leaves
layering the sticky mud.
Smooth mushrooms with
creamy spots and
thick white stems
erupting from the soft ground.
Sparkling bubbles with
golden fish and
deep emerald seaweed
clustering at the bottom.
Slippery blue pebbles with
thin silt and
sharp white sand
covering the discarded natural compost…
Spongy, silver, crisp, sticky, smooth, creamy, thick, soft, sparkling,
golden, deep, slippery, sharp…

Elsa Tonkinwise, Grade 5

Walking in the Meadow

I was walking in the meadow.
The sun was shining,
The wind was blowing gently.
The flowers were waving at me,
The grass was dancing.
I looked up in the sky.
There were fluffy clouds,
There were skinny clouds.
I picked up a flower and smelled it.
It smelled fresh.
I felt the water from the stem on my fingers.
The fresh breeze tickled me.
The meadow was beautiful.

Ho Young Jin, Grade 5

Dracula
Dracula
Pale, scary
Flying, hiding, biting
Pain in the neck
Vampire
Bryce Esposito, Grade 5

Christmas
Christmas is my favorite time of year,
full of fun and good cheer.
Wrapping presents and good food to eat,
even my dog, Zeke, gets a treat!
Say my prayers and turn out the light.
It's hard to sleep on Christmas Eve night.
Derek Cruise, Grade 4

Fall
Leaves, leaves everywhere.
As far as the eye could see.
Wind becoming stronger.
Days becoming shorter.
Bundle up everyone,
Cause fall's around the corner.
Alexa Teixeira, Grade 5

The World
The grass is green,
The sky is blue.
The stars are yellow
And the sun is too.
Birds are red, green, yellow, and blue.
Birds can fly, and I would too.
Jacob Maggard, Grade 5

Soccer Game
To the net I take the ball,
A goal to get is my coach's call.
I'm moving fast around a pick,
A chance at last for the winning kick.
The goal is made, it was such fun,
A game well played, now home I run.
John Duegaw, Grade 6

Surprise
At the school
Near a classroom
Around the corner
By the library
Above the lobby
Was a loud noise
Anna Nguyen, Grade 4

Art
I am a boy who loves to draw
I wonder what I will draw next
I hear the paint on the paper as I paint a beautiful flower on the white canvas
I see my flower with red, white and yellow petals
I want to be the best artist in the whole entire world
I am a boy who loves to draw

I pretend that my drawing can come to life
I feel that my art speaks to me, as I am drawing a picture
I touch my bumpy, dry painting
I worry that it might smudge if it is not dry
I am a boy who loves to draw

I understand that I have other things to do
I say that I am great
I dream to be a famous artist
I try my hardest with art
I hope that all my family and friends will support me
I am a boy who loves to draw
Luca Nero, Grade 5

Burning Memories
The way you burn at night,
Brightens up the street with light.
Someone smart enough to call,
Lets you enjoy your last few moments before you fall.

The sirens howling from down the street,
As your flames blow off much heat.
Neighbors are approaching the house full of smoke,
From under the blanket of darkness, the witnesses start to choke.

Smoke is blowing from inside,
As the firefighters fight from every side.
The family is crying on the sidewalk,
All because of your evil self that put them into terrible shock.

Finally you start to die down,
Now in the distance all it looks to be is a smoke filled town.
Family and friends gather around as it becomes daylight,
Hoping that all of the memories will wash away from this terrifying sight.
Marisa Schriner, Grade 6

I Am From
I am from paint splats, pencil sketches, and wooden splinters.
I am from the snow white house on Pine Road.
I am from Saturday morning TV and sleeping in an hour on Sunday.
I am from screeching cockatiel calls or cats meowing in the morning for food every day.
I am from biking down the road on the weekends.
I am from Indian and Pakistani blood coursing through my veins.
I am from eating pasta every day after school or in the morning.
I am from grapes sprouting on long wires that stretch long like metal snakes.
I am from shoveling the snow out of the driveway with my dad in the winter.
I am from the crackling of fireworks on the Fourth of July.
I am from me.
Andrew Smith, Grade 5

Coming Home

When my dog starts to bark I know you're home,
I follow the scent of your sweet cologne.

As I run down the never ending stairs,
I feel something that can't compare.

It is the love that I have deep inside,
Virtually impossible for me to hide.

I run to you with all my might,
And jump into your arms and hug you tight.

I feel the love, as we embrace,
I kiss your sweet, masculine face.

I treasure these times that we have together,
Wonderful memories that will live with me forever.

Susie Garrison, Grade 6

Dangerous Flowers

A flower can be many things.
They can be pretty or dull,
tall or short,
dead or alive,
mystical or magical.
Maybe that is hard to understand.
Well, it is very true.
You don't know?
What do you think happened to him?
You don't know?
He ate a magical flower and turned into a frog.
Now do you believe me?
Maybe not, but it is still true.
So you have to be careful.
No, not that flower!
Do not touch it!
Oh, I told you!

Felicity Sutton, Grade 4

A Christmas Tree

I am a Christmas tree,
How merry I am.
I am decorated every year.
Oh, how pretty I look on that special day,
With ornaments in my hair!
Children decorate me with all their favorite ornaments.
When Santa comes,
He puts presents under my outstretched arms.
My trunk is strong and straight.
My hair is green and prickly.
I am a kind Christmas tree.
I love to hear the children unwrapping presents.
I love hearing Christmas carols.
I love hearing children reading.
I am a Christmas tree.

Avrey Grischow, Grade 4

My Change

I used to walk through the hallways,
and just get ignored.
I used to have my own lunch table,
in my own corner of the cafeteria.
My color was black,
my vision was foggy.
And the wall of separation kept me from seeing
the bright side of life.

Now I'm more vibrant,
and so are my colors.
My table is fully,
and I love to smile and laugh.
What changed me,
you ask?
This happiness came from one simple word:
 a friend.

Julia Hynek, Grade 6

Stray Cat, My Cat

I heard a noise outside my house;
I really thought it was a mouse.

I looked around to find the sound;
you would never believe what I found.

It was a stray cat with lots of fur,
and all it did was purr, purr, purr.

I invited her inside to eat
and she snuggled by my feet.

I named her Bamboo because she was brown,
and because her eyes shined like a crown.

She is now my cat to keep.
I really love her so deep.

Aron Afzali, Grade 4

Yes, That's Me

Yes, that's me
Look and you'll see
My hair flows and curls naturally
My eyes glitter and sparkle like shining stars
My arms hugging people I care for
My hands giving friends presents
My heart beating like a drum
I'm good at making friends
I never try to hurt someone's feelings
My friends are extremely nice to me
I live to be funny
I hope to compose more piano pieces
I dream about winning the talent show
It's all clear as can be
That's positively, absolutely me

Ashleigh Clabaugh, Grade 6

An Ode to Dogs
This is a fuzzy pet.
It really loves chasing its tail,
And a stick is what dogs love to get.

Dogs like eating meat,
But they only eat dog food.
And they bark when they greet.

I had a dog, his name was Blue.
I also had a dog named Jackson.
Blue is the one who chewed my shoe.

Dogs are really big slobs,
But they are bundles of joy.
So be careful, they eat like hogs!
Kiersten Newton, Grade 4

Pink
Pink is sticky cotton candy
Pretty party dresses
And raspberry lipstick
It's like a beautiful rose
The color of fashion dresses
And my shirt with the bunny on it
Pink is for Valentine's Day
It tastes like bubble gum
Sweet juicy watermelons
And strawberry taffy
Pink feels like a soft pink bunny
And a magical unicorn
It smells like pink frosting
Pink sounds like Katy Perry.
Pink can sweeten your life!
Trinity Santiago, Grade 4

Cinnamon Valley
Tan valleys
Sprinkling cinnamon
Sweet cinnamon slides
Down the valley's mountain
Twinkling cinnamon flies through the sky
The valley field so wide and long
Cinnamon fills the land
Aubrey Wescott, Grade 4

Beatitudes
B lessed are the meek;
E very day they are pleasant.
A lso blessed are the clean of heart;
T hey keep God first.
I n the Beatitudes, All of
T he saying and teachings all lead
U p to one thing; treat everything with
D ignity and respect.
E very day we have to make these choices.
Christian Giamalis, Grade 4

I Am
I am nice and generous.
I wonder if we will have war with Syria.
I hear silence.
I see a blank piece of paper.
I want to become a financial manager.

I pretend I am in Minecraft.
I feel happy.
I touch the smoothness of this paper.
I worry about school.
I cry about other people's tears.
I am nice and generous.

I understand math.
I say be nice to each other.
I dream that there will be world peace.
I hope that everybody is happy.
I am nice and generous.
Robert Seifrit, Grade 5

Fall
Leaves are falling all around,
Start out green and end all brown.
Collecting food for winter's rest,
Animals run and build their nests.
Watching football on TV,
We trick or treat and get candy.
Picking apples from the tree,
We reach up high to get one sweet.
Fields of pumpkins for all to see,
Picking one that's too heavy.
Vibrant colors surrounding me,
Red, yellow, and orange are so pretty.
Breeze is blowing, branches bend,
Leaves take flight with the wind.
Leaping home I hear a sound,
Leaves are crunching with every bound.
Rake the leaves into a pile,
Jumping in makes me smile.
Sawyer Mapes, Grade 4

The Cat in My Hat
There's a deranged cat
In my voluminous hat
It's very warm where he sat
He likes my hat for his bed
Even when it's still upon my head
Outside in the snow
We really love to go
Where my hat is snatched,
By my feral brother, for we all know
Just how nice it can be
With something warm and fuzzy
Like a nonchalant cat
In your shroud-like hat
Jesse Hickman, Grade 6

Winter
Winter just barely begins
with frost on the window
and it kicks off cold winds
blowing

You can prove Winter
really has begun when
the first snow falls

It's definitely the middle
of Winter when carolers
are on your doorstep and
pots and pans are struck
on New Year's Eve

Sadly, Winter comes to
a close
as the cold, rainy February
fades away.
Emma Bishop, Grade 5

Midnight Fright
The sneaky skeletons roam around
as their bones make a clattering sound.
Witches laugh, black birds crow,
Gravestones wiggle and huge thorns grow.

Zombies try to dig out of the grass,
and ghouls and ghosts on the street pass.
Mummies and vampires haunt the street;
the fear of the night cannot be beat.

Crash! Bang! Boom! Splat!
The pumpkins are falling flat!
Jack-O-Lanterns light the town,
and autumn leaves are falling down.

As I go to sleep tonight,
I will think about the fright.
Zombies, vampires, witches, and ghosts;
I will think about them all tonight!
Sianna Bradley, Grade 5

My Best Friend is My Xbox
My best friend is a console.
Some people think it's crazy,
But I don't.
I can play it with my sister.
I can play it with my friends.
I play with friends at school.
But my real friend is my Xbox.
I had it since last Christmas.
I still have it now.
I keep it like a baby.
I love my Xbox.
Tylor Veney, Grade 4

The Babysitter's Warning
Were you about to push that girl?
Were you about to pull her curl?
Do you see that grape juice spill?
On the pillow that sits on the window sill?
I'm sure that Santa's watching close.
That vase you broke? I'm sure he knows.
Yeah, sure — it's weeks and weeks away
But be good for the sake of Christmas Day.
If you want to see a big wrapped box
(One that's not filled with homemade socks)
Under the tree, this December,
And toys in your stockings, then just remember:
If Christmas comes, just like it should,
Then Saint Nick will know if you've been good!
Sophia Leitner-Sieber, Grade 6

Hope
The winter woods are very cruel and dark,
My candle is my only flame of hope.
The snow flies 'round just like a morning lark,
My fear is weaving into a long rope,
I cannot hope to ever reach the end.
I'm cold and I have no way to escape,
I'm all alone and I have no true friend,
The snow falls 'round me like a magic cape.
My mother's arms bring me back home once more.
Hot cocoa soothing down my very weak dry throat.
Completely tired I lay down on the floor,
I sleep and am taken on a dream boat.
Here in my mother's embrace, I feel very warm,
I feel that I am safe from cold and scorn.
Isabella Pappas, Grade 6

Father Returns from War
Every night the children watched for Papa's return.
One night they heard a strange, distant noise
coming from far down the road.
They thought it might be their father coming.
They ran around the house, setting up decorations
and bringing out their special surprises.

When he got there, for it was indeed their father,
he found the lights off and nobody to welcome him.
He looked sad. Then all of the sudden the lights were on
and out jumped all the children shouting, "Surprise!"
Running and hugging him, they gave him their presents.
He just smiled because there was nothing else he could do
to show his joy at being home.
Bridget Andrews, Grade 5

Falling Leaves
F alling slowly, soaring by me in the air
A ll around
L ying gently on the ground
L and
I ncredibly soft
N early everywhere in the air
G liding by us

L ight hits
E very second
A round me is
V ery pretty
E very color like yellow and red
S ight we behold out our window, yellow, red, orange
Eliza Cole, Grade 5

Dance Class
I was not doing well in dance class
I couldn't get the hang of it
My dance teacher thought I was not a good dancer
Or that I was failing at it
Then I remembered the horrible death of my father
He wanted me to be a dancer
It made me work harder and harder
I pushed myself to the point where I was not confident anymore
I didn't think I could do it anymore
Making myself feel bad
I started spinning round and round
Trying my hardest to succeed
The rush of energy went through my body
This caused me to dance!
Kirsten Kanuika, Grade 5

My Daydream
I lay on my back in the sweet-smelling grass,
I look with bright eyes into the deep blue sky,
The sun is so orange and fiery bright,
And I see a baby bird learning to fly.

The sun slowly sets, sinking into the west,
And stars come from hiding, they pop into sight.
The moon is so full like a saucer of milk,
And skies fold around me as I step through night.

Sunrise opens the gates of day,
Hills rise from skyline like muffins when baked.
Clouds turning rosy cushion the sky,
And I am still smiling as slowly, I wake.
Quinlan Finamore, Grade 5

What Is Fall?
F irewood burning in the brisk autumn air
A gain the animals shelter for hibernation
L eaves falling gracefully down to the gentle ground
L ong, lazy days begin to form
Maggie Constantine, Grade 5

Magical Moments
Amber is a unicorn.
She's as shimmery as magic dust.
She likes jumping on trampolines,
cheerleading with her friends, and swimming in the Atlantic Ocean.
Amberlee Jack, Grade 6

High Merit Poems – Grades 4, 5, and 6

Lollipop Accident
I'm hungry
I think of that juicy rainbow lollipop
on the highest counter
I jump and jump onto the counter
until the highest one
I reach
get the lollipop
jump down
touch the juicy rainbow lollipop
take a lick
I feel so happy
not ready
for a bump on the shoulder
by my brother
as I jump
the lollipop
slips out of my hand
when I figure out
no lollipops for me.
Makayla Kelly, Grade 4

The Journey
Is it on its way?
the clouds are crying tears of anger
the wind is howling loud
the trees are bare and shivering
but it's still on its way

Is its journey almost over?
the rain is squeezing out of the clouds
the thunder is tired and bored
the lightning is lost and faint
for it's journey is almost over

Is it arriving?
the sun is smiling from ear to ear
the birds can't seem to settle down
the kids are happy and playing again
and
yes
happiness is arriving
Annabel Gerber, Grade 6

My Nature Walk
I feel the wind blow
The leaves crunch beneath my feet
It must be autumn

I walk down the street
See everyone bundled up
And people inside

The leaves are bright red
I can even see my breath
As the leaves fall down
Paige Audet, Grade 6

Snow Day
It's snowing
Hurray!
Maybe no school today
I wonder what I shall do
Should I make a snowman "dude"
I know what I can do
Finish my project it's overdue!
Art project what a doozy
I changed my mind,
all I want to do is be lazy
What show should I watch?
Maybe the Brady Bunch
I'm watching a show
And my mom says to shovel snow!
Luna Villamil, Grade 5

I Used to Be
I used to be a baseball
But now I'm a grand slam
I used to be a smile
But now I'm a frown
I used to be a giggle
But now I'm a laugh
I used to be incomplete
But now I'm finished
I used to be a grape
But now I'm a raisin
I used to be a piece of pizza
But now I'm eaten
I used to be a tiny baby
But now…I'm a grown man!
Nathan Dodge, Grade 5

Blue
I see the sky
Our school and the nice summer pool
They are all blue
When you hear the wind
And when you squirt out the glue
Then you run swiftly and hear blue
Even though the plums aren't blue
They taste like it
I think of juicy pie and custard too
When I feel a soft teddy bear
Or a squishy ball
They all feel blue
Blue can cheer me up
And get me excited!
Lourdes Torres, Grade 4

Halloween
Halloween is full of fear
Mummies, ghosts, and ghouls appear
Maybe death is here
It's okay if you drop a tear.
Genio Johnson, Grade 6

Dreams
My dreams are like trips to paradise.
Only bright happy colors
Appear in my mind.
A bright neon yellow sun
Shines my thoughts
Making every dream have a happy ending.
Light lavender represents the
Petals of beautiful lilacs.
Fusha pink is the cotton candy clouds
Floating above my head.
Making the air smell delectable
Baby blue is the sky clear and fresh
Like pure water.
Mint green standing as bushes
And beautiful plants surround me.
Every color in my dreams is
So majestic and gorgeous.
Jaclyn Berman, Grade 5

Kate
Kate
Creative,
Sweet,
Kind,
Wishes for an endless supply of chocolate,
Dreams of peace in the world,
Wants to make everyone happy,
Who wonders, "What lies beyond the sky?"
Who fears sadness.
Who likes dogs.
Who believes in fairies.
Who loves her family.
Who loves chocolate.
Who loves school.
Who loves Christmas.
Who plans to be a teacher.
Whose final destination is heaven.
Kate Haydel-Brown, Grade 5

Christmas
Santa, Santa
Flying through the sky.
Dropping presents by and by.
It's Christmas morning,
Whoopee! Whoopee!
Time to see what's under the tree.
Is it a bike?
Is it a train?
Is it a car?
Is it a plane?
Let's go and see
What is under the tree.
What's under the tree?
It's a Puppy for me!
And I named him Christmas Tree!
Anthony Mosca, Grade 4

Page 139

Lilliputian

I am only a knickknack in this nothing, yet more than an atom fills my soul.
You don't know me, yet all along that was my goal.
A destroyer is attacking me, and my humming bird family,
This makes me able to rest but not sleep, I must protect my surroundings from depriving me of knowledge.

Yet I have no say in what occurs around me,
I still have allies that try to help but can't.
I need more but more is being taken,
No one has met my destination, so I lose aplomb in myself.

I don't drown in knowledge, but a humming bird doesn't hum.
I don't have the capacity to know knowledge, I guess my soul feels numb.
I eat things smaller than myself, like a humming bird,
But truly, I feel as if I were the smallest thing, so I don't eat.

Knowledge was bigger yet I thought I could eat it.
I bit off more than I can chew,
And I found myself dead on the inside,
Because my forest is crackling and gray.

Soon I will move on from a humming bird
Because I am too endangered.
I die every day, but that will change,
It's not that I don't need the humming bird; Nobody needs…us.

Brandon Foster-Bagley, Grade 6

The Power of True Love

True love is when you would do anything for that special person.
You would risk your life to protect them.
Loving someone is when you find that person who completes you.
If you truly love somebody, they are the reason you exist.
There are some people who try to fake love just so they can say they are in love since true love is so rare.
Only the luckiest of people find true love.
If you happen to be one of those lucky people,
Hang on to it and don't let go.
Because true love is the strongest of all power.

Sarah McCloskey, Grade 6

Thanksgiving

Thank you
For all my tongue can taste,
The turkey with stuffing inside tender, sweet, and tasty
With that delicious apply pie
Put all that smooth, silky gravy on that turkey with mashed potatoes on the side

Thank you
For all my eyes can see,
The whole family sitting at the table
The beautiful leaves of all colors combined with the amazing, astonishing, sunset in the horizon

Thank you
For all my ears can see,
Birds singing as they fly away to the south,
Loud sounds on the TV from a football game,
And "clinging" and "Clanging" coming from all the pots and pans in the kitchen

Ryan Valdemira, Grade 6

The Soccer Field
The soccer ball goes on the field on top of the green grass.
It was being passed very fast.
Foot by foot there it goes.
I wonder if the players hurt their toes.
After that here comes the wave!
The crowd stands up as the players play.
Soon after someone kicks the ball!
Then soon it falls.
A team has won, hip hip hooray!
They leave with the trophy today.
Aidalina Cruz, Grade 5

Things I Am Thankful For
I am thankful for all my friends.
They make me feel glad when I am sad.

I am thankful for my mom and dad.
My mom and dad never make me feel mad…

If I could write all that I am thankful for —
That would be too much that's for sure!

I just can't write all the things I am thankful for.
Aolani Cruz, Grade 5

Darkness
As my mother closes the lamp
Nothing, but pure darkness
I stay as petrified as a mouse
All the things I wonder, pop out,
It's clear to me now
Darkness, I have to live with it every day
Just wait, you might see things you cannot believe
Well, as long you think of light you won't fear the dark
As soon as I close my eyes I dream of the best things
The sun is peaking and darkness…is light
Ali Latif, Grade 5

Dreams
I go to bed and say goodnight,
It's definitely not worth the fright,
I'm so eager to dream right now,
I could dream about a famous person taking a bow,
Think about it dreams do come true,
The main route of a dream is all about you,
A dream is something you should keep close to your heart,
A dream is a future with a brilliant start.
Heather Kwafo, Grade 6

Grandparents Are…
The folks I love.
People who put a smile on my face.
Those relatives who come and cheer me on at events.
Someone with whom I enjoy having conversations.
Friends who take me on adventures.
William Werner, Grade 6

Winter's Snow
I wake up in the morning, look out of the window
seeing the beautiful snow!
Such a beautiful sight, so white
With my winter coat I head out into the cold!
I pick up some snow and feel it, then smile,
For I haven't seen much snow in awhile!
Catching snowflakes in my mouth, having so much fun,
Then I am done, but not for long!
I walk in the house and drink warm hot chocolate,
Imagining what my next snowy adventure will be like!
Caitlynn Anderson, Grade 6

Run
Run
Hear the tap, tap, tapping as I run on the hard ground
Run
See the world whizzing by me
Run
Feel the wind on my face
Tap, tap, tap
Whiz, whiz, whiz
Blowing
Run
Hadley Kaeyer, Grade 6

Ode to Pomegranate
Oh, pomegranate,
Your juice is good; Your seeds are better,
But you are all of them together.
You're my favorite juice and fruit ever.

Your color is beautiful, but you taste a lot better.
You make my taste buds go on a heavenly ride.
I just love you so much.
I love your juice and your seeds.
I can't stand to be away from you.
Tye Lewis, Grade 4

My Sister
Heart of the house
stuck in my land of hope
But never wants to leave
Living in my dreams
sits on the seat of my heart forever
our relationship will forever stay stuck together like glue
Symbol of happiness
Always loved by me
Ava Folk, Grade 4

Thanksgiving Is Fun
Thanksgiving is fun.
It is a time to be thankful.
Come on and grab your friends and family
And have some fun while eating food and playing board games.
That is the true meaning of Thanksgiving!
Steven King, Grade 5

Life

I want to see life.
I want to cradle it in my arms, rest it upon my shoulders, wrap it around myself like a blanket, and never let go.
I want to leave a footprint in the fresh soil of the rain forest.
I want to taste the warm, creamy milk that sleeps inside a coconut,
Smell the cool, salty air that drifts above the oceans all around us.
I want to be part of the massive crowds of China, to experience the hustle and bustle of it all.
I want to press my hand to the chilly, snowcapped mountains of Russia,
Gaze up at the twinkling stars from a different place each night.
I want to see polar bears, great white sharks, speckled giraffes, sprinting cheetahs, and soaring eagles.
I want to stand on top of the world at the top of the Eiffel Tower.
I want to run free, roam free, touch the sky, fly!
I want to chase down and tackle my dreams.
I want to go out there and show the world who I am.
I want everything.

Grace Palmer, Grade 5

Halloween Night

Screams and shouts and a bunch of pouts
Twists and turns with no return
It's Halloween Night and your on the prowl
Looking for things that won't make you howl
You're afraid of ghosts and goblins jumping out at you
And witches making stew out of you
You duck and hide at the slightest 'creek'
Knowing the monster won't be so sweet
But you shouldn't be afraid of a slight sound
Because there's more out there, like a woman who drowned
You jump at the footsteps as you try to go to sleep
You peep towards your door and see that it's your friends who are yelling "TRICK-OR-TREAT!"
So don't be afraid on Halloween Night
Just have some fun, and don't let the vampires bite

Zoonash Syed, Grade 6

Paradise

Paradise
Paradise is like Wonderland
You are in a trance, yet wide awake
To see this world with open eyes, you are shocked
WHOOSH! There's the glistening waves crashing onto the glittering sands
You look up and see baby blue skies
All around you are a whole group of palm trees, swaying in the wind as a couple of coconuts fall

Then you notice a peculiar hut right in the middle everything
As you cautiously walk in you notice it has everything you need
It has books, clothes, supplies and a bed too!
Then it suddenly dawns on you,
This truly is paradise and…
I am truly home!

Kenneth Tang, Grade 6

Mountain

As I look through the open sky, I see a giant white cap and a bulky structure that stands up so high with a purpose.
As the birds fly over it, I think to myself, "What a beautiful landmark and what remarkable colors."
I see the galloping sheep jumping from ledge to ledge and the roaring mountain lion waiting to catch its prey.
What a beautiful mountain.

Nathan Sottak, Grade 5

Shopping Time
I went shopping with my Mom.
I got a charm.
She bought a toy car for my brother.
He was happy
And so was I.
Brianna Branch, Grade 4

Ducks
Ducks
Soft, floating
Flying, spying, quacking
Covered with brown feathers
Bird
Jackson Williams, Grade 5

Owls
Owls
Small, feathery
Scaring, hiding, living
They are nocturnal animals
Bird
Jacqueline Garst, Grade 5

Snow
Snow is so fun to play with
But not to get hit with.
It is beautiful on trees
But not when stepped on.
And is beautiful when untouched on fields.
Spencer A-R, Grade 4

Dogs
dogs,
cute, furry
sleeping, barking, playing
I love my dog
Lila
Anneliese Getola, Grade 4

Twins
T wins are sisters, but closer,
W ith each other at all times,
I dentical sometimes, fraternal sometimes,
N ever mean (well, usually not),
S tick together, that's what we do.
Emma Colton, Grade 4

World War II
World War II
Loud, terrifying
Bombing, running, shooting
The worst 6 years ever
Death defying
Ryan Jubulis, Grade 5

Holocaust
H ate being spread for religious reasons
O ne by one, they were each eliminated
L adies holding children, never letting go
O n the ground, little hope remains where the death camp stood
C autiously hiding, praying never to be taken away
A ton of people dying in front of people's eyes and doing nothing about it
U nsure when freedom will reveal itself, but almost positive it will
S orrow filled the air, if only Hitler was fair
T ears running down all the innocent people's faces
Madison Pascual, Grade 6

The Garden
The sun welcomes the new plants.
While the water gives them refreshments while they watch the beating sun.
The darkness replaces the beating sun.
Now the plants can see is darkness.
The plants wait for the beating to come back and welcome them.
They can still taste the refreshments from the water.
The sun comes back.
The plants cheer.
While they drink the refreshing water.
Hailey Rutherford, Grade 5

Winter
The colder it gets, the more you shiver…
Time to bring the blankets out and light the fireplace.
Soon it will be snowing.
Time for a cup of joe.
Let's make a snowman or a fort but don't catch a cold.
Next thing you know you'll be counting up to the twenty-fifth and singing Christmas carols.
Christmas lights and decorations fill our festive tree.
Oh my! Listen I hear the big red guy. Ho Ho Ho!
Boy do I love winter!
Jacob Learish, Grade 4

A Game of Tag
A game of tag and chase with him
with his eyes sparkling into my soul
with his golden face shining in the sun
sometimes the best thing to do with him is to play out in the open world
he wants me to spend time with him playing outdoors
he strikes my soul when I look at him
and we sing of freedom together and
happiness fills the air
Michael Blazo, Grade 4

Screaming
That's what I felt like doing
When I heard the horrible news
The loss of someone is hard on you
But not as difficult as anything you can imagine on me
Gifts didn't help
Sympathy made it worse
So every time I find myself thinking of Grandma, that's what I'm doing inside…
Screaming
Alexia Spicci, Grade 6

I Wonder Who...?!

I stared into a mirror and a bunny stared back
I stumbled back in surprise and hopped into an old brown sack.

I pulled my ears over my eyes I was filled with all sorts of whos, wheres and whys
I hopped over to the mirror once more when suddenly someone knocked at the door

In came a girl with bright red hair she had rosy cheeks and skin that was fair
I knew this girl very well she came in with a string and a jingly bell

She picked me up and took me out I still wonder what that thing was about
She put me down on the grassy ground while I still wondered what I found

I wondered who made that amazing thing was that an inventor who was a wearing a ring?
All these questions made me think more even if I had ideas I wasn't quite sure

I took a look at clear object and saw myself and smiled I wondered who made this magical thing he must be wild!
I thought and thought then thought some more! Even if I had ideas I still wasn't sure!!

I frowned no matter how hard I thought I wouldn't get it right! I looked up at the ceiling and squinted at the light
I took another look at the strange clear thing, you don't know what it is, do you?
The creator of this thing has to be really smart, hmm...I wonder who...?

Shachi Dahal, Grade 5

Dreaming

From the words that I think up
Daydreaming in a classroom
To the words that stick with me
That I end up writing down.
When your mind's always racing you learn to keep
An index card around. The first syllable's sound,
When it came out of my mouth it made my ear drums do a little dance.
As the notes pranced off the page and gripped my soul, I knew this was it.
It's the first word that turned out to sing a song.
You know me, I have O.W.D: Obsessive Writing Disorder.
But my first piece of writing was a joke.
It's like in a huge recital, when you hit a sour note. As it rumbles through the auditorium with a final screech, you can't speak.
When you say the wrong line in a musical, you want to run away but this drive inside forces you to stay and finish the play.
When I read my first piece of poetry they laughed at me.
Now I recite a poem I wrote and they reply "Wow, that was deep!"
Later that night it made me wonder.
"All of this just from one dream" The dream to be a poet.
Scribbles in a notepad turned out to define who I am. It's gotten to the point to when I sleep, I dream about the words
In my next piece of poetry. Sharing my thoughts makes me happy.
A way I can express myself. The joy I feel when I watch the led leap across the page, a tingly feeling. And no matter what people
Say about my silly little thoughts, sure enough, I will keep on Dreaming.

Brianna Jones-Hollis, Grade 5

Thanksgiving Spatial Fun

Thanksgiving is so fun because you help out with dinner and hanging with family. Watching movies with family is so fun. The best part about the meal is the golden brown turkey right out the oven. But I wouldn't say thanksgiving is my favorite. But it a time to sit with the family, AND my family watches the football game, and when we sit down to eat us give prays for thanking us food, Now we dig in and rip the turkey apart. After that we eat dessert like pumpkin pie with whip cream on top. When they take it out of the oven it smells like a 100 candles lighting up in one room. I like to drink Kelp juice with dessert. Then we line up to GIVE the chief our dinner plates. Then something weird about me
Is when it time for pumpkin pie, I eat in the back room, and watch TV while I eat whip cream

Alyssa Straile, Grade 6

Magic

Do you believe in magic?
Because it's always there
Do you believe in magic?
It's always in the air

Do you believe in magic?
I do, it's real
Do you believe in magic?
It's no prank, it's real

Magic is wonderful,
It lets your dreams fly
Magic is incomparable, it's no lie

Magic is beautiful
It helps you every day
Magic is sweet
It makes you just lay,

And look at all the wonders, of things big and small
Sweets, dreams, come one and all

Do you believe in magic?
Because it's always there
Do you believe in magic?
It's always in the air
Alyssa Melby, Grade 4

Mom

You brighten up my life with tender love and care
You reach out to me like a tree
You care

I am very thankful to have you as my mom
You make my heart glow
My future shine

I always think you over protect
But you just want me to be safe
And I am with you

Your brilliant brain thinking
Your opinions help
That is why I feel good on the inside

I feel so happy when I'm with you
You are such a good person
The greatest one around
You deserve your own special crown

Like I said before
You have a good heart
You're honest and true
I love you
Carly Beaulieu, Grade 6

Voice of Frogs

Blackness starts to spread,
twilight is calling,
little life lit eyes appear out of the crystal clear water,
and jump to join the grass,
croak,
you hear softly,
while songs of freedom whirl around you,
and dart through your head,
the darkness gets lighter
the little treasures come closer,
while the sun comes up slowly,
like it's the earth's rebirth,
they hide on the dawn bright lawn,
then disappear into the mist of the creek,
a small smiles comes to my face,
then they smile back at me.
Dakota Bishop, Grade 4

Thanksgiving

Leaves are warm and crisp, the sun is shining
Turkeys are ready for you specially made
Pumpkin pie oh so lovely
The feast is erupting, ready to be eaten
Turkeys are ready for you specially made
Macy's parade proud and thankful
The feast is erupting, ready to be eaten
Family together oh who couldn't be more thankful
Macy's parade proud and thankful
Board games set up and ready
Family together oh who couldn't be more thankful
Thanksgiving couldn't be better
Board games set up and ready
Pumpkin pie oh so lovely
Thanksgiving couldn't be better
Leaves are warm and crisp, the sun is shining
Alma Dardari, Grade 4

Thanksgiving

The beautiful cozy smell of turkey fills the air
I am grateful for all of the feast
My mom makes the best green rice in the world
I eat a fat juicy drumstick
I am grateful for all of the feast
I see my family all at once
I eat a fat juicy drumstick
My grandma makes a yummy pie
I see my family all at once
Back to Pittsburgh to see Grammy and Pappy
My grandma makes a yummy pie
We have yummy stuffing balls
Back to Pittsburgh to see Grammy and Pappy
My mom makes the best green rice in the world
We have yummy stuffing balls
The beautiful cozy smell of turkey fills the air
Alex Bartone, Grade 4

Long and Blazing Fire
It brings destruction,
When it comes it leaves ashes,
It is long lasting,
The color is red and dead,
Nothing remains afterward.
Joseph Knisley, Grade 6

Animals
Act wild and do tricks,
Different pets can walk or fly,
Some make weird sounds,
Different sizes and heights,
Pets listen to their owners.
Meghan Reilly, Grade 6

Winter Day
Looks freezing out there,
Lumberjacks chopping oak wood,
Wolves are howling now,
Plenty of wood to last a while,
The day is ending very soon.
Douglas Hild, Grade 6

My Missing Part of Family
Memories come back,
Of my great-grandfather's love,
A wonderful man,
A World War II veteran,
My missing part of family.
Abbie Thompson, Grade 6

Bears Hibernating
It's almost spring now,
All bears were hibernating,
The bears come outside,
All of the bears saw new life,
Now they go and eat.
Caroline Brooke, Grade 6

Settlers
Pilgrims
Thankful, giving
Talking to Indians
Make food to eat with Indians
People
Kylie Mastropolo, Grade 4

Swimming
We swim in the pool,
Or we swim in the ocean,
The water is warm,
That is what it is in the day,
And it is cool in the night.
Emidio Sciarretta, Grade 6

I Am
I am awesome and smart.
I wonder how I became the person I am.
I hear a bell ring when I get an answer right in my head.
I see a beautiful garden when I think of my BFF.
I want to always stay on top of my school work.
I am awesome and smart.

I pretend to be a dog whisperer.
I feel creative and like an artist.
I touch blankets soft as silk.
I worry when the time comes I might not be ready to grow up.
I cry about not seeing my BFF in school every day. (I always miss her.)
I am awesome and smart.

I understand that everybody has to grow up.
I say when you set your mind to something there is nothing you can't do.
I dream about being a singer.
I try always to get good grades.
I hope I can achieve always staying on top of my schoolwork.
I am awesome and smart.
Isabella Serra, Grade 5

Dancing Dreams
I am a girl who loves to dance
I wonder what dance will bring me?
I hear my dance teacher telling me to do all sorts of things like roundoff backhand springs
I see all of my friends doing their roundoff backhand springs
I want to make the competition team with my best friend Siara
I am a girl who loves to dance

I pretend I'm on stage doing my very best
I feel relieved after I do my front handspring and my teacher says fabulous
I touch the mats when cart wheeling
I worry that I might fall while I'm trying to land
I am a girl who loves to dance

I understand that I might not make competition team
I say I must try harder
I dream to be the best dancer
I try to land front handsprings
I hope to be on competition team and win a trophy
I am a girl who loves to dance
Elizabeth Petrangelo, Grade 5

Color Splits
It's a touch of rainbow and a touch of light.
It's a wonderful thing to see.
Especially, when green sees me.
Red, is the color of my lips and blood.
Blue, is the color of skies shining upon us.
Pink, is the color of my shirts and pants.
Purple, is the color of my family's feathers.
The paper is like a canvas of mazes of colorful rainbows that just needs to be filled.
So I paint and splat it until it's says I'm done.
Christina McCain, Grade 4

Teacher vs Parent
Teacher
Smart, happy
Teaching, working, playing
Morning, afternoon, Mom, Dad
Working, cooking, loving
Clean, fun
Parent
Martiah Fenelon, Grade 6

Girls vs Boys
Girls
Pretty, cute
Sharing, caring, learning
Salon, mall, practice, sports
Working, driving, playing
Handsome, strong
Boys
Anyjha Frazier, Grade 6

Jamestown
The new land
Beautiful land
Trees that are untouched
Native homes where Indians live
Wild animals running in fields
The teal colored ocean
Gently kissing a sandy shore
Jocelyn Tyree, Grade 4

Trees
Magnificent feature of nature
Swaying in the wind
Giving off oxygen
The main source to life
Brightly blazing in the sun
Seeing the world as it changes
Making the world lively
Lalana Kraiwan, Grade 5

My Seasons
Summer
Hot, sunny
Playing, laughing, drinking
Juice, skirts, coffee, sweats
Sitting, eating, sleeping
Cold, foggy
Winter
Kimberly Yanez, Grade 6

Beautiful
Beautiful is flowers blooming
Beautiful is the moon shining
Beautiful is music flowing
Beautiful is the leaves turning colors
And beautiful is me!
Ellyse Colón, Grade 4

The Most Important Thing About Apparitions
The most important thing about apparitions is you can't see them.
They whirl in the wind.
They make stairs creak.
They're the returning of the dead;
And some don't even have heads!
They may be animals or humans.
One day we'll all be them!
But the most important thing about an apparition is you can't see them.
Connor Maze, Grade 4

Attack of the Fish
It is early afternoon, early in the summer.
The light blue waves are crashing and the seagulls are squawking in the breezy blue sky.
I smell tangy seaweed and fresh ocean.
I feel a warm cool breeze. Also, cold water on my skin.
The neon yellow fish are attacking the light green turtle.
My mind is calm.
Will the turtle get away from the fish?
Cai Rogers, Grade 4

When I Am
When I am tired, I am as sleepy as a bear nestling for an upcoming hibernation.
When I am sad, I am like a puppy begging for a treat to nibble on.
When I am annoyed, I am as furious as a bull charging at a bright red sheet.
When I am happy, I am like a cheerful little girl on Christmas morning.
When I am embarrassed, I am as red as a fully bloomed rose in a garden.
When I am sick, I am like a light headed mess about to explode.
Paige Shannon, Grade 6

Water in the Ocean
I am the water in the foamy ocean.
Blue as an orchid, springing up from the ground.
I command the fish to swim eagerly.
I cough up waves when I get a cold.
I can deceive you of a nice, calm day, but I will really toss all of the swimmers around.
I am the water in the foamy ocean.
Audrey Murray, Grade 6

How to Have Fun
You can't have fun if you don't know how so pick up this poem and read it out loud. Play outside or pick up a book, watch TV or learn how to cook. That's just the beginning were not done yet, write a poem or get a pet. Ride your new scooter or climb up a tree, come to the park and play with me, we can go down the slide or play basketball, go on the swings or do nothing at all.
Michaela Fitzgerald and Ali Hoy, Grade 6

Fun Feast
The Thanksgiving Holiday is the best time to stuff your face.
Nobody can make turkey as good as my grandmother.
Games are the best part of my Thanksgiving Day.
My family and I play Monopoly, Scrabble, and other board games.
My Uncle Vinnie makes homemade mashed potatoes with gravy.
For dessert, my Aunt Ashley makes fresh brownies to finish the awesome day.
Eugene Zellman, Grade 6

A Blossom
I am a Blossom,
As I grow older I do not die nor wilt,
I grow stronger.

Sometimes it's hard. and other times easier,
But I still stand tall.
And when I fall, I stand taller,
And I grow stronger.

You see you too are a Blossom just as me.
You grow, and you learn,
You strive and you achieve,
You shine, and you inspire,
You are inspired.

So truthfully the definition of a Blossom,
Is You and Me.
Nia Phipps, Grade 6

It's About
It's about balls being hit
Home-runs being robbed
Playoffs being made

It's about never quitting
Always winning
First place taking

It's about games being won
Shutouts, no hitters, and perfect games
History being made

It's about eating food
Fans being cruel
Unfair calls

It's about the World Series being won
Max Pellegrino, Grade 5

An Ode to My Brother
Bub, I love you so much!
Even when you're mean sometimes,
But I still love you so much!

We always fight,
Even when you're nice,
It could last the whole night.

We can get along,
Most of the time we can't,
But we can when we play Ping-Pong.

You say you don't mean it,
I know you don't mean it,
Even though I say I don't believe it.
Jordan Hill, Grade 4

Black Heart
Go away
I'm not here
I'm not going to shed a tear
You have a cold heart
A black one too
I never realized
What you could do
You threw me away
Just like that
Never said bye
Never came back
Black heart is all I could say
Never going to see another day
Fine whatever,
Have your way
Just remember what you did
You smashed my soul
And threw it away
Julia Lazar, Grade 6

I Am
I am funny and loving
I wonder if I could ever fly
I hear barks
I see a butterfly
I want to touch the sky
I am funny and loving
I pretend to fly
I feel happy inside
I touch a shining star
I worry about my life
I cry when my friends are not nice
I am funny and loving
I understand God
I say funny things
I dream of being a singer
I try my best on work
I hope to live a good life
I am funny and loving
Elizabeth Pierce, Grade 5

Blue
Blue is bluebirds chip, chip, chipping
The blue shimmering water
And pretty blue flowers
Blueberries taste sweet
Like soft blue cotton candy
And juicy eggplant
Blue jays sparkle with fun
Blue diamonds shimmer so brightly
And blue shirts are soft
Blue feels hard and big like my jeans
It feels smooth like a car
Driving down the highway
Blue brings happiness.
George McComas, Grade 4

Sled Races
Snowy and cold
A blanket of white
We grab our sleds
To head off before night

We got to the top
All ready to race
And off goes the horn
We're gone in a flash

I'm in the lead
With no time to pass
There's the finish line
Nearer it gets

Off again goes the horn
Kali has won 7 seconds flat
Rematch my rivals yell
So I answered with a flash of my smile
Kali Tregler, Grade 6

My Favorite Days
I love dark and cold days
and hiding away in the trees
I love how the trees sway
and how they rock me to sleep

Other days I just want to walk
and listen to the wind whistle
I like not having to talk
and feeling nature around me

On days like these I feel free
as the wind whisks me away
Sometime I feel as happy as a bee
in a big flower field

Hello trees, hello birds
I am sorry but I have to go
Even though I love your songs and words
I will listen for you in the snow
Sarah May, Grade 6

Me
I am me,
simple me,
colorful me,
annoying me,
silly me,
sad me,
happy me,
tall me,
scared me,
curious me,
I am me.
Victoria Rafac, Grade 5

God Is Great and Loving

God is great, God is loving.
God does care for you.
He cannot make you do bad or good.
He brings great, he brings bad.
God makes animals and people.
That is great, that is loving.
God is great and loving!
Hannah, Grade 4

Pumpkin Patch

So full of orange
I will snatch
One of my own
Cut a latch and
Carve a face
Then bake a batch
Of pumpkin pie.
Geena DeMario, Grade 5

My Dad

My Dad is fun to be around.
But he is never on time.
He gets things I need
And he is fun to be with.
My Dad is fun, but can be boring.
I love my Dad
And it will always be like that.
Bari Muhammad, Grade 4

Sports

Baseball
Hit, outside
Stealing, catching, hitting
Dirty, long, bloody, sweaty
Skating, passing, shooting
Inside, cold
Hockey
Trevor Turkovich, Grade 5

The Holocaust

Holocaust
Hatred, hope
Burning, locked, gassed
Taking, killing, optimism, energy
Warming, protecting, unrelenting
Unforgettable, undeniable
Love
Jake Wilson, Grade 6

The Turkey

Turkey
Juicy, gravy
Turkey pecks at the ground
Tastes good with a lot of gravy
Yummy
Chris Sorrentino, Grade 4

Months

January it's cold and it snows. You have to have fun everybody knows
February love is in the air, that's when everybody starts to care
In March we say hooray, because it's Trevor Hubbard's birthday
April people joke around, they start to become the big class clown.
My flowers being to bloom. That means June is coming soon
June school is coming to an end, that means July is around the bend.
In July we go to the Fireman's Fair, there are fireworks every where
August it's a real bummer. It is almost the end of summer.
September it's the start of school, but I just want to swim in the pool.
In October it's Halloween, that's when scary faces are seen.
In November my dad was born. At Thanksgiving we eat corn
Every year a day to remember, it's always in the month of December.
Trevor Hubbard, Grade 5

Football

Boom, pound, crack, blood, sweat, hard work
Handoff — you bounce outside, yardage, then you get hit
You run your route, find the ball in your hands, but again get hit
You still get back up, you refuse to stay down
One more time you get the ball and one more time you get crushed
Your head is pounding as fast as your heart
There is pain, bruises and sprains, but you hop back up
You're on the goal line, the QB calls for another handoff, up the middle
The ball slams into your gut, you get popped but stay up
You keep going, you dive, a glance at the ref…
Touchdown! You are hurting, throbbing, but the pain melts away for the moment.
Timmy Flynn, Grade 6

Kiwi

Oh Kiwi, oh Kiwi, the wonders you held.
Yes, you are delicious or at least that is what I was told.
Oh, you look like a young cactus who's thorns will soon sprout
And you feel like a baby porcupine whose quills will soon come out.
When I peel you, you sound like someone sanding wood.
When I slice you, you sound like a baby chick coming out of its egg before it finally stood.
On the inside, you look like a short rocky cave.
And on the inside, you feel like a toad after it bathed.
When I sniff you, you remind me of a bouquet of flowers.
And you taste like sour candy that was left stale for hours.
Oh Kiwi, please tell me how you left me speechless with your taste of pure deliciousness.
Tyler Lagun, Grade 5

My Cats

They lay in the orange sun rays resting
when I'm gone
while the sun warms their black circular body
resting until I walk through the door
and almost trip over them
that's when they run away with their feet like golden jets
even though they are no longer young, they are still as fast as a black blur
when they finally slow down
they rub and purr against my feet
begging for me to pet them
and I do

Tyler Eckert, Grade 4

Fairy Tales

As I walk down the old dusty street, my nose starts to smell something sweet. I see a house made out of gingerbread bricks, with a roof made of lollypops that needed to be licked. I walk to the door and go inside, in the house there is a witch I feel I must hide. As I close the delicious candy door, I shake with fear and say, "Ah… is this yours?" She replied "Oh no that's okay, I needed some company anyway." We sat and ate candy galore, until at least we could eat no more. We said farewell and bid our goodbyes, I hope I can come there another time. This had taught me how fairy tales end, sometimes you can meet your very best friend.

Kassidy Burke, Grade 6

The Nazi Plaque

As black boots marched on the blood stained ground the hearts of Jews quickened their pace. And every hate filled step the Nazis took the terror grew. Like a deadly plaque the Nazis' hate spread all over Europe from one to another all from one hate filled man, Hitler. Soon best friends against each other fear of someone who they knew their whole life. Killed for something they could not help. Yet to Hitler Jews were game and he was the hunter. Stamped with stars and numbers the Jews were herded like animals to the camps. And even now the Holocaust left a hole of fear in their hearts.

Savana Patton, Grade 6

My Grandparents Are

Brave people from their generation.
An inspiration to me and to others to succeed in life.
A symbol of love and affection which reminds me of when I see my sister caring for her pet dog.
Role models for encouragement when I am sad.
An expression of strength and wisdom to our family.

Deepak Shankar, Grade 6

The Extraordinary Durham Road

My neighborhood is the irking growls and hisses from our beloved furry friends.
My neighborhood is the delicious aroma of crispy, cheesy pizza from RJ's down the busy hill.
My neighborhood is children running on the cool, soft grass as fast as a car swishing down the road.
And it is the elegant flowers the bloom in the spring with vivid colors.
And it is the loving, warm place I like to call home.

Sayida Afghani, Grade 6

Soccer

I am a champion with speed and skills.
I wonder if I will be successful.
I hear my family and friend cheering me on
while I run to the goal and score.
I see the soccer ball glide through the
green grass.
I want to meet my favorite soccer player on
the Mexican team.
I am a champion with speed and skills.

I pretend I am standing on a turf field.
I feel the soccer ball bounce off my foot
then hit it with my knee
I touch the ground to get up.
I worry I will sparing my ankle on the soccer field.
I am a champion with speed and skills.

I understand that I will lose some games.
I say to always believe.
I dream I will win the championship.
I try to always play hard.
I hope I won't sparing my ankle in the championship.
I am a champion with speed and skills.

Jordan Cruz, Grade 5

He Shoots, He Scores!

I am a fast and strong hockey player
I wonder if our team will win
I hear skate blades crunch against the
cold, hard, smooth ice surface that
the players skate on
I see the black puck come flying toward my stick
I want to try to score a goal to help my team
I am a fast and strong hockey player

I pretend that I'm playing in the National League
I feel the cool breeze up against my face
as I gain more speed
I touch the hockey stick's shaft
I worry about someone hitting me hard and me getting hurt
I am a fast and strong hockey player

I understand that our team might not win
I say that our team's good
I dream I will be a professional
I try to achieve that goal
I hope that our team will win the
USA Hockey Championship
I am a fast and strong hockey player

Nicholas Kanaczet, Grade 5

The Perfect Wave

As gigantic waves crash upon the shore
I see the best wave that I just can't reach.
I swim out again, but hit the sea floor
And just like that I am back on the beach.

Not riding any good waves is no fun
These waves are like bulls where they buck and swing
The light starts to fade, and down goes the sun.
And inside my head, a bell starts to ring.

I notice a pattern, it could help me
There is a spot where the wave crashes late
I swim over there, and then I am free
And on the horizon, the wave of fate

As I paddle up, I'm all about grace
And when I crash down, a smile's on my face.

Andy Cort, Grade 5

Jack and Jill

You know it isn't easy to be Jack

It's always the same thing every day
Jill and I go up the hill
no matter what

Clumsy Jill trips on her shoelace
rolls down the hill
(on to me)
breaks my leg

On top of that, I am soaked
Jill doesn't even notice
She walks away leaving me flat on the ground
for 30 minutes

What a good sister she is!

William Gordon, Grade 6

What a Veteran Must Do

You leave your family, friends, and home
To keep us safe and sound
And when it's time that you return
And since we love you dearly
We celebrate all around
It's amazing what you do for us
And we all love you very much
One thing I know about veterans
Is that there is no one like you
No, there is nonesuch
And when I see a veteran
And maybe even you
I think I know exactly, yes, exactly what you'd do
You'd bend down on your knees and say,
"Did you know I fought for you?"

Ally Sprow, Grade 4

My Pets

I am a girl who loves all pets
I wonder if my pets can talk
I hear my cats and dogs fight to sleep in my bed, they are so loud
I see my cats and dogs cuddling with each other
I want to see my pets get along every day forever
I am a girl who loves all pets

I feel my pet's fluffy fur and it is relaxing, so I fall asleep
I touch my cats and dogs
I worry that my pets will get hurt
I am a girl who loves all pets

I say I love my pets
I dream I have lots of pets
I try to keep them safe
I hope my pets love me unconditionally because I love them
I am a girl who loves all pets

Faith Parton, Grade 5

A Happy Place

Under a tree in a meadow,
Reading an awesome book,
Truly makes me feel mellow,
Inside my own little nook.
Under my covers in my cozy little bed,
Drifting to sleep,
A pillow under my head,
Climbing up the mountain of my mind so steep,
Truly makes me wish to fall asleep.
On the shoreline water lapping at your toes,
A beautiful day for a walk on the beach,
Cool breezes nipping at your nose,
While sucking on the sweetest peach.
Up in my tree house the best place of all,
I promise to you that I won't let you fall,
I stay in my tree house until my mom gives me a call…
That's why these are the best places of all.

Caitlin Bagdasarian, Grade 5

Dream Colors

Dreams are red

Red because of the roses, leaves, and blood running through your veins

Dreams are green like the grass. Green is outside, video games, and reality

Dreams are brown, like hair, or a bureau.

Dreams are blue like water which is important for life.
Blue like your reading folder.

Blue, Brown, Green, and Red are all the dream colors I love.

Andrew Carmona, Grade 5

The Season of Colors
Summer ending, school staring, the
Days becoming shorter,
The arrival of autumn is near
The brittle leaves drifting down,
Leaving trees bare
Cornucopias filled
With pumpkins and squash from the fields
The mouthwatering smell of baking apple pie
Kids in costumes running from house to house
Gathering as much candy as they can
Rainfall comes in barrages
The crimson and amber leaves
Look like a painted canvas
Parties for Thanksgiving,
With mashed potatoes that are clouds,
Fluffy and warm
The turkey drenched in gravy,
A pumpkin pie for dessert
Days are ending sooner, and the air becoming cooler,
The end of autumn is near,
Winter almost here!
Brandon Robayo, Grade 6

Goodbye Summer, Hello Autumn!
Leaves fall into the pool before we cover it up
Birds tweeting and chirping
As they prepare to migrate south for the winter
The warm feeling of gloves as I slip them on
Fast blowing leaves are a
Light mist floating through
The stormy sky
The rustling
As loud as a hurricane's violent winds
Crunchy amber leaves under my feet
Children walking into new schools
Families coming and
Traveling to get to loved ones before Thanksgiving
Scrumptious cinnamon-filled apple fritters
People picking pumpkins to use for tasty pie
Delicious gold corn at farm stands
After gorgeous fall
Winter comes
And snow drifts slowly down
Instead of
Leaves
Daniela Garey, Grade 6

Mystical Creatures
Have you ever seen a creature so beautiful and wonderful?
One that sparkles and gleams in light?
That hides until sunset's gone, but stays for the night?

Have you ever seen a creature so mystical and whimsical?
One that lives in the forest deep?
That lives and breathes but never sleeps?
Ashley Klein, Grade 5

James, the Seagull
Once there was a bird who loved to write.
But you might have thought it was someone bright.
Out of all the birds it was a really, small gull.
But he had one problem, his pencil was dull.
He said, "This can't be true, this is a fable."
But all he needed to do is go to Staples.
The only thing was it was too late.
He said, "What do I do? For goodness sake!"
For the store to be open, he prayed all night.
Until he saw the morning light.
When he was first in line he went berserk.
So he checked out his sharpener with the clerk.
When the clerk asked, "What's your name?"
The little gull said, "My name is James."
Ethan Choi, Grade 5

When I Grow Up...
I could be a builder!
I would build high to the sky!
Or I could be a policeman!
I would fight crimes, and stop bad guys!
I could be a firefighter!
I would put out fires!
Or I could be a boss!
I would fire and hire!
I could be a doctor!
I would help the sick!
Or I could be a farmer!
I would grow fresh vegetables that I would pick!
But when I grow up is the only time I have to worry.
And when I am I will be in a hurry.
William Rice, Grade 5

Fall
Big oversized sweater
With boots made out of leather

Leaves falling
But winter is calling

Watching TV with my Starbucks drink
Or maybe with some milk that's pink

What colors are in this season
Orange, red or gold—It's only nature's reason

Anyway off to the mall
To get myself some popcorn to start the fall
Kiara Chombo, Grade 6

A Dream
I had a dream that Mom and Dad gave me candy.
I had a dream that I helped Santa and his reindeer.
I had a dream that I helped elves at Christmas.
I had a dream that I got lots of gifts for being good.
Jadasia Watkins, Grade 4

Bring on the Olympics!
I am a brave girl who does gymnastics.
I wonder if I'll become an Olympian.
I hear my teammates cheering me on as
I hit the spring board and stick my landing.
I see the audience cheering and clapping as I compete.
I want to stick my beam routine and qualify for
state championships.
I am a brave girl who does gymnastics.

I pretend that no one is watching me on beam.
I feel the rhythm in my floor exercise as I get scored by judges.
I touch the shiny gold medals.
I worry about doing something wrong in front of the judges.
I am a brave girl who does gymnastics.

I understand that I cannot always win.
I say, "I believe in myself."
I dream of being a professional gymnast.
I try my best to succeed.
I hope I will always be able to do gymnastics forever.
I am a brave girl who does gymnastics.
Haley Farnoto, Grade 5

A Girl Who Loves Soccer
I am a girl who enjoys playing soccer.
I wonder if I'll win the game.
I hear the crowd cheering my name as
I dribble the ball, as I score the goal.
I see my family and team cheering my name loudly.
I want my team to go to Championships and win the games.
I am a girl who enjoys playing soccer.

I pretend my team always wins my soccer games.
I feel very happy when my team score and wins a game.
I touch my own Championship trophy.
I worry about getting hurt and not playing in the game.
I am a girl who enjoys playing soccer.

I understand I may not make the team.
I say it's ok to lose.
I dream playing on a great team.
I try to score a goal.
I hope I will score a goal one day this year.
I am a girl who enjoys playing soccer.
Karina Rivera, Grade 5

Fall
October air giving us a fright,
drifting through the air like an invisible breeze.
"Trick or treat!" you hear at your door all night long.
So scared in fall when the leaves fall right off the trees.
Get ready! Get ready! October has arrived
And it's here for a while.
Turkeys say gobble in the barn — it's all you hear.
Thanksgiving feast: turkey, stuffing, and cranberry sauce
Can be your family's meal for the night.
Nice nights in November.
All the leaves fall off the trees.
And cover the ground.
Two or three are blown away by a huge gust of wind.
"Brrr," you say on a November night.
December: Santa's coming 'round the corner.
Getting presents under the tree
hoping you got what you wanted.
Snowy days playing in the snow.
Dreaming of nice warm days in the summer.
Wish, whoosh, drop goes the snow:
it is bleaching the ground.
Kylie Brzezicki, Grade 4

Blue
Blue represents many things
like when a bird sings.
Colorful blue eyes, the same as the sky.
A wave in the ocean
when a surfer is in motion.
The smell of blueberry pie
or the first bite as you let out a sigh.
Blue stands for a boy, it's a color of joy.
Blue is a color of a flower
like violet soap scent in a shower.
Blue can be the wind on your face
when you're dreaming of another place.
Blue is bold and loud
for school colors standing proud.
Blue can be cozy and warm
when someone gives you a gentle touch on your arm.
Blue can be a song
when one knows they are wrong.
It could leave a sour taste in your mouth
when your day just goes south.
It is up to you to choose your blue!
Abigail Day, Grade 5

The Sun
Sun glowing so brightly
Its rays scream down to Earth
Orange, yellow, and burning red surround it
Its rays heat us like a microwave
Covered with red-hot burning fire
Shines like a bright lantern
What a beautiful thing.
Trey Cox, Grade 5

Ode to Hot Chocolate
Hot chocolate, chocolate, chocolate
With your marshmallows they make you so delicious
You also make me warm inside
You remind me of my dad sitting at his table
Every time I drink you
You make it feel like it's Christmas
I'll always love you all the time!
Jada Townsend, Grade 4

Christmas

Christmas is the time of year,
To celebrate all the joy and cheer.
Families putting up ornaments sipping their hot cocoa with piles of whip cream.
Kids sledding down white fluffy snow.
Having snowball fights all day long.
Parents saying 'time to come in,
Put your pajama's on'...
Sitting by the fireplace roasting up your feet.
Hanging up your stockings,
Reading books about jolly old Santa Claus.
Naming and finding your elves,
Mom and dad tucking you into bed,
Daydreaming about the presents that will be under the tree tomorrow morning.
Kids wake up the next morning running into their parents room saying 'Santa has come,
Santa has come, wake up, wake up, you got to see all the presents under the tree.'
They dump out their stockings looking through their toys, ripping open their presents from under the tree.

Emma Schueler, Grade 5

The Sea

Oh how I love the sea!
It's calming, soothing, and beautiful!
When I go to the glorious sea, I sit and imagine myself swimming with all the fish and sea creatures.
I also walk along the edge of the sea and see all the gorgeous shells.
Oh how pretty they are.
When it's time for lunch, I sit on the deck and listen to the sea and watch its waves go up and down again and again.
Listening to the ocean, I eat my lunch and admire how pretty the sea is.
After lunch, it's back outside!
Splashing and playing in the waves.
As dusk appears it's inside for all of us.
We sit and read calmly before dinner, but as we eat dinner,
we talk about our fun at the ocean and talk about what to do the next day.
As we are getting tucked into bed I think about the soothing waves and walking along the sand in my bare feet.
As I drift off to sleep I can't wait until the next day.
Now, dear reader, what do you love about the sea?
You heard my thoughts, what are yours?

Logan Dimpel, Grade 6

Why?*

Why were we different from everyone else?
Why did people not care for us?
Why were we forced into the ghettos and concentration camps with little food and water?
Why didn't people help us when we were thrown into boxcars and taken away?
Didn't they hear our screams and cries for help?
Why did the Nazi's torch only Jewish synagogues and buildings?
We are people too, we have feelings
When we were beaten and killed, why didn't they stop the Nazi's?
Didn't it occur to them that something was wrong, something wasn't the same?
We were taken away from our lives and families
Why did that evil, cold hearted man, Hitler, take pleasure in hurting us not only on the outside but in the inside
One more question, why didn't anyone standup for what they knew was right?
Why?

Mya Karvan, Grade 6
*Remember the Holocaust and what the Jewish people went through

Me Thinking…

In the very morning of a crisp winter's day,
Next to the log where I lay,
A little worm, right at the base,
Crawled out of its hiding place.
A bird started singing,
A bell started ringing,
A chicken started walking,
A skier started talking:
Hurry, hurry! In the lake!
Look! The ice is about to break!
Berries were ready to be picked
Balls were ready to be kicked.
As I lay there I tried to think about the best thing —
About the transition from winter to spring.

Elisabeth Nikolau, Grade 5

Making Friends

You look down the hall,
A new kid falls.
You run out to help
But you don't know what to say.
All you need to do is this:
Give them a smile,
It breaks the ice.
But if you ignore them,
And stay with your friends
It will send the message
That they are alone.
So just help,
And just maybe,
It can make both of your lives go the other way.

Olivia Shuff, Grade 5

June 21st

June 21 is when summer begins!
All animals appear!
Kids have a joyful time
playing and admiring all the animals.
Once June is here, give out a happy cheer!
June is when fireflies appear
and everybody loves to catch fireflies!
June fills the air with joy.
All the trees wake up and spread their beautiful green
leaves fill the trees like never before.
Butterflies are fluttering in the air,
bees are zooming and buzzing and getting their honey,
Then the birds zoom in the air and get food for their families.
June is when you get ready to have fun!

Lumaris Cora, Grade 4

I Wish

I wish I were a star so, I could shoot across the sky.
I wish I were the sun so, I could provide daylight.
I wish I were Cinderella so, I could dance the night away.
I wish I were me so, I could be myself.

Haley Dean, Grade 5

Hope

there's light in every darkness
laughter in every tear
a rainbow after every storm
courage blooms out of every fear

a white dove in a flock of crows
a green leaf when all is brown
a spark in every dying flame
a jewel in every crown

there's a rose peeking from every thorn bush
a birdsong in every still dawn
a child at play while all are working
a rabbit in every front lawn

there's something good in every bad
something happy in every sad
there's always something, some kind of thing
that makes a dying soul begin to sing

Johanna Hall, Grade 6

Christmas

The snow plow scraping across the road
Little drops of sugar float by
Lights fill the street
Sweet smells of apple pie

Joys fill the air with the carols of the night
Kids excited for Santa Claus
Cheering of the sled riders
The figure skaters get a round of applause

Families gather around the tree
Joys of Christmas everywhere
Wisps of the breezes of winter
Joys of Christmas fill the air

A family makes what we call love
 They cherish memories that last forever
Jingle bells play distant throughout
Last year was old new but this is the best December

Caelyn Pritschau, Grade 6

Waiting for Spring

I am waiting for Spring
I feel my little plants popping out of seeds
Sitting outside is peaceful
When I pick flowers, the scent remains on my hand
The awakening of Spring brings peace to the Earth
Grass turns green, buds turn into leaves
I have ideas that burst like a seed
When I learn something new, flowers bloom
Bees pollinate, birds chirp, flowers bloom, the wind blows
All at the same time
While I sit on a wooden bench and wait for Spring

Mishael Quraishi, Grade 4

Flowers
Flowers
Pretty, blossom
Planting, smelling, growing
It grows in dirt
Primrose
Kendall Feiler, Grade 5

Comet
Comet
Long, big
Running, jumping, licking
Has lots of spots
Dalmatian
Adam Bartosz, Grade 5

The Hatless Bear
There once was a bear that was fat,
He laid and slept on my front doormat.
He woke up and roared,
It was his loud snore.
It turned out he just lost his hat.
Mario Enamorado, Grade 6

The Friendly Dolphin
There once was a dolphin with a hue,
He splashes and dives in the deep blue.
Who had lots of good friends,
And his dream never ends.
But he will always be true to you.
Avianna Harris, Grade 6

Soccer
Soccer
Fun, hard
Running, kicking, scoring
Injuries can hurt badly
Sport
Liam Alexander, Grade 5

Horses
Horses
Beautiful, fast
Running, jumping, cantering
Riding them is fun
Wonder
Ana Maria Frujinoiu, Grade 5

Fair
Fair
Loud, amazing
Cheering, tiring, unending
The games are awesome
Amusement park
Julianna Grasso, Grade 5

Giving Is Great
Thanksgiving is great. My mom prepares the ham, my father welcomes the guests.
Soon the dinner table is full. Later, the food arrives and we dig in.
As we feast my uncle tells jokes to make us chuckle.
Only a few minutes later and I'm stuffed with no room to spare.
For the duration of the day we play games, watch the Eagles and tell stories.
Thanksgiving is an amazing time of the year
Nuno Pereira, Grade 6

Sharks
S hark eyes turn black when they eat so nothing can get in their eyes
H ammerheads have sensors in their heads
A Mako can catch a tuna fish
R are sharks like the short nose saw shark
K ids sometimes get killed by sharks
S o never go in the water after it rains
Caleb Crowley, Grade 5

Picking Apples
Driving up the mountains through the curvy winding roads.
The smell of the cool crisp air with the fall breeze running through our hair.
As we reached the top we discovered many fields of ripe colorful apples.
We started to walk through each field finding the apples that we wanted most.
Picking them one by one and tasting them to discover all the joy of a fresh picked apple.
Alexis LeRoy, Grade 6

Mr. Bogart
Mr. Bogart is my teacher and he makes me smile
Mr. Bogart is very kind and he treats me like his own child
Mr. Bogart is very nice and he makes learning fun.
Mr. Bogart is quite awesome and his personality is as bright as the sun!
Mr. Bogart is very enthusiastic and that is why I think he is fantastic!
Anoushka Herrala, Grade 5

Holocaust
One evil man mistreated the Guys that he despised they were the Jewish
Jewish people focused his hate men, women, and children were forced through the gates
At the death camps people cried while they died
The Nazis ruled and they made decisions to live and die
Towards the end of the war Hitler was losing and oozing and then he committed suicide
Dylan Makarovsky, Grade 6

The Willow Tree
The willow tree, so proud and strong, moves ever so slightly in the wind.
So proud and strong, the willow tree, as it sits upon the field.
I find peace with the willow tree as it sits upon the field.
When the wind gets mad the tree goes faster but never, ever less graceful.
When the wind gets mad and throws a tantrum, the willow tree calmly tames it.
Mica Frank, Grade 4

Grandparents Are…
Loving relatives who are always there for you.
Great people who will sacrifice many things for their descendants' freedom.
Wise, and share many life lessons.
There to cheer you up.
Happy to help in any way.
Emma Davis, Grade 6

Camping
Tonight, I look out, on the moon, in the dark night this tent is like a room,
In a sleeping bag that's old, it's too rainy and too cold.
I wonder why we're here for a week, how does everyone expect me to sleep?
I'll wait until the morning bright to complain about my night!
"Wake up, wake up!" I hear them say. Now this is the last day,
To fish and to wish I was gone. We're all packed up, time to go.
I get in the car, we are driving home, I can't bear to say that I miss camping more than anything!

Fiona York, Grade 5

Grantham's Great Thanksgiving Feast
Thanksgiving is fun with the Grantham family. "Hey Mom, Aunt Donna's here," I said. Aunt Donna brought some string and beads to make bracelets. Now, I can sit and make one. Kindness is used to remember everyone Mom is so kind. Games are fun to play with my family, because we add new directions into them. I will set the table for dinner tonight. I cook a turkey that we killed and served it with potato salad. Every year we pray before dinner. We thank God for our meal and why we are here. "Nice job Alyssa with cooking the turkey and the CHOCOLATE PUDDING looks delicious," gently spoke Mom. "Good job setting up the table tonight" everyone said to me that night. After dinner we all went into the living room and enjoyed watching the football game. We love the Dallas Cowboys, Eagles, and Steelers. Thanksgiving is fun with my family and I think you know why.

Alyssa Grantham, Grade 6

When I Am
When I am tired, I am as exhausted as a koala in the middle of the day.
When I am sad, I am like a little kid at the beach that just found out the ice cream man just ran out of treats.
When I am annoyed, I am as crabby as someone who was woken up at 5:00 a.m. on a Sunday.
When I am excited, I am like a squirrel that just got a life supply of nuts.
When I am silly, I am as giddy as a miner, striking gold for the first time.
When I am angry, I am like the fiery sun about to explode.

Samantha Lankowicz, Grade 6

The Robot
There once was a cold, hard, steel robot,
Its eyes glared at me,
I then wondered if it might somehow be alive,
It was dragging its steel legs as they clanked and clonked in a decisive pattern on the cold, hard floor,
In that cold, dark room it spotted me yet this time was different instead of glaring at me it just spoke through its cold dark artificial mouth and said "I will terminate" and then all the sudden it stopped speaking never to speak or move again.

Connor Hanks, Grade 5

A Girl!
War has rung like the Liberty Bell chiming endlessly.
I arrive in my battle armor, prepared to taste the bitterness of defeat, or the sweet taste of victory.
I bend down and smell a lone flower, the only one that hasn't been trampled over by the opposing team.
I suspect that they will find out sooner or later, but brains are over bronze.
They have cut my hair and changed my name to Sam. "A girl! A girl!" they would yell in outrage.
A girl *is* on the battlefield, but equality for the opposite gender does not exist.

Katy Meta, Grade 5

Blue
Blue is the sky where the planes fly so high. Blue is big waves crashing.
Blue is a bird chirping as loud as a cricket on a warm summer night.
Blueberries are so tasty and yummy, I feel them dancing in my tummy.
My grandma's garden is full of great smelling flowers like Blue Bells, Pansies, and Corn Flowers.
A blue sweater feels soft and warm, when you put it on in the winter frost.

Daniel Czebatul, Grade 5

The Yeti
The evergreens are crisp
There is snow on the ground
The Yeti is coming
He'll hunt you down

His claws are like daggers
and his teeth are like thorns
He never staggers
and he has sharp horns

He can lift up trucks
and turn them to scrap metal
He likes to eat ducks
and he'll never settle

So here's a tip
It will help you out
Avoid the Yeti
He'll make you shout
Jackson McVety, Grade 5

An Ode to Sloths
Oh, how I love you sloths!
You're so cute and furry
I don't mean to bug you,
But I really want to hug you!

Oh, sloth, you are superb!
With your dirty fur
You can climb a tree
Way better than me.

I could draw you all day.
I would paint you a picture.
You're so lazy I can admit,
But loving you I can't quit.

You remind me of myself,
I have not idea why.
Tell me, sloth, do you love me too?
Hopefully you do as much as I love you!
Kyndall Miller, Grade 5

All of Halloween and Fall
H appy days!
A wesome monsters,
L aughter and fun!
L iars and ghouls,
O utstanding costumes,
W itches and ghosts,
E ating candy,
E leven Reeses'!
N ever-ending fun.

I love Halloween
Timothy Schum, Grade 5

Little Love Star
I was born on a special day.
February 3 is my birthday.
My Mom was proud that she had
A baby girl.
She always wanted a baby girl
Named Makayla.
When I was four and I started
Head Start,
She gave me a kiss and called me
her star.
I will always be her star.
I love my Mom and she loves me.
Makayla Ward, Grade 4

Football
Flying through the sky
Cutting through the air
Running
Jumping
Reaching for the ball
Almost in your hand
You grab it
Now you're running for a purpose
Juke left
Juke right
Diving into the end zone
TOUCHDOWN!!
Joey Saiag, Grade 6

Believe
BELIEVE
You can
They can
We all can
We can believe
Believe we will win
Believe you can get in national sports
Believe
You can get there
Believe
So you achieve your goal
BELIEVE
Andrew Castronovo, Grade 6

Hallow's Eve
Moon full and bright,
Creepy cackles in the night.
Goblins, ghosts getting antsy,
As trick-or-treaters drop their candy.
Monsters, monsters everywhere!
Definitely quite a scare!
Crawling, black cats,
Numerous, flying bats
Always lots of frights,
Well, it is Hallow Eve's dreaded night!
Madalyn Karban, Grade 6

Prayer of the Lost Dog
All by myself in a large scary city
I must pray to find a loving family or at
least some food or shelter.
Marinda Cannon, Grade 5

Halloween Night
Halloween is near.
Candy and costumes galore.
Halloween is here.
Virginia Lohn, Grade 4

Zebra
Black, white, gray, and brown
Lives in the wild, eats grass
Zebras are so cute!
Alana Reader, Grade 4

Bats
bats are very cool
bats are very awesome too
bats are very fun
Isaiah Chhith, Grade 5

Soon
Sun said hi to moon
He said "You are blocking me."
"Shh, you'll be out soon."
Grace Cutler, Grade 6

Grades K-1-2-3
High Merit Poems

The Day Before School
The day before school,
I swam in my pool.
I sat on my raft
And stayed out of the draft.

I played with my friend
And didn't pretend.
We had some fun
Playing in the sun.

I bounced a ball
Right at a wall.
I shot a puck
Until it got stuck.

My dad came home,
I played with my Destroyer Dome.
I went to sleep
While my toys were in a heap.
Mario Martin, Grade 3

The Day Before Third Grade
I woke up thinking about school
But instead I dressed for the pool.
I raced to the car.
The pool wasn't too far.

I said hi to my friend.
In the pool we played pretend.
Then I went home to have some lunch.
I had some grapes in a bunch.

I sat down to read my book.
The cat shot me a funny look.
She tilted her head nice and sweet,
Looking for a kitty treat.

It was time to rest my head.
And finally I went to bed.
I was falling fast asleep.
And not a creature made a peep.
Caroline Marschke, Grade 3

Fall Is Coming
Leaves dancing here
Leaves dancing there
Please beware
Fall is coming
I stop running
No more slides
No more fun rides
Leaves change brown
I walk around and around
Time to go to sleep
Through the window I peek
Nakhai Wilson, Grade 3

Cooking
Oh my,
Chef, my fried pot pie was a little dry.
Put a little flour,
Baked it for an hour,
Then it was sour.

Asked the teacher,
She said stir it till nine,
Then bake it with some lime,
And it will be fine.
Olivia Magnini, Grade 1

Basketball
Basketball is fun!
I play basketball
on Monday, Tuesday,
Thursday, and Sunday.
Joey and I play
Super basketball
on the school courts!
We practice shooting
Awesome hoops!
Basketball is great!
Matthew Neely, Grade 1

Fall
I love fall.
The leaves change colors.
Fall is cold.
The leaves fall down.
We pick pumpkins.
We eat soup.
We eat pumpkin pie.
We go on trips.
We wear hats and scarves.
We drink hot chocolates.
Cassandra Cruz, Grade 2

I Am From
I am from my mom,
because she had me.
My mom is cute every day.
I am from chicken,
because I love chicken.
I am from a dog,
because I have a pet dog.
I am from Ohio,
because that is where I was born
I am Harmonie.
Harmonie Brown, Grade 3

Coloring Crayons
Coloring crayons
Red, yellow, blue and orange
On the gray, gray desk
Jenna Makuen, Grade 3

Dreams
Wonderland, Candy Land
Candy canes?
Alice? White rabbit?
Oh! Cotton candy trees!
AHHH! Queen!
Tiny doors?
Marshmallow bushes?
Where am I?
Oh it was just a dream!
Hailey Rumpf, Grade 2

Christmas
Christmas is so cold!
I like presents!
We decorate the
inside of our house.
Our Christmas tree is
extremely cool!
I get so excited
I could scream Now!
Merry Christmas!
Conner Thompson, Grade 1

Summer Rain
It was a nice summer rain.
I will play in the rain.
I will go on a black train.
It was a nice summer rain.

It was a nice summer rain.
Rain water goes down the drain.
There was a hole with a drain.
It was a nice summer rain.
Malaya Giesy, Grade 2

Swimming
One time I had a tie.
Second I won in fly.
Third I won in free.
Fourth I did IM with glee.
Fifth was my lane number for breast.
Sixth place was not my best.
Seventh race was in back.
Eighth was done then I had to pack.
Ryan Snyder, Grade 2

Halloween
A very scary night
Skeleton hanging from the ceiling
Kids playing tricks on everyone
Witches making noises
Kids scaring everyone with their costumes
Pumpkins with big and silly faces
Everyone is having a good time
On a scary Halloween night.
Enni Jiang, Grade 3

Untitled
Reading is fun
looking at beautiful
picture books can be interesting
I like
mysteries
Reading is better than science

time
if you read
you can read bigger
books
I like reading more than
going to Ocean City
Do you like reading?
Read!
it is good for you.
Henry Mucklow, Grade 3

Sky
I feel the soft wind blow
Across my face it will go.

When I look down I will see
a nice city with tiny things of glee.

And when it is time to go to bed
I will turn my head
and will see black
but it doesn't scare me.

Because I cause it
then it is time.

The sun open its eyes
then the process starts over again.
Jake Williams, Grade 3

Wonderful, Wonderful, Weather
Weather is rain falling from the sky
like rain drops of happiness.
Weather is a fresh breeze
of wind rushing through the air.
Weather is the sun beating
down with rays of joy.
Weather is snow drifting
down from the clouds
as young children laugh
with glee.
Weather is small icicles
falling down like pebbles.
Weather is fall leaves
falling onto the ground
in a heartbeat.
Wonderful, wonderful, weather
Maya Salzman, Grade 3

Sickness
I'm not getting out of bed.
My stomach hurts so much.
Call the school,
I am not hungry.
I skip breakfast.
I skip lunch,
But dinner is calling my name!
Maya Piezal, Grade 2

Thanksgiving
On Thanksgiving, I wish
That Santa Claus would come.
He came!!
We ate turkey, fish
and other food.
It was a good
Thanksgiving!
Anna Olszowka, Grade 3

Halloween Curse
The open road!
Twisty!
Turney!
Skeletons everywhere!
A Cyclops at my door!
It is Halloween.
It is…
Isaac Engler, Grade 2

America
A great country
Many people of the past
Enormous place
Royal love
It has a cool president
Caring with freedom
Amazing place to live in
Aaliya Sheikh, Grade 2

Awesome
A pple fritters
W hales
E .T.
S occer
O ctober
M e
E arth
Caden DeCesare, Grade 2

Dolphins
You must protect these creatures.
Some people hurt dolphins.
Some people hunt dolphins
I wish some people would care for them
like I do.
Maddy Devine, Grade 2

Fall
Leaves are falling
from the trees.
I think the squirrels
are going to flee.
That's why I like fall.
Widney Borgella, Grade 3

Bunny
Bunny
Bunnies are the best
Crawling, jumping, eating
Bunny likes celery
Holly
Zoe Naish, Grade 1

Cat
Cat
Black, fluffy
Licking, eating, playing
He likes to play
Fluffy
Lianelys Oviedo, Grade 1

Hyena/Africa
Hyena
Eats meat, brown spots
Laughing, running, hunting
He jumps on hippos
Africa
Nathaniel Loveless, Grade 1

Monkey
Monkey
Brown, black
Swinging, eating bananas
My monkey can swing high
Chimp
David Merullo, Grade 1

Autumn
Kids buckled up in jackets
Leaves falling changing colors
Warm and toasty fires
Cuddling up in your blanket
It is fall!
Tianna Smith, Grade 3

Soccer
Kick the ball
Score a goal
No touching the ball
Block the goal
Playing soccer
Alexander Groza, Grade 2

Halloween Fright
Halloween's going to give you a fright,
You will run for the hills.
On Halloween you will get some candy.
But watch out for the zombie family.
On Halloween night muwha!
Madison Regis, Grade 3

Fall
Fall is fun.
Fall is cool and cold.
The leaves fall down in the fall.
The leaves can change to red.
Fall is the best!
Danny Zhao, Grade 1

Turkey
Turkey
big, fat
pray, eat, giving
happy, memorable, exciting, careful
nice
Kevin Girdusky, Grade 3

Jenny
J ust Jenny
E ight
N ose wiggles
N ice
Y oungest
Jenny Parsons, Grade 2

Beach
B igger than a kiddie pool
E dge of the ocean
A lways fun
C rowded
H ot sand
Christopher Wessell, Grade 2

Fall
Fall is fall.
I like fall.
Fall is windy.
Fall is so much fun.
I love fall.
Andrew Mac, Grade 1

Outer Space
I'm in outer space.
Now I see the planets close to the sun.
There's the planets far away from the sun!
But where are the dwarf planets?
Where are they?
Shawn Eckhart, Grade 2

I Love
I love my family
I love ice cream
I love my elf
But most of all
I love my sister.
Giuliana Alvini, Kindergarten

Stripes
Stripes
Black, white
Jumping, running, napping
Zebras live in Africa
Zebras
Izabella Bartman, Grade 1

Carnival
Spinning Ferris wheel
Fast roll coaster
Slippery slide
Slow train
Lots of things at the carnival!
Valentina Barrios-Quintero, Grade 2

I Love
I love my dog
I love my turtle
I love my stuffed animals
But most of all
I love turkey.
Parker Schramm, Kindergarten

I Love
I love Batman
I love Spunky
I love number 3
But most of all
I love monkeys.
Christopher Scudder, Kindergarten

I Love
I love mommy and daddy.
I love my poppy.
I love my mom-mom.
But most of all
I love my b-mom.
Aubrey Kapusta, Kindergarten

I Love
I love pink
I love Monster High
I love puppies
But most of all
I love my Barbie Doll.
Emily Craiter, Kindergarten

The Day Before Third Grade
In the morning I was in a hurry,
But there was no need to worry.
Outside it felt cool,
So I went to the pool.

When I got home I played and played
On this hot summer day.
I played with my sister all day long
And we sang a bunch of songs.

After we ate dinner the sun went down.
I went inside and had a big frown.
I thought summer had been fun,
But I knew it had to be done.

My mom yelled, "Time for bed."
But I shook my head.
I couldn't stop thinking about school
Or my trip today to the pool.
Brooke Standish, Grade 3

The Day Before Third Grade
I woke up early to go to the pool.
The weather outside was a little cool.
My time at the pool was fun,
But now the swimming is done.

We made our last trip to Kennywood
Riding all the rides that we could.
My last ride was the Swings,
And all the fun that it brings.

It was time to go home and play
To end this summer day.
Hanging on a branch of a tree
Where there was a buzzing bee.

Last I went inside to bed.
On the pillow I put my head.
Finally I went to sleep
My covers around me to keep.
Zackary Waslosky, Grade 3

A Girl's Dream
A girl's dream is to speak to the flowers
To cry with the falling snow
To soar in the sky with the butterflies
To go with the wind
Watch it go, watch it go
To ride a purple pony
Who's very very fast
To get a diamond ring
To design a pair of stylish jeans
But ah, my dear
That's just a dream
Adalia Looney, Grade 3

My Best Friend

My best friend is a very special girl.
She is always there for me
And she always cares about me
I love her so much
She is like a sister to me
We have a special bond.
Caring, sharing, and doing cool things together
Makes our friendship unique.
We are always together doing fun things together.
My best friend is Viona.
She means the world to me.

Litzy Salazar, Grade 3

The Best Teacher

My best teacher is Ms. Betances
She teaches us a lot of different things.
I love her so much.
She teaches us magical tricks.

Ms. Betances is nice and kind too.
I love her so much.
Her gently smile and caring t

She is the best teacher in the world and I want to have her
Next year in the fourth grade.

Jenny Huang, Grade 3

Sheldon

When we first got you, you were a little ball of fluff.
You slept in a doghouse, ate lots of food and got into trouble,
You love to play rough.
You got a ripped ear and a very long body.

Mom says you're special
When you do something wrong.
Even though you don't like to be cuddled,
You wrestle the dog
You take leaps in faith and fly like a bat
Sometimes I forget you are a cat.

Samuel Schell, Grade 3

I Am From

I am from my mom
She's nice, she makes dinner for me and she has a job.
I am from Cleveland
I was born there.
I am from rice
It's my favorite food.
I am from cats
I have a cat.
I am smart.

Jaden Williams, Grade 3

Christmas

Comes one time a year
People go caroling time to time
Churches have plays
People have gifts bought
Decorating houses with lights
Everyone with heavy jackets
Snow blankets the ground

Bright lights on the tree
Everyone sees their family
Santa brings presents
Sleigh bells ring
Everyone bundles up around the fire

Schools are on Christmas break
People leave out cookies and milk for Santa
Everyone wants to be good
Kids make a wish list
Santa sees what he can do!

Santa eats the cookies and drinks the milk
He puts all of the goodies — wherever
Lay out carrots for his reindeer
Remember one for each.

Tyler Thompson, Grade 3

The Aquarium Is

The aquarium
is stingrays
floating like a
magic carpet.

The aquarium
is seeing water
sparkling like
crystals. The aquarium
is tiny little waves peeking
up. The aquarium is a blanket
of color covering the tanks.

The aquarium is a beautiful
rainbow underwater.
The aquarium is a rainbow
reef showing off its
colors. The aquarium is
tiny waves whispering to each other.

The aquarium is the
ocean smell that moves
to my nose.

Samara Ginsberg, Grade 2

Gingerbread Man
The smell of ginger,
Yummy, Yummy.
Snap! goes the gingerbread girl
Wow! She tastes buttery!
Her licorice shoes, shirt, and hair really pop out.
"You look fragile," I said to her.
Crack! Crunch! Crinkle!
There goes her body as I take a bite.
Aileen Fisher, Grade 3

Winter
Winter is the season for kids to play outside all day.
It is the season to build and make snow angels in the
park or the backyard.
It feels good to have fun in the snow and play with your friends
It is the time to have hot chocolate and stay warm.
It is time to sing and dance while playing with your friends
Winter is the season to have fun all day long.
Angeles Sierra, Grade 3

My Garden
Pumpkins, tomatoes, pickles all great food!
Leaves that fall in the garden I pick them up.
The deer that try to come into the garden can't come in.
I take out the weeds, I take care of my garden.
I take the food out of the garden before it gets too cold!
I have potatoes and lots more!
I like my garden.
Tess Nichols, Grade 3

The Gingerbread Cookie
This gingerbread cookie smells really spicy as it bakes.
With Skittles as eyes and M and M buttons,
His licorice mouth makes a zig zag smile.
This cookie was sad as he got closer and closer to my mouth.
Yummy!
Crunch! Crunch!
I pop him in my mouth.
Kaleigh Portella, Grade 3

Turtles
Turtles are great.
Turtles have a shell.
They can go into their shells.
Turtles are good.
Turtles sometimes eat cat food and sleep all day.
Turtles are amazing.
Henry Scallorns, Grade 1

Gingery Men
I walk down the stairs and smell a sweet smell baking.
Crack!
I bite into the gingerbread man.
The red and white cookie is delicious.
What a yummy gingerbread man.
Jack Kinzler, Grade 3

Black
Black is the color of my sweatshirt,
  the sweatshirt that I wear to school.
Black is the color of my pants,
  the pants that match my sweater.
Black is the color of my hair,
  the hair that matches my pants and sweater.
Gabriella Alvarado, Grade 3

Halloween
Zombies are black
zombies are gray
zombies are around you night and day
you can run
you can hide
but you're unlucky if you're the zombie's bride.
Madison Cochrane, Grade 3

Thanksgiving
T urkeys are good, thank God
U se your fork to eat the turkey
R ide your bike to the supermarket to buy some turkey.
K atie came to eat some turkey
E verybody likes turkey
Y our Thanksgiving will be great
Francesca Licari, Grade 3

Electric Guitar
Electric Guitar
dusty, wood
smooth, bumpy, rough
strings, plastic, wood, metal
rock, rock and roll, heavy metal, pressing, strumming
Samuel Nicolella, Grade 3

Cats
Cats
clean, fresh
furry, soft
orange, peach, nose, eyes
jumping, purring, playing, running, sleeping
Emma Greco, Grade 3

Cats
Cats
mice, food
soft, fluffy, smooth
paws, nose, ears, tail
purring, growling, walking, scratching, biting
Hailee Hamblin, Grade 3

I Came Across a Turtle
I came across a turtle, small as small can be.
Its shell was bright green.
I hid him in my room so my mom wouldn't see.
He was quiet until he was scared by a bee!
Lilly Ryann Metzger, Grade 3

High Merit Poems – Grades K, 1, 2, and 3

I Am Happy to Be Me
I am happy
to get new shoes.

I am happy
to be me now.

I am happy
in the world.

I am happy
to have a mother.

I am happy
to have a father.

I am happy
now.

I am happy
to be me.
Zaniyah Byard, Grade 3

Fall
Orange skies
Blanketing the city
red, yellow, orange and brown
leaves on the ground
Icy winds twirling
outside
"crunch!"
sound of leaves
when I step on them
"drip, drop, drip"
rain falling
Pumpkins red and orange
Pumpkin pie
I smell it
leaves falling
from the trees
grayish clouds
Thanksgiving
I love fall
Adair Nelson, Grade 3

I Am From
I am from Teresa Lavender.
My mom feeds me and she takes care
of me.
I am from my mom. She gave birth
to me the day I was born.
I am from lobster and crab legs.
Lobster is good and yummy.
I am from a chinchilla.
They are cuddly and good, and
good listeners.
Lauriana Bell, Grade 3

Seasons
Winter you can have lots of fun in the snow
you can build a snowman
that can play with you
like a friend

Spring rain puddles to play in
puddles to jump in
splash
puddles to splash in

Summer sunny days
and barbecues
good food
and fun for me and you

Fall leaves leaves
and more leaves
to jump and play in
and
apples
and
pumpkins to eat and bake
Jacob Mono, Grade 3

Amazing Animals
Tigers leaping
Dolphins swimming in the deep blue sea
Birds gliding high in the sky

A bear resting in a cave
Sharks searching for food
A rabbit hopping

Cheetahs racing each other
A panther sitting watching the sunset
A lion sitting with its cubs

A red panda eating in a tree
A polar bear teaching her cubs to swim
A seal swimming from polar bears

A whale jumping out of the water
A sea turtle on the beach hatching her eggs

These are amazing animals
Jasmyn Mendez, Grade 3

Feelings
My feelings are low
My feelings are high
I shall love Him up up high
He shall reign up up high
The dream of your life is coming true
The dream of your life is changing attitude
The dream of life is coming true
Eden Tam, Kindergarten

Dogs
Dogs
dirty, wonderful
soft, furry, fluffy
paws, fur, ears, nose
eats, plays, drinks, sleeps, barks
Aubrey Murphy, Grade 3

Gingerbread Man
Gingerbread Man
cinnamon, good
tasty, soft, rough
eyes, feet, buttons, hand
stir, shape, bake, decorate, eat
Ana Nieves, Grade 3

Owls
Owls
dirty, woodsy
fluffy, furry, soft
eyes, body, beak, feet
coos, flies, watches, perches, hunts
Kai Brennan, Grade 3

I Love
I love my mom and dad
I love my house
I love mashed potatoes
But most of all
I love Dad.
William Shields, Kindergarten

Cat
Cat
kennel, litter
furry, soft, skinny
fur, claws, babies, whiskers
meows, runs, hisses, scratches, cuddles
RyLeigh Wood, Grade 3

Michael Myers
Michael Myers is my name
and all the scaring is my game
no screaming
no yelling when you see me in fright
or you will lose your sight
Richard Torres, Grade 3

Water
Water
ocean, fresh
smooth, wavy, wet
clear, glistening, sparkling, bright
splashing, helping, quiet, peaceful, homey
Emerson Ryder, Grade 3

Eagles
Eagles are wild
I said to the child.
Eagles are awesome
like a pink cherry blossom.
Eagles are excellent
like miracles God has sent.
Eagles are my favorite bird.
Reese Tysor, Grade 1

The Eye
The eye it haunts every soul.
When it grabs on, it never goes.
A man took the eye, and took it swell.
And this man I know him well.
His name is death and all is well.
All is well.
All is well.
E. H., Grade 2

Autumn Falls
Autumn is here.
Leaves are falling off the trees.
Squirrels climbing down the trees.
Kids are coming back to school.
All animals are sleeping in their house.
Apples are falling off trees.
Fall is here, so be prepared.
Destine Munro-Richard, Grade 3

Chasety
C aring and careful all the time
H elpful at home and at school
A nxious to learn new things
S hy like a rock star
E very day full of energy and excitement
T hankful for friends and family
Y oungest girl in the family
Chasety Flores, Grade 3

Halloween
Candy, treats, and costumes
Beware!
Monsters all around.
Time to have fun trick or treating
All on the streets
Get Ready!
This is Halloween!
Aja King, Grade 3

Fall
The season fall is great
You get to jump in leaves and play
The different colors are beautiful
I look forward to all the holidays
The season fall is the best season of all
Anna Sanford, Grade 1

I Am From
I am from my mom.
My mom helps me take care of my dog.
I am from Toledo.
Some of my family lives there.
I am from ribs.
I like ribs.
I am from my dog.
His name is Pongo and he is a big puppy.
I am a Christian.
Deonna
Deonna White, Grade 3

Ode to Ice-Cream
Oh, ice-cream you make a day right.
You taste in all different flavors.
You feel think and look like snow.
You give me frostbite on my tongue.
You taste so sweet.
You're such a treat to get on a long car ride.
You make a hot day cool and icy.
I eat you in spring and summer.
I love you so much!
How would we live without you?
Cadence Clifton, Grade 3

Yellow
Yellow is the color of my football jersey,
The jersey I wear.
Yellow is the color of the sun,
The sun shines bright.
Yellow is the color of the shoes,
The shoes I walk in.
Yellow is the color of the dandelions,
The dandelions I give to my mom.
Yellow is the color of my house,
The house I live in.
Vincent Bottisti, Grade 3

Thunderstorm
Rain is falling from the sky
Hitting the ground
Splattering on rocks, wood, and roads
Trees flipping and flopping
Throwing leaves everywhere
Lightning splits the sky and thunder booms
It's all going to be over soon
Soon it's going to be over
Soon
Travis Bloom, Grade 3

The Mystery of the Missing Seven
Two and four coming through
What comes next six and eight
And then comes ten lappy looze
All numbers even looking for seven
Anya Vedbathiri, Kindergarten

I Love
I love my family.
I love my room
I love my Uncle Scott
But most of all
I love God.
James Bergmark, Kindergarten

Cat
Cat
Black, fluffy
Playing, meowing, running
Scares the birds away
Tag
Max Stehura, Grade 1

My Hamster
Hamster
White, black
Running, sleeping, eating
My hamster likes to play
Jacob
Yaimaris Vazquez, Grade 1

Dog
Dog
Black, happy
Running, eating, licking
He stares at people when we are eating
Aries
Nomar Rivera, Grade 1

Rabbits
Rabbits
I have a rabbit
My rabbit is white
Hopping, eating, napping
Rabbits
Anializ Quinones, Grade 1

I Love
I love Mommy
I love my Monster High pillow
I love my brother
But most of all I
I love Daddy.
Samantha Weinert, Kindergarten

I Love
I love my room
I love my dog
I love my stuffed animals
But most of all
I love God.
Max Brown, Kindergarten

My Brother
My brother's name is Trey
One day we went to San Diego Bay
My brother Trey is big
He looks like a big rig
He's so tall and I'm so small
His birthday is in Fall
I have fame
He has game
Shavar Smith, Grade 3

Falling Leaves
Falling leaves, raking leaves
orange, yellow, red leaves.
Birds flying south.
we see apple picking and pumpkin pies.
Cool breeze blowing by.
Kids dragging their feet.
Animals getting ready to hibernate.
me in my bed asleep.
Daniel Olton, Grade 3

Nolan
Little, annoying
Stinky feet
Nice and kind
Funny and sweet
He's my little brother
Good and bad
He's my best friend
When I am happy or sad
Cameron Wojnar, Grade 2

My Dog
My dog is great I love him
And he loves me too
I walk him
I feed him
I play with him
And also I love him
Forever and ever
With all my heart
Jordi Simbana, Grade 3

Fall
fall
fall leaves are falling
to the ground they are red,
yellow, and brown.
Do they come off the ground?
I miss summer
do you
I can jump in a leaf piles can you?
Dakota Pomerleau, Grade 3

Fall Is…
Fall is as red as apples.
Fall is as orange as fire.
Fall is as yellow as sunflowers.
Fall is colorful!
Brooke Szczepkowski, Kindergarten

The Pool Is the Best
Playing ball with friends
Off the diving board without fear
Often times we bring a picnic
Lounging in the hot sun
Luca Pickeral, Grade 1

Soccer
Soccer is awesome
Soccer is fun
It is great
Soccer is cool
Bennett X. Niemiera, Grade 1

Dogs
Dogs can run
Dogs can have lots and lots of fun
Dogs can lick your feet
And dogs are always sweet
Olivia L. Niemiera, Grade 1

Louis Is
Louis is young.
Louis is great!
Louis eats fast.
Louis is late!
Louis Semtner, Grade 1

Dogs
D o tricks
O utside or inside
G o to vets
S nuggle with you
Ramon Feliciano, Grade 2

Leaf
Leaves change color to red to brown.
Some leaves fall on the ground.
I like to play with my best friend.
The fall is so fun.
Benson Xue, Grade 1

Tacos
I like tacos with hard shells,
bacon, but no one tells,
even tomato yes, yes, yes.
It makes me want a treasure chest.
Bailey Johnson, Grade 3

Swim
Feeling the cold water on my body
When I dove into the cold water
Competing for the summer Olympics.
Winning the race
Cheering with joy
Nonstop smiling
When I hold
The golden medal
Seeing all the flash lights
Of cameras
Getting my picture taken
Going home
Holding my golden medal
People asking for my autograph
Going back to the Olympics
Winning again
But this time second place
My victory ended with a kick and splash
Stella Bryce Jann, Grade 3

My Third Grade Year
My third grade year
Is so much fun!
But I can't get
All my homework done.
No field trips, no recess
What a shame.
I can't even get
In the basketball game!
Math and reading
And science too.
But writing is
My favorite thing to do.
I really think
Ms. Collier is the best.
But I don't want to
Take another test.
I don't want
Another grade mess.
Stefan Farrar, Grade 3

The Only Tree
on the hill a fire started
it blew out the trees
one started to fall, tumbled the rest
but one stayed, the smallest of all
up on the hill
this tree made it better, he felt pretty good
but he was the only small tree on the hill
the end of the month, still lonely can be
he stared at where his family tree used to be
that spring a tree grew
it was his family tree
up on the hill was a real family tree
as happy can be, a family tree
Lily Brown, Grade 3

I Am Most Thankful for My Friends and Family
    T he stuffing is good
    H ave a nice Thanksgiving
    A lot of decorations
    N ice pilgrims
    K ind Native Americans
    S inging Thanksgiving songs
    G iving thanks to God for Thanksgiving
    I love Thanksgiving
    V ery good turkey
    I like to give thanks
    N ice Indians
    G ive me mashed potatoes
Emma Bogdan, Grade 3

Green
Green is a peacock's feather,
Waving in the peaceful breeze,
Green is the minty taste of gum that makes my tongue numb!
It's a whisper at night,
When everyone's asleep.
After the winter is spring, it makes green of everything!
Green is a leaf painting on a canvas,
The many shades of the rain forest,
Ivy snarled on a vine, mounds of green M&Ms are divine!
Girl Scout thin mints make me think "green."
Frogs leaping on a lily pad
Recycling keeps the Earth clean, these are all the signs of green!
Layla Reilly, Grade 2

Thanksgiving Poem
    T oo much Turkeys
    H appy Holiday
    A holiday of thanks
    N ever eat too much on Thanksgiving
    K now that it's that time of year we give thanks
    S o much fun and happiness
    G ive thanks
    I like to eat turkey
    V ote for turkey
    I love this holiday
    N o one is to be unhappy
    G o and Thank one another
Sophia Banzil, Grade 3

I Am From
I am from my step-dad.
He takes care of me, he cuts my hair, and he plays with me.
I am from the race track.
I want to be a race car driver.
I am from carbs,
because it is meaty.
I am from a lion
because it is King of the jungle.
Ethan Chaisson, Grade 3

Rainbow Loom
Looping, Breaking, Creating
all over the school,
Covering everyone's wrist and
some teachers too.
Walking, talking all types of rainbow looms
Tie-die, regular, glow-in-the-dark, you name it
They're just dreaming about it!
Feels like a family, connected around the globe,
Loomed with love and care, passion and fashion.
Thank you to the Rainbow Loom,
For bringing us all together.
Muskan Manchanda, Grade 3

The Silly Bear
Silly Bear is fat and he likes to read,
He is a student in Mrs. Kesler's class.

First grade is fun for him,
He has been the peacemaker of the month two times.

He likes to color,
He loves to read.

Silly Bear really likes Mrs. Kesler,
But most of all he loves his friends!
Brandon Bevins, Grade 1

Spaceship
Zoom! Zoom! Up in space
The ancient planets in that place
"No gravity rules," the astronaut says
A big murky space is the best
All the stars look so alike
And when you look at them they are so lifelike
And boom! A shooting star, I was in awe
Beep! Beep! Beep! went the satellite
And we'll have to get back
And Whoosh! went the ship
Now it's time to land the ship!
Theo Demopoulos, Grade 3

Ode to Milk
Oh, how good you look, like a white lake in that cup!
I drink a whole cup at least every night.
When I'm home from scouts I rush to the kitchen.
I often drink from the carton.
A cry I often hear "Enough milk!" yells mother.
"Who drank all the milk?," yells mother.
"Which would you like, orange juice or milk?"
"Milk!" I always say.
With cold, refreshing taste.
Ooops, we're out of milk!
Time to get more so I can taste that white taste again!
Elijah Rovito, Grade 3

Tacos

I like choco tacos with ice cream,
they make me want to scream.
That's how much I love them,
they taste like yummy gems.
Delaney Flynn, Grade 3

My Scary Pumpkin

My pumpkin is so scary,
it won't give a berry.
It will really glow at night,
it will really give a fright!
Jackson Huckins, Grade 3

Pets

P lay with them
E xercise with them
T each them
S it with them
Sulisnet Torres, Grade 2

The Shot

Ouch!
Pinch!
Long and silver
Stick it right in!
Nasear Glasgow, Grade 2

Fright Night

When I walk the streets at night
I'm in for such a fright
I see all the sights
And I think what a night
Loralie Taylor Landesman, Grade 3

I Love Turkey

I love turkey
It's color is golden brown
The turkey is juicy
Turkey is my favorite food
Luke Trinchillo, Grade 3

Hello Thanksgiving

Hello Thanksgiving!
How do you do?
I really want to celebrate with you!
Charles Chelstowski, Grade 3

Cat

C ute and cuddly
A ttacks mice
T ail is wagging
Emily Clouse, Grade 2

The Gingerbread Boy

The house was full of a delightful, gingery smell as the cookie baked.
I took a bite of the scrumptious cookie.
It was so delightful!
Crunch!
The crisp gingerbread man meets my teeth.
He was going to get eaten!
Yum!
Reed Wells, Grade 3

My Gingerbread Man

My gingerbread man has a strong smell of ginger when he comes out of the oven.
When I take a bite he tastes spicy, gingery, and sweet.
He has yellow buttons and green eyes made out of Skittles,
and a mouth made out of jelly beans.
He looks too yummy to eat.
Crack! Snap! Crunch!
My Christmas gingerbread man is the best ever!
Ryan M. Teicher, Grade 3

My Delicious Gingerbread Man

Gingerbread men have a gingery scent that fills the house while they're cooking.
With a candy cane mouth, and chocolate chips for eyes
Crunch!
Gingerbread has a cinnamony taste when I take a bite.
Snap! Crunch! Yum!
They're a great Christmas treat.
Ryan Anne Foley, Grade 3

The Haunted House

Don't go in the haunted house there are witches, ghosts, goblins, it is true
vampires werewolves are after you.
Hear the screams, hear the wails, look they're right on
you're tail.
Don't worry my child your mind was just going wild.
Emily Lindtveit, Grade 3

If I Were a Fish

If I were a fish I would eat all of the creatures in the ocean until I was the only one left.
I would swim all the way to the very bottom of the ocean.
I would also swim super, duper, muper fast through the entire sea!
Luke Dougherty, Grade 2

Ode to Candy

Yummy in my tummy
Oh, how good you are!
Sweet candy
Come in handy!

Lollipop, lollipop
My favorite in the world.
I'll never be without you
Or I'll pop.

What will you look like in my tummy?
Yummy, yummy, yummy!
Rachel Glancy, Grade 3

I Am Most Thankful for My Family

T oday is turkey day!
H ave a happy day!
A very good apple pie!
N ice decorations!
K inds of food!
S mell the corn!
G ive thanks to your family!
I love all the food!
V ery hot potatoes!
I love all my family!
N ice food!
G ravy on turkey!
Ava Zinser, Grade 3

America
A great place to live in
M any people live there
E veryone loves it
R esponsible country
I t has a president
C ountry that's great
A lot of freedom...
Khashiya Ranginwala, Grade 2

Fall
I love fall.
In fall I play with leaves.
In fall leaves turn colors.
In fall leaves fall.
In fall I play with my sister in leaves.
Fall is so fun.
Tiffany Zheng, Grade 2

I'm Born To...
I was born to live
Born to play
Born to live the day away
Born to laugh
Born to sing
Born to be happy with everything
Daniel Russell, Grade 3

Rain
It is no fun when it rains.
It is fun when it doesn't rain.
When it rains you get stains.
Skidding in the yard causes stains
And a great deal of awful pain.
It is no fun when it rains.
Ethan Adkins, Grade 2

Purple
Purple is the color of my shoes,
 the shoes that I wear.
Purple is the color of my hat,
 the hat that I wear,
Purple is the color of a butterfly,
 the butterfly that flies.
Kadance Francis, Grade 3

Black
Black is the color of my Xbox 360,
 the Xbox 360 that I play Minecraft on.
Black is the color of my shoes,
 the shoes that I wear,
Black is the color of Endermen,
 the Endermen that I fight on Minecraft.
Nicholas Belardo, Grade 3

Beagle
B arks
E ats doggie treats
A dorable
G oes to the vet
L ikes to walk and run
E ars flop
Marielis Rosado, Grade 2

Fun Day
Swimming in the pool
Play Legos
Going to the park
Riding my bike
Shopping at the mall
Having fun!
Julianna Garcia, Grade 2

Together
Going to the playground
Going to school
Going bike riding
Going skateboarding
Going to the movies
Going together
Alexander Wildgoose, Grade 2

Family
Watching TV
Going to the park
Swimming in the pool
Playing Xbox
Taking trips
Being with my family!
James Conover, Grade 2

Zebra
Z igs and zags
E ats grass
B lack stripes
R uns fast
A nimal
Devion Faboskay, Grade 2

Turkey
Turkey
delicious, good,
eating, gobble, wobble,
nice, yummy, exciting, happy,
hungry
Madison Persichette, Grade 3

Spring
Rain rain flowers grow
hibernating bears wake up
birds chirp a soft tune
Eli Duvall, Grade 2

The Stump
The memory of that one day
Came back as soon as I
Touched as if the Saturn rings
When it fell down to stay

That snowy night that it came down
I remember it like yesterday
Although I really didn't care
It looked like it had a snowy gown

As I counted one by one
I felt surprised to know 16
Only 16 years of growth
Was the only time you felt the sun
Maddie Granger, Grade 3

I Am From
I am from my mom,
because she buys my birthday cake
when it's my birthday.

I am from Maplerow,
because that is where I grew up.

I am from macaroni
because it is cheesy and good.

I am from a panda, because it is
clean.

I am a good listener to my teacher
Sharon White, Grade 3

Kelci Waters
K ind
E ducated
L oved by family
C ool
I ndependent

W icked cool
A wesome
T alented
E nergetic
R espectful
S uper awesome!
Kelci Waters, Grade 3

Dolphins
I like dolphins
beautiful sounds
they are cute
are cuddly looking
good tricks
very fun to look at
Flora Hernandez-Mekonnen, Grade 3

Dolphins

A dolphin is a slippery, slick wonder each and every day,
With a slim, rounded nose, colors of pink and gray.
Sounds like the whistling of wind and the tick tock of the clock,
It smells like a crisp spring morning breeze, down by the dock.
Dolphins feel like silk on a pretty, blue dress
Dolphins swim through the ocean with finesse.

Madison Kiesel, Grade 2

Pink

Pink is the color of my blanket,
　The blanket that I use when I go to sleep,
Pink is the color of my jacket,
　The jacket that I wear outside,
Pink is the color of my socks
　The socks that I wear in the house.

Angel McClanahan, Grade 3

Nature

The crickets chirp in the dawn of night,
The birds tweet in the morning air,
The frogs jump…in the sound of the water,
The bats come out at the night of the moon,
The rainbow comes out at the end of the rain,
The trees blossom in early spring.

Yechezkel Kirshenbaum, Grade 2

Purple

Purple is the color of my fake tree,
　The tree with ornaments.
Purple is the color of my name,
　The name my mom named me, Amethyst.
Purple is the color of my room,
　The room that has dragonflies on the wall.

Amethyst Earley, Grade 3

Black

Black looks like things you'd like to forget,
like monsters and nightmares.
Black sounds like something you don't want to know.
It's someone shrieking before he falls to the ground.
Black feels like a black cat sitting on the street
staring right at you.

Ben Heinrich, Grade 2

Thanksgiving

On Thanksgiving people give thanks.
There are parades and parties on Thanksgiving.
On Thanksgiving there's no school.
On Thanksgiving we eat turkey.
On Thanksgiving there's football.
On Thanksgiving you see a lot of your family.

Sofia DeLaRosa, Grade 3

A Golden Wish

My fish Goldie was a wish,
She was on my summer bucket list.
I saw her at the carnival night –
In the bowl, she looked so happy and bright.
I played and played the coin toss game,
I won – and my life was never the same!
The way she flapped her fins,
Made me feel like my life was a win.
I fed her and talked to her every day,
She was my best friend, and loved to play.
Goldie died today, but why?
I didn't have time to say good bye.
I gently placed her in the yard,
And made her a beautiful farewell card.
Now, my friend is up in the sky
In a place where she can swim… or fly!

Abrielle Brown, Grade 3

A Tale of Disaster and Hope

"I hate you!"
His screams echo through the playground.
Suddenly he lunges, left hand first!
I have no choice.
Thoughts relay messages through my head.
I tilt back, leap —
a tight roll that could make an acrobat proud.
I hit the ground with a satisfying thud,
sprint out of the dreadful place.
Then, I turn, hear a soft voice,
"Jonathan," his tone is full of concern.
"I'll always love you, Jonathan."
His words wash over me in a warm haze.
I hug him. He does the same.
After all, he is still a little brother. My little brother.

Jonathan Z. Schmidt, Grade 3

Blue

Blue is a frozen nose,
In the winter, it's the tips of your toes.
On the first spring day,
It's a robin's eggs and a blue jay.
Blue is twilight shadows on snow,
Sometimes the feeling way down low.
Blue is the color of sad,
But sometimes, blue is not that bad.
Like the color of joy,
At the birth of a newborn boy!
Blue is the sound of a river that flows,
It makes me feel like freshly washed clothes.
Blue is the color of the beautiful sky,
It's also the clouds just passing by.

Kennedy Ballak, Grade 2

Ms. Collier's Back to School
Ms. Collier is the best.
She will never let us rest.
Ms. Collier is as sweet as sugar.
But when it comes down to toast,
she's a cooker.

She shines like the sun.
But in class she's full of fun.
But when someone has a mood.
She isn't rude.
But some people are rude.

That's when people have gratitude
Finally when you hear the whistle.
I think it's time for dismissal,
Finally I get on the bus,
This is when you'll hear the fuss.
Savannah Wilson, Grade 3

Ode to Winter
When the wind brings snow
everybody knows
the winter of the year has come!

When huge evergreens
decorate city scenes
the winter of the year has come!

When kids yell, "WHOA!"
as they play in the snow
the winter of the year has come!

An ode to hot cocoa
an ode to snow
an ode to Santa's
"Ho, Ho, Ho!"
Ava Repka, Grade 3

What Is Turquoise
Turquoise is like the Caribbean Sea,
With no one on an island except me.
Turquoise smells like funnel cake,
Sometimes it's a blue lake.
It's a color as bright as the sun,
Turquoise is a color that's fun.
It tastes like cotton candy,
And it feels like a quite happy me.
It is not very serious,
At times, it can be mysterious.
Turquoise often makes people grin,
It's like a nice picture to be in.
A mermaid's tail,
This is not the color of pale.
I will love turquoise forever,
And the time I will hate it will be never!
Rhyan Lehman, Grade 2

America
A merica my beautiful country
M ost fairest of all.
E xcellent schools with knowledge
R esponsible for democracy.
I ncredible place to live in
C ourageous country.
A mazing America I love you!
Simrah Mansoori, Grade 3

Scary Train
I got on a scary train.
Oh my! I saw a bad ghost!
I ran, I saw a big brain!
Oh no! The ladder is broke.
I climb up the strange chain.
The roof is open. I jump off!
I ran away from the train.
Zachary Mazey, Grade 2

Fall Leaves
Falling leaves fall off the trees
The wind blows them side to side
And the leaves glide
Crunch! Crunch!
We rake them
There is a bunch
The leaves are dancing in the breeze.
Ethan Elson, Grade 3

America
A merica the free
M arvelous place to be
E ndless education in schools
R emarkable regions everywhere
I ndependence unlimited
C ultures growing every day
A wesome place to live in…
Reza Rehman, Grade 3

America
A beautiful place to live in
M agnificent landforms everywhere
E ntirely a free country
R adiant people of different cultures
I nteresting states to explore
C aring presidents that make history
A merica God bless you!
Somaya Tahir, Grade 3

Dogs
Dogs are so awesome
They are nice and fun to have.
Puppies are cute too,
It's fun to cuddle with them
and they are company too!
Nevaeh Kimball, Grade 3

Thanksgiving Family
Thanksgiving is family!
We eat together
Turkey, carrots, and
Really good stuffing!
We all take turns
Bowling super good
Spares and strikes.
Thanksgiving is family!
Giona Torres, Grade 1

School
My teacher's name is Kala,
Mine is too.
Abby B. is my friend,
So is Abby Hughes.
Kristen is quiet,
John is loud.
Everyone likes
To make the teacher proud!
Kayla Maggard, Grade 3

Trick or Treating
I like Halloween
It is scary
I get a costume
I put it on fast
I get some candy
In my big basket
Treat or Treating
Is so very much fun!
Joseph Blake, Grade 1

Halloween Fun
Halloween is Fun!
You put on really
scary costumes.
Then you go walking
and Trick or treating.
Grownups give you good
Candy to enjoy!
Halloween is Fun!
Jesse Little, Grade 1

Fall
I see fall when I go outside.
I pick up the leaf.
I like fall.
I go to the park and I see leaves.
I like fall because fall is so fun.
We get to play in the park.
I see leaves falling down.
I see leaves in the grass.
Winnie Li, Grade 1

Fall

I like to collect leaves on the ground.
Fall is very fun to play in the leaves.
The leaves look colorful in the trees.
I love to jump in the leaves with my friend.
I love to throw leaves on the floor with Livia.
I love the wind to go fast.
The leaves fall from the tree.
Fall is so colorful.
Fall is the prettiest of all.

Bella Li, Grade 2

Snowflakes

On a cold snowy night,
Snowflakes falling
What a beautiful site.
Branches of trees all dressed in bright white.
Winter is here,
Winter is here!
The dancing flakes you will see all night.
Snowflakes, Snowflakes!

Jonah Thakore, Grade 3

The Joy of Gingerbread Man

Snap! Crunch! Crack!
I bite into my gingerbread man.
He has candy blue eyes and red sprinkles galore.
He looks delicious.
He's a flat little man, as fragile as glass.
You have to be careful.
Gingerbread man I love them so much.
They are the best Christmas treat.

Angus Kenson, Grade 3

Grow Grow Little Flower

Grow grow little flower
Grow little flower you need a shower
Little flower if you don't grow I will make you as my dad
I got one I will make you feel sad
Or I am going to put you on a field
Or maybe I can put you on a shield
I got one I will put you on a line
Then I will just say fine

Makayla Watson, Grade 3

The Beach

My dog ran and sat in the sand.
I touch the water with my hand.
Me and my dog went to the water it was fun.
I ate an ice cream but it melted because of the sun.
I went to get shells but they were broken then went home.
I gave food to my dog she wanted more.
We went to the beach the next day.
We went and it was long and we went in May.

Kimberly Lainez Rodriguez, Grade 3

I Am From

I am from my Auntie.
My Auntie is sweet and caring. She
makes me feel special. I am from homes. It makes
me comfortable. I am from ice-cream
and cake and pizza. It is good.
I am from cats and dogs. They are
cute when they are puppies and
kittens.

Trinity Clemons, Grade 3

King's Dominion

When I went to King's Dominion there were some cool games.
Some other rides were lame.
I went to the pools.
I went to something cool.
I saw big trees.
They were all free.
That day was cool.
The next day I went to school.

Jonatan Tul, Grade 3

Nutter

There once was a cat named Nutter
He loved milk and toast with butter.
He sat on his bed
And scratched his head
And said, "I need to call my brother."
So he called his brother and told him
I sure do miss my dear sweet mother
Because she also liked milk and toast with butter

Ainsley Clark, Grade 1

The Big City

Honking cars,
100-foot buildings,
people everywhere.
I see toy stores, restaurants, train stations, and hotels,
Big Ben right overhead.
Across the ocean,
some people say it's better.
But that's not what I say.

Jack Plucker, Grade 2

The Beach

I went to the beach one day.
It was so fun because we got to play.
A big wave hit me right in the face.
We went to this place.
I made a castle of sand.
Then my dad smacked it with his big fat hand.
I went in the water and I grabbed a fish.
It was so fun to go to the beach but then the fish gave me a big wish.

Hadiyyah Neblett, Grade 3

Tacos

This taco is so very delish,
I wish they were always like this.
I would eat them every day and night,
Eating them is not a fright.
Tacos taste like chocolate and milk,
I like them with lettuce and sauce,
but some people think they taste like spider silk,
But I disagree with people who think they taste like moss.
Tacos, I love them, I said it again,
They are way more than a big piece of bread,
They are bread, sauce and lettuce,
But I hate them when they're dead.

Gage Tlapa, Grade 3

I Am Most Thankful for My Friends and Family

T he day for turkey
H appy people
A ll people like turkey
N ative American
K indness and happiness
S mells good
G ive people thanks
I love Indians and pilgrims
V ery good stuffing
I love Thanksgiving
N ice Indians
G ood people

Justin Trinchillo, Grade 3

I Am Most Thankful for My Family and Friends

T urkey
H appy Thanksgiving
A ll nice food
N ative Americans
K ind things from my family
S omething smells good
G ood day for turkey
I n the kitchen the food is good
V ery good gravy, mom
I love Thanksgiving
N ice things
G od is special

Christina Wessely, Grade 3

The World's Best Teacher

The world's best teacher is kind, caring and loving.
She teaches in a fine way to help us do well in school.
She finds ways to help us succeed in a kind way
She plays games with us
she makes the class smile.
She is really magical.
She teaches many things and wants us to move to fourth grade
I believe she is someone very special and I feel she is the world's best teacher.

Bin Ni, Grade 3

I Am Most Thankful for My Family and Friends

T hankful
H ow great this turkey is
A mazing holiday
N ice turkey
K ind
S melling good
G od
I like Thanksgiving
V ery good food
I eat with my family
N ovember 28, 2013
G ravy

Ava Campo, Grade 3

I Am Most Thankful for My Mom and Dad

T he stuffing is good
H appy Thanksgiving!
A happy day
N ice food
K indness
S mells good
G ive thanks
I 'm thankful
V ery good turkey
I 'm lucky for Thanksgiving
N ice day
G ravy on my food

Gianna DeSena, Grade 3

I Am Most Thankful for My Whole Family

T he turkey is good
H appy Thanksgiving
A really good day
N ice things
K indness
S mells of good turkey
G ive thanks
I love God
V ery good mashed potatoes
I love turkey a lot
N ice decorations
G ravy

Adriana Balacich, Grade 3

It's Halloween

It's Halloween!
When Halloween comes, the children get treats
When they go trick or treating.
They get treats on a very spooky night.
The children find this time a very enjoyable one.
They get many delicious treats from different houses in their neighborhood.
The children will always wear their costumes
And have a Happy Halloween.

Kristi Liu, Grade 3

An Identical Twin
Being a twin is so much fun
We are double trouble
And double the fun
The best thing about being twins is
No one can tell us apart
Especially because we are
   So smart.

My twin is not only my sister
But she is also my best friend in the world.
My twin sister is there when I'm happy and
She cheers me up when I'm sad.
We are there for each other.

We are not fantastic
We are TWINTASTIC!
Evva De La Cruz Valdez, Grade 3

I Am From
I am from God,
He made me
He makes me do the right thing.
I am from my house,
I stay warm, I play and I eat
there.
I am from shrimp, chicken
and Pizza. They are good.
I am from sheep and chickens.
I like to rub them.
I am gorgeous. I am from
Atlanta, Alaska, New York.
I am from Cleveland and Columbus
but mostly from Cleveland.
Hollywood. They have pools.
Janasia Starks, Grade 3

Summer
Summer is like
the world's best friend

Summer is like a party
that never ends

The days are longer
the nights are shorter
because it's summer

Having ice cream and
sodas dripping down your
chin

It's summer
Chuck Schaeffer, Grade 3

Police
P olite
O ut for missions
L aw abiding
I mportant
C atch bad guys
E arn medals
Dariel Aviles, Grade 2

Ninjas
N aughty
I nvisible
N imble
J ousters
A lone
S ilent
Landon Mullarkey, Grade 2

Elves
Elves are fun!
Elves look awesome!
Elves love sitting around.
They fly in the night!
Elves dig into candy.
They like to make a mess!
Ella Matthis, Grade 1

Thanksgiving
I love Thanksgiving!
I eat turkey.
I watch great football.
I play with my
Brother, Mom, Dad.
Thanksgiving is Fun!
Riely Armstrong, Grade 1

Blue
Blue is the color of a blue bird,
   A bird flying in the blue sky.
Blue is the color of my book bin,
   The book bin that I put my books in.
Blue is the color of the water,
   The water I swim in.
Juliana Barone-Lopez, Grade 3

Chubby Cheeks
Chubby cheeks dimpled chin.
Rosy lips, teeth within.
Curly hair, very fair.
Eyes are blue, lovely too.
Teacher's pet is that you.
Yes yes yes.
Laisha Pita, Grade 3

Things I Love
Swings — WEEEE!
Playing outside
Acorns
Bouncing the ball
Guitars
Playing on the drums
Zoe Fosco, Grade 2

Cats in a Lane
Cats in a lane
running in the wet rain.
Cats on a cute train
cuddling in a drain.
Chasing mice from the grain.
Three cats in a lane.
Lily Miller, Grade 2

Blue
Blue is the color of the water in my pool,
   The pool I swim in.
Blue is the color of the sky,
   The sky I breathe air in and out.
Blue is the color of my favorite jacket,
   The jacket I wear.
Brittney Ferlazzo, Grade 3

White
White is the color of my skin,
   The skin that I wear,
White is the color of snow,
   The snow that I play in.
White is the color of the clouds,
   The clouds that I look at.
Peter Hans, Grade 3

Summer
S wim in the lake
U se floats in the pool
M ake boats to float
M ake sand castles
E at watermelon
R ide a scooter
Bradley Negron, Grade 2

Fall
I like to play in the fall.
I love to play with my friends.
I like to fly a kite.
I like to go outside to play.
I love reading a book in the fall.
I love my teacher like Ms. Rose.
Sophia Chen, Grade 1

St. John
I love St. John
The water is so clear.
It is a clear as a diamond!
Fish scowl across the sea.
The sting rays frighten you when you're surfing,
As they jump through the ocean.
I am going back in 8 weeks.
It is in the U.S. Virgin Islands!
I relax in the hot sand.
Seriously!
If the fish could fly!
So I love it here.
Whew! We are home.
Yes, hip, hip, hooray!
Quinn McHugh, Grade 2

Ode to Dad's Chocolate Cookies
I love chocolate cookies
I love them, I love them, I love them
When they go in my tummy
The other foods will say yummy
When my dad makes them
Water comes out of my mouth
I'll die without the chocolatey taste
And the chocolate chips
My dad makes them warm, soft, and dark brown
I'll get to eat them for dessert
I like the cookie dough
Way down low in my milk
I love them, I love them, I love them
Bailey Warner, Grade 3

I Am Thankful for My Family and Friends
T he turkey is ready
H appy thanksgiving
A very awesome day!
N ice dinner, I see you set the table
K ind people
S mells like heaven
G ive me more turkey
I love Thanksgiving
V ery good food and dessert
I absolutely love today
N ature is where turkeys live
G ravy
Conor Roche, Grade 3

Fall
The bountiful leaves lie down on the ground
With the colors of fall all around.
Just as red and brown.
Their beauty shines bright in the sunlight.
The grass withers
The flowers fade
At the end of a fall day.
Lilly Short, Grade 2

Gardens
Gardens
pollen, grass
fruits, vegetables, soft
daisies, roses, hummingbirds, bees
petals falling, watering, fertilizing, buzzing, tweeting
Zander Chapin, Grade 3

Sunshowers
I like sunshowers.
Plants get to eat and drink at the same time.
I can do that too.
I drink the rain, but I can't eat the sun.
I eat pizza instead.
Ashley Malkin, Grade 1

Halloween
Zombies are thumping on the door
You're running from a vampire,
There's no where to escape on Halloween night,
And you manage to get out,
But where will you live?
Mikey Gueli IV, Grade 3

Summer Fun
The beach is so much fun.
Splashing through the sun it is like I am getting tan on the land.
The crabs are snapping at me.
Every day I am there I'm having more and more fun.
Taylor Buckley, Grade 1

Oh Fall
Leaves are changing colors.
And people jump in the leaves.
There are the green, red, yellow leaves.
I love fall because I love Halloween every fall.
Quinn Johnson, Grade 2

Halloween Night
On Halloween night, some people have a fright
For them, scare levels reach full height
But most times it's on a school day
That's the only bad thing I have to say
Damien Cavallo, Grade 3

Thanksgiving
Thanksgiving is a lot of fun.
People come over to give thanks.
People also come over to eat.
Thanksgiving is a time when we give thanks to God.
Isabella Muro, Grade 3

Fright Night
Two girls alone at night what a fright what a fright
Trapped inside a haunted house what a fright what a fright
Monsters coming from everywhere it's a fright it's a fright
Rheya Lasonde, Grade 3

Wonderful Weather

Summer sun as yellow as
Sunflowers smiling down at me
Watching the birds singing gracefully
Flowers dancing in the wind
Making me smile
Grass cold and wet
As I lie down on it
Clouds as white as cotton balls
Winter snowballs getting thrown
Wham! Wham! Wham!
while my boots step on crunchy snow
Crunch Crunch
Spring birds chirping
Chirp, Chirp, Chirp, Chirp
Flowers blooming children jumping in puddles making me smile
The beautiful autumn leaves falling from the trees
As I step on them crunching under my feet
Winter, Spring, Summer, Fall
I love the seasons
I love them all

Isabella Mintz, Grade 3

The Day Before Third Grade

It was the day before school,
And my grandma and grandpa were taking me to the pool.
I had lots of fun,
But soon I left and the fun was done.

After the pool
I got things ready for school.
I packed my lunch
To eat at school for brunch.

I looked in my bag for all my supplies.
And there they were right before my eyes.
I looked for a book to put in my bag.
The book was heavy so my arms started to sag.

I went upstairs to go to bed.
I lay down on my pillow soft under my head.
I was kind of excited for school.
I got tucked under my blankets because I felt cool.

Steve Duchi IV, Grade 3

The Grateful Elephant

In the Savannah, I am big and gray,
I use my trunk to work all day.
I am intelligent and I am smart,
I can even use my trunk to paint art.
My big ears keep me cool, protect me from rain,
I eat bamboo, roots, and sugarcane!
I have ivory tusks that protect me,
And my big eyes help me see.
Savannahs and rain forests are where I roam,
I am thankful to call these home.

Molly Hughes, Grade 1

My Delicious Donut Ode

Delicious, round, glazed, creamy,
However it comes,
Hole in the middle; I don't care.
When I see you I almost pass out.
Should I eat it or just be full?
It doesn't matter if I'm full,
I'll say I don't have a full stomach just to eat you.
Jelly or peanut—Hmmm, both!
Ooh, la, la, look it's triple chocolate!
Smells extremely delicious,
I don't know; I can't say.
It's just too good!
Oh, donut shop, here we come!
Maybe there are too many donuts to choose.
I'll buy the store.
Ah, now that's paradise!
Oops, big trouble,
There are no more donuts!

Avery Lamka, Grade 3

Two Things Equal Up to One

There are always two sides on one thing
in nature
fresh leaves and
dry leaves
different colors
different sides
two sides to the sky
sunny or rainy
water evaporating and
sun rays pointing up
the sun and the rain are both rising up
in the sky
sun makes you dry
water makes you wet
the sides can be similar or not alike at all
sometimes, if it's special
the sides mix and make something beautiful
like a rainbow

Elizabeth Lee, Grade 2

Christmas

Joy,
It snows.
It is wonderful.
I drink hot cocoa,
I build snowmen,
I build snowballs,
It's a great time of the year.
Then Santa comes to town!
I see a reindeer with a red nose,
it glows in the night and it shines in the day,
He pulls the sleigh and flies in the air.
And when he gets home he says, "Best day ever!"
It's the greatest.

Lydia Biviano, Grade 1

Pizza
Hot, cheesy pizza
Ham, pineapple and cheese
Round, warm, hot, spicy
Inviting me to sample
A slice that's most delicious.
Emily Dube, Grade 3

Rocks
R olling
O utside
C hunky
K een
S hiny
Kaelin Ballard, Grade 2

Cobra
C limbs trees
O utside
B rown and black
R ough skin
A ttacks people
Alize Lajeunesse, Grade 2

Water
W ell
A tlantic Ocean
T ributary
E stuary
R iver
Jaiden Gomez Mendez, Grade 2

I Love
I love Mom
I love school
I love the day
But most of all
I love God.
Timothy Crozier, Kindergarten

I Love
I love my dad
I love my room
I love my car
But most of all
I love ice cream.
Francisco Posada, Kindergarten

Cat
Cat
Black, fluffy
Running, eating cat food, crawling
She likes to play
Kitty
Julissa Rodriguez, Grade 1

Rabbit
Rabbit
White fur, orange carrots
Playing, hopping, chewing
I like my rabbit
Biscuit
Zanith Longfellow, Grade 1

Spiders
Spiders
Webs, Yellow
Running, spinning, planning
Eating juice from flies
Scary
Edilberto Gutierrez, Grade 1

Beach
Looking for seashells
Building sandcastles
Swimming in the ocean
Going to the beach
Michael Grzywacz, Grade 2

My Puppy
He spills his bowl
and fills my soul
He snuggles me at night
And fights away my fright.
Sophie Miller, Grade 2

Family Night
Popcorn, ice-cream, juice
Pillow fights, board games, movies
Excited, happy, fun
Family night
Hayley Slack, Grade 2

Camping
Sleep in tents
Making s'mores
Doing a scavenger hunt
Going camping
Jaelynn Dennis, Grade 2

Fall
F un
A lso autumn
L eaves fall from the trees
L eaves feel crunchy
Breana O'Brien, Grade 2

Fall Is…
Fall is as red as apples.
Fall is as orange as pumpkins.
Fall is as yellow as the stars and the moon.
Fall is colorful!
Sarah Hodum, Kindergarten

Thanksgiving
T ime to celebrate
H ot soup is waiting for me
A romas fill the air
N obody is unhappy
K nauss family has fun
S it at the big round table
G ive more, receive less
I t's time to say, "Thank you!"
V ictory time is harvest time
I nside our warm house, there's a FEAST
N one of our feast is left over
G ive thanks — Now!
Kristina Knauss, Grade 3

I Am Most Thankful for My Family
T urkey
H appy
A happy day
N ever stop eating
K ind
S tuffing
G ravy is good on turkey
I like Thanksgiving
V ery good turkey
I don't like stuffing
N ice food
G obble, gobble
Matthew Cipri, Grade 3

Blue
Blue is the color of the sky,
The sky I see.
Blue is the color of the book basket,
The book basket I read from.
Blue is the color of the sea,
The sea I swim in.
Blue is the color of the marker,
The marker I use.
Blue is the color of my chair,
The chair I sit in.
Blue is the color of the water,
The water I use to clean the dishes.
Jordan Olmack, Grade 3

The Whale
The whale
has a
silly tail
and can
go so far
down
that
it can
even
drown.
Sean Barnes, Grade 1

My Special Friend
Daniella is a special and sweet girl.
She is my best friend.
She always makes me laugh.
She cheers me up when I am sad.
Daniella is the best friend to have.

We always share and care about each other.
Although we don't get to be in the same class,
We get to chat at breakfast time and catch up.

Daniella is the best friend ever.
Ever and ever we will always be together.
We will try to always support one another.

Daniella is there for me and I am there for her.
She will always have a very special place in my heart.
I love my best friend Daniella.
Isabella Rodriguez, Grade 3

Ode to Pineapples
I love your yellowness, so juicy
So sweet, I love you on pizza too!

You make my mouth water just thinking about you.
You are my #1 favorite food.

You help my brain think right.
You're a fruit that I adore.
You are a good snack to have when I'm hungry.

You make my tongue tingle when I eat you cut up.
My family loves you too,
My dad likes you frozen, so do my sister and I.

You're really juicy. I like to drink your juice.
You are so good. Can't wait for snack time!
Eliyana Nelms, Grade 3

Winter
I love winter, winter is fun.
So much fun but I miss the sun.

I can go outside and run and play,
but Mom always says not all day.

Yes, it is true, it is very very cold
But playing in the snow never gets old.

I was born in March, the last winter month
so now everyone knows why I love winter so much.

There are 3 months in each season
Summer, spring, winter and fall.

Oh! My my my, I think I love them all.
Lariah Alija Jones, Grade 3

Irresistible Creatures
Bunnies are cute and adorable.
They are small but capable.

They are warm and sweet creatures.
They have smooth and furry features.

I love them greatly.
They are just so lovely.

I can't resist their chubby cheeks,
And how they have so much energy that they can hop for weeks.

Finally, bunnies are my favorite.
I even like them more than chocolate.
Noura Arbab, Grade 2

Airplanes
Flying high in the sky
All different colors: red, green, and blue

All different shapes and sizes
Different types of planes

Carrying passengers, carrying cars, carrying missiles
Soaring through the sky

Landing and taking off
As fast as a cheetah

Leaving white streaks in the sky
Floating down to land
Elia Powers, Grade 3

An Ode to My Best Friend
My best friend's name is Emily
She is very nice
She's like part of my family
Our friendship has no price!

Emily is very cool
Emily loves horses too
She's also very smart in school
That's why we're best friends too!

Emily and I are different in very many ways
I'm sure we are going to make it to the very end
We'll be friends until our last days!
That's why this Ode is for you, my friend!
Kimber Spaulding, Grade 3

Fall
Fall is a great time of the year.
The leaves come off the trees.
Animals hibernate and thanksgiving is here.
The fun is also here.
Nicholas Pearson, Grade 3

Outside in October

Outside in October the frost makes a very thin blanket on the ground or grass outside.
Outside in October the colorful and beautiful leaves fall slowly down off the trees as the trees become empty.
Outside in October I feel a shiver through my spine as the cold wind runs through my body and hair.
Outside in October I hear a silence fall over everything and I hear nothing.
Outside in October I smell all of the fresh nature.
Outside in October the trees blow in the wind as a strong breeze blows by.
Outside in October you hear the children run on the playground as they step on the leaves, which makes a crunching noise.
Outside in October you can see grown birds, which used to be little babies, fly away for winter. And the bears crawl into their dens to hibernate.
Outside in October you can hear the little children jump in leaf piles that they just made and you hear them working together to build it again for the next person to jump in.
Outside in October the stars come out and then become dark and you drift off to sleep.

Josephina Kamens, Grade 3

Lammy

Lammy, Lammy is so kind.
She cuddles and gives you hugs.
And she wobbles when she is hungry or wants to take a nap.
Sometimes she is cranky, but that's okay I still love her anyway.
She loves me, and it doesn't matter what's outside. All that matters is, who I am on the inside.
I will always love her.

Kelly McCain, Grade 2

Beach Sand

Twinkling in the bright sun, hiding beautiful seashells that washed up from the dark frigid ocean.
Wondering if it too, will get swallowed by the sea.
Imagining when the next beach party will be.
When the people leave it doesn't get lonely, it murmurs to the amazing sea and waits in anticipation for the sun to rise again.

Jadyn Genest, Grade 3

Love the World

We've only got one world
We have to treat it right,
Stop driving those cars when you don't need to.
We have to love the world
Or the world won't turn out right.
Start recycling.
Save those trees.
We need to breathe healthier air.
Kids are crying and almost dying.
Love the world
We have to treat it right.
Please stop smoking
Every time you start to smoke one person dies
Please stop smoking.
People filling lungs of little ones
Start walking
Stop using cars, motorcycles, planes
All those other vehicles.
We have to treat the world right
just like it treats us…
Love the world

Stephanie Kannon, Grade 3

I Am From

I am from mom.
She is nice to me. She loves
me. She takes care of me.
I am from Cleveland, Ohio,
because this is where I grew up and this is where
I live.
I am from greens.
They are good for you. They
are good, and that is my favorite
food.
I am from cats,
because my grandma has
a cat and my auntie has
a cat.
I am nice, pretty, I am
mommy's and daddy's girl.
I am a cutie pie and I
am good. I am gorgeous and a brat.
I am from Weather girl,
when I grow up?

Miracle-Storm Griffin, Grade 3

High Merit Poems – Grades K, 1, 2, and 3

My Dog, Meimei
My dog, Meimei, running faster than
the wind on my back
Her fur coat
softer than feathers
My dog, Meimei
sleeping with me
Meimei wrestling with
her sister, Ruby
Sadie Margolin, Grade 3

Bob the Chair
My chair is wearing some hair
and it just ate my pear.

I guess it doesn't care
And it gave me an evil glare.

Now, I don't want to share
With the chair that ate my pear.
Lucas Lindemann, Grade 3

Fall
In the fall leaves change color.
In the fall leaves fall down.
In the fall we see pumpkins.
In the fall it is a little bit cold.
In the fall we can eat pumpkin pie.
In the fall we can play at the park.
In the fall we can go trick-or-treat.
In the fall we can make apple pie.
Kristy Lei, Grade 1

I Am From
I am from mom.
She loves me and cares for me.
I am from Cleveland.
That is the best city to me.
I am from pizza.
It is good.
I am from dogs.
I always wanted a dog.
Santyana Thomas, Grade 3

My Puppy
My puppy likes to eat a bone
His dog house looks like a cone
He likes to swim in the lake
My puppy likes to try to eat the cake
We always have fun
We like to sit in the sun
My puppy is in a good mood
He likes to eat food
Durrell Woodson, Grade 3

At the Forest
Roses are red,
valleys are blue,
I love Aunt Donna,
and so do you.

The sun is yellow,
the sky is blue.
Don't forget
the clouds too.
Madeline Higgins, Grade 2

Fall
The leaves are falling to the ground.
It's really bound what I found.
There's Yellow, Green, Red and Brown.
I think I know what I found.
Fall
Is so beautiful but won't last long.
It will
come along again,
not too long.
Alyssa Archetti, Grade 3

My Baby Brother
I will play with Jake
Jake will play with me
He crawls everywhere
He knows everything in the house
He is sometimes naughty
He is sometimes cute
He bites on everything
And chews on his clothes
But he is the best baby brother
Adhana Blaise, Grade 1

Volcanoes
V alleys
O oze
L ava
C raters
A shes
N atural disasters
O penings in Earth
E xplosions
S urfaces move
Caden Daley-Rivera, Grade 2

America
A good place to live in
M any people from different countries
E ach person has many rights
R uled by a great president
I s a cool nation
C itizens of America
A ll grow together...
Ridwan Ismail, Grade 2

Saw
S harp
A ble to cut wood
W orks for you
Jordani Gonzalez, Grade 2

Chili
My favorite food
The opposite of its name
Turkey, beans, and chips
Sylvia Erdely, Grade 3

The Voyage
Sailing across the sea from year to year
no land in sight
just open water for all your life.
Kaylee Ferrier, Grade 2

Fall
Make a pie of leaves and
pick all of the leaves up and throw
the leaves in the air.
Neal Liu, Grade 1

Fall
I like fall
The leaves change colors.
And the leaves fall don on the tree.
Aaron Tan, Grade 1

Fall
fall is here
the breeze is coming
and bright leaves fall
Dan Khoi Nguyen, Grade 3

3D
Images from sheets,
Popping out before your eyes,
I just love 3D.
Kenny Russell, Grade 3

Index by Author

A-R, Spencer 143
Abood, Alexandra 54
Abraham, Elysse 24
Abramovich, Joshua 34
Acosta, Jovanni 87
Adam 45
Adams, Christina 110
Adams, Isaac 129
Adams, Olivia 110
Adase, Jack 34
Adkins, Ethan 172
Adu, Jennifer 115
Afghani, Sayida 150
Afzali, Aron 136
Agak, Martina 54
Ahmad Ali, Haajar 109
Ahmed, Azza 22
Ahmed-Syed, Iffath 83
Albert, Mia 69
Alcott, Abby 121
Alderfer, Eric 111
Alderfer, Jamie 51
Alegria, Amanda 122
Alexander, Liam 156
Alfrey, Matthew 115
Allah-Mensah, Joellen 48
Allen, Autumn 62
Allen, Ayrienna 45
Alloco, Sydney 90
Almanzar, Carlos 92
Altman, Brooke 110
Alvarado, Gabriella 166
Alvini, Giuliana 164
Amadio, Lily 27
Amaral, Anthony 86
Amico, Alexandra 39
Andersen, Erik 38
Anderson, Caitlynn 141
Anderson, Maia 40
Andre, Jadyn 64
Andrews, Bridget 138
Andrus, Giovanni 50
Angelis, Natalia 118
Apruzzi, Nick 130
Arbab, Noura 181
Archetti, Alyssa 183
Arencibia, Cassandra 117
Armentrout, Colin 71
Armstrong, Riely 177
Arrington, Beneé 118
Asbury, Natalie 122
Ashby, Logan 42
Askew, Mykayla 100
Attles, Simone 72
Auden, Abigail C 134

Audet, Paige 139
Audrey 130
Austin, Jack 104
Auth, John 105
Averett, Dekai 22
Aviles, Dariel 177
Azzarano, Kristian 76
Babu, Vivek 86
Baciak, Sydney 72
Bagdasarian, Caitlin 151
Bailey, Morgan 106
Bak, Riley 122
Balacich, Adriana 176
Ball, Tommy 50
Ballak, Abbie 132
Ballak, Kennedy 173
Ballard, Kaelin 180
Banzil, Sophia 170
Barbier, Julie 130
Barker, Tristan 70
Barnes, Sean 180
Barnes, Tyrone 111
Baron, Hayden 48
Baron, Mark M. 97
Barone-Lopez, Juliana 177
Barrickman, Ellie 44
Barrios-Quintero, Valentina 164
Barta, Parker 89
Barthelus, Elizabeth 29
Bartman, Izabella 164
Bartone, Alex 145
Bartosz, Adam 156
Bassford, Emily 69
Bates, Taylor 74
Bathula, Shreya 112
Beauchaine, Emily 72
Beauchamp, Fabian 82
Beaulieu, Carly 145
Beaulieu, Gabrielle 106
Beblar, Joshua 33
Becker, Connor 24
Beckett, Connor 77
Beckford, Kailey 59
Beckford, Madyson 107
Belardo, Nicholas 172
Belgaonkar, Nikhil 105
Belgiorno, Francesca 42
Bell, Lauriana 167
Benchimol, Mikaela 50
Berg, Connor 43
Berger, Tyler 95
Bergeron, Anabelle 91
Bergmark, James 168
Berkovic, Luka 36
Berman, Jaclyn 139

Bernal, Mercedes 98
Betts, Nora 102
Bevins, Brandon 170
Bhandari, Devang 96
Bhowmick, Aunnesha 131
Bianchi, Emma 74
Bianco, Zach 49
Bielecki, Kailyn 51
Billows, Maddy 40
Birt, Madison 56
Bishop, Dakota 145
Bishop, Emma 137
Biviano, Lydia 179
Bjornstad, Sarah 38
Blaise, Adhana 183
Blake, Joseph 174
Blankenship, Alison 125
Blankenship, Caleb 125
Blankenship, Micah 37
Blazo, Michael 143
Bledsoe, Mykala 123
Blevins, Kendal 113
Blizzard, Elizabeth 53
Bloom, Talia 41
Bloom, Travis 168
Blount, Daeviana 34
Boas, Jack 66
Bobbey, Wyatt 66
Boecker, Ian 46
Bogdan, Emma 170
Bolling, Dylan 58
Bonomo, Cristian 130
Boorse, Rebecca 60
Borgella, Widney 163
Bottisti, Vincent 168
Bowe, Kylie 27
Boyle, Brycen 44
Boyle, James 21
Bracco, Isabella 38
Bradley, Jacklyn 54
Bradley, Joseph 62
Bradley, Sianna 137
Branch, Brianna 143
Brandon, DJ 130
Bransfield, Danny 93
Breckenridge, Elizabeth 79
Brennan, Kai 167
Brewster, Donny 32
Brewster, Nolan 85
Brick, Sydney 67
Brinton, Andrew 116
Brogan, Ellie 60
Brokaw, Max 74
Brolly, Liam 24
Brooke, Caroline 146

Brooks, Caitie 36	Catalano, Jason 111	Coon, Bailey 29
Brooks, Emilee 85	Cauwenbergh, Ian 115	Cooperrider, Chloe 109
Brooks, Harrison 123	Cavada, Max 20	Copenspire, Kaylee 104
Brown, Abrielle 173	Cavalieri, Julia 134	Cora, Lumaris 155
Brown, Codie 92	Cavallo, Damien 178	Corfias, George 27
Brown, Elaineah 97	Cavanagh, Ryan 42	Coronado, Fernando 53
Brown, Elijah 62	Cavender, Jordan 26	Cort, Andy 151
Brown, Grady 60	Ceccio, Allison 46	Corvin, Ally 125
Brown, Harmonie 162	Cejpek, Michael 66	Cory, Isaac 20
Brown, John Andrew 36	Celaj, Emma 112	Coslove, Zachary 58
Brown, Josiah 95	Chaisson, Ethan 170	Costa, Isaiah 101
Brown, Kaleb 27	Chakrabarti, Abhirup 22	Costello, Jillian 124
Brown, Lily 169	Chapin, Zander 178	Cote, Caroline 78
Brown, Lorna 126	Chaput, Jack 114	Cote, Daniel 56
Brown, Macy 85	Charland, Valery 62	Cotter, Brandon 91
Brown, Maezee 48	Chelstowski, Charles 171	Cox, Gavin 98
Brown, Max 168	Chen, Claire 97	Cox, Trey 153
Brown, Mykayla 103	Chen, Sophia 177	Cozzone, Emily 112
Bryant, Justin 82	Chesen, Gavin 63	Craiter, Emily 164
Brzezicki, Kylie 153	Chew, William 46	Crandall, Chase 64
Buckley, Taylor 178	Chhith, Isaiah 158	Crihfield, Joshua 23
Bungatavula, Devesh 127	Chiapperino, Cole 67	Croft, Mackenna 59
Burgoyne, Eliza 29	Choi, Ethan 152	Crowley, Caleb 156
Burhans, Chloe 92	Choi, Jason 115	Crozier, Timothy 180
Burke, Abby 49	Chombo, Kiara 152	Cruise, Derek 135
Burke, Kassidy 150	Christensen, Emma 63	Cruz, Aidalina 141
Burks, Michael 57	Christensen, Rachel 27	Cruz, Aolani 141
Burns, Hardy 84	Chung, Julia 74	Cruz, Cassandra 162
Burns, Kristopher 24	Ciesla, Jackson 107	Cruz, Jada 109
Burrows, Gwen 43	Cincotta, Kelly 57	Cruz, Jordan 150
Burton, Bryn 58	Cipri, Matthew 180	Culkin, Sarah 41
Busch, Taylor 79	Clabaugh, Ashleigh 136	Curimbaba, Natasha 101
Butcher, Annie 102	Clark, Ainsley 175	Currier, Nicholas 61
Butcher, Ellie 38	Clark, Ed 119	Cusick, Lucas 39
Buynak, Johnathan 70	Clark, Jonathan 116	Cutler, Grace 158
Byard, Zaniyah 167	Clark, Kaytlee 45	Czebatul, Daniel 157
Bythrow, Aubrianna 117	Clark, William 44	D'Amato, Cristina 38
Bywaters, Lizzy 57	Clegg, Jaelynn 105	D'Amico, Jenna 92
Cabrera, Paige 81	Clement, Zachary 121	D'Angelo, Olivia 108
Calderon, Gabriella 86	Clemons, Trinity 175	Dahal, Shachi 144
Caldwell, Trisha 103	Clifton, Cadence 168	Daley, A.J. 55
Calibey, Jeana 93	Cline, Emily 68	Daley, Julia 46
Caligiuri, Sara 62	Cline, Morgan 50	Daley-Rivera, Caden 183
Cammarotta, Bryce 75	Clontz, Dakota 93	Danforth, Addison 75
Campbell, Clive 29	Clouse, Emily 171	Dapul, Clarisse 104
Campo, Ava 176	Coates, Hadiyah 49	Dardari, Alma 145
Cannon, Edward 66	Cobrinik, Jamila 101	Davan, Nicholas 114
Cannon, Marinda 158	Cochrane, Madison 166	Davis, Ashley 111
Cao, Guanyi 22	Cole, Aaron 87	Davis, Emma 156
Capaldi, Isabella 34	Cole, Eliza 138	Davis, Xzayvier 112
Capria, Vincent 66	Collins, Stacia 115	Day, Abigail 153
Capristo, Gia 36	Colón, Ellyse 147	De La Cruz, Ashley 50
Carey, Ryan 38	Colton, Emma 143	De La Cruz Valdez, Evva 177
Carmona, Andrew 151	Comas, Grace 58	Dean, Haley 155
Caron, Amelia 62	Combs, Larissa 103	Deane, Johnnie 131
Carr, Alicia 61	Commons, Kylie 44	DeCesare, Caden 163
Carroll, Brian 127	Conde, Sheik 69	DeJesus, Miles 34
Carroll, Carly 110	Conley, Olivia 99	DeLaRosa, Sofia 173
Carvalho, Julia 39	Conover, James 172	DellaRocco, Tyler 110
Cassada, Thomas 129	Constantine, Maggie 138	DeMario, Geena 149
Cassinera, Joseph 53	Cook-Hayes, Haleigh 19	Demopoulos, Theo 170
Castronovo, Andrew 158	Cooke, Andrew 87	Dennis, Jaelynn 180

Index by Author

Dennis, Laniyah 93
Depinet, Jacob 20
Deringer, Sydney 131
DeSena, Gianna 176
DeStefano, Caitlin 46
Devine, Maddy 163
DiFranco, Jacob 20
DiMaggio, Christina 45
DiMarzo, Colleen 117
DiMeo, Stephanie 112
Dimpel, Logan 154
Dively, Haleigh 42
Dobkin, Miranda 18
Dockery, Charlotte 47
Dodge, Nathan 139
Doherty, Molly 52
Dokos, David 91
Donahue, Olivia 96
Dongilli, Emily 105
Dooley, Chiara 26
Dorielan, Marlynn 29
Dotson, Jon 22
Dotson, Savannah 46
Dougherty, Luke 171
Douglas, Will 55
Dragas, Alex 25
Dreger, Halina 64
Driscoll, Delaney 95
Droxler, Elaine 134
Dube, Emily 180
Duchi IV, Steve 179
Duegaw, John 135
Duffy, Aidan 33
Dumminger, Alex 76
Dunlap, Sophie 52
Dunlop, William 54
Duvall, Eli 172
Eakins, Raelynn 25
Earley, Amethyst 173
Eaton, Zenna 100
Eber, Jocelyn 109
Eckenrode, Michael 91
Eckert, Tyler 149
Eckhart, Shawn 164
Edwards, Laurel 108
Egedy, Andrew 65
Egoroff, Amirrah 121
Eich, Julia 54
Ellis, Michael 115
Ellis, Nathan 104
Elrod, Ja'kiya 53
Elson, Ethan 174
Elswick, Brady 75
Emmanuel, Hephzibah 51
Enamorado, Mario 156
Endara, Emilia 90
Engle, Kyle 124
Engler, Isaac 163
Erdely, Sylvia 183
Espinoza, Pricila 81
Esposito, Bryce 135
Ettle, Maya 59
Evans, Amelia 81
Everett, Annabel 43
Faboskay, Devion 172
Fard, Ava 118
Farnoto, Haley 153
Farrar, Stefan 169
Federico, Trent 31
Feiler, Kendall 156
Feit, Juliana 89
Feliciano, Ramon 169
Fellows, Jackson 62
Fenelon, Martiah 147
Fennell, Claire 29
Ferguson, Kyle 124
Ferlazzo, Brittney 177
Ferrier, Kaylee 183
Figueroa, Keishla 125
Fili, Madison 51
Finamore, Quinlan 138
Finn, Abbey 19
Fischer, Michael 126
Fisher, Aileen 166
Fisher, Coyote 68
Fitzgerald, Michaela 147
Fitzsimmons, Tommy 87
Fleurmont, Kristy 87
Flores, Chasety 168
Fluet, Jaden 19
Flynn, Delaney 171
Flynn, Timmy 149
Foley, Nick 103
Foley, Ryan Anne 171
Folk, Ava 141
Fonarov, Anna 134
Fonseca, Isabel 109
Foos, Allison 40
Foos, Clemens 76
Forberg, Ethan 39
Ford, Ella 45
Forte, Autumn 33
Fosco, Zoe 177
Foster-Bagley, Brandon 140
Fox, Austyn 55
Fox, John 113
Francis, Kadance 172
Francis, Madison 74
Frank, Mica 156
Fratto, Alex 124
Frazier, Anyjha 147
Frederick, Drew 76
Freese, Caroline 85
Friesen, Colton 52
Frujinoiu, Ana Maria 156
Fu, Cecilia 51
Fulginiti, Brendan 90
Fuller, Gabriela 35
Fusaro, Bryan 88
Gabrie, Sasha 117
Gant, Gabriela 24
Garcia, Isaiah 24
Garcia, Julianna 172
Gardner, Jacob 22
Garey, Daniela 152
Garrison, Susie 136
Garst, Jacqueline 143
Garvey, Shannon 28
Gasparovic, Zakiy 55
Genest, Jadyn 182
George, Kelby 64
George, Leslie 77
Gerber, Annabel 139
Geres, Nicole 39
Gergies, Monica 82
Getchey, Natalie 83
Getola, Anneliese 143
Giamalis, Christian 137
Gianfrancesco, Kyleigh 40
Giangrasso, Adriana 90
Gibson, Miranda 112
Gieder, Kyle 76
Giesy, Malaya 162
Giglietti, Noah 30
Gilbert, Olivia 32
Gillingham, Nina 48
Ginsberg, Samara 165
Giovannetti, Sky 41
Girdusky, Kevin 164
Givone, Sarah 64
Glance, Brenna 33
Glancy, Rachel 171
Glasgow, Nasear 171
Goerlich, Miranda 39
Gomez, Andrew 78
Gonzalez, Jordani 183
Gordon, Dayjanea 20
Gordon, William 151
Gorelin, Mikayla 120
Goremusandu, Kennedy 47
Gould, Jacob 56
Graboski, Jack 18
Graf, Matthew 91
Granados, Clarissa 99
Granados-Martinez, Kaylee 61
Granger, Maddie 172
Grantham, Alyssa 157
Grasso, Julianna 156
Gray, Jessica 23
Greco, Emma 166
Greco, Sarah 59
Gregorie, Tasmir 42
Griffin, Estella 46
Griffin, Miracle-Storm 182
Grischow, Avrey 136
Grisius, Julia 92
Grosk, Ivy 23
Groves, Madeline 61
Groza, Alexander 163
Grubb, Josh 108
Gruss, Ava 42
Grzywacz, Michael 180
Guanio, Cristina Noelle 61
Gueli IV, Mikey 178
Guillen, Carlos 57
Gundecha, Manav 32

Guo, Kobe	61	
Gupta, Puneet	56	
Gutierrez, Edilberto	180	
Guy, Lauren	33	
Gwiazdowski, Hanna	94	
H., E.	168	
Haas, Madyson	94	
Habicht, Isabella	76	
Hafer, Nathan	77	
Hall, Johanna	155	
Hall, Tobias	46	
Hamblin, Hailee	166	
Hamer, Colby	55	
Hamilton, Haley	18	
Hamman, Kerstin	31	
Hammond, Maya	101	
Hampton, Morghan	125	
Hanks, Connor	157	
Hannah	149	
Hannis, Maggie	68	
Hans, Peter	177	
Hanselmann, Stephen	123	
Happel, Elizabeth	81	
Harding, Jordan	21	
Harne, Elliot	75	
Harnett, Riley	84	
Harris, Avianna	156	
Harris, Marli	27	
Harrison, Paige	120	
Hart, Emily	33	
Hart, Katie	71	
Hart, Meghan	114	
Hart, Torgyn	92	
Hart, Walden	59	
Haugen, Natalie	28	
Haydel-Brown, Kate	139	
Hayden, Gabriella	61	
Hayes, Kaelea	57	
He, Devin	66	
Heaphy, Jack	78	
Heasley, Ben	110	
Hedgemond, Elijah	70	
Heil, Michael	77	
Heinrich, Ben	173	
Hendricks, Molly	93	
Henley, Avery	119	
Henry, Belinda	45	
Henry, Danny	70	
Herman, Maci	63	
Hernandez-Mekonnen, Flora	172	
Herner, Chayla	84	
Herrala, Anoushka	156	
Herrey, Alanna	115	
Hessler-Burdick, Noah	115	
Hickey, Shannon	33	
Hickman, Jesse	137	
Higginbotham, Alexander	44	
Higgins, Kendal	71	
Higgins, Madeline	183	
Hild, Douglas	146	
Hill, Dejah	126	
Hill, Jordan	148	
Hillier, Sage	21
Himes, Haley	51
Hirsawa, Ramil	22
Hobart, Katie	69
Hoch, Hannah	77
Hodum, Sarah	180
Hoffman, Hailey	59
Hohmann, Thomas	82
Homan, Leah	109
Horan, Baileigh	97
Horne, Raelyn	65
How, Rachel	113
Howell, Patrick	102
Hoy, Ali	147
Hrebinko, Abby	120
Hronich, Ashley	90
Hronich, Brittany	49
Huang, Jenny	165
Hubbard, Christiana Tsai	47
Hubbard, Trevor	149
Huckins, Jackson	171
Huggler, Jason	44
Hughes, Amaya	78
Hughes, Molly	179
Hurley, Jonathan	42
Hurley, Logan	29
Hynek, Julia	136
Hynes, Brionna	50
Hynes, Nathen	36
Iberis, Joey	56
Igbinobaro, Janice	106
Impastato, Dante	43
Ingegni, Makala	96
Innocent, Domonic	92
Internicola, Ember	132
Isbrandt, Vanessa	44
Ismail, Ridwan	183
Isaac	116
Iyer, Rhea	114
Jabbar, Rashad	93
Jack, Amberlee	138
Jackson, Kyle	67
Jackson, Michaela	55
Jamal, Riaz	71
Jann, Stella Bryce	169
Jaquez, Ashley	53
Jasinski, Christopher	130
Jaworski, Bryce	113
Jencks, Laura	78
Jennewine, Mitchell	67
Jenny, Dylan	21
Jensen, Christian	84
Jiang, Enni	162
Jin, Ho Young	134
Joe, Gabrielle	129
Johnson, Bailey	169
Johnson, Genio	139
Johnson, Quinn	178
Jokhadar, Haya	71
Jones, Abby	25
Jones, Ashley	93
Jones, Brandon	62
Jones, Bryce	34
Jones, Hannah	95
Jones, Justice	113
Jones, Lariah Alija	181
Jones, Madison	82
Jones, Maya	61
Jones, Mikael	63
Jones, Tristan	64
Jones-Hollis, Brianna	144
Jordan, Nylah	85
Jubulis, Ryan	143
Judge, Gia	89
Justus, John A.	105
Justus, Kaylee	129
Kaeyer, Hadley	141
Kaitlyn	33
Kamens, Josephina	182
Kanaczet, Nicholas	150
Kannon, Stephanie	182
Kantor, Sam	130
Kanuika, Kirsten	138
Kapoor, Sid	120
Kapusta, Aubrey	164
Karban, Madalyn	158
Kareem, Adeeba	85
Karimova, Sabrina	64
Karvan, Mya	154
Kauffeld, Emily	113
Kauffman, Brandon	94
Kaymak-Loveless, Kaeli	88
Kaza, Isha	59
Kazanjian, Alyssa	31
Keane, Martin	68
Keane, Reagan T.	58
Keddy, Niko	11
Keller, Megan	47
Kelley, Gabe	43
Kelly, Liam	118
Kelly, Makayla	139
Kemp, Ryan	110
Kennedy, Joelle	97
Kennedy-Jensen, Caitlin	94
Kenson, Angus	175
Kern, Owen	66
Kiesel, Madison	173
Kilmurray, Matthew	26
Kimball, Nevaeh	174
King, Aja	168
King, Steven	141
Kinney, Kailah	101
Kinzler, Jack	166
Kirshenbaum, Yechezkel	173
Kitchen, Sammy	93
Klein, Ashley	152
Klein, J.T.	131
Knauss, Kristina	180
Knierman, Ryder	114
Knisley, Joseph	146
Kogan, Sarah	103
Kohnke, Elise	19
Kollmar, Jack	39
Komasz, Ava	108

Koykka, Brenden 44
Krader, Kyle 96
Kraiwan, Lalana 147
Krall, Cadence 73
Kramer, Emma 92
Kramer, Sophie 102
Krivak, Aubry G. 41
Kuhns, Kori 133
Kwafo, Heather 141
Lacava, Jessica 37
Lachman, Jonathan 111
Laferrara, Anthony 71
Lafkas, Christina 10
Lagun, Tyler 149
Lahiry, Trisha 91
Lainez Rodriguez, Kimberly ... 175
Lajeunesse, Alize 180
Lambert, Robert 105
Lamitola, Michael 50
Lamka, Avery 179
Landaverde, Cassandra Rose ... 67
Landi, Julianna 68
Lane, Kaitlynn 114
Lange, Ellie 84
Langenbach, Hailee 73
Lankowicz, Samantha 157
Larimer, Mackenzie 36
Larkin, Sean 62
Lasonde, Rheya 178
Latif, Ali 141
Lavallée Harris, Michelle-Ann ... 85
Lawson, Andrew 127
Lazar, Julia 148
Leach, Isaiah 66
Learish, Jacob 143
Lee, Chris 122
Lee, Elizabeth 179
Lee, Rachel 96
Lee, Sharon 93
Lees, Reese 60
Legersky, Maya 103
Lehman, Rhyan 174
Lehman, Turner 56
Lei, Kristy 183
Leinheiser, Jaydon 73
Leininger, Amber 126
Leitner-Sieber, Sophia 138
Lenkaitis, Ryan 112
Leopold, Henry 67
LeRoy, Alexis 156
Lessing, Jamie 77
Levine, Benjamin 65
Lewis, Alaina 29
Lewis, Graclynn 104
Lewis, Gregory 62
Lewis, Haley 57
Lewis, Keyontae 25
Lewis, Tye 141
Li, Bella 175
Li, Winnie 174
Libby, Erin 50
Licari, Francesca 166

Lindemann, Lucas 183
Lindtveit, Emily 171
Little, Jesse 174
Liu, Kristi 176
Liu, Neal 183
Locke, Noah 52
Loew, Sammy 64
Logan, Elijah 130
Lohn, Virginia 158
Long, Sorrell 21
Longfellow, Zanith 180
Looney, Adalia 164
Lord, Jack 63
Lorenzo, Gianna 70
Loughran, Maggie 50
Loveless, Nathaniel 163
Luna, Michael 66
Lundrigan, Brooke 72
Lutz, Erin 40
Mac, Andrew 164
Madiedo, Marcus 25
Maggard, Jacob 135
Maggard, Kayla 174
Magnini, Olivia 162
Mahoney, Allyson 54
Makarovsky, Dylan 156
Makuen, Jenna 162
Malazarte, Keara 44
Malhotra, Rhea 117
Malkin, Ashley 178
Manchanda, Muskan 170
Mann, Spencer 29
Manning, Hannah 118
Mansoori, Simrah 174
Mapes, Sawyer 137
Margolin, Sadie 183
Mariani, Ashley 36
Marschke, Caroline 162
Martin, Emma 61
Martin, Ian 102
Martin, JaQuez 133
Martin, Mario 162
Martinez, Giovanni 55
Massey, Aaron 39
Mastromonaco, Vito 50
Mastropolo, Kylie 146
Mathur, Kunaal 110
Matkevich, Kristina 103
Matthew, Jessica 93
Matthews, Quincey 43
Matthis, Ella 177
May, Justin 81
May, Sarah 148
Maze, Connor 147
Mazey, Zachary 174
McAlister, Tyler 74
McCain, Christina 146
McCain, Kelly 182
McCallum, Stuart 37
McCann, Isabella 121
McCarrick, Sadie 121
McClanahan, Angel 173

McCloskey, Sarah 140
McComas, George 148
McCurrie, Katie 18
McDonald, Emma 29
McDunnah, Madison 119
McElroy, Joachim 56
McGowan, Emily 72
McGuire, Madison 53
McHugh, Quinn 178
McKeta, Colby 133
McLaughlin, Asia 107
McQuaide, Elle 40
McVety, Jackson 158
Meade, Daniel 96
Meadows, Madison 26
Mehta, Sahuj 130
Meininger, Naomi 45
Melby, Alyssa 145
Melita, Andrew 91
Melkote, Anika 28
Menand, Sara 58
Mendez, Jaiden Gomez ... 180
Mendez, Jasmyn 167
Mendez, Rimervi 34
Meriwether, Natalie 120
Merrick, Paige 121
Merriman, McKenna 56
Mertz, Emma 133
Merullo, David 163
Meta, Katy 157
Metro, Lauren 118
Metzger, Lilly Ryann 166
Michaels, Grace 103
Michaud, Augustin 85
Michaud, Rebecca 127
Michnik, Anna 89
Mika, Casper 56
Mikalonis, Sydney 42
Mikkelson, Noah 111
Mikolajczak, Ryan 23
Miller, Blake 19
Miller, Ella 103
Miller, Ellie 75
Miller, Kyndall 158
Miller, Lily 177
Miller, Sam 22
Miller, Sophie 180
Mink, Sadie 44
Minnick, Jacob 102
Mintz, Isabella 179
Mioduski, Elisabeth 129
Miranda, Nicole 131
Miron, Benjamin 19
Mitchell, Tsampica 67
Mo, Felix 74
Mohrey, Isabella 113
Monaghan, Dylan 39
Monahan, Connor 88
Monfort, Jalyn 42
Mongeluzi, Anthony 89
Mono, Jacob 167
Montag, Kiersten 71

Monti, Joey	41	
Moore, Eva	94	
Moore, Hannah	60	
Moore, Quintin	73	
Moore, Victoria	28	
Morello, Gabriella	71	
Morgan, Jackson	89	
Morman, Abigail	125	
Morra, Sofia	81	
Morrison, Breonna	52	
Morrissy, Katelyn	20	
Mosca, Anthony	139	
Moser, Dana	89	
Moser, Deanna	89	
Mowery, Carolyn	105	
Mucklow, Henry	163	
Muhammad, Bari	149	
Mullarkey, Landon	177	
Muller, Riley	20	
Munro-Richard, Destine	168	
Muro, Isabella	178	
Murphy, Alexander	70	
Murphy, Aubrey	167	
Murray, Audrey	147	
Murtagh, Cormac	96	
Naish, Zoe	163	
Nankishore, Miguel	40	
Napoli, Peter	69	
Neale, Jordan	82	
Neblett, Hadiyyah	175	
Neely, Matthew	162	
Negron, Bradley	177	
Nelms, Eliyana	181	
Nelson, Adair	167	
Nelson, Ben	27	
Nelson, Courtney	129	
Nero, Luca	135	
Newman, Ivy	95	
Newton, Kiersten	137	
Nguyen, Anna	135	
Nguyen, Dan Khoi	183	
Nguyen, Ethan	98	
Nguyen, Judy	45	
Ni, Bin	176	
Nica, Sylvia	81	
Nichols, Matthew	18	
Nichols, Tess	166	
Nickerson, Veronica	22	
Nicolella, Samuel	166	
Niemiera, Bennett X.	169	
Niemiera, Olivia L.	169	
Nies, Erik	43	
Nieves, Ana	167	
Nigro, Katherine	96	
Nikolau, Elisabeth	155	
Nilles, Rebekah	65	
Nittoli, Michael	119	
Nock, Matthew	90	
Novick, Rachel	62	
Nutt, Chelsey	67	
O'Brien, Breana	180	
O'Connell, Carson	25	
O'Connor, Natalie	21	
O'Hara, Saoirse	87	
O'Melia, Nick	73	
O'Reilly, Haley	115	
Obrimah, Ogaga	47	
Oedy, Collin	62	
Ogbolu, Jason	53	
Okurowski, William	25	
Olmack, Jordan	180	
Olosunde, Oluwafemi	100	
Olson, Katie	99	
Olszowka, Anna	163	
Olton, Daniel	169	
Oreski, Madison	53	
Ortiz, Stephanie	42	
Oswald, Hannah	27	
Oviedo, Lianelys	163	
Owens, Lexy	83	
Paliouras, Nina	36	
Palmer, Grace	142	
Panati, Dani	114	
Pappas, Isabella	138	
Parelius, Samantha	69	
Parker, Olivia	37	
Parsons, Jenny	164	
Parton, Faith	151	
Pasch, Adalia	76	
Pascual, Madison	143	
Patel, Dilan	58	
Patel, Diya	127	
Patel, Priya	25	
Patton, Savana	150	
Paynton, Lauren	104	
Pearson, Nicholas	181	
Pearson, Teddy	79	
Pellegrino, Max	148	
Pendleton II, Robbie	67	
Penkrat, Christian	38	
Penny, Gabe	124	
Peperak, Baylee	99	
Peralta, Alejandro	96	
Percival, Ronnie	78	
Pereira, Alexandra	102	
Pereira, Nuno	156	
Perreault, Kaylee	109	
Persichette, Madison	172	
Petell, Perrin	22	
Petrangelo, Elizabeth	146	
Petrucci, Thomas	120	
Phifer, Alexxus	81	
Phillips, Ashley	19	
Phillips, Witt	129	
Phipps, Nia	148	
Phung, Brian	95	
Pickeral, Luca	169	
Pidruchna, Olga	106	
Piechocki, Matthew	50	
Pieper, Carson	75	
Pierce, Elizabeth	148	
Pierson, Kevin	85	
Piezal, Maya	163	
Pike, Kayla	109	
Pimentel, Jacob	31	
Pinci, Mary Angela	31	
Pineda, Vianca	89	
Piontkowski III, Robert	104	
Piscatello, Dilan	49	
Pita, Laisha	177	
Plucker, Jack	175	
Podvorec, Lydia	79	
Poerio, Tegan	58	
Poirier, Noah	130	
Polanofsky, Krista	38	
Poliviou, Kira	27	
Pollard, Georgia	105	
Pomerleau, Dakota	169	
Portella, Kaleigh	166	
Porter, Cole	45	
Porter, Destiny	92	
Portillo, Ashley	53	
Portzline, Raiden	63	
Posada, Francisco	180	
Postel, Katie	37	
Potope, Ashley	47	
Potter, Will	88	
Powers, Elia	181	
Prestigiacomo, Julie	96	
Prioleau, Mark	64	
Pritschau, Caelyn	155	
Prouty, Clay	122	
Provonsha, Andrew	76	
Purcell, Chloe	80	
Quain, Kevin	86	
Quinones, Anializ	168	
Quintino, Natalie	36	
Quraishi, Mishael	155	
Rabaev, Rivka Bella	80	
Raczka, Jenna	37	
Radcliff, Isaiah	58	
Rafac, Victoria	148	
Raftery, Niamh	122	
Ragno, Ian	102	
Rahman, Aamin	56	
Rakach, Arkasha	45	
Ralph, Laurel	75	
Ramirez, Francisco	46	
Ramoy, Elizabeth	104	
Ranginwala, Khashiya	172	
Rapposelli, Giovanni	55	
Rashkind, Ethan	78	
Reader, Alana	158	
Reading, Megan	49	
Reamon, Soraya	112	
Reckner, Justice	103	
Reed, George	60	
Reed, Kendra	86	
Reed, Stephen	80	
Regis, Madison	164	
Rehman, Reza	174	
Reilly, Layla	170	
Reilly, Meghan	146	
Reinhart, Josh	126	
Reiss, Lara	47	
Renzetti, Danny	66	

Repka, Ava	174	
Reyes, Leslie	121	
Reynolds, Kelsey	117	
Rice, William	152	
Richter, Joshua	50	
Riegert, Fiona	35	
Rieker, Kara	78	
Rieser, Lianna	46	
Riley, Arissa	32	
Rinebolt, Sean	126	
Rivera, Karina	153	
Rivera, Nomar	168	
Riveron, Kylie	124	
Rizzotti, Kylie	130	
Roballo, Jamie	64	
Robayo, Brandon	152	
Roberson, Amanda	73	
Roberts, Alyssa	81	
Robins, Rayce	97	
Robinson, Briana	40	
Robinson, Camryn	113	
Robinson, Harley	115	
Roche, Conor	178	
Rodic, Aleksa	132	
Rodrigues, Catarina	21	
Rodriguez, Gisell	70	
Rodriguez, Isabella	181	
Rodriguez, Julissa	180	
Rodrique, Sophie	132	
Roesch, Raquelle	27	
Roesener, Max	67	
Rogers, Cai	147	
Rom, Samantha	60	
Roman, Angelius	118	
Romandi, Kelly	36	
Romero, David	85	
Roos, Julia	75	
Rosado, Marielis	172	
Rosario, Cristian	122	
Roscoe, David	25	
Rosenthal, Sara	18	
Rosiek, Lydia	111	
Rosser, Gabriel	112	
Rostucher, Brenden	59	
Roth, Abigail	74	
Roth, Ryan	126	
Rothfus, Helen	100	
Rouffiac, Anne-Emilie	68	
Rought, Cecelia	26	
Rovito, Elijah	170	
Rozik, Lily	133	
Ruggiero, Timothy	133	
Rumpf, Hailey	162	
Rush, Isaiah	34	
Russell, Daniel	172	
Russell, Imayla	91	
Russell, Jessica	129	
Russell, Kenny	183	
Rutherford, Hailey	143	
Ryan, Braden	117	
Ryan, Brooke	56	
Ryan, Sydney	41	
Ryder, Emerson	167
Safferstein, Kira	31
Saiag, Joey	158
Saidi, Tala	129
Salazar, Litzy	165
Saltzer, Max	39
Salzman, Maya	163
Sanchez, Ali	126
Sanchez, Eliya	50
Sanchez, Leonardo	133
Sanchez, Marcos	76
Sandler, Margaret	26
Sanford, Anna	168
Santiago, Trinity	137
Santos, Kieran P.	102
Sarubin, Samantha	63
Satcowitz, Kendall	116
Saul, Kameron	70
Scallorns, Henry	166
Scanlon, Joseph	118
Scanlon, Steven	118
Schaefer, Elizabeth	57
Schaefer, Graham	66
Schaeffer, Chuck	177
Schauwecker, Sydney	38
Schell, Samuel	165
Schermerhorn, Logan	36
Schildtknecht, Nicholas	43
Schindler, Nathan	63
Schmenk, John	54
Schmidt, Jonathan Z.	173
Schmidt, Maggie	74
Schmidt, T. Sabrina	95
Schneble, Caroline	87
Schnupp, Erin	65
Schramm, Parker	164
Schriner, Marisa	135
Schroeder, Julie	72
Schueler, Emma	154
Schum, Timothy	158
Schumacher, Nicholas	39
Schumaker, Dillon	116
Schuman, Jaclyn	28
Schurr, Ryan	60
Schwed, Andrew	64
Sciarretta, Emidio	146
Scott, Annie	99
Scott, Madyson	84
Scott, Noah	97
Scricco, Maria	60
Scudder, Christopher	164
Seifrit, Robert	137
Selby, Ava	57
Selfe, Elizabeth Erin	34
Semelsberger, Makenzy	109
Semtner, Louis	169
Sensenig, Jordan	50
Senz, Ian	40
Serpico, Sean	131
Serra, Isabella	146
Severns, Ashley	98
Shabazz, Madina	102
Shah, Avan	88
Shank, Landon	88
Shankar, Deepak	150
Shannon, Michael	110
Shannon, Paige	147
Shao, Lucy	42
Sharon, Megan	92
Shearer, Gianna	61
Shearon, Kelsey	115
Sheikh, Aaliya	163
Shenefield, Tommy	49
Sheridan, Chloe	58
Sherry, Taylor	102
Shields, Leah	112
Shields, William	167
Shifflett, Henry	43
Shore, Lily	128
Short, Lilly	178
Shrock, Brooke	113
Shuff, Olivia	155
Siani, Aasjot	84
Sicinski, Melissa	79
Sidhu, Ruheen	79
Sierra, Angeles	166
Silva, Brett	59
Simbana, Jordi	169
Simonds, Jake	88
Simone, Lena	81
Simone, Lydia	49
Singh, Sonali	71
Singh, Sonali	109
Singleton, Braeden	82
Sisler, Kendall	10
Skalli, Yasmine	90
Skelly, William	43
Skorupski, Sophia	130
Skowron, Connor	30
Slack, Hayley	180
Slate, Carl	27
Slone, Jackson	42
Slotterbeck, Kevin	49
Smaciarz, Mazey	81
Smith, Andrew	135
Smith, Luke	79
Smith, Mason	132
Smith, Sarah	67
Smith, Shavar	169
Smith, Tianna	163
Smondyrev, Katerina	88
Snyder, Ryan	162
Sollie, Cal	91
Sonricker, Summer	125
Sorrentino, Chris	149
Sottak, Nathan	142
Southwick, Jordan	80
Spaulding, Kimber	181
Spayd, Evelyn	86
Spearin, Payton	87
Spicci, Alexia	143
Spicer, Troy	130
Spinner, Lauren	122
Sprow, Ally	151

Squires, Simon...........98	Thorpe, Makayla...........81	Ward, Makayla...........158
Stacy, Bethany...........39	Ticknor, Ella...........12	Warner, Bailey...........178
Stacy, Cody...........42	Tillman, Travis...........114	Waslosky, Zackary...........164
Stamps, Gavin...........43	Tlapa, Gage...........176	Waters, Kelci...........172
Standish, Brooke...........164	Tonkinwise, Elsa...........134	Watkins, Jadasia...........152
Stann, Olivia...........98	Torres, Cynthia...........87	Watson, Makayla...........175
Stant, Kaydee...........120	Torres, Giona...........174	Waugh, Kyleigh...........55
Stark, Kevin...........128	Torres, Lourdes...........139	Weatherspoon, Melanie...........115
Starke, Erin...........96	Torres, Richard...........167	Weaver, Matthew...........24
Starks, Janasia...........177	Torres, Sulisnet...........171	Webb, Caroline...........126
Starner, Dylan...........76	Torrey, Ashley...........24	Webster, Lasarina Hope...........12
Stehura, Max...........168	Tower, Brandon...........101	Wei, Kelly...........41
Stern, Aaron...........41	Townsend, Jada...........153	Weightman, Holly...........67
Stevenson, Eric...........98	Toyberman, Randy...........121	Weimer, Luke...........55
Stewart, Delaney...........60	Traband, Emily...........124	Weinert, Samantha...........168
Stewart, Dillan...........121	Tran, Tyler...........75	Weisman, Joey...........132
Stidham, Olivia...........75	Tregler, Kali...........148	Wells, Alexandria...........107
Stitz, Samuel...........117	Triandafilou, Charlie...........63	Wells, Andrew...........40
Stoehr, Isabelle...........25	Trinchillo, Justin...........176	Wells, Reed...........171
Stone, Jason...........45	Trinchillo, Luke...........171	Wender, Danielle...........116
Stough, Colby...........119	Tripodi, Daniel...........119	Werner, William...........141
Straile, Alyssa...........144	Troyer, Cayla...........57	Wescott, Aubrey...........137
Streckfus, Chloe...........35	Tsang, Gloria...........123	Wessell, Christopher...........164
Strogach, Lilly...........41	Tucker, Josiah...........53	Wessely, Christina...........176
Stutmann, Jakob...........78	Tucker, Sebastian...........24	West, Evelina...........30
Su, Yiming...........32	Tul, Jonatan...........175	West, Lachie...........127
Suda, Zhen...........37	Turkiewicz, Justin...........123	Wetzel, Emmeline...........78
Sudbey, Erin...........38	Turkovich, Trevor...........149	White, Deonna...........168
Summers, Catie...........97	Turner, Lucy...........84	White, Gabriel...........98
Suriel, Eileen...........76	Turnwald, Maxwell...........126	White, Kayanna...........79
Susie, Julia...........35	Tyree, Jocelyn...........147	White, Sharon...........172
Sutton, Felicity...........136	Tysor, Reese...........168	White, Travell...........98
Swartley, Austin...........48	Tzanakis, Abby...........63	Whitt, Ben...........20
Sweeney Benzon, Ellie...........19	Vaia, Sammy...........129	Wienecke, Kendall...........104
Syed, Zoonash...........142	Valdemira, Ryan...........140	Wilcoxson, Eryce...........133
Sylvor Greenberg, Abigail...........94	Valeri, Nathien...........104	Wildgoose, Alexander...........172
Szczepkowski, Brooke...........169	Van Wezel, Sofie...........89	Wilke, Jack...........83
T., Makira...........106	VanGils, Spencer...........81	Wilkins, Taja...........58
Tahir, Somaya...........174	Vazquez, Yaimaris...........168	Willett, Brendan...........114
Tam, Eden...........167	Vedhathiri, Anya...........168	Williams, Alexis...........92
Tan, Aaron...........183	Velez, Christian...........107	Williams, Jackson...........143
Tang, Kenneth...........142	Velsor, Jonathan...........87	Williams, Jaden...........165
Taylor, Francesca...........77	Veney, Tylor...........137	Williams, Jake...........163
Taylor, Jakob...........110	Verdun, Hannah...........111	Wilson, Abigail...........70
Taylor Landesman, Loralie...........171	Vescera, Isabella...........66	Wilson, Alana...........82
Teicher, Ryan M...........171	Vickers, Jake...........125	Wilson, Isabela...........45
Teixeira, Alexa...........135	Villamil, Luna...........139	Wilson, Jackson...........117
Tejeda, Charlize...........36	Viscuso, Julia...........83	Wilson, Jake...........149
Telysheva, Dasha...........130	Vitelli, Marrianna...........62	Wilson, Nakhai...........162
Tetil, Kristen...........48	Voloshen, Christian...........118	Wilson, Savannah...........174
Thacher, Benson...........80	Vuillemot, Ryan...........29	Winch, Cameron...........74
Thakore, Jonah...........175	Wadhwa, Mrinalini...........107	Winn, Lauryn...........54
Thierry, Conner...........59	Wagner, Hannah...........55	Winneg, Max...........108
Thoman, Sophia...........124	Waite, Mackenzie...........106	Wireman, Spencer...........42
Thomas, Santyana...........183	Walker, Aidan...........127	Wise, Emoni...........79
Thompson, Abbie...........146	Walker, Chase...........95	Wiseley, Ashton...........97
Thompson, Abby...........115	Wallace, Madison...........67	Wiza, Anna...........22
Thompson, Conner...........162	Walsh, Cal...........48	Wojnar, Cameron...........169
Thompson, Emily...........45	Walter, Luke...........122	Wolfus, Zoe...........19
Thompson, Joe...........126	Walter, Lydia...........41	Woo, Jocelyn...........70
Thompson, Rodneyka...........65	Walz, Margaux...........27	Wood, RyLeigh...........167
Thompson, Tyler...........165	Ward, Jada...........83	Woodford, Hannah...........80

Woodside, Lowrie 23
Woodson, Durrell 183
Woodward, Belle 102
Woodward, Caroline 61
Woodward, Connor 37
Worsham, Caris 69
Wriker, Amanda 84
Xue, Benson 169
Yahner, Jessie 28
Yan, Jason 92
Yanez, Kimberly 147
Yang, Sophie 12
Yarish, Mikayla 90
Yeaw, Kathrine 117
Yeung, Alex 128
York, Ayanna 79
York, Fiona 157
Younes, Jerod 133
Young, Darrah 120
Young, John 103
Young, Kevin 54
Yup, Kayla 133
Yup, Tyler 67
Zadrozny, Zade 133
Zaman, Wasif 88
Zeak, Autumn 63
Zecchini, Brooke 83
Zellman, Eugene 147
Zereoue, Amos 71
Zhao, Danny 164
Zheng, Tiffany 172
Zhou, Hannah 38
Zinser, Ava 171
Zittle, Billy 46

Index by School

Abraham Joshua Heschel School
New York, NY
Abigail Sylvor Greenberg 94

Al-Ghazaly Elementary School
Teaneck, NJ
Ridwan Ismail 183
Simrah Mansoori 174
Khashiya Ranginwala 172
Reza Rehman 174
Aaliya Sheikh 163
Somaya Tahir 174

Alexander Adaire School
Philadelphia, PA
Matthew Graf 91

Allenwood Elementary School
Allenwood, NJ
Ashley Hronich 90
Brittany Hronich 49

Ann Antolini School
New Hartford, CT
Ivy Grosk 23

Arbor Intermediate School
Piscataway, NJ
Anika Melkote 28

Arts Academy Charter School
Allentown, PA
Isabella Mohrey 113

Ashland Elementary School
Manassas, VA
Shachi Dahal 144

Aston Elementary School
Aston, PA
Jacklyn Bradley 54
Kylie Brzezicki 153
Lumaris Cora 155
Madison Fili 51
Emily Kauffeld 113
Hannah Moore 60
Rebekah Nilles 65
Madison Oreski 53
Luke Smith 79
Evelyn Spayd 86
Jake Vickers 125

Avenel Middle School
Avenel, NJ
Janice Igbinobaro 106

Avon Grove Intermediate School
Hockessin, PA
Emily Hart 33

Avon Grove Intermediate School
West Grove, PA
Caitlin DeStefano 46

Avonworth Elementary School
Pittsburgh, PA
Luke Walter 122

Bala Cynwyd Middle School
Bala Cynwyd, PA
Sophie Yang 12

Bankstreet School for Children
New York, NY
Mrinalini Wadhwa 107

Barrington Elementary School
Upper Arlington, OH
Natalia Angelis 118
Ava Gruss 42
Connor Hanks 157
Anoushka Herrala 156
Lexy Owens 83
Emma Schueler 154
Matthew Weaver 24

Bartle Elementary School
Highland Park, NJ
Jaclyn Berman 139
Andrew Carmona 151
Miranda Dobkin 18
Hephzibah Emmanuel 51
Torgyn Hart 92
Justice Jones 113
Robert Lambert 105
Chris Lee 122
Rimervi Mendez 34
Samantha Parelius 69
Olga Pidruchna 106
Max Roesener 67
Timothy Ruggiero 133
Katerina Smondyrev 88
Ellie Sweeney Benzon 19
Dasha Telysheva 130
Alana Wilson 82

Bell Academy
Bayside, NY
Gloria Tsang 123

Belmont Middle/Jr High School
Belmont, NH
Brian Carroll 127
Isaiah Costa 101
Nathan Sottak 142
Alexandria Wells 107

Bensley Elementary School
Richmond, VA
Kimberly Lainez Rodriguez 175
Hadiyyah Neblett 175
Shavar Smith 169
Jonatan Tul 175
Makayla Watson 175
Durrell Woodson 183

Bethel Springs Elementary School
Garnet Valley, PA
Ben Heinrich 173

Birches Elementary School
Turnersville, NJ
Aubrianna Bythrow 117
Guanyi Cao 22
Brandon Cotter 91
Emily Cozzone 112
Christina DiMaggio 45
Brendan Fulginiti 90
Patrick Howell 102
Jessica Lacava 37
Alaina Lewis 29
Jacob Minnick 102
Olivia Parker 37
Robert Piontkowski III 104
Soraya Reamon 112
Ashley Severns 98
Chloe Sheridan 58
Nathien Valeri 104
Kelly Wei 41
Abigail Wilson 70
Ashton Wiseley 97
Caroline Woodward 61
Connor Woodward 37

Birchwood School
Cleveland, OH
Kevin Stark 128

Bishop Hoffman Catholic School - St Joseph Campus
Fremont, OH
Alex Dumminger 76
Allison Foos 40
Clemens Foos 76
Drew Frederick 76
Isabella Habicht 76
Adalia Pasch 76
Andrew Provonsha 76
Marcos Sanchez 76

Blackrock School
Coventry, RI
Anthony Amaral 86
Emily Beauchaine 72
Gabrielle Beaulieu 106
Carly Carroll 110
Jackson Ciesla 107
Mackenna Croft 59
Jordan Cruz 150
Haley Farnoto 153
Olivia Gilbert 32
Avery Henley 119
Laura Jencks 78
Nicholas Kanaczet 150
Julianna Landi 68
Asia McLaughlin 107
Quintin Moore 73
Luca Nero 135

Faith Parton 151
Elizabeth Petrangelo 146
Jacob Pimentel 31
Karina Rivera 153
Brett Silva 59
Benson Thacher 80
Joey Weisman 132

BOCES
Mastic Beach, NY
John Young 103

Boonsboro Elementary School
Boonsboro, MD
Natalie Asbury 122
Riley Bak 122
Mykala Bledsoe 123
Johnnie Deane 131
Josh Grubb 108
Elizabeth Happel 81
Natalie Haugen 28
Haley Himes 51
Cadence Krall 73
Alyssa Melby 145
Abigail Morman 125
Baylee Peperak 99
Ashley Phillips 19
Sean Rinebolt 126
Maggie Schmidt 74
Ava Selby 57
Kendall Sisler 10
Olivia Stann 98
Aubrey Wescott 137

Boyce Middle School
Upper St Clair, PA
Vivek Babu 86
Tyler Berger 95
Claire Chen 97
Jason Choi 115
A.J. Daley 55
Claire Fennell 29
Katie Hobart 69
Dylan Jenny 21
Katie McCurrie 18
Emma Mertz 133
Ben Nelson 27
Harley Robinson 115
Aleksa Rodic 132
Cal Sollie 91
Maxwell Turnwald 126
Emmeline Wetzel 78

Brookfield Middle School
Brookfield, OH
Breonna Morrison 52

Burgettstown Elementary Center
Burgettstown, PA
Macy Brown 85
Stacia Collins 115
Geena DeMario 149
Aubry G. Krivak 41
Turner Lehman 56
Virginia Lohn 158
Elisabeth Mioduski 129
Noah Poirier 130

Caroline G Atkinson School
Freeport, NY
Jadyn Andre 64
Joseph Cassinera 53
Kiara Chombo 152
Fernando Coronado 53
Ja'kiya Elrod 53
Kennedy Goremusandu 47
Tobias Hall 46
Kyle Jackson 67
Ashley Jaquez 53
Genio Johnson 139
Brandon Jones 62
Ashley Portillo 53
Cynthia Torres 87
Josiah Tucker 53
Travell White 98
Emoni Wise 79
Amos Zereoue 71

Catherine A Dwyer Elementary School
Wharton, NJ
Caroline Cote 78
Andrew Gomez 78
Rashad Jabbar 93
Sid Kapoor 120
Kylie Mastropolo 146
Jessica Matthew 93
Ronnie Percival 78
Sophia Skorupski 130
Chris Sorrentino 149
Jakob Stutmann 78

Cedar Bluff Elementary School
Cedar Bluff, VA
Codie Brown 92
Annie Butcher 102
Ellie Butcher 38
Ainsley Clark 175
Morghan Hampton 125
Lilly Short 178

Chelsea Elementary School
Chelsea, ME
Amelia Evans 81

Chickahominy Middle School
Mechanicsville, VA
Azza Ahmed 22
Taylor Bates 74
Anabelle Bergeron 91
Sydney Deringer 131
David Dokos 91
John Duegaw 135
Jessica Gray 23
Madyson Haas 94
Leah Homan 109
Bryce Jones 34
Nylah Jordan 85
Andrew Lawson 127
Alexis LeRoy 156
Felix Mo 74
Ogaga Obrimah 47
Amanda Roberson 73
Rayce Robins 97
Jessica Russell 129

Steven Scanlon 118
Ian Senz 40
Kelsey Shearon 115
Henry Shifflett 43
Aasjot Siani 84
Kenneth Tang 142
Aidan Walker 127

Children's Village
Philadelphia, PA
Sophia Chen 177
Cassandra Cruz 162
Quinn Johnson 178
Kristy Lei 183
Bella Li 175
Winnie Li 174
Neal Liu 183
Andrew Mac 164
Aaron Tan 183
Benson Xue 169
Danny Zhao 164
Tiffany Zheng 172

Christ the King Catholic School
Toledo, OH
Mazey Smaciarz 81

Clearview Elementary School
Bethlehem, PA
Daeviana Blount 34

Clover Hill Elementary School
Midlothian, VA
DJ Brandon 130
Ed Clark 119
Andrew Cooke 87
Haley Dean 155
Nathan Dodge 139
Ashley Klein 152
Jackson Morgan 89
William Rice 152
Sonali Singh 109
Lauryn Winn 54

Clover Street School
Windsor, CT
Iffath Ahmed-Syed 83
Madyson Beckford 107
Lorna Brown 126
Ellyse Colón 147
Isaiah Rush 34
Leonardo Sanchez 133
Makayla Thorpe 81
Lydia Walter 41
Jada Ward 83

Columbus Preparatory Academy
Dublin, OH
Yasmine Skalli 90

Commodore Perry Elementary School
Hadley, PA
Dylan Bolling 58
Johnathan Buynak 70
Jocelyn Eber 109
Riley Harnett 84
Hannah Jones 95
Ryder Knierman 114
Mackenzie Larimer 36

Index by School

Hannah Manning 118
Sarah May 148
Isabella McCann 121
Sadie Mink 44
Alexander Murphy 70
George Reed 60
Noah Scott 97
Brooke Shrock 113
Kali Tregler 148

Commonwealth Connections Academy
Dublin, PA
Sophia Leitner-Sieber 138

Commonwealth Connections Academy
Harrisburg, PA
Mary Angela Pinci 31

Copper Beech Elementary School
Glenside, PA
Sam Miller 22

Cortland Christian Academy
Cortland, NY
Chloe Burhans 92
Michaela Jackson 55
Raiden Portzline 63

Crocker Farm Elementary School
Amherst, MA
Jonathan Z. Schmidt 173

Currie Elementary School
Cortland, OH
Ethan Adkins 172
Riely Armstrong 177
Joseph Blake 174
Malaya Giesy 162
Jesse Little 174
Zachary Mazey 174
Lily Miller 177
Matthew Neely 162
Conner Thompson 162
Giona Torres 174

Delta Elementary School
Delta, OH
Kristopher Burns 24
Justice Reckner 103
Ally Sprow 151

Derryfield School
Wilton, NH
Benjamin Miron 19

Dickinson Avenue Elementary School
East Northport, NY
Julie Barbier 130
Mark M. Baron 97
Mikaela Benchimol 50
Emma Bishop 137
Edward Cannon 66
Marinda Cannon 158
Ryan Cavanagh 42
Valery Charland 62
Nicole Geres 39
Kaylee Granados-Martinez 61
Cristina Noelle Guanio 61
Kobe Guo 61
Trevor Hubbard 149
Dante Impastato 43

Amber Leininger 126
Emma McDonald 29
Daniel Meade 96
Tsampica Mitchell 67
Matthew Nock 90
Dilan Piscatello 49
Samantha Rom 60
Lauren Spinner 122
Caroline Webb 126

Dobbins Elementary School
Poland, OH
Wyatt Bobbey 66
Ellie Brogan 60
Gabriella Calderon 86
Kylie Commons 44
George Corfias 27
Julia Eich 54
Avrey Grischow 136
Joey Iberis 56
Connor Maze 147
Michael Nittoli 119
Eliya Sanchez 50
Luke Weimer 55

Donegal Elementary School
Mt Pleasant, PA
Kaelea Hayes 57

Dutch Neck Elementary School
West Windsor, NJ
Muskan Manchanda 170

E Russell Hicks Middle School
Hagerstown, MD
Zoonash Syed 142

East Woods School
Oyster Bay, NY
Grace Cutler 158

Edwin Forrest School
Philadelphia, PA
Brianna Jones-Hollis 144

Ethel M Burke Elementary School
Bellmawr, NJ
Francesca Belgiorno 42
William Chew 46
Madeline Groves 61
Brenden Koykka 44
Marcus Madiedo 25
Carson O'Connell 25
Priya Patel 25
Aamin Rahman 56
Alana Reader 158
Danny Renzetti 66
David Roscoe 25
Braden Ryan 117
Gianna Shearer 61

Ettrick Elementary School
Ettrick, VA
Jennifer Adu 115
Ayrienna Allen 45
Tyrone Barnes 111
Kylie Bowe 27
Brianna Branch 143
Paige Cabrera 81
Dakota Clontz 93

Laniyah Dennis 93
Keyontae Lewis 25
Bari Muhammad 149
Destiny Porter 92
Chloe Purcell 80
Leslie Reyes 121
Carl Slate 27
Tylor Veney 137
Makayla Ward 158
Jadasia Watkins 152

Fairfield Woods Middle School
Fairfield, CT
Noah Giglietti 30

Fayerweather Street School
Cambridge, MA
Tommy Shenefield 49

Ferry Farm Elementary School
Fredericksburg, VA
E. H. 168

Fishing Creek Elementary School
Lewisberry, PA
Anna Nguyen 135
Max Saltzer 39

Floyd T Binns Middle School
Culpeper, VA
Ali Sanchez 126

Foster Elementary School
Pittsburgh, PA
Maia Anderson 40
Jack Austin 104
Luka Berkovic 36
John Andrew Brown 36
Gia Capristo 36
Andy Cort 151
Natasha Curimbaba 101
Haleigh Dively 42
Delaney Driscoll 95
Katie Hart 71
Abby Hrebinko 120
Abby Jones 25
Maya Jones 61
Maya Legersky 103
Erin Lutz 40
Elle McQuaide 40
Sara Menand 58
Katy Meta 157
Gabriella Morello 71
Nina Paliouras 36
Arkasha Rakach 45
Kira Safferstein 31
Lucy Shao 42
Isabelle Stoehr 25
Yiming Su 32
Trevor Turkovich 149
Ryan Vuillemot 29

Frisbie School
Wolcott, CT
Isabella Bracco 38

GATE-Central Academy
Middletown, OH
Matthew Alfrey 115
Tristan Barker 70

Kendal Blevins 113
Brycen Boyle 44
Josiah Brown 95
Ryan Carey 38
Cadence Clifton 168
Haleigh Cook-Hayes 19
Isabel Fonseca 109
Rachel Glancy 171
Jordan Hill 148
Emma Kramer 92
Avery Lamka 179
Sean Larkin 62
Graclynn Lewis 104
Tye Lewis 141
Lucas Lindemann 183
Noah Locke 52
Emma Martin 61
Kyndall Miller 158
Eliyana Nelms 181
Kiersten Newton 137
Gabe Penny 124
Ava Repka 174
Arissa Riley 32
Elijah Rovito 170
T. Sabrina Schmidt 95
Kimber Spaulding 181
Troy Spicer 130
Jada Townsend 153
Bailey Warner 178
Eryce Wilcoxson 133
Alexis Williams 92

Gilmore J Fisher Middle School
Ewing, NJ
Heather Kwafo 141

Gloria Dei Montessori School
Dayton, OH
Michael Burks 57
Marli Harris 27
Nathan Schindler 63
John Schmenk 54
Zhen Suda 37
Rodneyka Thompson 65

Graham Intermediate School
Bluefield, VA
Derek Cruise 135
Darrah Young 120

Grandview Elementary School
Derry, PA
Makenzy Semelsberger 109

Great Meadows Middle School
Great Meadows, NJ
Amanda Alegria 122
Morgan Bailey 106
Maddy Billows 40
Paige Harrison 120
Christian Jensen 84
Jamie Lessing 77
Nick O'Melia 73
Maria Scricco 60
Delaney Stewart 60
Sammy Vaia 129

Greenwich Country Day School
Greenwich, CT
Charlotte Dockery 47
Annabel Gerber 139
Megan Keller 47
Matthew Kilmurray 26
Anne-Emilie Rouffiac 68
Margaret Sandler 26
Madina Shabazz 102
Lily Shore 128
Connor Skowron 30

Greenwich School
Greenwich, CT
Eva Moore 94

Hahntown Elementary School
North Huntingdon, PA
Abrielle Brown 173

Hampton Elementary School
Lutherville, MD
Ryan Snyder 162

Harding Middle School
Lakewood, OH
Halina Dreger 64

Hawthorne Christian Academy
Hawthorne, NJ
Erik Andersen 38
Ethan Choi 152
Cristina D'Amato 38
Andrew Egedy 65
Rachel How 113
Christiana Tsai Hubbard 47
Michael Lamitola 50
Cormac Murtagh 96
Georgia Pollard 105
Mark Prioleau 64
Kameron Saul 70
Luna Villamil 139

Hawthorne Park Elementary School
Willingboro, NJ
Kelly McCain 182

Haycock Elementary School
Falls Church, VA
Kristina Knauss 180

Heron Pond Elementary School
Milford, NH
Emily Dube 180
Delaney Flynn 171
Jackson Huckins 171
Bailey Johnson 169
Nevaeh Kimball 174
Gage Tlapa 176
Kelci Waters 172

Highland Elementary School
Abington, PA
Quinlan Finamore 138

Hillcrest Middle School
Trumbull, CT
Wasif Zaman 88

Hillsboro Christian Academy
Hillsboro, OH
Elizabeth Pierce 148

Hillside Elementary School
Needham, MA
Talia Bloom 41

Holy Family School
Flushing, NY
Aron Afzali 136
Keara Malazarte 44
Jenna Raczka 37
Cristian Rosario 122
Felicity Sutton 136

Homeschool
NH
Elliot Harne 75

Homeschool
NY
Adalia Looney 164
Daniel Russell 172
Kenny Russell 183

Homeschool
OH
Alexandra Abood 54

Homeschool
VA
Sean Barnes 180
Isabella Pappas 138

Honeoye Falls-Lima Manor School
Honeoye Falls, NY
Kaitlyn 33
Connor Becker 24
Cole Chiapperino 67
Will Douglas 55
Abbey Finn 19
Ember Internicola 132
Cai Rogers 147
Lydia Rosiek 111
Summer Sonricker 125

Hurley Elementary/Middle School
Hurley, VA
Logan Ashby 42
Alison Blankenship 125
Caleb Blankenship 125
Micah Blankenship 37
Emily Cline 68
Morgan Cline 50
Jon Dotson 22
Savannah Dotson 46
Jonathan Hurley 42
Logan Hurley 29
John A. Justus 105
Kaylee Justus 129
Jackson Slone 42
Bethany Stacy 39
Cody Stacy 42
Spencer Wireman 42

Hutchinson Elementary School
Pelham, NY
Sharon Lee 93

Indian Hill Middle School
Cincinnati, OH
Cecilia Fu 51

Indian Hill School
Holmdel, NJ
- Jason Yan 92

Indian Valley Middle School
Harleysville, PA
- Nicholas Currier 61

Interboro GATE Program
Prospect Park, PA
- Abbie Ballak 132
- Kennedy Ballak 173
- Julia Cavalieri 134
- Theo Demopoulos 170
- Elaine Droxler 134
- Kyle Gieder 76
- Dayjanea Gordon 20
- Jesse Hickman 137
- Molly Hughes 179
- Madison Kiesel 173
- Sammy Kitchen 93
- Rhyan Lehman 174
- Layla Reilly 170
- Sean Serpico 131
- Ella Ticknor 12

J Harold Vanzant Elementary School
Marlton, NJ
- Elisabeth Nikolau 155

Jack Jackter Intermediate School
Colchester, CT
- Abigail C. Auden 134
- Caitlin Bagdasarian 151
- Abby Burke 49
- Jordan Cavender 26
- Shannon Hickey 33
- Brandon Kauffman 94
- Augustin Michaud 85
- Sydney Mikalonis 42
- Noah Mikkelson 111
- Ryan Mikolajczak 23
- Grace Palmer 142
- Megan Reading 49
- Sara Rosenthal 18
- Andrew Smith 135

Jack Jouett Middle School
Charlottesville, VA
- Johanna Hall 155

Jane H Bryan Elementary School
Hampton, VA
- Hadiyah Coates 49

JC Stuart Elementary School
Willingboro, NJ
- Christina McCain 146

JCDS, Boston's Jewish Community Day School
Watertown, MA
- Josephina Kamens 182

Jefferson Middle School
Pittsburgh, PA
- Madison Jones 82

John Mandracchia Sawmill Intermediate School
Commack, NY
- Lilly Strogach 41

Kathleen H Ryerson Elementary School
Madison, CT
- Lasarina Hope Webster 12

Keith Valley Middle School
Horsham, PA
- Jack Kollmar 39

Kingsview Middle School
Germantown, MD
- Joellen Allah-Mensah 48

Kipps Elementary School
Blacksburg, VA
- Adhana Blaise 183

Knollwood Elementary School
Fair Haven, NJ
- Alex Fratto 124

Laddie A Decker Sound Beach School
Miller Place, NY
- William Dunlop 54
- Ivy Newman 95

Lake Avenue Elementary School
Saratoga Springs, NY
- Katie Olson 99

Lakewood Catholic Academy
Lakewood, OH
- Lilly Ryann Metzger 166

Lee Eaton Elementary School
Northfield, OH
- Bailey Coon 29

Lehman Alternative Community School
Ithaca, NY
- Gwen Burrows 43

Liberty Corner Elementary School
Liberty Corner, NJ
- Sophie Kramer 102
- Casper Mika 56
- Nicole Miranda 131
- Rachel Novick 62
- Dilan Patel 58
- Alexandra Pereira 102
- Julia Roos 75
- Andrew Schwed 64

Liberty Corner School
Liberty Corner, NJ
- Maggie Hannis 68

Licking Valley Intermediate School
Newark, OH
- Elizabeth Erin Selfe 34

Licking Valley Primary/Intermediate School
Newark, OH
- Abby Alcott 121
- William Clark 44
- Olivia Conley 99
- Chloe Cooperrider 109
- Michael Ellis 115
- Kelby George 64
- Makayla Kelly 139
- Ellie Lange 84
- Rachel Lee 96
- Reese Lees 60
- Madison Meadows 26
- Cole Porter 45

- Clay Prouty 122
- Dillon Schumaker 116
- Dylan Starner 76
- Dillan Stewart 121
- Olivia Stidham 75
- Colby Stough 119

Lincoln Elementary School
Pittsburgh, PA
- Alex Bartone 145
- Emma Bianchi 74
- Max Brokaw 74
- Julia Chung 74
- Chase Crandall 64
- Alma Dardari 145
- Molly Doherty 52
- Carlos Guillen 57
- Benjamin Levine 65
- Megan Sharon 92
- Jack Wilke 83

Louise Archer Elementary School
Vienna, VA
- Adeeba Kareem 85
- Tala Saidi 129

Maddux Elementary School
Cincinnati, OH
- Sylvia Nica 81

Madison Middle School
Madison, OH
- Mykayla Askew 100
- Ian Cauwenbergh 115
- Alex Dragas 25
- Zenna Eaton 100
- Caelyn Pritschau 155

Mapleshade Elementary School
East Longmeadow, MA
- Jadyn Genest 182

Maria Hastings School
Lexington, MA
- Nikhil Belgaonkar 105

Marie Curie Institute
Amsterdam, NY
- Gabriella Alvarado 166
- Dariel Aviles 177
- Kaelin Ballard 180
- Juliana Barone-Lopez 177
- Izabella Bartman 164
- Nicholas Belardo 172
- Vincent Bottisti 168
- Kai Brennan 167
- Zander Chapin 178
- Emily Clouse 171
- Caden Daley-Rivera 183
- Amethyst Earley 173
- Devion Faboskay 172
- Ramon Feliciano 169
- Brittney Ferlazzo 177
- Kadance Francis 172
- Jordani Gonzalez 183
- Emma Greco 166
- Edilberto Gutierrez 180
- Hailee Hamblin 166
- Peter Hans 177

A Celebration of Poets – East Grades K-6 Fall 2013

Alize Lajeunesse 180
Zanith Longfellow 180
Nathaniel Loveless 163
Angel McClanahan 173
Jaiden Gomez Mendez 180
David Merullo 163
Landon Mullarkey 177
Aubrey Murphy 167
Zoe Naish 163
Bradley Negron 177
Samuel Nicolella 166
Ana Nieves 167
Breana O'Brien 180
Jordan Olmack 180
Lianelys Oviedo 163
Jenny Parsons 164
Anializ Quinones 168
Nomar Rivera 168
Julissa Rodriguez 180
Marielis Rosado 172
Emerson Ryder 167
Max Stehura 168
Sulisnet Torres 171
Yaimaris Vazquez 168
Christopher Wessell 164
RyLeigh Wood 167

Marion Elementary School
Belle Vernon, PA
   Caitlynn Anderson 141
   Sydney Baciak 72
   Hayden Baron 48
   Elizabeth Breckenridge 79
   Jaelynn Clegg 105
   Logan Dimpel 154
   Emily Dongilli 105
   Autumn Forte 33
   Nina Gillingham 48
   Colby Hamer 55
   Baileigh Horan 97
   Raelyn Horne 65
   Nathen Hynes 36
   Mitchell Jennewine 67
   Joelle Kennedy 97
   Kori Kuhns 133
   Gianna Lorenzo 70
   JaQuez Martin 133
   Sarah McCloskey 140
   Emily McGowan 72
   Colby McKeta 133
   Victoria Moore 28
   Chelsey Nutt 67
   Robbie Pendleton II 67
   Lydia Podvorec 79
   Kendra Reed 86
   Alyssa Roberts 81
   Lily Rozik 133
   Kristen Tetil 48
   Hannah Wagner 55
   Chase Walker 95
   Holly Weightman 67
   Zade Zadrozny 133

Marsh Grammar School
Methuen, MA
   Alyssa Archetti 183
   Madison Cochrane 166
   Mikey Gueli IV 178
   Rheya Lasonde 178
   Emily Lindtveit 171
   Dan Khoi Nguyen 183
   Nicholas Pearson 181
   Laisha Pita 177
   Dakota Pomerleau 169
   Richard Torres 167

Mary Walter Elementary School
Bealeton, VA
   Travis Bloom 168
   Donny Brewster 32
   Nolan Brewster 85
   Ally Corvin 125
   Colton Friesen 52
   Lalana Kraiwan 147
   Veronica Nickerson 22
   Teddy Pearson 79
   Elia Powers 181
   David Romero 85
   Taylor Sherry 102
   Tyler Thompson 165
   Jocelyn Tyree 147
   Ben Whitt 20

Massabesic Middle School
East Waterboro, ME
   Ashley Davis 111

Matapeake Elementary School
Stevensville, MD
   Kaylee Ferrier 183

Medway Middle School
Medway, ME
   Isaac Adams 129
   Madison Birt 56
   Daniel Cote 56
   Addison Danforth 75
   Austyn Fox 55
   Jordan Harding 21
   Kaitlynn Lane 114
   Madison McDunnah 119
   Kaylee Perreault 109
   Francisco Ramirez 46
   Mason Smith 132
   Jordan Southwick 80
   Payton Spearin 87
   Brandon Tower 101
   Madison Wallace 67
   Ayanna York 79

Midview East Intermediate School
Grafton, OH
   Jacob Depinet 20
   Jacob DiFranco 20
   Sky Giovannetti 41
   Chayla Herner 84
   Madalyn Karban 158
   Sadie McCarrick 121
   Nicholas Schumacher 39
   Mikayla Yarish 90

Miles School
Cleveland, OH
   Lauriana Bell 167
   Harmonie Brown 162
   Ethan Chaisson 170
   Trinity Clemons 175
   Miracle-Storm Griffin 182
   Kailah Kinney 101
   Janasia Starks 177
   Santyana Thomas 183
   Deonna White 168
   Sharon White 172
   Jaden Williams 165

Miller City-New Cleveland School
Miller City, OH
   Collin Oedy 62
   Kaydee Stant 120
   Cayla Troyer 57
   Sofie Van Wezel 89

Mills Parole Elementary School
Annapolis, MD
   Makira T. 106

Moravian Academy Middle School
Bethlehem, PA
   Elysse Abraham 24
   Liam Brolly 24
   Taylor Busch 79
   Emma Davis 156
   Maya Ettle 59
   Miranda Gibson 112
   Sage Hillier 21
   Isha Kaza 59
   Rhea Malhotra 117
   Deepak Shankar 150
   Leah Shields 112
   Conner Thierry 59
   William Werner 141
   Kathrine Yeaw 117

MOT Charter School
Middletown, DE
   Shreya Bathula 112

Munsey Park Elementary School
Manhasset, NY
   Juliana Feit 89

Mystic Middle School
Mystic, CT
   Amelia Caron 62
   Jonathan Clark 116
   Eliza Cole 138
   Maggie Constantine 138
   Caleb Crowley 156
   Jada Cruz 109
   Xzayvier Davis 112
   Olivia Donahue 96
   Bryan Fusaro 88
   Hanna Gwiazdowski 94
   Hailee Langenbach 73
   Angelius Roman 118
   Jake Simonds 88
   Lucy Turner 84
   Margaux Walz 27

Index by School

Nayaug Elementary School
South Glastonbury, CT
- Jack Plucker.................175

Nazareth Area Intermediate School
Nazareth, PA
- Nick Apruzzi.................130
- Cristian Bonomo.................130
- Eliza Burgoyne.................29
- Jamila Cobrinik.................101
- Julia Daley.................46
- Chiara Dooley.................26
- Trent Federico.................31
- Michael Fischer.................126
- Sasha Gabrie.................117
- Sarah Givone.................64
- Jacob Gould.................56
- Tasmir Gregorie.................42
- Maci Herman.................63
- Hannah Hoch.................77
- Jason Huggler.................44
- Brionna Hynes.................50
- Mya Karvan.................154
- Owen Kern.................66
- Dylan Makarovsky.................156
- Vito Mastromonaco.................50
- Natalie Meriwether.................120
- Haley O'Reilly.................115
- Madison Pascual.................143
- Savana Patton.................150
- Carson Pieper.................75
- Kevin Pierson.................85
- Ashley Potope.................47
- Josh Reinhart.................126
- Joshua Richter.................50
- Catarina Rodrigues.................21
- Raquelle Roesch.................27
- Ryan Roth.................126
- Cecelia Rought.................26
- Jordan Sensenig.................50
- Ruheen Sidhu.................79
- Sarah Smith.................67
- Eric Stevenson.................98
- Daniel Tripodi.................119
- Christian Voloshen.................118
- Melanie Weatherspoon.................115
- Jake Wilson.................149
- Amanda Wriker.................84
- Jerod Younes.................133

Nesaquake Middle School
Saint James, NY
- Lily Amadio.................27
- Sara Caligiuri.................62
- Rebecca Michaud.................127

NEST+m School
New York, NY
- Elizabeth Lee.................179

Nether Providence Elementary School
Wallingford, PA
- Bryce Cammarotta.................75
- Abhirup Chakrabarti.................22
- Anna Fonarov.................134
- Kirsten Kanuika.................138
- Alyssa Kazanjian.................31
- Dylan Monaghan.................39
- Riley Muller.................20
- Giovanni Rapposelli.................55
- Camryn Robinson.................113
- Gabriel Rosser.................112
- Robert Seifrit.................137
- Jason Stone.................45

New Freedom Christian School
New Freedom, PA
- Nicholas Schildtknecht.................43
- Sophia Thoman.................124

New Town Elementary School
Owings Mills, MD
- Kayla Yup.................133
- Tyler Yup.................67

New York Institute for Special Ed
Bronx, NY
- Justin Bryant.................82
- Sheik Conde.................69
- Aolani Cruz.................141
- Ashley De La Cruz.................50
- Elijah Hedgemond.................70
- Ramil Hirsawa.................22
- Steven King.................141
- Eileen Suriel.................76

New York Institute for Special Education
Bronx, NY
- Mikael Jones.................63

Nitrauer Elementary School
Lancaster, PA
- Maddie Granger.................172

Noble Academy-Columbus
Columbus, OH
- Kaytlee Clark.................45
- Walden Hart.................59
- Ali Latif.................141

Noble Leadership Academy
Passaic, NJ
- Noura Arbab.................181

Norman J Levy Lakeside School
Merrick, NY
- Joshua Abramovich.................34
- Andrew Brinton.................116
- Mikayla Gorelin.................120
- Clarissa Granados.................99
- Christina Lafkas.................10
- Sammy Loew.................64
- Kira Poliviou.................27
- Lara Reiss.................47
- Joey Saiag.................158
- Kendall Satcowitz.................116
- Jaclyn Schuman.................28
- Aaron Stern.................41
- Randy Toyberman.................121
- Justin Turkiewicz.................123
- Danielle Wender.................116

Northwood Elementary School
Hilton, NY
- Mia Albert.................69
- Sydney Alloco.................90
- Alexandra Amico.................39
- Andrew Castronovo.................158
- Spencer Mann.................29
- Andrew Melita.................91
- Brian Phung.................95
- Kylie Rizzotti.................130
- Alexia Spicci.................143
- Emily Thompson.................45
- Anna Wiza.................22

Norton Middle School
Norton, MA
- Aunnesha Bhowmick.................131

Norvelt Elementary School
Mt Pleasant, PA
- Madeline Higgins.................183
- Krista Polanofsky.................38

O'Donnell Middle School
Stoughton, MA
- Tyler Tran.................75

Oak Ridge Elementary School
Harleysville, PA
- Isaac.................116
- Eric Alderfer.................111
- Jamie Alderfer.................51
- Dekai Averett.................22
- Tommy Ball.................50
- Devang Bhandari.................96
- Dakota Bishop.................145
- Michael Blazo.................143
- Devesh Bungatavula.................127
- Lizzy Bywaters.................57
- Tyler Eckert.................149
- Ava Folk.................141
- Monica Gergies.................82
- Jack Graboski.................18
- Molly Hendricks.................93
- Liam Kelly.................118
- Kyle Krader.................96
- Allyson Mahoney.................54
- Ian Martin.................102
- Justin May.................81
- Joey Monti.................41
- Carolyn Mowery.................105
- Kayla Pike.................109
- Sophie Rodrique.................132

Oakdale-Bohemia Middle School
Oakdale, NY
- Sayida Afghani.................150
- Elizabeth Blizzard.................53
- Colleen DiMarzo.................117
- Laurel Edwards.................108
- Ethan Forberg.................39
- Daniela Garey.................152
- Adriana Giangrasso.................90
- Niko Keddy.................11
- Ryan Kemp.................110
- Samantha Lankowicz.................157
- Brooke Lundrigan.................72
- Katie Postel.................37
- Brandon Robayo.................152
- Kelly Romandi.................36
- Michael Shannon.................110

Paige Shannon 147
Ryan Valdemira 140
Mackenzie Waite 106
Alex Yeung 128
Brooke Zecchini 83

Ohio Connections Academy
Worthington, OH
Victoria Rafac 148

Old Mill Road School
Merrick, NY
Jordan Neale 82

Old Saybrook Middle School
Old Saybrook, CT
Joseph Bradley 62

Olentangy Hyatts Middle School
Powell, OH
Sahuj Mehta 130

Orion Academy
Cincinnati, OH
Stefan Farrar 169
Lariah Alija Jones 181
Savannah Wilson 174

Osborn Elementary School
Ashland, OH
Graham Schaefer 66

Our Lady of Hope School
Middle Village, NY
Adriana Balacich 176
Sophia Banzil 170
Emma Bogdan 170
Ava Campo 176
Vincent Capria 66
Damien Cavallo 178
Charles Chelstowski 171
Matthew Cipri 180
Sofia DeLaRosa 173
Gianna DeSena 176
Kevin Girdusky 164
Francesca Licari 166
Isabella Muro 178
Anna Olszowka 163
Madison Persichette 172
Madison Regis 164
Conor Roche 178
Loralie Taylor Landesman ...171
Justin Trinchillo 176
Luke Trinchillo 171
Christina Wessely 176
Ava Zinser 171

P.S. 100 Coney Island
Brooklyn, NY
Amirrah Egoroff 121

P.S. 158
New York, NY
Samara Ginsberg 165

Parkway School
Greenwich, CT
Ashley Malkin 178

Pemberton Elementary School
Henrico, VA
Adam 45
Audrey 147

Emilee Brooks 85
Harrison Brooks 123
Grady Brown 60
Thomas Cassada 129
Lucas Cusick 39
Aidan Duffy 33
Brady Elswick 75
Jackson Fellows 62
Nathan Hafer 77
Devin He 66
Amaya Hughes 78
Makala Ingegni 96
Sam Kantor 130
Elise Kohnke 19
Ethan Rashkind 78
Abby Thompson 115
Joe Thompson 126
Spencer VanGils 81
Caris Worsham 69

Pennridge North Middle School
Perkasie, PA
James Boyle 21
Timmy Flynn 149
Belinda Henry 45
Ava Komasz 108
Henry Leopold 67
Sorrell Long 21
Courtney Nelson 129
Lauren Paynton 104
Kylie Riveron 124
Brooke Ryan 56
Ryan Schurr 60
Melissa Sicinski 79
Austin Swartley 48

Pierre Van Cortland Middle School
Croton on Hudson, NY
Michaela Fitzgerald 147

Pierre Van Cortlandt School
Croton on Hudson, NY
Ali Hoy 147

Pike Delta York Middle School
Delta, OH
Michael Eckenrode 91
Ella Ford 45
Hailey Hoffman 59
Abigail Roth 74
Sydney Schauwecker 38

Pine Hill Waldorf School
Wilton, NH
Jaden Fluet 19

Pittsburgh Online Academy
Pittsburgh, PA
Haajar Ahmad Ali 109

Plainedge Middle School
Bethpage, NY
Thomas Petrucci 120

Pocopson Elementary School
West Chester, PA
Ellie Barrickman 44
Jack Boas 66
Rebecca Boorse 60

Hardy Burns 84
Emilia Endara 90
Shannon Garvey 28
Manav Gundecha 32
Meghan Hart 114
Kaeli Kaymak-Loveless 88
Ryan Lenkaitis 112
Ashley Mariani 36
Jackson McVety 158
Dani Panati 114
Max Pellegrino 148
Witt Phillips 129
Caroline Schneble 87
Annie Scott 99
Travis Tillman 114
Ashley Torrey 24
Sebastian Tucker 24
Cal Walsh 48
Hannah Zhou 38

Pond Road Middle School
Robbinsville, NJ
Nick Foley 103
Jonathan Lachman 111

Pope John Paul II Catholic School
New Britain, CT
Kailyn Bielecki 51

Pope John Paul II School
New Britain, CT
Julia Hynek 136

Public School 131
Brooklyn, NY
Evva De La Cruz Valdez 177
Chasety Flores 168
Jenny Huang 165
Enni Jiang 162
Kristi Liu 176
Bin Ni 176
Isabella Rodriguez 181
Litzy Salazar 165
Samuel Schell 165
Angeles Sierra 166
Jordi Simbana 169
Jonah Thakore 175

Public School 183
Rockaway Beach, NY
Oluwafemi Olosunde 100

Public School 235 Lenox
Brooklyn, NY
Widney Borgella 163
Ethan Elson 174
Aja King 168
Destine Munro-Richard 168
Daniel Olton 169
Tianna Smith 163
Nakhai Wilson 162

Public School 48
Staten Island, NY
Sarah Kogan 103

Public School 50
Staten Island, NY
Eden Tam 167

Index by School

Ramsay Elementary School
Mt Pleasant, PA
- Eli Duvall 172
- Kyleigh Gianfrancesco 40
- Bryce Jaworski 113
- Gavin Stamps 43
- Cameron Wojnar 169

Richlands Elementary School
Richlands, VA
- Gavin Cox 98
- Jacob Maggard 135
- Kayla Maggard 174

Riderwood Elementary School
Towson, MD
- Parker Barta 89
- Ian Boecker 46
- Joshua Crihfield 23
- Kyle Engle 124
- Zakiy Gasparovic 55
- Michael Heil 77
- Jack Lord 63
- Blake Miller 19
- Samantha Sarubin 63
- Chloe Streckfus 35
- Emily Traband 124

Riverside Middle School
Riverside, NJ
- Christina Adams 110
- Giovanni Andrus 50
- Cassandra Arencibia 117
- Elijah Brown 62
- Alicia Carr 61
- Julia Carvalho 39
- Larissa Combs 103
- Zachary Coslove 58
- Jillian Costello 124
- Nicholas Davan 114
- Mario Enamorado 156
- Pricila Espinoza 81
- Martiah Fenelon 147
- Anyjha Frazier 147
- Miranda Goerlich 39
- Alyssa Grantham 157
- Avianna Harris 156
- Gabriella Hayden 61
- Alexander Higginbotham 44
- Amberlee Jack 138
- Jaydon Leinheiser 73
- Elijah Logan 130
- Giovanni Martinez 55
- Aaron Massey 39
- Quincey Matthews 43
- Alejandro Peralta 96
- Nuno Pereira 156
- Erin Starke 96
- Alyssa Straile 144
- Kimberly Yanez 147
- Eugene Zellman 147

Riverton Public School
Riverton, NJ
- Aileen Fisher 166
- Ryan Anne Foley 171
- Angus Kenson 175
- Jack Kinzler 166
- Kaleigh Portella 166
- Ryan M. Teicher 171
- Reed Wells 171

Robert Frost Middle School
Rockville, MD
- Rhea Iyer 114

Roosevelt Elementary School
Kearny, NJ
- Alexa Teixeira 135
- Julia Viscuso 83

Roosevelt Elementary School
Rahway, NJ
- Beneé Arrington 118
- Simone Attles 72
- Elizabeth Barthelus 29
- Kailey Beckford 59
- Clive Campbell 29
- Miles DeJesus 34
- Marlynn Dorielan 29
- Kristy Fleurmont 87
- Gabriela Fuller 35
- Domonic Innocent 92
- Anthony Laferrara 71
- Tyler Lagun 149
- Cassandra Rose Landaverde ... 67
- Isaiah Leach 66
- George McComas 148
- Judy Nguyen 45
- Saoirse O'Hara 87
- Stephanie Ortiz 42
- Diya Patel 127
- Kevin Quain 86
- Gisell Rodriguez 70
- Imayla Russell 91
- Trinity Santiago 137
- Julie Schroeder 72
- Charlize Tejeda 36
- Lourdes Torres 139
- Jonathan Velsor 87
- Jocelyn Woo 70

Sacred Heart Elementary School
Pittsburgh, PA
- Natalie O'Connor 21

Sacred Heart School
Oxford, PA
- Danny Bransfield 93
- Caroline Brooke 146
- Jeana Calibey 93
- Jenna D'Amico 92
- Douglas Hild 146
- Ashley Jones 93
- Joseph Knisley 146
- Meghan Reilly 146
- Kara Rieker 78
- Emidio Sciarretta 146
- Abbie Thompson 146
- Abby Tzanakis 63
- Marrianna Vitelli 62

Seven Generations Charter School
Emmaus, PA
- Caden DeCesare 163
- Maddy Devine 163
- Luke Dougherty 171
- Shawn Eckhart 164
- Isaac Engler 163
- Zoe Fosco 177
- Nasear Glasgow 171
- Quinn McHugh 178
- Maya Piezal 163
- Hailey Rumpf 162

Somerset Elementary School
Chevy Chase, MD
- Jake Williams 163

South Elementary School
Andover, MA
- Avan Shah 88

Springside Chestnut Hill Academy
Philadelphia, PA
- Olivia D'Angelo 108

St Alexis School
Wexford, PA
- Steve Duchi IV 179
- Caroline Marschke 162
- Mario Martin 162
- Brooke Standish 164
- Zackary Waslosky 164

St Andrew School
Johnstown, PA
- Joshua Beblar 33
- Jacob Gardner 22
- Ian Ragno 102
- Jessie Yahner 28

St Anselm Elementary School
Philadelphia, PA
- Giuliana Alvini 164
- James Bergmark 168
- Max Brown 168
- Emily Craiter 164
- Timothy Crozier 180
- Estella Griffin 46
- Kendal Higgins 71
- Sarah Hodum 180
- Gia Judge 89
- Aubrey Kapusta 164
- Anna Michnik 89
- Anthony Mongeluzi 89
- Kiersten Montag 71
- Dana Moser 89
- Deanna Moser 89
- Francisco Posada 180
- Lianna Rieser 46
- Parker Schramm 164
- Christopher Scudder 164
- William Shields 167
- Brooke Szczepkowski 169
- Samantha Weinert 168

St Bartholomew School
Bethesda, MD
- Martina Agak 54
- Gavin Chesen 63

Emma Christensen 63
Rachel Christensen 27
Trey Cox 153
Sarah Culkin 41
Caroline Freese 85
Julia Grisius 92
Danny Henry 70
Ho Young Jin 134
Gabrielle Joe 129
Gregory Lewis 62
Maggie Loughran 50
Sofia Morra 81
Charlie Triandafilou 63

St Bernadette Elementary School
Westlake, OH
Lachie West 127

St Brigid School
Portland, ME
Emily Bassford 69
Carly Beaulieu 145
Jack Chaput 114
Ava Fard 118
William Gordon 151
Caitlin Kennedy-Jensen 94
Erin Libby 50
Michael Luna 66
Kristina Matkevich 103
Tyler McAlister 74
Erin Schnupp 65
Taja Wilkins 58
Jackson Wilson 117
Hannah Woodford 80

St Dominic School
Brick, NJ
Sianna Bradley 137

St Hilary of Poitiers School
Rydal, PA
Kristian Azzarano 76
Isabella Capaldi 34
Emma Celaj 112
Grace Comas 58
Daniel Czebatul 157
Abigail Day 153
Puneet Gupta 56
Martin Keane 68
Reagan T. Keane 58
Joachim McElroy 56
Madison McGuire 53
Lauren Metro 118
Katelyn Morrissy 20
Joseph Scanlon 118

St James School
Basking Ridge, NJ
Julia Lazar 148

St James School
Sewickley, PA
John Auth 105
Kassidy Burke 150
Susie Garrison 136
Leslie George 77
Brenna Glance 33
Lauren Guy 33

Haley Hamilton 18
Helen Rothfus 100
Marisa Schriner 135
Landon Shank 88
Julia Susie 35
Francesca Taylor 77

St John Neumann Academy
Blacksburg, VA
Brandon Bevins 170
Lydia Biviano 179
Taylor Buckley 178
Olivia Magnini 162
Ella Matthis 177
Bennett X. Niemiera 169
Olivia L. Niemiera 169
Luca Pickeral 169
Anna Sanford 168
Henry Scallorns 166
Louis Semtner 169
Reese Tysor 168

St John Neumann Regional Academy – Elementary Campus
Williamsport, PA
Kyle Ferguson 124
Michelle-Ann Lavallée Harris 85

St John Vianney Regional School
Allentown, PA
Christian Giamalis 137

St Joseph Montessori School
Columbus, OH
Hannah 149
Spencer A-R 143
Sydney Brick 67
Sophie Dunlap 52
Coyote Fisher 68
John Fox 113
Mica Frank 156
Gabriela Gant 24
Maya Hammond 101
Kate Haydel-Brown 139
Noah Hessler-Burdick 115
Thomas Hohmann 82
Sawyer Mapes 137
McKenna Merriman 56
Anthony Mosca 139
Olivia Shuff 155
Braeden Singleton 82
Kevin Slotterbeck 49
Simon Squires 98
Fiona York 157

St Joseph School
Mechanicsburg, PA
Max Cavada 20
Dejah Hill 126
Jacob Learish 143
Isabela Wilson 45

St Joseph School
North Grosvenordale, CT
Jack Adase 34
Paige Audet 139
Niamh Raftery 122

St Joseph School-Fullerton
Baltimore, MD
Olivia Adams 110
Liam Alexander 156
Brooke Altman 110
Colin Armentrout 71
Adam Bartosz 156
Connor Berg 43
Caitie Brooks 36
Allison Ceccio 46
Michael Cejpek 66
Kaylee Copenspire 104
Clarisse Dapul 104
Tyler DellaRocco 110
Nathan Ellis 104
Bryce Esposito 135
Kendall Feiler 156
Ana Maria Frujinoiu 156
Jacqueline Garst 143
Julianna Grasso 156
Ben Heasley 110
Haya Jokhadar 71
Kunaal Mathur 110
Miguel Nankishore 40
Erik Nies 43
Jason Ogbolu 53
Vianca Pineda 89
Elizabeth Ramoy 104
Kelsey Reynolds 117
Briana Robinson 40
Logan Schermerhorn 36
Samuel Stitz 117
Jakob Taylor 110
Kyleigh Waugh 55
Andrew Wells 40
Jackson Williams 143
Billy Zittle 46

St Mary Elementary School
Shrewsbury, MA
Trisha Lahiry 91

St Marys School
Lee, MA
Kieran P. Santos 102

St Mary's School
Lee, MA
Zach Bianco 49
Gabe Kelley 43
Ellie Miller 75
Perrin Petell 22
Laurel Ralph 75
Lena Simone 81
Lydia Simone 49

St Michael the Archangel Regional School
Clayton, NJ
Stephanie DiMeo 112
Sarah Greco 59
Christopher Jasinski 130
J.T. Klein 131
Brenden Rostucher 59
Autumn Zeak 63

Index by School

St Paul's School for Girls
Brooklandville, MD
Nia Phipps 148

St Peter Cathedral School
Erie, PA
Ryan Jubulis 143

St Peter School
Washington, DC
Kendall Wienecke 104

St Rose of Lima Academy
East Hanover, NJ
Connor Beckett 77
Kelly Cincotta 57
Grace Michaels 103
Katherine Nigro 96
Julie Prestigiacomo 96
Natalie Quintino 36
Timothy Schum 158
Isabella Vescera 66

St Rose of Lima School
Newtown, CT
Erin Sudbey 38

St Sebastian Elementary School
Pittsburgh, PA
Sydney Ryan 41
Madyson Scott 84

Stratfield School
Fairfield, CT
Tristan Jones 64

Swiftwater Intermediate School
Swiftwater, PA
Isabella Serra 146

Tandem Friends School
Charlottesville, VA
Jack Heaphy 78

Tenakill Middle School
Closter, NJ
Naomi Meininger 45

The Bethlehem Childrens School
Slingerlands, NY
Anya Vedhathiri 168

The Ellis School
Pittsburgh, PA
Annabel Everett 43
Tegan Poerio 58
Fiona Riegert 35
Elizabeth Schaefer 57
Catie Summers 97
Elsa Tonkinwise 134
Lowrie Woodside 23

The Fenn School
Concord, MA
Tommy Fitzsimmons 87
Riaz Jamal 71
Stuart McCallum 37
Connor Monahan 88
Peter Napoli 69
William Okurowski 25
Will Potter 88
William Skelly 43
Max Winneg 108

The Holy Name of Jesus Academy
Massena, NY
Bridget Andrews 138

The Lutheran Academy Scranton
Scranton, PA
Nora Betts 102
Sarah Bjornstad 38
Jason Catalano 111
Matthew Nichols 18
Tess Nichols 166

The Masters School
West Simsbury, CT
Matthew Piechocki 50

The Town School
Brooklyn, NY
Brandon Foster-Bagley 140

Thoreau Elementary School
Concord, MA
Mishael Quraishi 155

Torah Institute of Baltimore
Owings Mills, MD
Yechezkel Kirshenbaum 173

Troy Intermediate School
Troy, PA
Autumn Allen 62
Elaineah Brown 97
Kaleb Brown 27
Maezee Brown 48
Aaron Cole 87
Emma Colton 143
Isaac Cory 20
Raelynn Eakins 25
Anneliese Getola 143
Haley Lewis 57
Paige Merrick 121
Hannah Oswald 27
Kevin Young 54

Tunbridge Public Charter School
Baltimore, MD
Mykayla Brown 103

Tyrrell Middle School
Wolcott, CT
Gabriel White 98

Village School
Marblehead, MA
Bryn Burton 58
Alanna Herrey 115
Hadley Kaeyer 141
Christian Penkrat 38
Hannah Verdun 111
Brendan Willett 114
Cameron Winch 74
Belle Woodward 102

Walter J Paton School
Shrewsbury, MA
Ethan Nguyen 98
Zoe Wolfus 19

Wellesley Middle School
Wellesley, MA
Vanessa Isbrandt 44

West Elementary School
Andover, MA
Zachary Clement 121

West Woods Upper Elementary School
Farmington, CT
Sonali Singh 71

Westgate Alternative Elementary School
Columbus, OH
Mercedes Bernal 98
Trisha Caldwell 103
Isaiah Chhith 158
Madison Francis 74
Kerstin Hamman 31
Jalyn Monfort 42
Alexxus Phifer 81
Isaiah Radcliff 58
Stephen Reed 80

Weston Elementary School
Manville, NJ
Valentina Barrios-Quintero 164
James Conover 172
Jaelynn Dennis 180
Julianna Garcia 172
Alexander Groza 163
Michael Grzywacz 180
Hayley Slack 180
Alexander Wildgoose 172

Wickersham Elementary School
Lancaster, PA
Jovanni Acosta 87
Carlos Almanzar 92
Fabian Beauchamp 82
Aidalina Cruz 141
Keishla Figueroa 125
Isaiah Garcia 24
Hailey Rutherford 143
Christian Velez 107
Kayanna White 79

Willard School
Sanford, ME
Stephen Hanselmann 123

William M Meredith School
Philadelphia, PA
Lily Brown 169
Zaniyah Byard 167
Sylvia Erdely 183
Flora Hernandez-Mekonnen 172
Stella Bryce Jann 169
Stephanie Kannon 182
Jenna Makuen 162
Sadie Margolin 183
Jasmyn Mendez 167
Isabella Mintz 179
Jacob Mono 167
Henry Mucklow 163
Adair Nelson 167
Maya Salzman 163
Chuck Schaeffer 177

Winn Brook School
Belmont, MA
Sophie Miller 180

Winthrop L Chenery Middle School
  Belmont, MA
    Ella Miller 103
Wooster Christian School
  Wooster, OH
    Ashleigh Clabaugh 136
    Natalie Getchey 83
    Audrey Murray 147
Yeshiva Shaare Tzion
  Highland Park, NJ
    Rivka Bella Rabaev 80
Young Scholars of Western PA Charter School
  Pittsburgh, PA
    Sabrina Karimova 64

Author Autograph Page

Author Autograph Page